MARKETING MANAGEMENT FOR NON-MARKETING MANAGERS

Improving returns on marketing investments

Heather Fitzpatrick, CPA, CGMA

Chartered Global Management Accountant®

Powered by

Notice to Readers

Marketing Management for Non-Marketing Managers: Improving Returns on Marketing Investments does not represent an official position of the American Institute of Certified Public Accountants, and it is distributed with the understanding that the author and the publisher are not rendering legal, accounting, or other professional services in this publication. If legal advice or other expert assistance is required, the services of a competent professional should be sought.

1 2 3 4 5 6 7 8 9 0 PIP 1 9 8 7 6 5 4 3

ISBN: 978-1-93735-267-7

Publisher: Linda Prentice Cohen
Acquisitions Editor: Robert Fox
Developmental Editor: Suzanne Morgen
Project Manager: Amy Sykes

To Brad, Emma & Ryan,
the three most important people in my life

PREFACE

Shortly after the AICPA asked me to write this book, I asked a friend, who is a CFO, to read the draft outline.

'Very interesting,' he said with a rather unconvincing nod, and he slid the outline back toward me.

'What's wrong?' I asked. 'You don't like it.'

'It's not that I don't like it,' he said. 'It's just that I'm not sure I'd read it. What does marketing have to do with me? I'm the CFO, not the marketing director.'

It's a reasonable question, and if someone else put this book in your hands, as I did with my CFO friend, you may be asking yourself the same question. In that case, let me explain what this book can do for you—and then provide the simple suggestion that turned my CFO friend from a sceptic into an enthusiastic fan.

Does your company do these things?

- Work continually to improve the company's ability to serve its customers?
- Cultivate a culture of curiosity that gives exceptional insight into the market's needs?
- Align everything the company does with the goal of meeting the needs of the market?
- Execute unwaveringly on plans to improve performance?
- Consistently outperform its competition?

If it does, this book is for you.

If this describes your company, you are probably working within a company that is a leader in the market. This book is about how your company got there, and what you need to do to stay there.

If it doesn't, you should still read this book.

If this description doesn't match your company, this book will share the secrets of companies that do fit that description. You'll find out that they don't define marketing the way you do, and that the way companies who *do* outperform their competitors define marketing as the key to their success. Companies that outperform the rest of their peers do so because they understand the concepts in this book.

You will too, if you read it. And that could make an enormous difference to your company, your career, or both.

And if you still have doubts, read the ending first.

But if you still need some encouragement, I have another suggestion. Read the ending first.

That's right, it's okay to peek. See how the story ends. More specifically, sharpen your pencil and take the Marketing Performance Evaluation in chapter 17.

The Marketing Performance Evaluation is based on my company's research about what makes a market leader's marketing so much more effective. By comparing the best practices of market leaders to those of your own company, you'll know where to focus your attention and what areas of this book will be especially relevant to your company's situation.

You might find the evaluation itself provides some value. That was the impact it had on my CFO friend. When I followed up with him after sharing an earlier draft, my reluctant reader had become much more interested.

'Okay, your evaluation got me thinking and hooked,' he said. 'I am interested in reading your book.' In fact, he offered to read and comment on the draft and to be the first paying customer.

So, if you're sceptical about whether this book is relevant to you, go ahead and read the ending first. Then, I hope you'll return to the beginning and resume the journey to becoming a market leader.

ACKNOWLEDGEMENTS

My mission, and that of my company, is to help organisations generate better returns on their marketing investments. It's my passion, and I have been studying the subject for more than 20 years. One of the most important things I've learned is that, in most cases, marketing results are more heavily influenced by non-marketing managers than by marketing managers. In this book, I've highlighted what I've learned in my research and through my experience as a management consultant so that you, the reader, might benefit from the insight I have gained.

I owe many people thanks for that insight and for their help with this book.

First of all, I would like to thank my colleague Ann Janikowski for reading, editing and pushing back on every concept in this book. Ann, your editorial skills are exceptional, and your insight and thoughtful questions are even better.

I would also like to thank my husband and business partner Brad Sturgill for reading, commenting and playing the devil's advocate. Brad, this book is much better for the scepticism you brought to the process. I appreciate your patience over the past year of writing, and your continued support with this obsession I have with improving returns on marketing investments. Your commitment and support have made possible everything I do professionally.

My third in-house editor, Olivia Doyle, PhD, reviewed many of the market research references in the book and provided some of the examples I used in the book. Olivia, thank you for lending your experience and insights to this book.

I could not have produced this work without the insight, support and willing participation of my clients. Thank you for both your business and for your support.

Mike Flynn, the retired publisher of the *Puget Sound Business Journal*, was instrumental in helping me launch my research study in 2001. Mike, thank you for introducing me to the executives of so many market leaders, for encouraging their participation in that first focus group, and for your support and mentorship over the past 20 years. To that original group of executives, an added thanks for sharing your insights. I am particularly interested to hear your feedback on where your input led me during the ten years of research that followed.

I am indebted to Ron Rael, writer, speaker and consultant with The High Road Institute, for his introduction to Robert Fox in the AICPA's publishing division. Ron, thank you for your encouragement, advice and enthusiasm.

I would also like to thank Robert Fox and the AICPA for understanding the importance of effective marketing management to their audience and for helping me share my approach with non-marketing managers and executives around the world. Robert, I have particularly enjoyed our conversations about marketing, publishing and life. I look forward to continuing our work together.

Many fellow Rotarians, business leaders, and other friends in the community helped test the Marketing Performance Evaluation and provided feedback or advice on other aspects of this book. Thank you for your help, for listening to me talk about concepts from case studies to chapter topics, and for providing feedback. Thank you to the many volunteers in the Seattle # 4 Rotary who helped bring in exceptional speakers. Some of the market leaders you introduced to the club were included in this book as a result of your efforts. Thank you!

I also learned about market leaders from one in my own family. To my Dad, Don Fitzpatrick, Jr., thank you for all the stories around the dinner table that gave me insight into what really mattered in business and for modelling the behaviours of a market leader.

To my Mom, Cheri Greene, thank you for believing in me. Your support, especially in recent years, has been incredibly important to me. Thank you.

And last, but certainly not least, I thank my two children, Emma and Ryan, who are, along with my husband Brad, the most important people in my life. Thank you for being so patient with me while writing this book, for giving me hugs, kisses and encouragement, and for believing in me. I love you all very much.

ABOUT THE AUTHOR

Heather L. Fitzpatrick is the founder, president and CEO of MarketFitz, Inc., a management consulting firm focused on helping clients deliver measurably improved financial returns on market-facing investments. Her clients include Fortune 500 corporations, middle-market companies and regional for-profit and not-for-profit organisations. As a keynote speaker, Fitzpatrick has worked with trade and professional organisations across the United States to help their members understand how to manage marketing so that it delivers better results. As a CPE instructor and trainer, she has conducted in-house training programmes and public courses on a broad range of marketing topics.

A licensed CPA and CGMA with over 20 years' experience as a marketing professional, Fitzpatrick brings unusual insight to her quest to help clients more effectively manage their marketing efforts. Her firm, MarketFitz, combines marketing, financial and management consulting in order to help clients better understand their market, tailor their operations, services or products and processes to customer needs, and manage their brand reputation in the marketplace. MarketFitz facilitates strategic, business and marketing planning using proprietary and proven methodologies to develop customised, actionable strategies and tactics that generate solid financial returns. With a plan in place, MarketFitz also coaches clients through execution, helping them forecast, manage and measure returns in ways that dramatically enhance the likelihood of success.

Fitzpatrick earned her MBA from the University of Washington and her BA from Colgate University. Before launching MarketFitz in 1998, Fitzpatrick spent six years at Deloitte's Seattle office, initially as a member of the tax team and subsequently as the firm's Director of Marketing. In addition to her passion for improving returns on market-facing investments, Fitzpatrick is committed to community service. She has served on numerous non-profit boards and committees in leadership roles and is an active member of the Seattle Rotary # 4. She is a member of both the AICPA and the Washington Society of CPAs, where she has served in leadership roles on the organisation's board of directors.

She lives with her husband, Brad Sturgill, and children, Emma and Ryan, in Edmonds, Washington.

To learn more about Heather Fitzpatrick and MarketFitz, Inc., please visit www.MarketFitz.com.

Heather Fitzpatrick
President & CEO
MarketFitz, Inc.
PO Box 1839, Edmonds, WA 98020
206-624-7470
hfitzpatrick@ marketfitz.com

CONTENTS

Section 1

WHAT IS MARKETING?

1

A MARKET LEADER'S DEFINITION OF MARKETING

How do you define marketing?

When I ask managers this question, the answers are surprisingly diverse, even among marketing managers. But there is one group that defines marketing in very similar terms, and that group shares an important characteristic: they are market leaders.

In almost every industry, the competitive landscape looks similar. The majority of the players are engaged in a bloody battle for market share, competing fiercely with other organisations of their size, and generating about the same *margin*. I call these companies *average performers* because they all seem to perform within a narrow profit margin range.

Behind them are the battle-weary under-performers; their bottom lines are red and creditors are circling. These companies are still battling for business, but they're not getting it. They're not yet gone, but they are certainly on their way.

And then there are the market leaders. These companies consistently out-perform their market. They attract the best customers and do so at a better margin. And, compared to the fierce battle in which average performers are engaged, they seem to do so effortlessly.

What frustrates many marketing and non-marketing managers at average-performing companies is that an analysis of market leaders' marketing expenses and activities doesn't seem to provide insight into their success. Benchmarking studies show that both types of companies spend about the same percentage of their overall expenses on marketing, but they aren't generating the same results. Market leaders are getting more from those same dollars. Even more frustrating to average performers is that market leaders seem to do the same sorts of things average performers do, from a marketing perspective.

At first blush, it might seem that their secret lies somewhere else. But it doesn't.

Marketing is the key to market leaders' success. And it is the key both because they *define* marketing differently and because they *manage* marketing differently.

This book will help you understand how market leaders define marketing and why it makes a difference in the results they are able to drive. It will also give you insight into how they manage their marketing operations and how you can emulate their best practices. Let's begin with a closer look at the market leader's definition of marketing.

HOW MARKET LEADERS DEFINE MARKETING

For the past 20 years, I have been working with clients to help them improve the financial returns they receive on marketing investments. Initially, I focused on improving operational efficiency in marketing, which I knew from personal experience contributed to sub-optimal returns. Although improving operational efficiencies did deliver substantial financial returns, the changes weren't enough to produce financial returns rivalling market leaders. So, in 2001, I launched a study to identify why market leaders generate superior results on the same marketing investments and how average performers can adjust their behaviour to match their outcomes.

The research began with a focus group comprising executives from middle-market organisations who were market leaders in a diverse set of industries. I looked for companies that were recognised as leaders by their peers and whose financial performance was better than the average in their markets for at least ten years. In several cases, they had out-performed their competitors for decades. The participants were selected from industries that are fiercely competitive, with well-established competition and alternatives to purchasers. Focus group participants included executives from both business-to-business and business-to-consumer companies, as well as the executive director of a successful not-for-profit organisation.

Because I was particularly interested in how marketing was being managed among market leaders, the first point of discussion was to define marketing so that we could be sure our conversation covered the same basic content. Because definitions of marketing among managers can vary widely, ranging from sales alone, to promotional activities such as advertising, to a full list of the classic four 'P's of marketing, I fully anticipated spending time coming to consensus on what marketing is and what activities it includes.

There was no such need. Their definitions were the same. And that wasn't the only surprise. Not only did all the participants agree, their definition of marketing was far broader than the one used by companies waging battle at the middle of the average performance pack.

> *Marketing* is the profitable management of the interface between the market and its needs, and an organisation's ability to meet those needs for the purpose of producing mutual benefit.

For these market leaders, and the others with whom I've spoken since that initial focus group, *marketing* is defined as the profitable management of the interface between the market and its needs, and an organisation's ability to meet those needs for the purpose of producing mutual benefit. It is why they are in business.

On the other hand, when I ask managers and executives within average performers to define marketing, the definitions are operational in nature. They are focused on the specific activities they are undertaking that will help them increase sales. Marketing is simply what they do to drive business in the door.

See the difference?

The market leaders' definition of marketing focuses on a broader objective. For them, marketing is all about understanding and aligning their business with the needs of the market. In the market leaders' definition of marketing, there is no mention of the need to sell a product or service. The market leader's definition of marketing focuses on addressing customer needs. By serving market needs, they produce mutual benefit, which results in profit.

For market leaders, marketing doesn't drive business to the company; it defines the business the company is in.

Make no mistake. The executives at market-leading companies are, by no means, altruistic. They are in business to build successful, profitable companies. However, they believe that by thoroughly understanding and continually improving their ability to serve their customers' needs, profitability will result. Because they know that one size rarely fits all customers, they begin by focusing on the customers whose needs they are best able to serve profitably, leaving the others to their competitors. This intense focus on the market whose needs they can best serve, coupled with a carefully cultivated culture of curiosity about the customer, enables them to generate products and services that are more effective at meeting customer needs.

Building a 'market orientation' has been a popular concept among business leaders and management consultants for many years, and yet, most average performers haven't integrated this concept into their core culture. They are still intensely operationally focused, seeing themselves primarily as a vendor of whatever product or service they sell. Although they may understand the benefit they deliver, very little of their focus is on understanding market needs or even understanding which segments of a larger market will be best served by the type of solution they offer.

By contrast, the executives of organisations that are market leaders use the knowledge they generate from their passionate pursuit of a better market understanding to guide virtually every aspect of their business. All of their operational activities are aligned with their understanding of the market.

Because all activities must be aligned, market leaders do not consider marketing to be distinct and separate from strategy. *Marketing strategy* is business strategy, and the executives within market-leading companies are at the helm of both strategic and marketing leadership.

This, for market leaders, is marketing, and they consider it the key to their financial success.

MARKETING, THE DISCIPLINE, VERSUS MARKETING, THE FUNCTION

After listening to this market-focused description from the executives of market leaders about how they lead marketing, you may be wondering where the marketing department exists in this equation. After all, the market leaders' description doesn't talk much about the aspects of marketing that other definitions include, such as advertising or sales. Where do they fit in?

Before answering that question, it should be noted that market leaders make a distinction between marketing, the discipline they champion as CEOs, and marketing, the function. Marketing, the discipline, is all about understanding the market at an intimate level and using that information to guide marketing strategy, which is indistinct from business strategy. It is the paramount responsibility of the executive team. Marketing, the function, is operational in nature and supports the company's ability to meet the objective of marketing, the discipline: delivering value to customers. Both market leaders and average performers recognise the operational nature of the function of marketing. The difference between market leaders and average performers relative to the function of marketing is how it is managed.

In many ways, marketing definitions reflect the evolution of marketing as a field.

The original 'marketing' was the reputation of the person who made the item. You trusted the quality and made the purchase because you trusted the vendor.

As it became easier to sell across broader geographies, marks (small imprints, brands or signatures on products) were used to connect the product with the manufacturer, reassuring the purchaser that the item was genuine, and the quality was good. Around 1561, the term *marketing* emerged as a way to describe this practice.

When the industrial revolution made mass production more common, marketing moved from reassurance about quality to attempts to differentiate and persuade, and tools such as advertising and packaging emerged.

It wasn't until the mid twentieth century that the focus began to shift to understanding market behaviour. In the 1960s, Dr. Jerome McCarthy proposed that there are many ways to satisfy customer needs, and they can be grouped into four categories: product, price, place and promotions. Although still functional in nature, this definition was based on research about what influenced customer purchasing behaviour.

Since that time, marketing and business strategy academics have continued to refine and expand the definition of marketing. Dr. Phillip Kotler, one of the leading minds in the marketing profession, defines *marketing* as 'the science and art of exploring, creating, and delivering value to satisfy the needs of a target market at a profit. Marketing identifies unfulfilled needs and desires. It defines, measures and quantifies the size of the identified market and the profit potential. It pinpoints which segments the company is capable of serving best, and it designs and promotes the appropriate products and services.'*

This definition encompasses the discipline of marketing, the primary aspects of the function of marketing, the connection between business strategy and marketing strategy, and the importance of understanding the market. It is also the closest to the definition of marketing used by the market leaders in my research.

*Source: Philip Kotler's website: www.kotlermarketing.com/phil_questions.shtml#answer3

The structure of the marketing function varies depending on the organisation and particularly on the organisation's size. In large organisations, the marketing function may consist of a number of different groups within the organisation, from product management to communications, who guide decisions on all four 'P's of marketing, including product recommendations, distribution channel selections, pricing guidelines and promotional efforts. The executive team often has a limited role, consisting primarily of oversight approval.

In smaller companies, the executive team may actively manage a portion of the marketing function themselves. With more limited personnel, they are more likely to assume responsibility for product- or service-offering decisions, pricing approaches, and sometimes channel selection or management. They may also be more actively engaged in the promotional aspects of marketing.

> Marketing, the discipline, is all about understanding the market at an intimate level and using that information to guide marketing strategy, which is indistinct from business strategy. Marketing, the function, is operational in nature and supports the company's ability to meet the objective of marketing, the discipline: delivering value to customers.

Regardless of size, a key distinction between market leaders and average performers is that oversight of the marketing function isn't delegated away from the executives. Like all aspects of the company's operations, from finance to IT, human resources to logistics, marketing is carefully monitored by the executive team to ensure alignment with the customers' needs and the company's business and financial objectives.

To support this alignment, the marketing teams within market-leading companies are intimately acquainted with the organisation's objectives, the market's needs, corporate strategy and the aspects of promotions that are most likely to influence success. This deep understanding of their company's goals and their alignment with the marketing discipline, as led by the CEO, ensures greater marketing department focus and efficiency. The marketing department is in lockstep with the leadership of companies at the forefront of their industry.

Contrast this to the typical relationship between the marketing discipline and the executive team in companies embroiled in fierce competition at the middle of the competitive pack, and perhaps even your own company. In these companies, the executive team is more likely to have the traditional, internally-focused definition of marketing. It is not uncommon for a CEO, a CFO or a COO to see marketing as largely promotional in nature and not their 'responsibility' as leaders. Because the executive team's focus is on selling products or services, rather than understanding customers, the marketing department is tasked with ensuring that the company's products or services bring in revenue, often operating outside of the broader business or financial context. In many cases, the only attention the department receives from the executive team is criticism when the company fails to meet sales objectives or wants a budget increase.

Organisations that lack the market orientation and marketing discipline at the executive level and relegate marketing to a function within the organisation are rarely synchronised in their march toward success. Each team member or function within the organisation is moving in a slightly different direction, with a slightly different pace, and the result is wasted energy and resources. This is why they fail to generate the returns that their more successful competitors do on their marketing investments.

MARKETING IN YOUR ORGANISATION—AND IN THIS BOOK

How does your organisation define marketing? Do you use the century-old definition of marketing as 'the sales and promotions efforts managed by a marketing department within your company'? Does marketing include the broader scope of the classic four 'P's: product or service selection, pricing strategies, promotional efforts and placement? Or, do you currently use the market leaders' definition, aligning everything you do as an organisation with your market's needs in an effort to generate profitable, mutually beneficial solutions?

Regardless of which definition your organisation uses, I suspect you would prefer to be a market leader, generating superior profitability, instead of an average performer, struggling at the middle of the pack. This book was written for managers and executives whose training and experience has largely been focused on the financial or operational aspects of business. The objective is to give you, the non-marketing manager, the marketing knowledge required to help your organisation move toward market leadership or, if you are already a market leader, to maintain your competitive edge.

To accomplish this objective, you will need to understand how to effectively lead the discipline of marketing. This is the topic of the next section, 'Managing the Discipline of Marketing.' You will also need to understand the fundamentals of marketing strategy development in order to effectively evaluate marketing strategies developed by your marketing team. Also, as a manager or executive with a fiduciary responsibility to your organisation's shareholders, partners, stakeholders, funders or investors, you also have a responsibility to ensure the company's funds are generating the required rates of return. These are the topics of the third section of this book, 'Evaluating Proposed Investments in the Marketing Function.'

The fourth section of the book, 'Managing Marketing Operations,' provides information about how to manage the marketing function effectively and efficiently, so that the benefits of the investments are realised, and the expenses and risk are minimised. Finally, the last section of the book includes four tests to ensure a marketing plan is ready for approval and a self-assessment tool that allows you to evaluate how well your organisation compares to the behaviours of market leaders.

CHAPTER 1 SUMMARY

Marketing means different things to different people. Definitions sometimes include one or more of the following components:

- Advertising and other forms of promotion
- Sales and efforts to generate sales
- The *four 'P's of marketing*: product, price, promotion and place (or placement)

However, my research and experience reveals that the leaders of companies at the forefront of their industries, the market leaders, share a common definition. Further, that definition is one of the keys to their organisation's financial success. For market leaders:

> *Marketing* is the profitable management of the interface between the market and its needs and an organisation's ability to meet those needs for the purpose of producing mutual benefit.

This definition of marketing has a significant impact on the way market leaders manage marketing and their companies. Among the most striking differences between market leaders and the average performers competing against them with less success are that market leaders:

- **Stay intensely focused on the customer market.** The market leaders' definition of marketing centres around the customer and their needs, not the competitive market or internal operations.

- **Consider marketing strategy to be business strategy.** Market leaders consider marketing to be inseparable from strategy. Marketing strategy is business strategy. As a result, the CEO leads the company's marketing.

- **Nurture a culture of curiosity.** Market leaders share an intense curiosity about their markets and a passion for finding out more about their needs so that they can more effectively serve them. This passion is supported by a culture that encourages ongoing learning about customer needs, which is leveraged to continually improve company performance. This culture is considered key to marketing success, and nurturing a culture of continual learning is one of the CEO's primary marketing responsibilities.

- **Focus on the markets whose needs they can best serve.** This deep understanding of the market allows market leaders to be more focused and produce better financial results. They pursue the markets they know they can best serve, leaving less profitable markets to competitors, and they understand how to communicate the value of their solutions to their market more effectively than less curious competitors.

- **Ensure alignment between all corporate activities and the markets' needs.** Market leaders drive all decision making from this definition of marketing. Although they draw a distinction between marketing, the discipline, led by the CEO, and marketing, the functional department, everyone's activities, including those of the marketing department, are coordinated in pursuit of the executive's marketing vision.

Market leaders also make a subtle distinction between marketing, the discipline, which they lead, and marketing, the function, whose performance they oversee and manage. Although they are different in many ways, they work in tandem, and understanding and managing both effectively is critical to success.

The remainder of this book is based on the market leaders' definition of marketing and covers both marketing, the discipline, and marketing, the function, including the effective management of the marketing function within an organisation and the financial analysis of marketing investments.

Section 2

MANAGING THE DISCIPLINE OF MARKETING

2

THE DISCIPLINE OF MARKETING: THE FOUNDATION FOR BUSINESS STRATEGY

Has it ever seemed to you that some market leaders must have a crystal ball?

They just seem to know how the market will react to a new product or service, how to effectively communicate with people to persuade them to purchase their products, or what to do next in order to remain the leaders in their industry. They don't have one, of course. What they do have is something that is just as powerful.

They have a culture of curiosity about their customer that provides them with a continual stream of feedback, combined with an intense focus on a defined market or market segment, and an executive team that is deeply committed to addressing the market's needs. This combination provides them with what I call the *Crystal Ball Effect*: the vague impression that somehow they have more information than their competitors do. (See box 2-1 for more explanation.)

And they do.

They have more information because they are constantly gathering it, listening carefully to what they hear and tweaking their model to make it even more effectively aligned. It affects every aspect of their business, especially the function of marketing. Every decision, from what products and services to offer, to what the company's technology priorities are, to whom the company hires, is affected by this deep understanding of who they serve and what they need.

This intense focus on the discipline of marketing, listening to the market and aligning everything they do with the market's needs, at a strategic level, is the key to their success. Because it is led by the executive team and it affects every aspect of what they do, the discipline of marketing forms the market leader's business strategy.

Box 2-1: The Crystal Ball Effect

> The 'Crystal Ball' Effect is the impression among competitors that market leaders are better at predicting where the market is going and what will succeed. Although they don't have a glass orb that predicts the future, market leaders do have something that is almost as effective: a culture that is intensely curious about, listens to and aligns its activities with the market.

WHY THE DISCIPLINE OF MARKETING PRODUCES THE CRYSTAL BALL EFFECT

The management teams within companies that are market leaders have their eyes open and are listening carefully to the market at all times. Although this may sound like a natural thing to do, and many executives and managers believe they are listening to the market, it is actually relatively unusual.

Instead, most managers hear what they want to hear from the market and ignore the rest. For example, many years ago, I worked with a company that was considering expanding into a new retail venture. The board and executive team were extremely enthusiastic, except for a small band of individuals who were worried. They weren't convinced that there was sufficient foot traffic to support the business.

They hired my company to help them evaluate the size and potential interest within the market. Our finding supported the concerns of the naysayers, and we advised them not to move forward with their plans. However, this wasn't what the executive team or the majority of the board wanted to hear. So, they moved forward anyway. Two years and several hundreds of thousands of dollars later, they shuttered the retail operations. As we had predicted from our conversations with the market, there wasn't enough business to support it.

Smaller companies aren't the only ones who make these types of mistakes. Even market leaders are susceptible. Consider Coca-Cola's efforts to change the recipe for its classic Coke product. Like my client, they tested the market before they launched the new product. They conducted blind taste tests, surveyed people on results and conducted focus groups. In general, on a blind basis, people preferred the new, sweeter formula. However, when they asked focus group participants how they would react to a change in Coke's flavour, about 10% of the population became fiercely opposed to the idea. They, in turn, affected the opinions of those around them.

Coca-Cola had an indication of how the market would react, but they chose to ignore what they'd heard. They decided that the lone voice of a participant in a focus group was swaying the opinions or drowning out the voices of the others in the group. Unfortunately, in a broad consumer market in which consumers do talk to one another and influence the opinions of their friends, the focus group was a good proxy for the market environment. However, the real launch, unlike the focus group, didn't end after an hour or two. It continued, and those voices of dissent gathered others behind them. Coca-Cola was eventually forced to reintroduce the old product.

By listening to the market, companies generate some important benefits. First, they reduce the risk that their business and marketing plans will fail by turning assumptions about market needs into facts. Because this reduces the number of mistakes they make in their marketing or business strategy, it can dramatically improve their profitability.

Second, they are more likely to see new opportunities before their competitors do. For example, consider Sam Walton, who founded Wal-Mart. Walton didn't start the discounting concept. There were already several chains that were thriving by 1962, the year he founded Wal-Mart. In fact, Kmart and Target were both founded that same year. But because Walton was particularly good at listening to the market and responding to its needs, he saw an opportunity that the rest of the market did not.

Sam Walton and his wife, Helen, didn't particularly like cities. They liked the people and the atmosphere in smaller towns. So when Walton saw the rise in the discounting business in other cities, and the price advantages it brought to local residents, he wanted to bring that to his friends and neighbours as well.

He tried to persuade the Ben Franklin store where he worked to try out the discounting approach, but they weren't interested. It wouldn't work, they told him. The market just wasn't big enough, and people wouldn't buy from a discounter. But he didn't believe them. So he continued to mull it over.

Eventually, he started his own discounting company, and, for the first few years, competitors wrote him off as crazy. They assumed that a discounting operation could not be successful in a small town environment. None of Walton's competitors, including Kmart and Target, would go into towns of less than 50,000 people. Even the smaller chains wouldn't touch a town with a population below 10,000 or 12,000 people. Walton was putting discounting operations in towns with 5,000 people. And he did that because he made a different assumption about the market.

Sam Walton made a different assumption about the potential demand, and he based his assumption on a deep understanding of his market and the opportunity it presented. And, as a result, he stayed out of the competitive fray. While the big players battled for market share in big cities, Wal-Mart gained loyalty and secured 100% of the discount store market share in smaller locations. Within 20 years, they were the largest discount retailer in the United States. Now Wal-Mart is the world's largest non-military employer.

The thing about Walton's assumption is that it wasn't truly an assumption. It was a fact that he knew because he knew the market inside and out. He spent time talking to his customers, learning about who they were, what they valued and the type of merchant they preferred, and he tailored his business to match. He knew what influenced their decision to purchase from him or from a competitor, and he based his marketing strategy on those facts. By contrast, his competitors stuck to another assumption: the assumption that the best opportunities were in major markets. In the end, this assumption and their failure to recognise the opportunity first cost them their competitive leadership.

LEVERAGING MARKET INSIGHT

The insight market leaders generate from their version of a crystal ball, the marketing discipline, gives them three critical pieces of information:

- Information about opportunities that exist in the market in the form of unmet needs or opportunities to improve existing solutions

- Information about the solutions that exist, including the competitive threat posed both by others in the industry and by alternative solutions

- Information about the reputation of the company, also called its *brand*, which can represent opportunities, threats or both to an organisation

Almost any executive who has been through business school will recognise these factors as the key components of the 'opportunities' and 'threats' elements of a SWOT analysis. Often used as the basis of strategic planning, the SWOT analysis process facilitates the identification of the internal *strengths* and *weaknesses* of an organisation, the external *opportunities* in the market place, and the *threats* to success posed by competitors, customer perceptions and other issues. Many companies still use this process, or a variation of it, when they update or frame a strategic plan. Although some organisations make assumptions about the opportunities and threats the market presents, the market leaders' assessments are more likely to be based on a deeper and more accurate understanding of the market. This reduces the risk associated with assumptions, increases the likelihood they will spot opportunities before their competitors and makes them more adept at both defensive and offensive competitive strategies.

Opportunities: Identifying Unmet, Untapped or Underserved Market Needs

The first benefit of the discipline of marketing is that it gives the astute listener an opportunity to recognise opportunities, or the untapped potential in existing solutions, before the competition does.

For example, the story of Starbucks is, in many ways, similar to that of Wal-Mart. Starbucks was not the first coffeehouse chain, but it was the result of the identification of an underserved need in the market. Starbucks was conceived after Howard Schultz, who, at the time, was the director of retail operations and marketing for a roaster and retailer of whole beans and coffee-making equipment, took a trip to Italy. While he was there, he became intrigued with the Italian café, a community gathering spot, between home and work, where the barista knows everyone's name, and people can stop in for a quick cup of coffee or linger for a longer chat. The Italian café filled a need within the community—a need for a place to connect with others and build relationships. And Schultz realised that this was a need he saw in Seattle and in other places he visited.

When he returned from Italy, he tried unsuccessfully to persuade his employers to pursue it. Undaunted, he left the company to start a successful chain of coffee houses called Il Giornale. In 1988, he bought the assets of his former employer's roasting chain, Starbucks, and renamed his own coffee houses using that name. Then, he began expanding in other urban areas across the United States.

Of course, if Schultz had not already been steeped in the coffee drinkers' world, first as a salesman of coffee-making equipment and then as the head of marketing for the early coffee-roasting version of Starbucks, watching trends and studying the industry around the world, it is unlikely he would have recognised the need as readily. He was successful because he understood the market and saw an unmet need.[1]

Similarly, Guy Laliberte, CEO and founder of Cirque de Soleil, already knew the entertainment business. But for him, the concept of a reinvented, upscale circus without the expensive and controversial use of animals that encompassed dance, drama and daring wasn't the result of a single brainstorm. It evolved based on input from the market.

Laliberte was passionate about the type of performances he and his fellow performers enjoyed doing, including acrobatics, fire breathing, dancing, acting and many of the other forms of entertainment that had, for so many years before Cirque du Soleil was founded, been the core offerings of street performers. He was passionate, and he listened to the feedback he got as a street performer himself. As he added people, and as his troop grew, he continued to listen and tailor his product to match what he heard. The concept wasn't always the upscale product that we know today. It was the result of constant tailoring.[2] Laliberte's efforts created a new market for the circus industry, an art form that was long considered to be a dying industry. Now, almost 30 years later, the organisation is considered a market leader, not only within the circus industry, but within the entertainment industry overall, and performs around the world.

Although many concepts are born from a founder's ability to spot a need, market leaders gain their prominence in the market by continuing to listen and using what they hear to constantly innovate the ways in which they serve their market's needs.

Cirque du Soleil would not have been the success it has become if Laliberte had not listened continuously to feedback. Although other organisations have imitated the model, creating similar circus performances in cities around the world, Cirque de Soleil remains the market leader within the genre because it has continued to identify opportunities for growth in response to needs within the market.

Similarly, Starbucks has used market input derived from feedback from such sources as front-line employees (eg, baristas), from customers directly, from market research and from the intuition and deep understanding of the market at the leadership level to refine and innovate its product lines. Schultz developed those feedback mechanisms from the organisation's infancy, creating structures to solicit input. However, at some point, the company stopped listening as carefully. When Schultz returned to Starbucks as its CEO in 2008, feedback coming from the market was that the Starbucks experience was no longer a 'comfortable community coffeehouse.'

Push-button technology replaced hand-pulled espressos, similarly-styled interiors made all Starbucks stores feel like clones of one another, and long lines gave baristas little time to chat with their customers. The third place between home and work that Schultz envisioned had disappeared. Instead, Starbucks had become an impersonal, fast food, coffee-on-the-run experience. Fast-food industry king McDonald's probably made the comparison even more evident when it introduced the 'McCafe' concept, offering higher-end coffee and espresso-based coffee beverages in its stores at about the same time.[3] And the feedback Schultz and his team were hearing was that the market didn't like it.

Market feedback about returning to the local coffeehouse feel and the threat from fast-food competitors prompted a new innovation in Starbucks' approach to gaining and incorporating market feedback. Schultz gathered a group of employees and asked them to tell him how they would design a coffeehouse that would compete with Starbucks. He gave them a modest budget, and they created 15th Ave. Coffee & Tea, inspired by Starbucks. With hand-pull coffee makers, locally baked food, coffee and tea tastings in the mornings and poetry readings and open-mic music, accompanied by wine and beer at night, his employees proposed a return to the community concept. Schultz agreed and funded their vision. On July 24, 2009, the first 'de-branded' Starbucks opened in Seattle.[4]

This new Starbucks was located in the same space a branded Starbucks had been, and it still served Starbucks coffee, but the furniture and décor were local and secondhand. The concept provided a means of experimenting with ways to improve the customer experience and was successful enough that Schultz made over two other Starbucks stores shortly thereafter.

Although the initial concept store has since been rebranded with Starbucks name and logo, the feedback the company received about the facility, the service, the products they served and the environment helped guide decisions about other changes that were required to return the chain to its community gathering spot roots. For example, Starbucks stores around the world are being given a facelift. Instead of the same standard décor to which customers have become accustomed, stores will be tailored to suit the personality of the neighbourhoods in which they are situated.[5]

Threats: Understanding the Competition

Market leaders also leverage their understanding of the market and its needs to assess their competitors' strengths and weaknesses, representing threats or opportunities, respectively, within the market place. Sometimes, great insights come from listening to what customers are saying about competitors vying for the same market share.

Consider, for example, the U.S. market for household cleaning products. At the beginning of the 21st century, the market was relatively flat and dominated by a few players, like Proctor & Gamble and Unilever. New product innovations were seen by most as the key to expanding market share, but the related market share acquisition was typically modest.

In 2004, Clorox Company marketing executive Jessica Buttimer was talking with mothers of newborns and young children in Marin County, California, where she lived. A new mother herself, she heard and understood their concern for safer, more environmentally friendly cleaning products. At the time, the market for green solutions was still relatively small. The Clorox Co. executive team was reluctant to move forward without more information. In this case, they supplemented their executive team's listening skills with market research.

The market segmentation research further defined the characteristics of these parents. They were consumers who wanted greener products but were not necessarily strongly committed to addressing environmental issues. They might, for example, want to purchase a chemical-free product to protect their families' health but might still own and drive SUVs or make other purchasing decisions without regard to environmental impact. Although they were interested in green products, they were sceptical about the efficacy of products offered by competitors, were more price-sensitive than the more environmentally-focused segment of the market, would not travel extra distance in search of a green solution and wanted solutions from brands they trusted. Clorox called this segment 'chemical avoiding naturalists.'

More importantly, the research indicated that the existing competitors had weaknesses against which Clorox could compete: They were relatively unknown brands, not widely available and offered at a higher price. Clorox had the advantage of existing shelf space in almost every common market and the buying power to drive down prices. In addition, none of Clorox's major competitors had decided to pursue this segment.

When Donald Knauss joined Clorox in 2006, he recognised the value in the trend Buttimer had identified. Despite the small percentage of market share currently held by existing 'green' brands like Method, Knauss agreed that there was larger potential. Forty-four per cent of consumers said they would be interested in purchasing 'green' cleaning products if they were effective, reasonably priced and convenient. Knauss updated the company's strategic plan, adding a new strategy to 'leverage environmental sustainability for top line growth.' He also gave Buttimer the go ahead to develop and launch a new product line, Clorox Green Works, which was available beginning in January 2008.

Growth in the product line exceeded expectations. During the first year, Green Works captured 40% of the market for green cleaning products. In fact, the launch was so successful that the promotions and credibility that Clorox brought to the market inadvertently boosted sales for other makers of green cleaning products. In addition, the green market experienced such a boost from Clorox's success that the competition also enjoyed overall sales growth.[6]

In 2008 and 2009, Clorox benefited from its understanding of market needs, existing competitors' weaknesses and its major competitors' reluctance to enter into the green market.

Opportunities and Threats: Your Company's Reputation

Clorox's leadership understood something else that was critical to its success when pursuing the growing chemical avoiding naturalist market. It knew how the company was perceived in the market. It had a tremendous opportunity because, as the makers of Clorox bleach products and other chemical-based cleaners, it was known for producing extremely efficient cleaning solutions. However, these same chemicals were the products its *target market* was trying to avoid. Its reputation, the Clorox brand, was both an asset and a liability in this pursuit. (See box 2-2 for the relationship between reputation and brand.)

Clorox needed to retain the brand association because it had the trust and recognition that were key competitive advantages over Method, Seventh Generation (a Vermont-based company) and other new players in the market.

However, they needed to convince a sceptical market that they could produce an environmentally friendly product.

Box 2-2: Reputation = Brand

> The term *brand* is used in many different ways, even within the marketing field. A company's brand is its reputation in the community. The brand reputation must match the market's image of the vendor with whom they would like to do business, or the company's efforts to bring solutions to that market will be less effective.

With a lesser understanding of the market, Clorox's leaders may have missed either the benefit the Clorox brand would bring to chemical avoiding naturalists, who trusted Clorox to bring products to market that were effective or the liability that the brand's connection with chemicals could pose if left unaddressed. Fortunately, Clorox recognised both and worked proactively to build Clorox's green image.

At the recommendation of Joel Makower, founder and executive editor of GreenBiz.com, Clorox mitigated the liability associated with its chemical-heavy history by partnering with another organisation long associated with environmental protection and widely respected among its customer base: The Sierra Club. In exchange for an undisclosed contribution to the United States' largest environmental non-profit organisation, The Sierra Club allowed Clorox to use its logos as a seal of approval on its new Green Works products.

In an interview with Anya Kamenetz, of *Fast Company* magazine, Knauss described the decision. 'We looked around, and no one had greater credibility than the Sierra Club,' she explained. 'They were the Good Housekeeping Seal of environmental groups.'[7] While the move was controversial in the environmental community, it was successful with the chemical avoiding naturalists. The Sierra Club's seal of approval mitigated the risk posed by Clorox's long history of producing chemical-based solutions.

THE OTHER HALF OF MARKETING: MEETING MARKET NEEDS

So far, this chapter has focused on the first portion of the market leaders' definition of marketing: its external focus. Understanding the market and its needs is critical, but it is only half of the marketing equation. The other half is tapping what your company does well in order to meet those needs and identifying where you can make money doing so.

Most average performers begin with this. It's the easy part, relatively speaking. It's the internally reflective aspect of marketing, when the CEO marketer identifies her or his company's strengths and weaknesses as an organisation and looks at the markets the company should pursue in order to make money. It's where your company envisions the future and what the company will achieve.

It is also when the company's executive team, and sometimes the marketing team, answers basic questions about how you will achieve that vision, including

- what market or markets you serve;
- how you can best leverage your strengths to serve them;

- what your organisation needs to do to provide those solutions; and

- what financial outcomes are possible.

Most executive teams analyse their own passions, strengths and weaknesses at some point in the process of deciding what they are going to do. They might decide they like serving a particular type of client or delivering a particular product better than another or that they are better at it. Or, the decision might be based on where they currently make the most money.

The difference between average performers and market leaders is that average performers often begin and end with that internal perspective. Market leaders tie their analysis of strengths and weaknesses and their decisions about the markets they will serve and the businesses they will be in to the customers they choose to serve and their understanding of those customers' needs.

CHOOSING A MARKET: THE CHALLENGE OF SERVING MANY MASTERS

In our research, we identified five key behavioural differences between market leaders and average market performers, the first of which is an unwavering focus on the market (see chapter 1, 'A Market Leader's Definition of Marketing,' for an overview of these behaviours).

Market leaders begin with an exceptional focus on a single market or set of markets (sometimes called *market segments*). Decision-makers in the chosen market or markets share common needs and common purchase decision criteria. Sometimes these markets are defined by geography, profession, a demographic characteristic, and sometimes by other factors. Just as importantly, market leaders can easily define who isn't a part of their market.

Market leaders don't disregard a market segment or consider it to be outside their market because they don't believe there is profit potential in that market. Those segments might, in fact, be quite lucrative. They are eliminated as target markets because the executive team isn't passionately concerned about the market's needs, doesn't know or understand that market's needs as well or believes the segment's needs are adequately addressed by other competitors or existing solutions.

When they expand, market leaders take one of two approaches, and often both. They look for new needs within the markets they already serve, broadening their product or service offering in ways that are consistent with their company's reputation, or they expand into new markets whose needs and decision criteria are quite similar to those of their existing market. Market leaders identify new opportunities based on their understanding of their market.

Average performers often take a different approach. Their companies are frequently driven by an internal, sales-centric perspective. They consider what they want to sell, and then look for purchasers who could buy that product or service. Their initial markets tend to be broad, and when they expand, they follow common industry approaches or try to mirror the product or service offerings of larger competitors, regardless of whether these approaches serve the needs of their most natural customer base.

This lack of focus is particularly common in small and mid-sized companies. This may be the result of trying to compete with larger players, whose target markets have diversified as they have grown, or it may be because they believe they need to generate sales wherever they can find them. Either way, they fail to recognise the financial cost of this approach.

> Serving many markets simultaneously, especially as a small or mid-sized organisation, can be both inefficient and costly, and is one of the most significant causes of diminished returns on marketing investments.

Serving many markets simultaneously, especially as a small or mid-sized organisation, can be both inefficient and costly and is one of the most significant causes of diminished returns on marketing investments. Different market segments have, by definition, different needs and different decision-making criteria. To serve a specific market, an organisation must tailor the products, pricing, promotions and distribution choices to address that customer's needs. When an organisation tries to serve multiple markets, it incurs added costs as it tailors its products, pricing, promotions and distribution choices in response. Expanding the markets served can be an important way to grow, but the market leader CEO makes those choices carefully, staying as close as possible to the original market, and expanding through avenues that do not force the organisation to drive costs up in unsustainable ways.

Let me illustrate these issues with a few examples.

The Cost of Market Diversity

This first example, like most in this book, is not based on a single client. Instead, it is a composite based on the types of issues frequently seen when consulting with executives looking for improved marketing outcomes.

In this case, let's assume the client organisation is a custom technology application development company called Tailored Solutions, Inc., or TSI. TSI has been reasonably successful. It is a mid-sized player in a crowded industry, and it has grown because of strong customer retention and referrals. Although the company has experienced solid returns consistent with those of its middle-market competitors, the CEO wants TSI to be a market leader.

When asked to define his market, the CEO responds that almost every company has some technology pain. He provides solutions to alleviate that pain, so the potential market is huge. Virtually any company could be a client. With some prompting, he concedes that small companies are unlikely to be good targets because his fee structure would not be within their budget, and extremely large companies are unlikely to use his company because they generally have in-house resources. However, he insists that the remaining companies—all middle-market companies—are his target market. And, in fact, that is how he has been pursuing business.

In the company's early years, this worked, not because the market was so large, of course, but because the company was so small, and each incremental project represented significant growth. During the first few years, most of TSI's business came from referrals through the CEO's former employer and by virtue of being in the right place at the right time, performing well and providing excellent customer service. Now that the company had grown, its growth rates had slowed, and the company needed to add business more quickly than it had historically if it wanted to continue to grow aggressively. Unfortunately, relying on existing relationships, referrals and the occasional client who found them via their website was no longer producing enough new business to sustain the growth rates the CEO wanted to achieve.

To address this sales need, TSI's CEO decided to invest in 'marketing.' He looked at what his competitors were doing and invested in many of the same activities: social media, newsletters and the occasional technology trade show. Unfortunately, he has seen very limited returns. He's frustrated, and he doesn't know how to fix his marketing problem.

The problem this CEO is facing isn't with *marketing, the function*. It is with marketing, the discipline, the portion that he is leading as CEO. His problem is a lack of market focus, which is limiting his ability to connect with and understand his market. His market is simply too broad.

When I work with clients who have this problem, I recommend that the executive team walk through their most recent client or customer acquisitions and describe how they got the business. In most cases, they are soon able to see the issue. In this example, each customer engaged the business to address very different types of problems, and each customer approached his or her search for a solution in a different way. Each customer consulted different resources, from peer organisations to trade publications to blogs that covered similar concerns. Sometimes, the decision maker was a CEO, whereas other times the selection was made entirely by a CFO, COO or a programme manager. There were few common needs other than the pain around a data issue.

However, there *were* some patterns in TSI's problems. There were industries for which the company had addressed the same type of pain multiple times, and the decision makers and processes were consistent across all clients of a particular industry. There were also common pain points, like inventory controls, for which the decision maker and the criteria were the same across all industries that the company had served. TSI and its executive team understood these customers' needs and could demonstrate the cost benefit of their solution. And by identifying these industries, the company's markets were now well-defined. The executive team could count the number of companies that could be clients and estimate the number that might require TSI's solutions.

With a more refined focus, the company could pursue those markets more effectively. Instead of a scatter-shot outreach approach, it could communicate more directly, in ways that reflected its understanding of the targeted segment's specific needs, and greatly increase its odds of winning any particular client. When the CEO estimated the potential returns with focus on specific markets, the impact of narrowing the company's focus was significant.

If this seems like a natural decision, you may wonder why more companies don't do this. Why don't more companies narrow their focus to improve their returns? The answer is that narrowing means placing some customers on the back burner. Other times, it means turning down a type of business that isn't lucrative in favour of another that is. Turning down business or ignoring a potential source of revenue can be difficult when you are in the midst of the bloody battle between average performing competitors. Narrowing your focus requires a deep understanding of the market and its needs and a strong faith that you can provide a superior solution. In average performers, the executive team often lacks understanding, faith or both.

The Benefits of Market Focus

Consider, by contrast, one of the market leaders in our study: the School Employees' Credit Union of Washington and its related companies. During the Great Depression, Robert Handy, a high school teacher in Washington State, supplemented his income by selling insurance to his fellow teachers. As he sat with his clients, talking through their needs, he found that they had a common challenge. As teachers, they had a difficult time securing loans to purchase homes and fund other needs. Banks were leery of a profession they considered to be unstable and were not convinced that lending to teachers would be safe, particularly in the wake of the market's recent collapse. Handy knew that the banks were wrong.

In 1936, just three years after the Washington State legislature had authorised the formation of credit unions, Handy set out to form the Seattle Teachers' Credit Union. For the next ten years, Handy continued to teach while working on the side to promote the credit union to and for teachers. He knew the market well because he was a teacher himself. He knew what they needed, and he knew how to communicate with them. Although he was certainly in business to make money, he wasn't in business to build a credit union. He was in business to serve teachers' needs.

By 1946, the bank was big enough that it required a full-time executive, and Handy left teaching to become its first full-time CEO. In 1949, the bank extended its market. While Handy could have chosen to serve people other than teachers and remain in its current geography, Handy chose instead to grow the bank's capabilities to allow it to serve teachers across the state of Washington. He stayed true to the market: teachers and their needs. By 1960, Handy's organisation was serving teachers across the State and had become the state's second largest credit union.

Then, in 1972, it expanded its market again, offering its services to a group of customers with similar needs and a similar decision-making process: all school employees. In 2002, the organisation changed its name to more accurately reflect its scope: the School Employees' Credit Union of Washington.

Handy was focused. Not only did he remain focused on his market, school teachers and eventually school employees, but he continued to be passionately interested in their needs. From that passion was born a second set of companies, the PEMCO insurance companies. As Handy talked through the financial needs of his customers, he found another challenge shared by teachers throughout Seattle: access to reasonably priced fire insurance for their homes.

As a former insurance agent, he knew that teachers were relatively low risk and that the prices they were being charged didn't reflect their cautious nature. So, in 1948, just two years after assuming full-time leadership of the Seattle Teachers' Credit Union, Handy founded the Public Employees Mutual Insurance Company (PEMIC) to offer home fire insurance. Two years later, he founded the Public Employees Mutual Casualty Company (PEMCO) to offer liability insurance.

By 2001, when current PEMCO CEO Stan McNaughton participated in my company's research study, Handy's legacy included the credit union, a bank and three insurance companies, all focused on the same market: school employees in Washington State. In addition, PEMCO Corporation, another affiliate, provided centralised accounting and technical support services to other credit unions and remains a regional leader in financial automation and clearinghouse services.[8]

Robert Handy, and the executives who followed in his steps within these organisations, had a passionate understanding of their market. They certainly could have served other markets, but they maintained their focus. As a result, nearly 80 years later, the organisations he founded remain market leaders and enjoy stronger-than-average returns.

Focus Made the Difference

Look at the first 20 years of each of these two organisations, Tailored Solutions, Inc. (TSI) and Robert Handy's family of companies. Within the first 20 years, growth had levelled off for TSI. Handy's companies, on the other hand, were booming. By 1956, the School Employees Credit Union of Washington was the third largest credit union in Washington, well on its way to becoming the largest, and PEMCO and PEMIC were growing steadily. Focus and market understanding made a significant difference in the success each organisation enjoyed.

Because TSI's leadership team's target market was so broad and their decision-making processes were so diverse, the few promotional activities that the CEO conducted were not enough to catch the attention of the majority of the market. When they did attract a prospective client's attention, through social media or newsletters, for example, the message was often not a good fit. The reader did not share that particular pain, was not the decision maker or simply found the issue irrelevant. For every dollar spent on these broad-based tactics, the company received almost no return.

Handy, on the other hand, was exceptionally focused and he, too, enjoyed early growth because of personal relationships, referrals and services teachers couldn't find at traditional banks. For the first ten years, he spent his days teaching, meeting his customers in their work environment. Of course, he only interacted with a small number of them. All the same, he knew the issues—and he knew how to reach them.

Handy tailored his products and his message to the market in ways that would particularly appeal to them. The first credit union office was a small desk in the Education Department at the Seattle Public Library. His first promotional pieces were mimeographed flyers, printed on the same mimeograph presses used by teachers, and distributed through the principal's boxes at the central office.[9] To this day, the School Employees Credit Union website assures teachers that the organisation understands their unique needs, explaining that 'unlike many credit unions across Washington, School Employees Credit Union has not opened membership to the general public. We've chosen to buck the trend so we can stay focused on our unique and responsible membership base, offering them exclusive benefits that they've earned and deserve.'

By focusing, Handy was better able to spot new opportunities for growth, both through new services and through geographical expansion, minimise promotional expenses and tailor his distribution channels to meet his customers' unique needs. Although there were undoubtedly many other reasons Handy succeeded, market focus played a significant role in his financial success.

Choosing a Market

What do you do if you recognise yourself in these contrasting pictures, and your company is more like TSI than the School Employees Credit Union of Washington? How do you go about narrowing your focus? Begin by understanding how your most lucrative market (or markets) perceives you and your competition, and compare that to your company's passions and strengths.

Several years ago, I worked with one of our clients to help their executive team reassess where they should focus. For the purposes of this example, let's call them Widget Manufacturing, Inc. We began by assembling a list of their best customers. These customers were profitable, referred them business, used them nearly exclusively for the business they had and paid promptly. Next, we assembled a list of the customers that met this description who were no longer customers of the company and prospective customers whose business my client had not succeeded in winning and who were working with competitors.

I scheduled interviews with customers and prospective customers in a broad range of industries and for whom Widget Manufacturing had delivered a broad range of services. During the interviews, I focused my questions on the value these organisations believed Widget Manufacturing delivered to the market, why they did or did not choose to use them as a supplier and what they perceived to be their competitors' strengths and weaknesses. I also asked them about their decision-making process and selection criteria. After the interviews were completed, I used the input to create a map of how my client and each of its competitors were perceived relative to the competition.

The results were quite clear. From the market's perspective, Widget Manufacturing delivered a specific type of value: an ability to handle particularly complex customer needs promptly without unneeded costs or operational interruption. It excelled in this and was the market's first choice with work of this type.

Several weeks later, at a strategic planning retreat, we discussed the management teams' favourite customers and the factors, other than profitability and prompt payment, which made those customers stand out in their minds. We also talked about the company's own strengths. Not surprisingly, these matched. The management team liked challenging projects. They were more interesting, and they were particularly proud of their ability to deliver cost-effectively without client disruption.

> A company's *value proposition* is the unique set of skills and abilities they bring to the market. It's the company's source of value, from the customer's perspective.

They had discovered their value proposition.

A company's value proposition is the unique set of skills and abilities it brings to the market. It's the company's source of value from the customer's perspective. In this case, its value proposition was that it could address incredibly complex situations, delivering cost-effective, innovative solutions quickly and without significant operational interruption.

When we returned to its customer list, we found that a majority of its most profitable and satisfied customers had a large number of these types of needs. More importantly, certain industries shared those needs quite consistently. By contrast, its least profitable customers tended to be companies whose requirements were more routine.

As a result of this research, and the internal comparison of the market perception with internal strengths and passions, Widget Manufacturing was able to narrow its focus to a finite set of markets. Each of these target markets shares the needs Widget Manufacturing is best able to address, values the innovation and creativity the company brings to the table and will pay accordingly, and shares the company's own core values. Equally importantly, these markets are big enough to support growth and provide opportunity for expansion.

TRANSLATING VALUE PROPOSITION INTO PRODUCTS AND SERVICES

Your company's value proposition represents the value your company brings to addressing market needs. Your value proposition won't appeal to every market. That's why it is important to understand it. It gives you guidance about which markets are the best fits for your company, what it can deliver and which ones are unlikely to deliver a healthy margin. It also helps you stand out against your competition, particularly those average performers who don't understand what makes them different.

Your value proposition is based on your company's *core competencies*—that set of knowledge, skills and experience your organisation brings to delivering value to the market. Your core competencies generally mirror your company's values and its culture. A company that delivers innovation is skilled in thinking outside the defined lines of traditional procedure, is creative in how it approaches problems and employs people who like a challenge. A company that delivers low cost products to a thrifty market is excellent at process and operational efficiency and has a team that operates with precision on standardised procedures.

According to Deloitte's *Global Powers of Retailing* report, UK-based hypermarket/superstore Tesco PLC is the world's third largest retailer. It has gained that position by focusing on a single but very large market: consumers who are looking for inexpensive and convenient goods they use every day.

Tesco was founded in 1919 by Jack Cohen, who found he could make a significant profit by buying surplus armed services supplies and selling them to customers who wanted a bargain. Tesco's market was the price-sensitive, post-war homemaker, who needed everyday goods at lower prices.

Like many successful superstore retailers, Tesco's core competencies were negotiating for products customers used every day and selling them at cut rates in extremely efficient retail environments. Profitability in this business relies on rapid turnover of stock and large volumes of business.

In 1956, Tesco expanded from groceries, its core product selection, into broader superstore offerings, including apparel and household items. In the 1980s and beyond, Tesco has expanded its offerings to include financial services, gas stations, child-care facilities and consumer-oriented financial services. It also diversified the distribution channels through which it sells, offering both superstores and convenience stores, and adding Web-based home shopping in 2000.

By focusing on buying goods that people need every day in bulk and closely managing operations in order to sell them at a discount relative to its competitors, Tesco has become a market leader.

The CEO at the helm of a market leading company understands the value the company delivers to the market and how its core competencies affect what types of businesses the company will engage in to address customer needs. By contrast, average performers sometimes wander to wherever they see opportunity, regardless of whether the new business venture leverages the company's core competencies.

To illustrate, let's return to the Robert Handy example. School teachers clearly have other needs beyond access to credit and insurance. Some of these are shared by the population as a whole, like groceries or clothing. Others are more likely to be shared by more limited markets, such as access to textbooks and teaching supplies. Although Handy could have served his market in those ways, he didn't. The former insurance agent-turned-CEO stayed focused on delivering the products and services his market had trouble accessing. He also stuck to his company's areas of expertise: finance and insurance.

But knowledge of a particular type of service or product isn't the only form of core competency. In some cases, it's a focus on a particular population's interrelated needs. Many social service organisations provide diverse but complementary services to address the related needs of a particular population. For other organisations, their core competency is a distribution mechanism or some other operational asset. Amazon.com, for example, launched its business as a book retailer, using an exclusively online sales approach. Its core competencies are its ability to build and sustain the online infrastructure, technology and partnerships that allowed its original business to thrive. Now, it has leveraged those resources and that knowledge to offer a full range of goods, including groceries, to consumers around the world.

Being market-focused works because it provides market leading executives with an understanding of who the market is, how the company's core competencies can be leveraged to serve them and when either the market or the company's core competencies are not a good fit for a particular opportunity. Walking away from business opportunities is hard, even for companies who are market leaders.

Consider one of the world's leading retailers, UK-based Tesco. According to Deloitte's *Global Powers of Retailing* report,[10] issued in January 2012, hypermarket/superstore Tesco PLC is the world's third largest retailer. It has a strong track record of success, and with retail sales growing at an impressive 9.3% compound annual growth rate between 2005 and 2010, the company is slowly gaining ground on the two industry leaders ahead of it, Wal-Mart Stores, Inc. and Carrefour S.A.

Tesco has focused, for most of the last 90 years, on what it does well: buying in bulk goods that people need every day and closely managing operations in order to sell them at a discount relative to its competitors.[11] However, even market leaders make mistakes and venture outside their core competencies, value proposition and market.

One of the more recent divergences from Tesco's core competencies happened in 2010, when Tesco acquired online automobile retailer Carsite to sell cars to the consumer market. Tesco certainly understood some parts of the business. It entered the petrol sales market in the 1970s, and it understood its consumer: the price-sensitive shopper. And it was working within the bounds of its equation for success: Tesco negotiated purchases on fleet cars, purchasing in bulk at a discount and passing along a 15% to 20% savings to customers. However, although it was a product its cost-sensitive customer needed every day, it wasn't something they purchased routinely. On April 3, 2012, they closed Tesco Cars.[12]

Although the company publicly claimed that the closure was due to its inability to generate sufficient stock to sell, *CarDealer* magazine's autopsy of the failure cited an unnamed company executive who said the real issue was volume. 'There clearly was not enough customers,' the source explained in the article. 'The original goal was a five-year plan and within three years they wanted to be as big as Car Craft, selling 40,000 cars a year.' Well, look at the numbers they were doing and it was clear they weren't going to get anywhere near that.' When Tesco Cars closed its doors, it was selling 150 cars per month.[13]

When an organisation strays from its core competencies, it weakens its ability to serve the market, either because it diverts key resources to build new competencies or because it does not know the market and the competitive environment, relative to this new need, well enough to serve it. Product or service choices should be made based on the executive and marketing teams' understanding of the market they serve, the value they deliver, and the core competencies they bring to developing and delivering solutions.

ALIGNING YOUR BUSINESS ACTIVITIES

For the market leader, understanding the market and looking for opportunities that match the company's core competencies is just part of the equation. Next, the management team must work continually to adjust operations to align with the market's expectations and the value proposition the company wants to deliver. Their job—your job—is to ensure that every aspect of the business supports that alignment. As examples, the way the receptionist answers the phone, the products the company sells, the way accounting bills clients, the company's policy on returns and the way the company communicates the culture that reinforces behaviour must all align with market needs and the company's value proposition.

The Point C Principle

Market leader executives understand that if everything the company does, including the function of marketing, is aligned with the market's needs and the company's value proposition, the result will be superior financial performance.

Market Leaders Follow the Point C Principle

Market leaders understand that the most effective way to drive superior financial performance is to continually align their marketing and other operations with the market's needs in ways that reflect the company's unique value proposition. Their focus on more effectively meeting customer needs drives the superior financial outcomes that are the hallmark of their leadership.

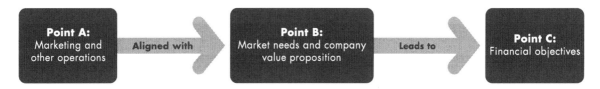

By contrast, average performers tend to view many aspects of operations, including marketing, as a simple means to an end. By 'doing' marketing and other operations, the company makes sales.

Average Performers Use Marketing to Drive Sales

In contrast to market leaders, most average performers see marketing as a means to an end. If revenues are lagging, average performers look to the function of marketing to drive sales. Their internal focus may drive improved performance, but rarely propels them into leadership positions.

By focusing on aligning their operations with Point B, the discipline of marketing, market leaders prioritise and manage operational changes differently. The *Point C Principle* sometimes leads market leaders to make less traditional choices relative to operations, and those innovations often lead to the company's ability to outperform competitors.

For example, consider how Starbucks' recruiting and human resources policies are influenced by the Point C Principle. Starbucks understands the value baristas bring to the management team's ability to understand the market. They are an extension of the leadership team, a way to gather critical information and innovate in ways that will keep the company at the forefront of its industry. They are also a key component of the company's distribution strategy, acting as a sales force, and they are a part of the product they sell, the experience.

In this 'third place' between work and home, customers want community. Community means familiar faces, greeting them by name and knowing what they typically order. If the person pouring their steaming coffee beverage changes with the weather, he or she can't build a relationship with that individual, and the experience, for which they will pay a premium over the cost of a traditional cup of coffee, is lost. When baristas turn over, Starbucks loses the sense of community it sells and a key source of feedback and information about the market.

For these reasons, Starbucks' employee retention strategies are critical to its success in serving the market. So, the company spends more money than the average fast food company on recruiting and training the right people and offers unusually generous employee benefits to make sure they stay on board. The results indicate these innovations are working. Whereas the rate of employee turnover in a fast food restaurant chain can reach 400% or more, Starbucks' rate is 65%. The company's cost to hire and train a barista is about $3,000, which adds up to more than the cost of the employee benefits that make Starbucks such an attractive place to work. But it's the other potential costs associated with turnover that represent real money to Starbucks: the cost of customers who will no longer see Starbucks as their local coffeehouse, and the cost of the market intelligence lost with the departure of a member of the company's primary market research team, its baristas.[14]

The Point C Principle also affected PEMCO Insurance Company's information technology priorities. PEMCO, one of Robert Handy's family of companies, understands that the experience a customer has during a transaction with an insurance company, particularly during a time of strain, is important. In 2007, in order to improve the experience, PEMCO bucked the trend toward automation, replacing automated phone respondents with live customer service personnel. 'When we asked our members what we could do to serve them better, we heard—loud and clear—answer the phone instead of dropping callers into a phone tree,' said PEMCO spokesperson Jon Osterberg in a PEMCO press release. 'Connecting with our members in real time allows us to build stronger relationships with them while separating ourselves from our competitors.'[15]

For executives at the helm of a market leading company, this is marketing strategy—and business strategy. Before any significant decision is made, whether about the markets they serve, the solutions they offer or how they operate the business, the executive team spends time envisioning what the business will look like, assessing what critical elements are needed to succeed and ensuring alignment with their understanding of the market and the value proposition they plan to deliver.

The Importance of Vision

We all have heard about how great athletes envision their success, running a race or making a successful play in their minds. It's a mental rehearsal for the real thing. Executives at the head of a business race do it, too. They envision success and take careful stock of what is required to make it happen and what will occur when it happens.

When I am interviewing a prospective client whose CEO is trying to grow business, I often ask what success looks like. Where do they want to be in five years? I'm always surprised by the number of executives whose descriptions are tentative, filled with words like 'hope' and 'if.' When there is sufficient vision to justify it, my next question is what do they believe they need to do differently in order to get there. Generally, their response is 'marketing,' often in the sales and promotions sense. My third question is about how they will handle an increase in business if it arrives. If they shrug off the question, I know that they have not visualised what success looks like.

Yet, without this vision of where you want to be, it is very difficult to plot strategies to get there. To paraphrase the author Lewis Carroll, 'If you don't know where you are going, any road will take you there.' The more clearly you see the goal, the easier it will be to identify the specific activities that will be needed in order to achieve it.

If you find yourself within an organisation that has no clear vision, creating one may be one of your most important marketing tasks. Based on your understanding of the market and its needs, and your capabilities as an organisation, what mutually beneficial future will you create for yourself and your market?

Developing Vision

Many approaches can be taken to developing such a vision, and the one you select will depend on your team, the size and complexity of your organisation and your culture. A strong vision builds on your understanding of the market and its needs, your core competencies and the value you deliver to the market, and predicts what that understanding could deliver, with focus, in some defined timeframe.

The timeframe you use will depend on your industry and your company. For technology companies, whose horizons change more rapidly, a three-year window might be perfectly appropriate. For a law firm or accounting firm competing in more established markets, a five- to seven-year window might be more appropriate. In some industries, such as commercial construction, in which the sales cycle is long, competition is established, and economic cycles make a significant impact, creating an even longer vision might be appropriate.

Regardless of the timeline, a good vision should be easy to describe to others within the company and be a realistic stretch, building on your strengths as an organisation. Executives should be able to articulate how this vision will benefit the customer, company employees and shareholders or owners in both financial and non-financial terms. The vision should also anticipate how competitors have reacted to specific initiatives and what the organisation has done to maintain its advantage. Most importantly, the vision should be detailed enough that it is easy to identify the differences between where you are currently and where you want to be.

Gap Analysis

Identifying the gaps between your vision and your current reality is the next step. In order to achieve the vision you have identified and meet the market's needs in ways supported by your core competencies and values, the market leader's executive team looks at those aspects of operations that need to change and creates a roadmap to do so. There are many approaches to doing this, and they are well covered by strategic planning texts.

This is where marketing strategy and business strategy meld together. This hazy line is the reason that the CEOs of market-leading companies consider themselves the head of their companies' marketing efforts—they equate marketing strategy to business strategy. It is also why so many elements of a company's management, including human resources, finance, the marketing function, operations, manufacturing, distribution, quality assurance and customer support fall into a market leader's definition of marketing.

Marketing, the discipline, defines the direction of the company, the markets it serves, the ways it addresses customer needs and the operations required to support those activities. As the company's marketing leaders, the executive team is responsible for understanding the market and its needs, establishing the vision for the company, defining how the company will address market need, communicating the vision to the entire company and holding the entire team responsible for progress toward the vision.

SETTING BUSINESS AND FINANCIAL OBJECTIVES

The executive team is also responsible for ensuring the financial viability of the company's marketing strategies. This is the final component of the market leader's definition of marketing: Marketing is the profitable management of the interface between the market and its needs, and an organisation's ability to meet those needs, for the purpose of producing mutual benefit.

The strategies involved in the market leaders' definition of marketing are virtually all-encompassing. As the company anticipates the ways it will address weaknesses identified in the *gap analysis*, improve on existing strengths and pursue new opportunities in the market, it will be important to ensure that the financial outcomes justify the expenditures.

To do this, we return to the beginning of this chapter, to our understanding of the market, its needs, current solutions and the competitors providing them. We also return to the markets we identified as those most likely to value the solutions delivered.

Many times, the marketing planning process skips lightly over the competitive realities of the market. Business and financial objectives are set, even within carefully selected markets, without regard to current market share, potential competitor response and whether the anticipated growth is feasible.

To wrap up the planning process, market leaders include a careful analysis of the financial feasibility of the company's marketing strategies and projected outcomes, both from a revenue perspective and an expense perspective. Then, based on their understanding of the market, they adjust those expected outcomes for potential risk and evaluate the anticipated returns against those that could be achieved elsewhere. The process at this level of marketing planning is very similar to the financial evaluation that exists at the functional level, which will be covered more closely in chapter 11, 'Evaluating Returns on Marketing Investments.'

The outcome of this financial evaluation at the conclusion of the marketing planning process is the development of business and financial objectives created in the context of the vision and based on an understanding of the market, which provide the foundation for the more functional aspects of marketing. These business and financial objectives should be clearly defined, measurable, realistic and achievable in the timeline identified.

QUESTIONS FOR NON-MARKETING MANAGERS TO ASK ABOUT THE DISCIPLINE OF MARKETING

As a non-marketing manager within your company, you have a responsibility to maximise your company's profitability and performance. If your company wants to move from the bloody war in the middle of the competitive pack to the superior performance of market leadership, your organisation must embrace the discipline of marketing. To help your organisation get there, consider asking the following questions of yourself and your fellow managers:

- How can we become more effective at listening to our market?
- How do we use the information we already receive? Are we responding to trends we see in the feedback we get?
- When we do business planning, are we making assumptions about what our market wants and needs, or are we basing our plans on facts?
- What market or markets do we serve? Are they distinct, with common purchasing decision criteria, or broad-based, with few common influencing criteria?
- What are our organisation's strengths that set us apart from our competitors? Do we know what they are, measure them and talk about them? Or are we mostly repeating what our competitors say?
- What is our company's value proposition?
- How well are our operations aligned with the value we deliver to the market? If there are aspects of our business that are out of alignment, are we proactively addressing them?
- Is our executive team committed to the discipline of marketing? If not, what can I do to help change that?

- Regardless of whether the executive team is committed to the discipline of marketing, do I practice it personally? How do I listen to the market? What do I do with the information I hear? How do I use it to continually improve our company's ability to serve their needs?

CHAPTER 2 SUMMARY

Many average competitors marvel at the market leader's ability to understand where the market is going and get there first. After all, who knew so many people would be willing to pay $3 for a cup of coffee? It's almost as if the market leader has a crystal ball.

Of course, this Crystal Ball Effect does not come from a crystal orb. Instead, it comes from another very powerful source: the discipline of marketing. The discipline of marketing leverages information generated through the market leader's carefully cultivated curiosity about the market, hones it through intense focus on a single market or set of related markets and matches it to the company's own passions and core competencies. The management team then works to align every aspect of company operations with this vision of how the company delivers value to the market, resulting in a smoothly-operating, market-driven machine.

The reason that market leaders appear to make decisions that beat the normal odds in business planning is because those decisions are more likely to be based on facts about the market than assumptions. Because assumptions represent risk, market leaders reduce risk—and improve profitability—by basing their business plans on the feedback they generate from the discipline of marketing.

By listening carefully and focusing on understanding the markets they serve, they are more likely to identify unmet or underserved needs, competitor weaknesses or strengths and potential issues with their own brand reputation. This marketing activity provides market leaders with the ability to spot opportunities before many of their competitors do simply because they are paying attention. It also makes them more adept at both defensive and offensive competitive strategy.

The other half of the marketing equation is the company's internal reflection about how they can best serve the needs they see within their target market. Effective management of the discipline of marketing provides clarity around the markets the company is best able to serve, allowing it to successfully focus on a finite set of markets. It matches the company's core competencies to the needs in the market, allowing the company to serve the market's needs in ways other organisations cannot or do not.

The discipline of marketing also guides the company's prioritisation of activities, as market leaders align all of a company's activities and operations with the target market and the core competencies their company brings to addressing market needs. Finally, the discipline of marketing helps companies identify the possible outcomes of doing so, facilitating the process of setting realistic business and financial objectives that are the basis of the company's business strategies. This alignment between the company's operational activities, the market's needs and the company's value proposition leads to superior financial results. The understanding that this alignment drives better returns is what I call the Point C Principle, and it is one of the important differences between market leaders and their less successful competitors.

It is at this point that the distinction between marketing strategy and business strategy becomes blurry. It is probably this haziness that prompted many of the executives included in my study of market leaders to argue that marketing strategy is business strategy, and that it is, and should be, led by the CEO.

Endnotes

1 Sources for information about Starbucks included the following:

The Starbucks Corporation website (www. starbucks.com)

Presentation to UCLA students by Howard Schultz, available on YouTube.com: www.youtube. com/watch?v= _kAiEO6jP48&feature= related

'Starbucks at 40: Java juggernaut branches out,' USA Today (online edition), March 10, 2011. www. usatoday.com/money/industries/food/2011-03-07-starbucks07_CV_N.htm

'Forty years young: A history of Starbucks,' *The Telegraph*, May 11, 2011. www.telegraph.co.uk/ finance/newsbysector/retailandconsumer/8505866/ Forty-years-young-A-history-of-Starbucks.html

Schofeld, Jack. 'Starbucks lets customers have their say,' The Guardian, March 24, 2010. www. guardian.co.uk/technology/2008/mar/24/netbytes. starbucks

Seattle Wikia: http://seattle.wikia.com/wiki/ Coffeehouses

2 For more information about Cirque du Soleil, see The Cirque du Soleil website: www.cirquedusoleil. com; http://static01.cirquedusoleil.com/en/~ / media/press/PDF/cds/cirque-du-soleil-at-glance.pdf

History of Cirque, http://vegascirquedusoleil.com/ home/history-of-cirque

3 Milletto, Matt. 'McDonalds $100M ad campaign and McCafe roll out,' Barista Exchange.com, May 6, 2009. www.baristaexchange.com/forum/topics/ mcdonalds-100m-ad-campaign

4 Berfield, Susan. 'Starbucks: Howard Schultz vs. Howard Schultz,' *Bloomberg Businessweek*, August 6, 2009. www.businessweek.com/ magazine/content/09_33/b4143028813542. htm?chan= magazine+ channel_top+ stories

Weston, Nicole. 'Debranding Starbucks?,' Brewed Daily Blog, July 30, 2009.

5 'Starbucks returns: The 15th Ave Coffee & Tea Experiment is over,' *The Capitol Hill Blog*, January 7, 2011. www.capitolhillseattle.com/2011/01/ starbucks-returns-the-15th-ave-coffee-tea-experiment-is-over/

6 Information for the Clorox case study came from: Neff, Jack. 'Green Works from Clorox: A Marketing 50 Case Study,' *Advertising Age*, November 17, 2008. http://adage.com/article/ news/green-works-clorox-a-marketing-50-case-study/132403/

Cammarata, Craig; Gough, Jennifer; Moss, Brian; Nowygrod, Ashley; Springer, Nathan; under the supervision of Hoffman, Andrew & Jongejan, Arie. 'The Clorox Company Goes Green,' The William Davidson Institute at The University of Michigan, Case # 1-428-989, May 12, 2010.

Schwartz, Ariel. 'Method: Only Inauthentic "Green" Cleaning Products Are Failing,' *Fast Company*, May 13, 2011. www.fastcompany. com/1753171/method-only-inauthentic-green-cleaning-products-are-failing

Kamentz, Anya. 'Clorox Goes Green,' *Fast Company*, September 1, 2008. www.fastcompany.com/958579/ clorox-goes-green

7 Kamentz, Anya. 'Clorox Goes Green,' *Fast Company*, September 1, 2008. www.fastcompany.com/958579/ clorox-goes-green

8 In addition to the PEMCO Corporation website, www.pemco.com, sources for this case study included the following:

Virgin, Bill. 'Nimble Pemco looks to grow,' *Seattle Post-Intelligencer*, June 23, 2005. www.seattlepi. com/default/article/Nimble-Pemco-looks-to-grow-1176756.php

Crowley, Walt, Creative Commons and HistoryLink.org, 'HistoryLink File # 2162: PEMCO Financial Services,' September 25, 2003. www.historylink.org/_content/printer_friendly/ pf_output.cfm?file_id= 2162

9 From the School Employees Credit Union Website: www.secuwa.org/home/about

10 www.deloitte.com/assets/Dcom-Global/Local%20 Assets/Documents/Consumer%20Business/dtt_CBT_ GPRetailing2012.pdf

11 Sources for information about Tesco include the following:

Wikipedia: http://en.wikipedia.org/wiki/Tesco

Clark, Tim. 'A history of Tesco: The rise of Britain's biggest supermarket,' *The Telegraph*, April 15, 2008. www.telegraph.co.uk/finance/

Endnotes, continued

markets/2788089/A-history-of-Tesco-The-rise-of-Britains-biggest-supermarket.html

Tesco's website: www.tescoplc.com

World Retail Hall of Fame website: www.worldretailcongress.com., article on Jack Cohen & Tesco PLC: www.worldretailcongress.com/hall-of-fame-member-detail.cfm?id= 203

Funding Universe website: www.fundinguniverse.com, article on Tesco PLC history: www.fundinguniverse.com/company-histories/tesco-plc-history/

Kaplan, Robert S. 'Tesco's Approach to Strategy Communications,' *HBR Blog Network*, September 2, 2008. http://blogs.hbr.org/hbr/kaplan-norton/2008/09/tescos-approach-to-strategy-co.html

Liptrot, Hannah. 'Tesco: Supermarket Superpower,' BBC Money Programme, June 3, 2005. http://news.bbc.co.uk/2/hi/business/4605115.stm

12 Sources of information about Tesco Cars include the following:

The Tesco Cars website: www.tesco.com/cars/
Center for Retail Research list of 'Who's gone bust in retailing 2010–2012?' www.retailresearch.org/whosegonebust.php

Wikipedia profile of Carsite: http://en.wikipedia.org/wiki/Carsite

Peacock, Louisa. 'Tesco closes second-hand car website after just a year,' *The Telegraph*, April 3, 2012. www.telegraph.co.uk/finance/newsbysector/retailandconsumer/9184616/Tesco-closes-second-hand-car-website-after-just-a-year.html

13 Baggott, James. 'The inside story on why Tesco Cars closed,' *CarDealer. Magazine*, April 3, 2012. www.cardealermagazine.co.uk/publish/exclusive-the-inside-story-on-why-tesco-cars-had-to-close-its-doors/63420

14 Flintoff, John-Paul. 'How One Brand Changed the World,' *CNBC Magazine*, January 2011. www.cnbcmagazine.com/story/how-one-brand-changed-the-world/1297/1/

15 PEMCO Insurance Company press release: 'PEMCO Insurance Acts to Improve Customer Service,' April 20, 2008. www.pemco.com/about_us/Pages/Live_operators_now_answer_calls.aspx

3

BRAND MANAGEMENT FUNDAMENTALS

One of the most important ways executives improve profitability and corporate value is by effectively managing their company's brand. A strong brand can increase the value of a company by more than 40% relative to a competitor with the same assets and customer base.[1] Even more importantly, a strong brand can dramatically reduce the cost of generating new business. Market leaders intuitively know this, and they carefully manage their brand in the market.

By contrast, the executives of many average performing companies, particularly small and mid-sized organisations, fail to proactively and effectively manage their brand reputation. There are four common reasons this happens. The first is that they do not understand what 'brand' is and, as a result, delegate 'brand management' to their marketing or creative teams instead of proactively managing it at the executive level. The second is that they aren't familiar with the building blocks of a strong brand, so they don't effectively align all of their activities with their desired brand reputation. Third, they don't understand the impact a strong corporate brand has on revenues, expenses and corporate valuation. Finally, they simply don't understand the fundamentals of *brand management*, including the tools and best practices used by market leaders to manage their brand. This chapter examines each of these in turn.

THE DEFINITION OF BRAND

Part of the reason brand is neglected by many companies is that the word 'brand' is somewhat confusing. Like the word 'marketing,' the term *brand* means different things to different people. *Brand* is used to describe anything from a logo, to the visual identity of an organisation, to a product or group of products, to the organisation's reputation. Although the quantity of academic research on corporate reputation and the impact it has on profitability has soared, the mix of terms used, ranging from *brand*, to *corporate image*, to *corporate reputation* has only made brand more difficult for many people to define.

Many people still associate the concept of brand with a name or the logo of the company or product line. This has its roots in the history of the word brand but is no longer a complete picture of what a *brand* represents. (See sidebar 3-1, 'A Brief History of Brand,' that follows.) Contemporary perspectives on brand are much broader.

> A company's *brand* is the reputation it has within the market, shaped by its corporate values, operating philosophy, value proposition and corporate social responsibility, which facilitates the customer's decision-making process.

A company's *brand* is its reputation within the market. It includes the public's perception of its corporate values, operating philosophy, value proposition and corporate social responsibility, based on how the company actually acts rather than what those documents say. A company's brand facilitates the customer's decision-making process. When known in advance, a company's brand reputation, like a person's reputation, makes it easy to decide whether you trust what they say or do and whether you want to do business with them.

Sidebar 3-1: A Brief History of the Concept of Brand

The concept of 'brand' has been around for more than 5,000 years. Marks were originally used in ceramics, stonemasonry and other works to indicate who owned or made it. Later, the English began using the word *brand* to distinguish one craft person's mark and skills from others.

When markets were small, the brand or mark was connected with an individual whose reputation was associated with the product. However, as the industrial revolution made mass-produced products more widespread, unknown producers had to compete with locally-produced products, and manufacturers began putting a trademark, or logo, on packaging, along with messaging designed to reassure the public that the mass-produced product was as good as, or better than, their local producer's products.

The manufacturer's expectation of the brand had expanded. Now, in addition to indicating who was responsible for making the product, it was also expected to promote familiarity and encourage trust.

In the early 1900s, manufacturers expanded the items used to convey that trust, creating advertising slogans, taglines and other communications vehicles to communicate messages to the market. By the 1940s, manufacturers had begun to study the association between the brand identity and the company's reputation in the market and became more focused on how they managed the market's perception of the company overall. The aspects leveraged to manage the brand were expanded beyond the promotional realm and beyond the four 'P's of marketing, eventually encompassing all of a company's operations.

Although there is still significant debate within academic circles about how brand, corporate reputation, image, identity and other terms are used, contemporary students of brand generally acknowledge that more comprehensive definitions more accurately reflect what we know about customer decision-making behavior.

A company's brand is a reflection of the executive team's mastery of the marketing discipline and its ability to anticipate and mitigate the potential impact the opinions of individuals outside its customer base might have on its customers' desire to make a purchase decision. A company's brand is its corporate reputation.

Because brand is a reflection of the company's effectiveness in managing both the discipline of marketing and those aspects of the company's reputation that affect purchasing behaviour, managing a brand effectively cannot be done by the marketing team alone. Certainly, the marketing team plays a key role by ensuring that the products and services an organisation sells, the ways they promote and distribute them and the pricing strategies they use are consistent with the reputation the company wants to maintain and the organisation's corporate visual identity is consistently applied.

However, decisions made in all areas of the company can affect brand by changing the value proposition the company is delivering in unexpected ways. In many cases, the management team is best positioned to identify and take action on these inconsistencies. To do so, the management team must clearly understand the building blocks of a strong brand.

THE BUILDING BLOCKS OF A STRONG BRAND

Brands become strong because they share four characteristics.

Strong Brands Reflect the Company's Value Proposition

First, companies with strong brands excel at the discipline of marketing and ensure everything they do aligns with their understanding of the market and the value they deliver to it. When aspects of that equation are out of alignment, the message to the market becomes confused, and the brand becomes weaker.

Companies with strong brands ...

- Reflect the company's value proposition
- Base their brands on truth
- Are good corporate citizens
- Are visually, verbally and behaviourally consistent with the image of the merchant with whom their customers would want to do business

To illustrate, consider the impact of Starbucks' decision to move from grinding coffee in the retail stores to selling pre-ground, packaged coffee and using automated espresso makers. The goal of these changes was to speed up service to customers while making the coffee experience more consistent. Certainly, these things are important to customers. Unfortunately, however, there was an unexpected negative consequence.

The new automation eliminated the smell of freshly ground beans and hot brewed coffee, a key component of the overall experience, and a critical part of that 'third place' experience that customers had come to associate with Starbucks.[2] Some argue that freshly ground coffee also tastes better. Market perception was shifting Starbucks from a provider of a high quality solution to their need for community, to a provider of fast, hot coffee, in the same category as fast food purveyors such as McDonald's. To be successful, and to align actions with market expectations, Starbucks had to improve speed and consistency while still providing the aroma of coffee to its stores.

In 2007, to realign business operations with market perceptions and business objectives and fix the damage to the brand, Starbucks announced that it was returning to its previous practice of grinding the beans in the store so that the scent of freshly ground beans would return.[3] Then, in 2008, Starbucks simultaneously closed all 7,100 of its U.S. stores for a three-hour training programme to ensure that baristas were delivering a consistent customer experience with high quality product.[1]

There are many other ways that brand inconsistencies can manifest. For example, there are companies whose pricing approach is inconsistent with the brand they are trying to sustain. This is most common in companies that are positioned as premium product or service providers but whose prices do not reflect the value they deliver. Often, especially in smaller companies, this is because the management team is concerned about what might happen to revenues if they increase their prices. Specifically, they are worried about losing customers.

This is also related to how well they have defined their market. They are stretching their brand reputation to be both 'exceptional product' and 'a relatively inexpensive solution.' Yet, if someone tells you something is both cheap and high quality, how likely are you to believe them? Not very. You are likely to reason that one or the other of these statements is not true.

In many cases, this means that some business is derived from people who believe they are relatively expensive, but not good, and pay a lower price as a result. These are the clients they will lose if they increase their prices. Keep in mind these people probably do not value the exceptional product that is the company's true value proposition. Conversely, there are undoubtedly a number of people who do value exceptional product but who reason that they must not truly have exceptional product if their prices are so low. By increasing their prices, they gain the portion of the market that simply expects to pay a premium for exceptional products, and they will increase their margins as a result.

Strong Brands Are Based on Truth

At some point in our lives, we have all met someone who is trying to be something he or she is not. Whether the person is simply trying to impress a potential employer with misrepresentations or is the proverbial wolf in sheep's clothing that lies and deceives to achieve his or her desired ends, the end result is the same. It may work for a short period of time, but once the deception is discovered, trust will be lost. The person's reputation will be discredited, temporarily or permanently, and any real value the person could have delivered will be forgotten.

A company's brand is similar. By definition, brands are the market's opinion. Just as we can see through a person whose behaviour does not match his or her true values, it is extremely hard to hide a disconnection between corporate values and actions for a sustained period of time. A company that deliberately tries to misrepresent itself to the market will eventually be discovered and discredited. In some cases, the customer may simply decide she or he doesn't know enough about the company, or feels a level of mistrust, and will shop elsewhere. This brand is likely to remain, at best, an average performer, whose true values are unclear and reputation is muddy.

However, with more serious deceptions, the customer is more likely to tell others, file a complaint with an oversight organisation or pursue legal redress. In this case, the brand may suffer much more serious challenges, potentially becoming a liability to the company that draws down not only sales but also corporate value.

To illustrate, consider the recent damage suffered to JPMorgan Chase & Co. in the wake of the company's $6.2 billion trading loss write-off. For many years, JPMorgan was considered one of the strongest banks in the United States. Then, in 2012, a single trader in its London office cost the company a significant loss. Although the bank argued that it was an isolated incident, the Office of the Comptroller of the Currency and the Federal Reserve both ruled that the bank was engaging in unsafe or unsound banking practices and violations of law or regulation. Finally, the Office of the Comptroller downgraded JPMorgan's management rating.

The company's market value slipped along with its brand reputation. After the May 2012 disclosure, stock prices plummeted from $41 to $31 in just 23 days. A year later, the company was still suffering from investor and consumer distrust.[5]

Companies With Strong Brands Are Good Corporate Citizens

Companies with strong brands are good corporate citizens. This doesn't mean that everyone agrees with everything they do or that they are philanthropically inclined. What it does mean is that they operate ethically and within the boundaries of the law. They also do their part to improve the communities they serve in ways that are consistent with their value proposition. When they make decisions about policies that affect their community, they consider both the impact on the bottom line and on that community, whether it is local, regional, national or international.

For example, many companies are moving toward using 'fair trade' coffee in corporate coffee makers. Although the coffee is often more expensive than other products, it improves the lives of small scale coffee farmers by improving wages, providing access to technology and capital and linking them to distribution channels. Fair trade coffee is becoming increasingly popular among both consumers and employees. By favouring fair trade coffees over more economical competitors, companies signal to their employees and the customers with whom they interact that they care about the welfare of others.

Many companies demonstrate their commitment to the community through their selection of suppliers whose labour standards comply with those of the world's more developed countries. For example, the Japanese company Marubeni posts its supply chain management policies prominently, just two clicks away from its home page. The policy describes its commitment to choosing suppliers that share the company's respect for human rights and the environment and how it will address suppliers that are found to violate the policy.

This does not mean that a company's policies, even when motivated by a strong sense of corporate social responsibility, will be uniformly popular. After all, not everyone agrees on the best approach to addressing a particular issue or concern. Microsoft, for example, acknowledged that the company's open support of gay rights legislation was likely to be controversial with some people, including some employees. However, the company felt that it was both an issue of equity for employees and an important recruiting concern for the company. For Microsoft, it made sense from both a business and a corporate citizenship perspective.

Of course, corporations do make mistakes. Companies are managed by humans, and people do make mistakes. Often, the public weighs the gravity of the situation by its management team's response to the situation.

Crisis managers, public relations professionals who are experts in navigating the outcomes of bad decision-making, or even bad luck, will generally tell clients that the best way to minimise negative impact is to correct misstatements promptly, acknowledge true problems, admit responsibility if applicable (with legal input and guidance) and address the situation so that it cannot re-occur. This is what the community/market would expect an upstanding citizen to do if he or she made a poor choice that hurt others in the community.

Strong Brands Reflect the Image of the Merchant With Whom Their Customer Would Like to Do Business

Companies with strong brands behave in ways that are visually, verbally and behaviourally consistent with the image of the type of merchant with whom their customer base would like to do business. This is more difficult than it sounds, and yet, it is probably the most important determinant of successfully building your brand.

To be visually, verbally and behaviourally consistent in a relevant way requires first that the company understand the personality and reputation of the type of person with whom a customer would want to do business if the company was a person, rather than a group of people. This is, of course, part of the discipline of marketing, and it tends to be relatively easy for the executive team, and particularly for the founder. Often, the founder was successful in business because he or she was the type of business person with whom the customer wanted to do business. As the company grew, the founder selected employees who looked and behaved similarly, reinforcing that brand reputation.

However, when a company becomes very big, maintaining that reputation becomes much more challenging. Successfully sustaining a brand's reputation from the founder's early days to a size in which the founder no longer has direct influence is very difficult, and few companies do it successfully.

To be successful, the company must become very deliberate about managing and reinforcing the brand image that it wants to project. Decisions regarding policy, operating procedures, internal and external communications, visual identity and other aspects of a company's business management are often made on a decentralised basis, particularly as a company grows. In order to maintain consistency, the business must have a way of ensuring that the decisions are made in the same way a single individual (the merchant with whom its customers would most want to do business) would make decisions if he or she were to control all corporate decisions.

Successful companies use many approaches to ensuring that decisions made internally are consistent with the company's desired brand image. Some companies rely heavily on cultural indoctrination, hiring selectively and providing extensive training as part of the on-boarding process. Other companies have strict policies, internal review procedures and centralised decision-making, which offers a greater degree of control. In some cases, the culture itself reinforces behaviour. Although these companies allow their employees great latitude relative to decision-making, the culture ostracises individuals who don't behave in ways that are culturally correct.

THE VALUE OF A STRONG BRAND

Non-marketing managers should be concerned about their brand because it has such a significant potential impact on corporate valuations. A strong brand can add significantly to a company's overall value, whereas a weak brand represents untapped opportunity.

Sidebar 3-2: Brand Valuation

There are several companies that assess the financial value of brands to large companies, and each has a slightly different approach.

While I looked at several for this book, I particularly liked the approach used in *The BrandZ Top 100 Most Valuable Global Brands* report.

This company begins by attributing financial data to individual or sub-brands (like Pampers) when a parent company (like Proctor & Gamble) has more than one and then removes the financial and other corporate factors that differentiate two similar businesses, leaving just the financial value of the branded business.

Then, the company factors in the results of consumer research that mirrors the confidence investors and consumers alike have in the brand in current terms. This process eliminates the inherent retrospective picture provided by financial data and provides a financial estimate of a given brand's value.

For example, the 2012 BrandZ report estimates that Apple's brand, the most valuable one on its list, is worth just under $193 billion of its business value. Without the positive association customers have with Apple's brand reputation, the company would be worth a fraction of its current value. Wal-Mart tops the retail list with a 2012 brand value of over $34 billion. Starbucks' brand, when isolated from the value of its financial assets and volume of business, accounts for over $17 billion* of its $39 billion in market value.

*For more information on the methodology and approach, review the WPP Brandz website: http://www.wpp.com/wpp/marketing/brandz

Although a brand's value can be calculated in different ways,[6] there is little doubt the impact on valuation is significant. According to a 2010 survey of participants in the World Economic Forum, a gathering of the CEOs of the world's largest corporations, non-profits and political entities, 60% of the forum participants said their brand, and their corporate reputation, represented more than 40% of their company's market capitalisation.[7]

Large, publicly-held companies are not the only ones to benefit from strong brand value. Research shows that companies with stronger brands, whether they are large or small, out-perform those with weaker brands on profitability, market-to-book value, total sales and total equity return bases.[8]

The stronger the brand is, the larger its impact will be on a company's overall value. Although market leaders enjoy a significant financial advantage, companies whose brands do not distinguish them from the hordes of alternatives in the industry receive no positive impact. On the other hand, companies with an exceptionally bad reputation in the market may have negative brand impact because they make unattractive acquisition targets. In these cases, their only exit strategy could be liquidation.

SOURCES OF ADDED VALUE ATTRIBUTED TO BRAND

Research indicates that there are several reasons a strong brand helps a company's ability to meet market needs and serves as a multiplier on its financial performance.[9] The most important sources of added value derived from a strong brand include the following:

- Increased customer preference
- Reduced promotional costs
- Reduced price sensitivity
- Ability to recruit and retain top talent
- Easier access to capital and financial markets
- Public benefit of the doubt

Increased Customer Preference

This is, perhaps, the most obvious benefit of a strong brand. Because customers recognise the brand, they have a strong understanding of the value it delivers. If both the value that the product or service delivers and the values that the company demonstrates in the market match the customer's own values, they will choose that brand over lesser known competitors.

People prefer to do business with someone they trust and who they believe shares their priorities and values. According to the *Brandz Top 100 Most Valuable Global Brands 2012*, a company with a solid reputation, perceived as trustworthy, has a 35% greater chance of standing out in a meaningful way among competitors.[10]

Consider your own behaviour. When you are choosing between a well-known brand and an unknown alternative, do you choose the well-known brand? Most people do, especially if the product, service or values are important to them. For example, if you need a sensitive surgery, you will choose the physician and hospital with the best reputations for success. If you are going to dinner for a special occasion, you will probably choose a restaurant you know or at least one about which you have heard good things. Some will favour a brand of attire that is well-known, like Hermès or Nike, because they want to be associated with the type of people who choose their products.

Reduced Promotional Cost

Market leaders talk about the importance of consistent investments in marketing initiatives, including brand management. Creating a strong market perception of what a brand represents takes time and investment, but once that brand reputation is created, the costs of maintaining it decrease. Although sustained investment is important, the overall expenditures drop dramatically when a brand is well-recognised.

Reduced Price Sensitivity

In the same vein, a strong brand provides a distinct advantage relative to price sensitivity. A simple trip down the grocery aisles in your local supermarket makes that obvious. The generic or house brand is often made by the same manufacturer as the premium brand to its side, but the prices are significantly different. Despite few or no differences in product, a significant portion of the market will pay the extra price for the brand name product.

As evidence, consider the coffee comparisons presented by the UK magazine *Which?* and *Consumer Reports* in the United States. In 2008, both magazines presented assessments of the quality of Starbucks relative to its coffee house competition. Both Starbucks and its competitors offered the same benefits as a local gathering spot. The primary difference was the coffee that was served. Starbucks serves its own brand, whereas other coffee shops serve other products. *Which?* magazine pronounced Starbucks to be more expensive and of inferior quality.[11] *Consumer Reports* also rated Starbucks' in-store coffee and found McDonald's espresso beverages to be of better quality, and its ground products in grocery stores had a similarly lacklustre review.[12] Yet, despite these apparent quality issues, even before Starbucks reverted to freshly ground products in the stores, Starbucks remained the world's largest coffeehouse chain. The average Starbucks customer pays a premium for his or her loyalty, spending an average of $3.50 during each of his or her 18 visits to the store each month.[13]

Ability to Recruit and Retain Top Talent

In addition to the clear advantage when it comes to selling products or services, a strong brand also has a distinct recruiting advantage. A comparison of lists for top workplaces and top brands show a significant correlation. Just like the consumers of a company's products and services, prospective employees find assurance in the clear values inherent in a strong brand. According to a 2011 study by Interbrand, 20% of employees under the age of 30 would prefer to have a lower-paying job with a brand they believe in than a higher wage job with a brand they feel is a poor fit or is weak.[14]

Strong brands provide a retention advantage as well. About 80% of employees between 18 and 30 years old say they will leave a company if it has a weak brand reputation.[15]

Easier Access to Capital and Financial Markets

According to research done in 1997 on behalf of Ernst & Young's Center for Business Innovation, 'not only do non-financial measures matter to corporate executives … investors take these measures into account when valuing companies.'[16] Financial analysts and others providing capital to companies use the company's reputation to help adjust financial output. In fact, nearly 35% of investment decisions are based on factors such as reputation and image, rather than financial data.[17] By facilitating access to capital, companies with strong brands can more quickly tap the resources they need to respond to the market opportunities uncovered as they listen to their market.

Public Benefit of the Doubt

Finally, a strong brand provides some insulation against minor missteps. Consider the personal 'brand' of a criminal: a mastermind at taking illegal advantage of others with a reputation for dishonesty and misconduct. If, after serving a sentence for misdeeds, the criminal's behaviour completely changed, he or she would still have difficulty persuading his previous victims to trust him or her again.

Conversely, when we first learn of the misdeeds of a popular public persona whose image was previously untarnished, many will defend him or her on the basis of reputation alone. We give that person the benefit of the doubt because of his or her reputation and prior behaviour. Strong corporate brands enjoy a similar benefit of the doubt, at least with respect to minor indiscretions.

Brand strength can only mitigate the impact of negative news within the market. Significant missteps, whether through continual failure to perform or a failure to live up to core values within the community, can be devastating. In many cases, they can significantly damage or even destroy a brand's ability to encourage preferential purchasing behaviour. According to The Conference Board, it is 'harder to recover from a reputation failure than to build and maintain reputation. It takes approximately three and a half years for a company to recover from a reputation failure, and companies with strong track records for corporate responsibility find it easier to recover.'[18]

Consider the tremendous blow to Martha Stewart's company, Martha Stewart Living Omnimedia, Inc., when its namesake and CEO was imprisoned for lying about insider trading. Despite efforts to use her five months in prison constructively and her energetic return to the company after her release, the company's stock has never recovered. In the five years after her arrest, the company's stock dropped in value by more than 60% in a period when the Standard & Poors (S&P) 500 increased by 20%. Despite the company's strong track record in other aspects of brand, such as product quality and fit for the market, the public is considerably more sceptical and less tolerant of any signs of potential misbehaviour, and the impact is most visible in the company's stock price.[19]

BEST PRACTICES AND TOOLS OF THE BRAND TRADE

Many average performers, particularly in small and mid-sized companies, are simply unfamiliar with the tools and best practices market leaders use to help manage their brand reputation. The tools are designed to help ensure visual, verbal and behavioural consistency: graphics standards, *key messaging*, talking points and brand audits. Familiarity with brand architecture helps managers appreciate how brands work together, and a basic understanding of crisis communications can help a company's executive and management team better prepare for an unexpected assault on their organisation's reputation.

Graphics Standards

There is an old saying that 'a picture is worth a thousand words.' A picture, or visual image, brings back memories and associations that would take pages of text to describe. The same can be true of components of an image, like a well-worn stuffed animal that reminds you of your childhood, or a battered, black, leather-bound text that reminds you of a favourite book of poems or your family Bible.

An individual's personal appearance also carries associations that are quite personal, just as a company's visual identity can carry associations that vary depending on whether you are part of the market. For example, a picture of a friend paints a broader picture of her reputation to you because you know her. However, the same picture given to someone who doesn't know her might communicate something entirely different. The way she looks might seem friendly or threatening, professional or unprofessional, formal or casual, depending on the person and his or her needs.

A company's *visual identity* paints a picture of a company's brand in much the same way. If the brand is unknown, one of the first impressions a company makes on a particular customer will probably be based, in part, on its visual appearance. Its logo, corporate colour scheme, the way it designs stores or facilities, the colour and design of its packaging, and the way employees look all help paint that first impression.

The colours, style, typeface and pictures a company chooses as part of its visual identity also play an important role in creating a first impression. Most people are familiar with warm tones and cool tones in colours. Warm colours tend to be associated with outgoing, energetic things, whereas cool tones are more reserved. However, colours carry more meanings than just warm and cold. For example, green is often associated with nature or health. Blue tones indicate trustworthiness or security. Yellow can communicate warmth and optimism.[20] Font choices, shapes, images and other elements of design also communicate visually with the market. For example, images that incorporate windows or glass can imply transparency. Images of identifiable landmarks, like the Eiffel Tower, suggest geographic boundaries and cultural values the brand might have.

The language of visual identity is complex. If your company is considering revising its visual identity, particularly its logo and other graphic elements, you should consider investing in professional design assistance. Changing your visual identity is costly because you will need to update all your printed materials, from business cards to paint schemes on company vehicles, and it can also be potentially confusing to the market.

To put this into perspective, have you ever run into a business colleague in a social setting and not recognised who he or she was? Perhaps the person generally wears a suit, and you met up with him or her while grocery shopping with his or her kids. Or maybe his or her work attire is a uniform, and you ran into him or her at the gym or at a formal event dressed in a tuxedo. You probably spent several minutes trying to place the person in your mind, searching for a mental association because they were dressed differently and appeared when you were not expecting them.

The same thing happens when a company changes its visual identity—it can take some time for the market's association with that identity to catch up. When a manufacturer changes packaging, for example, a shopper who is accustomed to picking up a quickly recognised product might opt for a competitor's product, rather than spending the time required to identify the same product in its new packaging, particularly if he or she considers the brands to be close substitutes.

Although an organised change in visual identity is manageable when needed, the more troublesome problem many organisations face is the inconsistent application of their existing visual identity. This is surprisingly common, even among bigger companies.

It happens for many reasons. Sometimes, it is because there is a specific need for graphic elements, and the current visual identity doesn't work. For example, consider a company that has a rather long name. When posted on a banner next to competitors at a conference, it is relatively difficult to read. So, designers change it, but not consistently. Sometimes, they simply stack the text, make it larger or change the font to block letters. The problem the company has is that the market won't study it to figure out why it looks familiar, as you would a friend you didn't immediately recognise. Its prospective customers are more likely to glance at the logo without reading it, even when the font is big enough, because it doesn't look like the one they know.

One tool companies use to prevent these sorts of issues and ensure consistency in their visual identity is a *graphic standards document*. This document contains guidelines on how the company's logo or logos, taglines, corporate colours, images and other visual elements should be used.

It typically also provides both examples of common applications and templates. For example, a manufacturer with corporate delivery vehicles might include its paint scheme and indicate what messages, logos and colours should appear and where. A retailer with common design elements in each of its stores, like the Gap or Nordstrom, might include both required design elements and guidelines relative to optional or local additions. A company whose employees are uniformed or have clothing guidelines that ensure a uniform look or feel, such as Federal Express or a high end hair salon, may include those standards within its graphics standards.

As a non-marketing manager or executive, you play an important role in managing your company's visual identity. Although most decisions about company-wide design projects will be managed by in-house marketing teams within larger companies, the greater risk for missteps relative to visual elements is with non-marketing professionals. Human resources teams, technology professionals, accounting and finance team members will, from time to time, create in-house or external newsletters or other collateral, staff booths at recruiting fairs or other events or promote the company's visual identity in other ways using internal non-marketing or external contract design assistance. In the process, it is easy for the brand's visual identity to become inconsistent and lose some of its power to shape market opinion. When equipped with graphics standards, non-marketing managers are often in the best place to spot these issues and stop them before they become public.

In smaller companies, the executive may monitor decisions directly. Larger companies have marketing teams or brand watchdogs within the company who are responsible for monitoring the brand's visual identity and who have final approval on all design decisions.

One other role the non-marketing manager often plays relative to the company's visual identity has to do with visual identity protection. The executive team or the company's legal counsel is generally responsible for trademark protections and for ensuring that the company does not violate other organisations' trademarks or copyrights. From a corporate protection perspective, executives should ensure that logos, proprietary design schemes and other important elements of the company's visual identity are protected appropriately under national and international trademark laws.

From a defensive perspective, the executive team should ensure designers and others who are responsible for developing elements of the firm's identity, such as the website, understand the copyright laws well enough to prevent inadvertent use or misuse of an image created by someone else or another company's

Sidebar 3-3: Common Elements in a Graphics Standards Document

- Company mission, vision and values
- A description of desired brand attributes
- Company and related names and how they must be used
- Brand architecture (how the company uses parent brands, sub-brands and product level brands)
- The logo or logos and any other official icons, often with a description, and sometimes with examples of prohibited designs or styles
- Website naming and design protocols
- Elements of the graphic identity, including company colours, typography and the appropriate placement of logos and icons
- Examples of how the logo is applied in different situations, such as letterhead, business cards, banners, advertisements and websites
- Templates for PowerPoint and other common tools
- Guidelines on the selection of images

Many graphics standards examples can be found online. In each case, the standards are tailored to the organization's specific requirements. For example:

US Agency for International Development (USAID): http://transition.usaid.gov/branding/USAID_Graphic_Standards_Manual.pdf

Rotary International: www.rotary.org/RIdocuments/en_pdf/547en.pdf

Larger companies often have approved images, including logos with trademark restrictions and other requirements regarding its use in the press section of their website. These help ensure that external users who are doing stories about the company or its products or services correctly reflect the brand reputation they wish to project.

For example:

Microsoft Corporation: www.microsoft.com/en-us/news/imagegallery/default.aspx

trademarked design elements. The cost of retooling a company's visual identity is substantial, and a company can incur substantial legal costs when it fails to safeguard against trademark infringements.

For example, the UK-based New English Tea Company incorporated a red, double-decker bus into its tea tin designs. A competitor, Temple Island Collections, had already been using the red bus image and discovered the apparent infringement and brought legal actions against them. New English Tea Company lost the case and was required to change the design and compensate Temple Island Collections for damages. However, the revised design still used the red bus image inappropriately, and the two companies engaged in a second court battle resulting in additional redesign costs and fines levied against the New English Tea Company. These costs might have been averted with more aggressive efforts to investigate potential infringements prior to approval of the tea tin design.[21]

Key Messages

The second tool companies use to help ensure that the market perceives the brand in a consistent manner is a *key messaging document*. Key messages help ensure that what the company says, whether in a press release, advertising or collateral materials describing the company's products and services, accurately reflects the reputation the company wishes to have in a consistent manner.

One of my favourite movies is the 1952 MGM classic, *Singin' in the Rain*, featuring American actors Gene Kelly, Donald O'Connor and Debbie Reynolds. In its opening scenes, we see actress Jean Hagen portraying the glamorous looking leading lady, Lina Lamont, as the popular star of the silent picture industry. It isn't until much later that we hear her voice. When we do, it paints an entirely different picture of Lina Lamont who portrays a sophisticated star on the screen. Lina's grating voice, incorrect grammar and self-serving statements betray the poorly educated, selfish actress behind the glamorous looks.

When Lina argues to the media manager and studio owner that she ought to be able to address 'her public,' the publicity manager protests that 'the studio's got to keep their stars from looking ridiculous at any cost,' to which Donald O'Connor's character, Cosmo Brown, quips 'no one's got that much money.' Her true character had been shielded from the public because the studio refused to let her talk. However, when it comes to a company and the individuals who speak on its behalf, this is hardly a realistic approach to protecting the brand.

The message that a company communicates is important. Marketing lore suggests there is a 'Rule of Seven,' which says that the customer must hear the same message an average of seven times from a company before they remember it. In messaging, as in visual imaging, frequently repeating the same behaviours in exactly the same way is how you improve retention.

In my experience, the Rule of Seven might be closer to the Rule of Twelve, or perhaps the Rule of Twenty. In our world of 24/7 communications via television, Internet and other media, getting one message to stand out and capture someone's attention is extremely difficult. There is too much competition. Unless the message happens to be relevant at that particular time for that particular customer, it will probably be missed altogether.

To be retained, the same message needs to be repeated in a consistent voice and spoken with consistent language that is meaningful to the target market every time it is communicated. A key messaging document reinforces the image with which the market should be left as a result of the communications, defines the key messages the market should hear and, hopefully, keeps the company from looking ridiculous.

Messaging documents can be prepared for the company overall or for a product or service line within a company, or both. For example, Proctor & Gamble likely has messaging both for the company overall, and for its divisions, such as Pampers.[22]

The biggest mistake I see when companies create messaging documents is that they don't write the messaging from the customer's point of view. In order to make an impact, the messages must be true, credible and relevant:

- **True.** As noted previously, a company rarely succeeds in claiming it can do something it actually does not have the capacity to do. When it does, it is generally caught, and the company's reputation suffers.

- **Credible.** Often, a company claims something within its messaging that is true and can be supported with proof points but that the market simply may not believe. For example, a new 'green' cleaning product company may produce something that is more effective than its less environmentally-friendly counterparts, but, according to research by Clorox, the market is unlikely to believe the message. The company may choose to include the message within its messaging document, along with ample proof points, but it should also offer other compelling reasons to make the purchase.

- **Relevant and important.** Finally, the message must be relevant and important to the market that receives it. For example, a company may offer a car that is both safe and attractive. If the messaging is limited to the beauty of the design, and the market is more interested in safety, the company's message may not be heard.

Sidebar 3-4: Common Elements in a Key Messaging Document

Key Messages:

- Statements about the benefits of doing business with a particular organisation that answer the question 'why should I purchase something from you?'

- Not intended for rote memorisation and parroting; rather, they are guides to a consistent 'voice,' reflecting a view of the company's principles, distinguishing characteristics and competitive advantages

- Based on brand attributes, factors that influence the purchasing decision and the value proposition

- Generally limited to the three to seven messages considered most important

- Change over time, adjusting to the company's understanding of its market

Proof Points (also called Substantiating Statements or Qualifying Statements):

- Provide evidence that the company offers the benefits that each key message describes, answering the customers' call to 'prove it!'

- Often describe the features and capabilities

Boilerplate:

- Two to four sentence description of the company and what it does; a variation of the value proposition

- Most often used at the bottom of press releases, award or directory submissions and in other short descriptions of the company's capabilities

Competitive Positioning:

- Analysis of competitors' messaging and how the company's own messaging contrasts to it

- Less commonly included in messaging documents

Creating and ensuring consistent use of a key messaging document for external communications helps ensure that what the market hears from the company is consistent, spoken in the same corporate voice and supported with evidence that proves the point. Although key messaging documents should be updated periodically, doing so too frequently is also a mistake. Returning to the Rule of Seven, if the message changes too frequently, the market may not hear it as many times as are required to retain it.

Talking Points

Talking points are closely related to, and generally derived from, key messages. *Talking points* outline the most important points to be made in a specific situation or by a specific person. Like the key messages in a messaging document, they generally provide the principal point, supported by proof points, from which the speaker or writer can draw. They are often prepared in bullet-point form, with concise supporting data. Unlike key messages, talking points are designed to be quoted verbatim and are often provided to the media to assist them in writing stories about a company.

Talking points are often prepared for executives or other managers for use in discussing specific events or situations, such as acquisitions or layoffs, with either internal or external audiences. They can also be used by executives who speak on a regular basis so that their presentations communicate the same information, using the same basic stories, to multiple audiences.

Like key messages, when used consistently, talking points help ensure that internal and external audiences hear the same messages from a variety of sources within the organisation. They help an organisation portray a consistent and unified front when used during a crisis and can make it easier for executives to field tough questions from audiences, including the media.

Brand Audits

Although messaging and visual identity are commonly associated with brand and heavily influence its external promotions, it is often the myriad of small, behavioural details that prove or disprove the visual and verbal image a company is trying to portray. For example, imagine booking a stay at a luxury hotel. The company's materials look elegant, the descriptions of the rooms and services all look appealing and the amenities are what you would expect for the premium price you pay.

When you arrive, the hotel is just as beautiful as expected. Visually, it's a display of elegance. You check into your room, slip out of your shoes and pad your way toward the sliding door to the balcony. It turns out to be somewhat of a challenge to open. Although you manage to open it enough to slide through, you decide to request that it be fixed. A call to the hotel's facility management desk rings several times before ending up in voicemail. You leave a message. After another 30 minutes pass, you try again. This time, a rather gruff voice greets you and says they will try to work it in within the next two days.

This brand inconsistency, a failure of one part of the organisation to behave with the same gracious elegance associated with the brand overall, may cost them your patronage. More importantly, you may leave the hotel with no intention to return without telling the management about your dissatisfaction and without letting the management know where their brand failed.

One tool that companies use to prevent this type of brand failure is a *brand audit*. Although there are many variations on the tool, most begin with a clear understanding of 'who' the brand wants to be. This includes the value proposition, brand attributes and core values.

Depending on the size of the company and the nature of the brand audit, the company may conduct an entirely internal assessment of where its operations are consistent or inconsistent with its desired brand reputation. The most common brand audits examine promotional materials, internal or external communications and common visual expressions of the company's *brand identity* to look for inconsistencies. These types of audits call attention to violations of the company's *graphics standards* (or a need to develop them), messaging that is inconsistent with the company voice or positioning and similar issues.

However, more comprehensive brand audits also include feedback about the brand's reputation from the broader market, including both customers and non-customers, and an examination of elements beyond the visual and verbal expressions of brand personality. This is where behavioural challenges to brand consistency, such as the repair team's slow, gruff response, are most likely to be identified.

Brand audits can also uncover hidden inconsistencies. One increasingly common challenge to brand consistency is the use of agents or subcontractors to accomplish work in the company's name. In many cases, agents sell products on a company's behalf, either as representatives or in a retail environment. Although they may be working for another organisation, when they represent a company's brand, the market often associates them, and their behaviour, with the brand itself. Because these individuals are likely to be customer-facing, their appearance, communications approach and behaviours have the potential to make a very strong impact on what the market believes about the product.

In 2009, passengers on a Continental Airlines flight were retained on a plane on a taxiway for more than six hours, overnight, when they could have allowed passengers off the plane and into the terminal. Although Continental Airlines suffered the damage to its reputation, the flight was actually operated by a subcontractor, ExpressJet, an independent company. Even though ExpressJet was identified in news stories, most of the negative press carried the Continental name.[23]

By conducting a thorough brand audit, a company can identify weaknesses both within its own company and within its partner relationships that can lead to brand damage.

BRAND ARCHITECTURE

The majority of this chapter has discussed brand as if the market associates the company with a single monolithic brand name and reputation. Although most companies have only one corporate brand name with which the market does business, many manage multiple brand names and personas in order to differentiate themselves or expand into different markets. The relationship between those brands, and the degree to which the market understands that they are related to one another, is called the *brand architecture*, and it is similar to the related reputations within a family in many respects.

Some companies extend a corporate brand, or parent brand, by adding additional descriptors or following consistent visual identity protocols. These are called *sub-brands*, or *sponsored brands*. Although this may help to differentiate a product or service line from others within the company, the brand reputation must be consistent. For example Deloitte Touche Tohmatsu Limited uses Deloitte as its parent brand name. However, it uses sub-brands around the world to denote specific divisions. For example, in the United States, Deloitte & Touche LLP provides audit services, whereas Deloitte Consulting LLP does management consulting.

Because sub-brands are more of an extension of a brand's name, they are most successful when they are fundamentally consistent. When a company lends its corporate brand name to a sub-brand that appeals to a different market or has a substantially different reputation, the sub-brand is likely to suffer. Gallo wines, for example, is one of the United States' leading producers of wines. However, the brand is most closely associated with inexpensive jug wines, rather than premium products. In the 1980s, as demand for low priced, non-premium wines was dropping and the market for premium wines was growing, Gallo attempted to enter the market with a more upscale wine using the sub-brand Gallo Estates. Although product reviews were positive, consumers still associated the product with its jug wine parents, and the product was a failure.

In terms of brand architecture, sub-brands are closely associated with their parent, or corporate, brands. In many cases, sub-brands reflect a naming protocol, rather than true differences in markets or the reputations those markets attribute to the companies serving their needs.

However, some companies' individual product brands are managed so independently of the parent brand that they are only tangentially associated. In many cases, the market is unaware that they are managed by the same corporation and perceives them to be completely separate companies. Yum! Brands, for example, owns KFC, Taco Bell and Pizza Hut. However, the brands of each of those restaurants have reputations that exist exclusive of Yum!'s involvement.

Individual product brands, when sufficiently separated from a company's parent brand reputation, can generate independent brand reputations. This makes the use of product brands a popular way to capture new market share outside of the company's existing market or compete with competitors that are leveraging different operating models with widespread appeal. Wal-Mart, for example, competes with warehouse retailer Costco through its Sam's Club stores. Sam's Club is, of course, a tip of the hat to founder Sam Walton, so in some ways, the brand acts as a sub-brand. However, the models appeal to slightly different markets. The association, if it is understood, does not detract from the parent brand because both are variations on discount retail operations.

Gallo found the solution to its premium wine market dilemma by using a product line branding solution. Three years after the failure of its Gallo Estates brand, it re-entered the market under a new brand name: Turning Leaf Vineyards. The new brand did not mirror its parent company's visual identity or name, and, thus, benefited from a separation of association with non-premium wines. The product line brand was far more successful than its sub-branded predecessor.[24]

Understanding a company's brand architecture is critical to the effective management of its reputation with the markets it serves. Although a company's brand architecture often mirrors its corporate structure, with each sub-brand or product line brand managed within a freestanding organisation, this isn't necessary. In fact, where brands have similar attributes, leveraging shared operational resources makes strong financial sense.

MITIGATING AND ADDRESSING BRAND DAMAGE

Warren Buffet famously quipped that 'it takes 20 years to build a reputation, and five minutes to ruin it. If you think about that, you'll do things differently.' Unfortunately, brand reputation damage can happen quite easily—and very quickly.

Protecting the company's reputation from damage requires careful management to ensure the company's words, appearance and behaviours are consistent with the reputation it wishes to maintain, and prompt attention to potential threats, including employee misconduct, legal allegations, customer discontent and media criticism.

Although internal inconsistencies can often be addressed effectively by management, some of the most rapid sources of damage come as a surprise from external sources. For example, a company may suffer from negative external perceptions that are inherent to the business model, as Wal-Mart has, relative to its compensation structures and heavy use of part-time personnel in order to reduce costs.

A company might also incur damage due to misbehaviour or perceived misbehaviour by employees, including executives or by subcontractors. McDonald's, for example, came under heavy criticism in April 2013 for a regional ad that parodied issues surrounding mental illness. The ad, McDonald's said, was not approved, and its advertising agency confirmed the accusation. Still, McDonald's reputation is suffering the negative impact.[25]

It might also be damaged by intentional or unintentional mistakes made by the company, such as tainted meat products, which must subsequently be recalled. For example, the Swedish company Ikea recently recalled meatballs and other products due to the discovery that their meat source had included horse meat with the beef used in the products. Unfortunately, this was preceded by a discovery that their chocolate cake contained unusually high amounts of coliform bacteria, which is found in faecal matter.[26]

In these cases, the reaction of the company and its executives will often determine how much damage will be done to its reputation. When the stakes are high, retaining an experienced crisis communications professional and, if needed, legal counsel is required. In addition, every company should have a *crisis communications* plan that outlines how the company will handle a crisis situation.

In general, even before a crisis arises, non-marketing professionals, including the executive team, should make sure that every employee understands how to handle inquiries about sensitive topics from external sources, including, but not limited to, the media. When a crisis surfaces, the company should have a designated company spokesperson with expertise in media relations that coordinates communications and is the only person to speak with the media. Executives and other employees should refer all inquiries about the crisis to that individual.

Because the truth will always be discovered, any communications should be factual. If the facts are not yet known, let the person making the inquiry know and call them back as soon as you have additional details you can release. Although crises can sometimes be embarrassing to the company, the executive team and other managers who do talk to the public should not speculate on, lie about or deliberately mislead the press about the situation. Trying to cover up the truth is rarely successful and makes the company look guilty. Once a brand is associated with misconduct, it can be years before the market's opinion improves, causing the company to lose customers, valued employees and strategic relationships with vendors and other partners and incur extensive marketing and legal expenses associated with its defence and reparation.

QUESTIONS FOR NON-MARKETING MANAGERS TO ASK ABOUT BRAND MANAGEMENT

As a non-marketing manager, you can play a critical role in helping your company maintain an effective and consistent brand reputation. To help you get started, consider the following questions:

- If my company were a person, how would I describe him or her?
- Is that description the type of individual with whom our target market(s) would like to do business?
- Are all of our operations and activities consistent with the reputation we would like to have in the market? If not, what are we doing to address those variances?
- Are we acting as a good corporate citizen, making decisions that are good for the community in addition to being good for business?

- Are we trying to persuade the public that we are, in fact, something that we are not?

- Do we have graphics standards and key messages?

- Do we use talking points when communicating important messages to key internal and external audiences?

- Do we conduct internal audits of our brand consistency?

- If we use more than one brand name, or are considering using more than one brand name, does the brand architecture make sense?

- Do we have a crisis communications plan ready so that we are prepared for the unexpected?

CHAPTER 3 SUMMARY

A company's brand is the reputation it has within the market, shaped by its corporate values, operating philosophy, value proposition and corporate social responsibility, which facilitates the customer's decision-making process. A strong brand can increase the market valuation of a company by 40%, reduce the cost of new customer acquisitions, improve customer loyalty and contribute to attracting and retaining great talent.

A company's brand is affected not only by its visual identity and communications with the market but also by its operational processes, the role it plays in the communities it serves and the way it treats employees and vendors. Because brand is affected by almost every aspect of business, brand management, like the discipline of marketing, is the ultimate responsibility of the CEO and the management team.

Companies with strong brands share several characteristics:

- They excel at the discipline of marketing and ensure everything they do aligns with their understanding of the market and the value they deliver to it.

- They base their brands on truth.

- They are good corporate citizens.

- They are visually, verbally and behaviourally consistent with the image of the merchant with whom their customers would want to do business.

Companies with strong brands also think carefully and proactively about what they want the brand to be, tailoring their communications, visual identity and behaviours to fit that personality. However, no brand can successfully portray a false image to the market on a sustained basis. The market will eventually discover the truth. As a result, all brand positioning should maintain a consistent focus on conveying brand attributes that are already true about the company, credible in the eyes of the market in order to be believed and relevant and important to the market and the way they make purchasing decisions.

This chapter also provides an overview of tools non-marketing managers can use to more effectively manage their brand:

- Graphics standards documents

- Key messaging documents

- Talking points
- Brand audits

Although most companies operate under a single brand name, many organisations use sub-brands or product level brands to further differentiate themselves or reach different markets. The relationship between the corporate brand and the sub-brands or product line brands is called a company's brand architecture. Understanding brand architecture is especially critical when a company uses sub-brands or manages brand names with very different brand reputations.

Even with careful management, brands do come under fire. The more successful and well-known the brand becomes, the more likely it is that the brand will experience some attack. In this case, the best defence is to be prepared with a crisis communications plan, address the issues truthfully and openly and retain professional crisis communications expertise if the situation is serious or has the potential to significantly affect brand reputation.

Endnotes

1 Brigham, Alexander and Linssen, Stefan. 'Your Brand Reputation is Irreplaceable. Protect It!,' *Forbes.com*, February 1, 2010. www.forbes.com/2010/02/01/brand-reputation-value-leadership-managing-ethisphere.html

2 Saporito, Bill. 'Starbucks: Wake Up, Smell the Coffee,' Time Business, February 26, 2007. www.time.com/time/business/article/0,8599,1593723,00.html

3 Horovitz, Bruce. 'Starbucks going back to grinding beans,' *USA Today*, March 20, 2008. http://abcnews.go.com/Business/story?id=4478266&page=1

4 Grynbaum, Michael. 'Starbucks Takes a 3-Hour Coffee Break,' *The New York Times*, February 7, 2008. www.nytimes.com/2008/02/27/business/27sbux.html?pagewanted=print

5 Sources:
Burne, Katy and Colchester, Max. 'J.P. Morgan Blunder Puts Bank in Regulators' Crosshairs,' *Wall Street Journal*, May 11, 2012. http://blogs.wsj.com/marketbeat/2012/05/11/j-p-morgan-blunder-puts-bank-in-regulators-crosshairs/?KEYWORDS=jp+morgan+london+whale
Vigna, Paul. 'The Hit to J.P. Morgan's Reputation "Really Hurts",' *Wall Street Journal*, May 11, 2012. http://blogs.wsj.com/marketbeat/2012/05/11/the-hit-to-j-p-morgans-reputation-really-hurts/?KEYWORDS=jp+morgan+london+whale
McIntyre, Douglas A. 'America's Nine Most Damaged Brands,' 24/7 Wall St Blog, April 10, 2013. http://247wallst.com/2013/04/10/americas-nine-most-damaged-brands-2/3/

6 2012 BranZ Top 100 Most Valuable Global Brands report, produced by WPP, BrandZ, and Millward Brown Optimor: www.millwardbrown.com/BrandZ/Top_100_Global_Brands.aspx

7 Brigham, Alexander and Linssen, Stefan. 'Your Brand Reputation is Irreplaceable. Protect It!,' Forbes.com, February 1, 2010. www.forbes.com/2010/02/01/brand-reputation-value-leadership-managing-ethisphere.html
World Economic Forum website and publications: http://www.weforum.org/

8 Sources:
Roberts, Peter and Dowling, Grahame. 'Corporate Reputation and Sustained Superior Financial Performance,' *Strategic Management Journal*, September 19, 2002. http://goizueta.emory.edu/upload/155/rad5b4ed.pdf
'Reputation Risk: A Corporate Governance Perspective,' published by The Conference Board, Research Report R-1412-07-WG, 2007. www.complianceweek.com/s/documents/ConfBReputation.pdf
Iwu-Egwuonwu, Ronald. 'Corporate Reputation & Firm Performance: Empirical Literature Evidence,' *International Journal of Business and Management*, April 2011.

9 'Reputation Risk: A Corporate Governance Perspective,' published by The Conference Board, Research Report R-1412-07-WG, 2007. www.complianceweek.com/s/documents/ConfBReputation.pdf

10 Gerzema, John and Roth, David. 'Reputation, Purpose and Profits: Bridging the Gap,' 2012 BrandZ Top 100 Most Valuable Global Brands report, 2012. www.millwardbrown.com/BrandZ/Top_100_Global_Brands.aspx

11 'Independents beat Starbucks for value,' *Which? Magazine*, January 24, 2008. www.which.co.uk/news/2008/01/independents-beat-starbucks-for-value-130057/; 'Which? Magazine survey: UK coffee chains,' posted in The Shot (blog) on January 24, 2008. http://theshot.coffeeratings.com/2008/01/starbucks-nero-costa-uk/

12 Sources:
'A triple-venti-American surprise? Consumer Reports finds McDonald's coffee better than Starbucks,' Food Inc. on NBCNews.com, February 4, 2007. www.nbcnews.com/id/16951509/
'Consumer Reports' Ground Coffee Tests Reveal Some of the Best Coffee Costs the Least,' *Consumer Reports* press release, February 2, 2009. http://pressroom.consumerreports.org/pressroom/2009/02/consumer-reports-ground-coffee-tests-reveal-some-of-the-best-cost-the-least.html
Ancil, Robert. 'Starbucks Roasted by McDonalds,' posted in Restaurant Consultants: The Next Idea

Endnotes, continued

Blog, December 21, 2009. www.thenextidea.net/content/blog?bid= 6

13 Keller, Kevin Lane. 'The Brand Report Card,' *Harvard Business Review*, January 2008. http://hbr.org/2000/01/the-brand-report-card/ar/1

14 Oswald, Nina. 'Employer Branding—Hit or Miss? Boost the value of your brand by clearly positioning your company on the job,' Interbrand website. www.interbrand.com/Libraries/Articles/Interbrand-EmployerBranding-EN.sflb.ashx

15 Brigham, Alexander and Linssen, Stefan. 'Your Brand Reputation is Irreplaceable. Protect It!,' Forbes.com, February 1, 2010. www.forbes.com/2010/02/01/brand-reputation-value-leadership-managing-ethisphere.html

16 *Measures that Matter*, Center for Business Innovation (CBI), Cap Gemini Ernst & Young, December 1997.

17 'Reputation Risk: A Corporate Governance Perspective,' published by The Conference Board, Research Report R-1412-07-WG, 2007. www.complianceweek.com/s/documents/ConfBReputation.pdf

18 *Ibid.*

19 McIntyre, Douglas A. 'America's Nine Most Damaged Brands,' 24/7 Wall St Blog, April 10, 2013. http://247wallst.com/2013/04/10/americas-nine-most-damaged-brands-2/3/

20 Williams, John. 'Your Brand's True Colors,' Entrepreneur., March 7, 2007. www.entrepreneur.com/article/175428

21 Sources:
Macdonald, Dids. 'Safeguarding Design Assets: A UK Perspective,' *WIPO Magazine*, February 2012. www.wipo.int/wipo_magazine/en/2012/01/article_0005.html
Temple Island Collection website news releases: 'Temple Island Collection v New English Teas. Second Court Judgment,' 'Temple Island Collection v. New English Teas,' and 'ACID News Flash: Temple Island Score Copyright Victory over New English Teas.' www.templeisland.com/new_english_teas_red_bus_copyright.asp
Cheesman, Chris. 'Photographers face copyright threat after shock ruling,' *Amateur Photographer*, April 1, 2012. www.amateurphotographer.co.uk/photo-news/534352/photographers-face-copyright-threat-after-shock-ruling

22 Sources for information on messaging:
Morrison, Maureen. 'McDonalds to launch ad campaign focused on growers,' *Advertising Age*, December 14, 2011. http://adage.com/article/news/mcdonald-s-launch-ad-campaign-focused-growers/231579/
Wikiquote.com: Advertising Slogans: http://en.wikiquote.org/wiki/Advertising_slogans
Wikipedia.com: Advertising Slogans: http://en.wikipedia.org/wiki/Advertising_slogan
'McDonald's Advertising Taglines and US Milestones,' *QSR Magazine*, June 30, 2000. www.qsrmagazine.com/news/mcdonalds-advertising-taglines-and-us-milestones
McDonald's Website: www.mcdonalds.com

23 Brigham, Alexander, and Linssen, Stefan. 'Your Brand Reputational Value is Irreplaceable. Protect It!,' Forbes.com, February 1, 2010.

24 Sources:
(KENDALL JACKSON WINERY LIMITED v. GALLO WINERY, 1998). http://caselaw.findlaw.com/us-9th-circuit/1139723.html
Funding Universe profile of E&J Gallo: www.fundinguniverse.com/company-histories/E-amp;-J-Gallo-Winery-company-History.html

25 Horovitz, Bruce. 'McDonald's pulls mental illness parody,' USA Today, April 12, 2013. www.usatoday.com/story/money/business/2013/04/11/mcdonalds-advertisement-mental-illness-nami/2075089/

26 Kavoussi, Bonnie. 'Ikea Horse Meat Controversy Hurts Company's Reputation: Analysis,' *The Huffington Post*, March 26, 2013. www.huffingtonpost.com/2013/03/22/ikea-horse-meat-reputation_n_2933891.html

Section 3

EVALUATING PROPOSED INVESTMENTS
IN THE MARKETING FUNCTION

4

EVALUATING MARKETING PLAN ALIGNMENT

Even among market leaders, some doubt always exists about the efficacy of marketing investments and the return they are actually delivering. With average performers, that slight doubt increases to substantial uncertainty. In fact, in many companies, the executive team is so sceptical about the value their marketing delivers that it is invariably the first line item cut when times are tough. However, the source of their doubt and the way they manage their marketing function are closely connected.

In fact, the executive teams within average performers are often correct to be sceptical about the returns they are receiving on marketing investments. They probably aren't getting the returns they could get, and they certainly aren't getting the returns market leaders are getting. And it's their own fault.

They could be getting better returns on their investments in the marketing function if they were evaluating plans accurately, managing them effectively and measuring the results.

WHAT DRIVES RETURNS ON MARKETING INVESTMENTS

The financial returns on the marketing function investments are greatest when the function of marketing is aligned with the discipline of marketing. It's what was described in chapter 2, 'The Discipline of Marketing,' as the Point C Principle.

Companies who adhere to the Point C Principle align everything in the company with the market's needs and the company's value proposition, from operations to brand management. The function of marketing is part of the operations that must be aligned.

Yet, frequently it isn't. This causes poor returns on marketing investments.

So, why are plans misaligned? There are four common reasons.

Four Common Reasons the Marketing Function Is Misaligned With the Marketing Discipline:

1. The plan is developed without insight derived from the discipline of marketing.
2. The plan has no strategy or objectives, just tactics or actions.
3. The marketing tactics or activities were poorly selected.
4. The plan was never evaluated for financial impact prior to approval.

First, many times, the plan, or part of it, is developed without insight from the discipline of marketing. Instead, the plan is based on assumptions about how the market will respond to a particular activity.

Every company makes assumptions when it is developing projections about its marketing performance. You assume that you know who will want to purchase your product or service, what features or benefits must be included in order for it to be appealing, how much they will pay, where they will look to purchase it and what will influence their purchasing decision. Those assumptions are common—and they represent risk. In fact, they form the most significant form of risk because they are such basic assumptions. If you get any one of these assumptions wrong, your product won't sell, or at least, it won't sell to its potential. And the consequences could be significant. The company loses money, time and, potentially, its competitive position.

The key is to use the discipline of marketing to ensure that you are not basing your entire marketing plan on assumptions that may be completely unfounded. Focusing on the marketing discipline and using it to inform marketing strategy is the first step toward improved alignment.

The second reason that plans tend to be misaligned is that the plan has no strategy or objectives, just tactics or actions. This is surprisingly common. In fact, even as a marketing consultant I am frequently asked to develop marketing plans without strategic guidance. Prospective clients sometimes give me a look of surprise when I ask for copies of their strategic and business plans or a specific outline of the business and financial outcomes they are trying to achieve. This is a good sign that they view marketing as an important but disconnected activity and that it is unlikely to be aligned.

In many respects, the relationship between a marketing professional and the management or executive team is similar to the relationship between an investment manager and his or her client. Ideally, the client gives the investment manager the goals, describes any special circumstances or anticipated needs, provides guidelines about the types of investments he or she is willing to make and his or her tolerance for risk, and the investment professional develops the plan to get the client to his or her goal. The investment manager must be knowledgeable, but he would not be able to operate effectively without some guidance about the client's goals. Conversely, the client has hired an investment manager to achieve optimal returns and should provide him or her enough information and guidance to perform that job without telling him or her how it should be done.

In some organisations, particularly large, consumer-focused retailers, which have a longer tradition of market-focused activity, the marketing discipline and the marketing function are well coordinated. These companies are at one end of the spectrum. At the other end of the spectrum, we frequently see professional services and other highly technical companies. In these organisations, the executive team may have unclear goals for the marketing function, may be failing to be effective in the discipline of marketing or may try to micromanage the marketing function, effectively dictating where marketing funds should be invested. In each case, these companies are leaving potential financial returns on the table.

For example, imagine a company that provides only limited information about its business plans to the marketing team, gives them a defined budget and then, at the end of the year, is frustrated at what the marketing team delivered. In our financial services analogy, this would be like a client who asks her financial manager to 'make money' and then is frustrated because the approach the financial manager took was too aggressive, too conservative or did not deliver the results she secretly hoped to achieve. Marketing investments, like financial investments, vary. Some take years to become effective but deliver far greater financial returns. Others are quick to deliver but have limited long-term impact.

When the executive team fails to clearly define business and financial objectives, the marketing team must guess about company priorities. In the end, the marketing department often ends up simply managing the same activities in which the company has always engaged, occasionally adding something new to try to keep up with market leaders.

The key to preventing this type of misalignment is to ensure that the marketing function is well informed about the company's overall objectives and to hold the marketing team accountable to its role in helping the organisation achieve those objectives.

The third common reason the marketing function is misaligned with the discipline of marketing is that the planning team made a poor selection of marketing tactics. Any given marketing tactic will be more appropriate for some markets, products or services, and organisations than others. Choosing the wrong tactic can mean that it is inefficient, exposing the company to segments of the population that will never be customers, or ineffective, failing to achieve its strategic objective.

The non-marketing manager may or may not influence the selection of marketing tactics. In smaller organisations, the non-marketing manager or executive is far more likely to play a role in identifying tactics, whereas in larger organisations, this is less likely to be the case. However, in either case, the non-marketing manager can play an important role in monitoring for tactical misalignment.

To help keep the marketing plan in alignment, non-marketing managers should understand the basics about how the various tactical categories (product, price, distribution and promotions) function and how approaches are chosen in each one.

Finally, the fourth common reason marketing plans are poorly aligned is that the plan was never evaluated for financial impact prior to plan approval. Marketing plans can, and should, be aligned with both business objectives and financial outcomes. To optimise returns, marketing plans should be evaluated in financial terms both before the plan is approved, to ensure the plan is well conceived, and after the plan has been executed, to evaluate how successful the plan was.

To help non-marketing and marketing managers alike, I developed a framework for assessing alignment of the marketing function and its activities with the discipline of marketing. I call it the *Marketing Alignment Map*, and it can be very useful in helping allay fears about marketing's effectiveness.

THE MARKETING ALIGNMENT MAP

The Marketing Alignment Map™ (see figure 4-1) is a flow chart that describes how each of the components of a marketing plan relates to the other for the purposes of aligning marketing activities with business objectives and assessing financial returns on the marketing function investments.

Figure 4-1: Marketing Alignment Map™

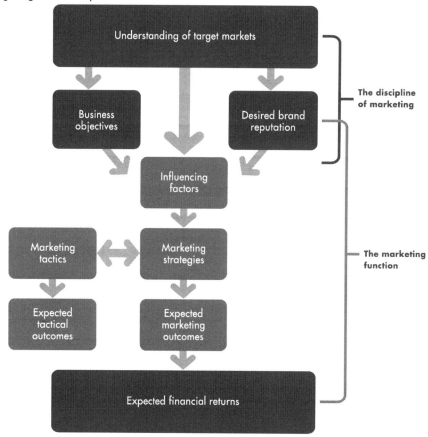

The Marketing Alignment Map begins with the work led by the executive team: the discipline of marketing. Based on the company's understanding of its market or markets, the executive team sets short and longer term business objectives, envisions the brand reputation they hope to achieve relative to the market place and estimates the financial outcomes they believe are possible to achieve if they work steadily toward those goals.

Targeted Business and Financial Objectives

The business objectives must be clear and realistic, based on a solid understanding of the size of the market, the organisation's own strengths and weaknesses and those of its competitors and its current market share and brand strength. Business objectives should also be tied to targeted financial objectives. Business objectives answer the following questions:

- How will we address our customer's needs?
- How will we drive financial results for our company?
- How will we know we have been successful?

For example:

- A retailer might set a goal to expand sales of a particular product by a certain percentage, resulting in a specific increase in gross profits.

- A professional service provider might decide to start providing services in an area in which its clients are currently underserved, with specific financial objectives, including targeted revenues.

- A not-for-profit might decide to build an endowment to sustain operations during an economic downturn, with a specific fundraising goal by a certain date.

- A business services company might be aggressively pursuing a certain share of a specific market, specifying that it would like to increase its market share from X% to Y% within a specific timeframe, and connecting that increase to specific changes in revenues and profitability.

- A company might decide that it needs to reduce overall operating costs by 2% to remain competitive, with a targeted date and total estimated savings associated with any changes that are made.

Although the company should set goals that are ambitious, the goals should also be realistic. They must also be communicated to the marketing team.

Desired Brand Reputation

The company should also envision the brand it would like to create. Although the market determines what the brand is, the executive team can manage the company's image by ensuring consistency among words, image and actions. The executive team is responsible for ensuring that the company's entire operational structure is aligned with its desired brand, ensuring that the brand elements (including messaging and the company's visual identity) are codified, and communicating and reinforcing the brand within the organisation.

The marketing function often plays an important role in helping to define the brand and creating key components of the brand management toolkit, such as the key messaging document and the graphics standards. Whether the marketing team created the standards, inherited them from previous team members or had them presented to them by internal and/or external advisers, because of their external focus, the marketing team plays a significant role in implementing and enforcing them. Consequently, it is exceptionally important that the marketing team understand how the brand elements relate to the market, its needs and the company's value proposition.

Influencing Factors

A strong marketing plan begins with an understanding of the customer's purchasing decision process and the factors that influence a company's success in making a sale. This includes knowing both who the decision-maker is and who influences the decision. For example, a technology company might sell its solutions to the chief information officer (CIO), but the users, the CFO and CEO, may heavily influence the decision. As a result, it is not sufficient to cater to the CIO alone. The company must also understand what is likely to influence the recommendation made by other team members.

Generally, many factors influence a purchasing decision. The marketing team must understand how each is weighted in the mind of the purchaser and how the company measures against them relative to its competition. A marketing team can rarely focus on all influencing factors. By prioritising and evaluating, the team can focus on those most likely to produce an impact.

It is the responsibility of the executive team, and others who oversee the marketing function, to ensure that these influencing factors are consistent with their understanding of the market, the brand the company is trying to create and the company's business objectives.

Marketing Strategies

Marketing strategies describe the marketing function's efforts to affect influencing factors in order to achieve business objectives. Another way to think about it is that strategies identify *what* the organisation wants to accomplish. The strongest strategies, when articulated, incorporate the impact they are trying to make on influencing factors.

> Marketing strategies describe what the organisation wants to accomplish.

For example, when Starbucks launched Via, its first foray into the instant coffee market, it understood the market's scepticism about whether the flavour of an instant coffee could rival that of its freshly brewed competitor. Perception about taste was one of the most significant factors influencing the customer's purchasing decision. In many respects, it was more important than product awareness, another key influencing factor. Starbuck's strategy was to change customer perceptions that instant coffee was inferior to freshly brewed coffee.[1]

In another example, imagine that a performing arts organisation's business objective was to increase the number of new patrons trying the theatre. Through conversations with new patrons, it discovered that most patrons who tried the theatre were invited to do so by someone whose taste and judgement they respected. The influencing factor for these patrons was whether or not such a person encouraged them to attend the theatre. Its marketing strategy was to increase the number of influential patrons who recommended a performance to their friends.

Similar to Starbucks, Airborne Express also developed a strategy to address perception. Until its 2003 acquisition by the German delivery company DHL, Airborne provided express delivery services to clients across the United States. Its core competency was its logistics framework, and its brand was known for operational efficiency and correspondingly low prices. For its customers, the most important influencing factor was whether the company could deliver packages on time. Despite a track record that matched or exceeded its rivals, aggressive competitor positioning had resulted in customer perception that on time and low cost were incompatible. Its key strategy, therefore, was to change that perception.

Although the key to developing strong marketing strategies is to understand what needs to change within the market to encourage increased purchasing behaviour, these changes must be consistent with the company's value proposition and its desired brand reputation. For example, a customer may not shop at Hermès because they believe the store's product lines are too expensive. This doesn't mean that Hermès should try to prove its products to be inexpensive. It simply suggests that the marketing team may be targeting the wrong audience.

Marketing strategies, like business objectives, must also be realistic. I met recently with a company that wanted to expand its sales across the country. Its marketing team knew that most customers had a need the company could address and that they were simply unaware the company existed. Although increasing awareness among those target customer groups was a laudable marketing strategy, the market was so broad and disconnected that doing so would be costly and take a significant period of time. The executive team agreed to narrow their market focus and concentrate their awareness efforts on specific, highly lucrative segments.

Marketing Tactics

A company's *marketing tactics* are the specific activities the company undertakes to execute its marketing strategies. Whereas strategies address *what* an organisation wants to accomplish, tactics address *how* it will be done. Marketing tactics are most often drawn from the four 'P's of marketing. They include product and service changes and introductions, pricing approaches and temporary pricing incentives, the selection of distribution channels and the management of the sales team and process and promotional approaches, such as newsletters, advertising and social media.

Marketing tactics describe how the organisation will meet its strategic objectives.

In some cases, especially for smaller companies, the executive or management team may actually craft significant portions of the tactical marketing plan, selecting product or services to add to the mix, establishing pricing policies, identifying sales channels and influencing the selection of promotional tactics. In larger companies, these functions are handled entirely by a diverse group of marketing professionals, often organised into multiple teams by expertise. In these cases, the marketing plans are likely to be extremely complex and integrated.

Returning to the prior example of Starbucks and its launch of Via instant coffee, its marketing strategy was to change the perception that instant coffee was inferior to freshly brewed coffee. To do so, the company hosted taste tests at its stores across the United States, inviting people to try Via and its traditionally brewed coffee to see if they could tell the difference. In exchange, participants were given a gift certificate for a free coffee beverage for their next visit, and a $1 coupon for their first purchase of Via products. This in-store campaign was one of the company's marketing tactics. Other tactics included distribution through recreational equipment retailers, bookstores, and other new channels, rather than exclusively within its own stores. It also included an interactive social media campaign, traditional advertising and outreach to radio disc jockeys and television personalities, encouraging them to try the product to see if they could tell the difference.[2]

The theatre that was referenced earlier could have used direct mail and e-mail outreach, discounted pricing offers, referral rewards and a variety of other tactics to encourage existing patrons to share theatre with their friends. Airborne, whose lean operating culture was advertising-averse, used a combination of case studies and statistics distributed by its sales force, outreach with business and general press regarding its model and financial guarantees to execute on its marketing strategies.

Choosing the right tactics, like choosing the right investment instrument, is critical to success. In general, the tactics must have the potential to influence behaviour, be consistent with the brand and be the most cost-effective and efficient option among those presented. Chapter 6, 'Aligning Marketing Tactics With Influencing Factors,' addresses the selection of tactics in greater detail.

As a non-marketing manager overseeing the marketing function, it is most likely not your responsibility to select the appropriate tactics. Instead, you should understand the basic principles of tactical selection and be able to ask informed questions about why the tactics were selected in order to be assured that the selection process was thorough. Chapters 7–10 review each of the major categories of marketing tactics, in turn, providing an orientation to each discipline and including a list of questions you can use at the end of each chapter.

Even if it isn't your job to select tactics, it is your responsibility to understand that marketing tactics are not marketing strategies. In many companies, especially smaller ones, the marketing plan is a list of tactics, rather than strategies and related tactics. For example, I recently looked at the marketing plan of a professional service organisation that listed social media, a new website, special events and advertising as their marketing strategies. Although these are popular choices among professional service organisations, their choices left me scratching my head and asking why they had selected them and what they hoped to achieve.

It soon became clear that these activities were what the executive team expected and their plan had been crafted to imitate those of their larger competitors. Unfortunately, without strategies guiding what the organisation was trying to achieve, the tactics were subject to two potential risks. First, they might not be the most appropriate choice of tactics to achieve the organisation's objectives. Second, because tactics, by nature, can be used to achieve any of a variety of objectives, there was little assurance that the way they would be used would help the company move forward in ways that were profitable.

Expected Tactical Outcomes

Each tactic should have at least one metric associated with it so that the marketing team, and the executives who oversee them, can determine whether it was successfully executed and if the market has responded to this tactic as anticipated. Marketers use a variety of metrics to assess where they stand according to plan. They generally fall into three categories:

- *Completion metrics.* Indicate whether the work was completed on time and answer the question 'how will we know we are done?'

- *Intermediate marketing metrics.* Indicate whether the marketing tactic operated as expected and answer the question 'how will we know this tactic was successful?'

- *Financial metrics.* Are more directly connected to the company's financial performance and also answer the question 'how will we know this tactic was successful?'

For example, if a new service line, social media, a new website, special events and advertising are the chosen tactics, the completion metrics might include the anticipated launch date for the service line and website, the number of social media posts, the number of special events and the completion of a specific advertising flight.

The corresponding intermediate marketing metrics might include the number of clients secured within a specific timeline (for the service line), the number of friends on Facebook or the number of responses to a blog post (for social media), the number of visitors to a new website (for the website), the number of special events or number of prospective clients who attend (for special events) or the number of ads placed or impressions (for advertising). The financial metrics might include revenue per new client or revenues generated from a special event.

Some of the most common metrics are included in chapters 7–10. As you review these metrics, it is important to remember that although completion and intermediate metrics may help a marketing department track progress, they often do not translate to financial metrics.

When I speak to audiences about metrics and marketing analytics, I am often asked whether it is possible to measure the potential financial return of an individual tactic. The answer, as you will discover in chapter 11, 'Evaluating Returns on Marketing Investments,' is 'sometimes.' Most marketing tactics work in collaboration with other tactics. For example, social media often assumes the presence of a website. Special events frequently produce better outcomes with a strong media relations plan. Thus, although tactical metrics and expected tactical outcomes are an important management tool, they are no substitute for the broader financial metrics that should be associated with marketing strategies.

Expected Marketing Outcomes

Expected marketing outcomes can, and should, be measured in both financial and non-financial terms.

For example, Starbucks expected that between 8 million and 10 million people who liked Starbucks and were willing to pay a premium for the quality they offer would take the coffee taste test during the first week of the campaign.[3] Of those individuals, Starbucks would have had an expectation that a certain percentage would find no difference or even prefer the instant version.

The market for instant coffee is significant. Internationally, consumers spend about $23 billion annually on instant coffee.[4] In the US, about 7% of the U.S. population currently drinks instant coffee daily, and a larger percentage drink it while travelling, camping or on other occasions.[5] Internationally, those numbers are even bigger. In Japan, 60% of the coffee sold is instant. In the UK, 80% of coffee sold is instant. Although the expected marketing outcomes from Starbucks' marketing campaign are not public, if even 5% of the millions of consumers in the initial markets of the US, the UK, Japan, and Canada began to purchase Via on a regular basis, the revenues would be significant.

The intermediate marketing metrics Starbucks marketers used to estimate the impact of this strategy might have included the number of people who took the taste test, the number of people who redeemed the coupon to expand their taste test experience and the number of people who purchased Via in a period immediately following the campaign. They also undoubtedly had financial projections that allowed them to evaluate the financial impact of their marketing efforts.

Chapter 11 provides a framework for translating intermediate marketing metrics into financial metrics and evaluating potential financial returns on marketing investments.

Expected Financial Returns

As a part of the business planning process, the executive team should develop financial projections that reflect the expected financial outcomes associated with those business objectives. Like the business objectives, the expected financial returns should be based on market realities. They should also be adjusted for risk associated with market uncertainty.

At the end of the marketing assessment process, the non-marketing manager should be able to assess the impact expected from marketing activities on the expected financial returns. If the two do not align, either the marketing plan or the business and financial objectives should be revisited.

EVALUATING MARKETING ALIGNMENT

The Marketing Alignment Map provides a framework that companies can use to achieve the natural alignment market leaders have because of their adherence to the Point C Principle. By using the Marketing Alignment Map to evaluate marketing plans prior to approval, a company's management team can significantly improve the performance of its marketing function.

As you walk through the functional marketing plan for your company, beginning with the company's objectives, the plan should reflect the company's understanding of the factors that will influence behaviour and should prioritise strategies that will make the most significant impact on them. The selected tactics should be consistent with the value proposition and brand reputation the company is trying to achieve. Walking through the Marketing Alignment Map, you should be able to envision how each piece of the marketing puzzle fits together with the discipline of marketing.

Although it is the marketing team's responsibility to bring experience and expertise to the selection of marketing tactics, they should also be able to explain how they were selected and why those particular tactics will be most effective. Your marketing team, whether internal or external, should be able to tell you how they estimated the impact the strategies will have and why they selected the tactics they will use. They should also be able to tell you how they arrived at the financial estimates they used.

Finally, after hearing the marketing team's explanation of how the marketing strategies and tactics were selected and estimates were made, you should feel confident that the risk-adjusted returns delivered by the marketing investments and the investments that will be required to achieve them, are consistent with the company's overall financial return expectations.

THE BENEFITS OF ALIGNMENT

The Marketing Alignment Map can be used either as a framework for evaluating marketing plans or as a process for creating them. Either way, ensuring alignment improves your financial returns in several ways:

- *Aligned plans are more likely to be implemented.* When marketing strategies are not aligned with business and financial goals, executive commitment is weak, and initiatives are more likely to be altered or discontinued before they have an opportunity to produce a return. Because many marketing investments, such as advertising, generate optimal returns after an extended investment (sometimes for several years), abandoning the investment prematurely results in wasted funds.

- *Aligned investments reduce the risk of brand damage.* When marketing tactics are inconsistent with brand reputation, it creates market confusion that can result in decreased profitability. For example, Colgate has long been known for addressing customers' oral and dental health needs. When the company ventured into frozen dinners, the market was confused, and the new product line failed. The result was a costly loss to the company. Brand damage can also happen when marketing tactics are abandoned before they become effective. If a company experiences a rapid series of abandoned campaigns, the market can also become confused about the brand and its message.

- *Projects without impact are tabled or discarded.* The Marketing Alignment Map provides an easy way to evaluate current marketing initiatives against desired objectives, making it easier to spot poorly selected tactics or 'copycat' behaviour with no strategic purpose. It also provides a strong framework for evaluating unexpected opportunities and new ideas that arise after the marketing plan is underway. By leaving budget for these sorts of plans and establishing targeted financial impacts, unexpected opportunities can be quickly evaluated and either seized or ignored.

QUESTIONS FOR NON-MARKETING MANAGERS TO ASK ABOUT EVALUATING MARKETING PLAN ALIGNMENT

As a non-marketing professional with oversight responsibility for the marketing function, you should be focused on three questions:

- Is the plan consistent with our understanding of the market, our business objectives and our brand?

- Is the logic behind the development of the marketing strategies, tactics and expected outcomes solid?

- Do the risk-adjusted financial returns expected as a result of our investments in marketing match or exceed our expected financial returns?

If the answer to all three of these questions is yes, your marketing plan is aligned with your company's business and financial objectives, and with your market and brand, and you can feel confident you are making a solid investment. If the answer is no, or you are not sure, subsequent chapters of this book should provide you with the understanding required to make an accurate assessment.

CHAPTER 4 SUMMARY

Non-marketing professionals are frequently asked to provide input and approval on key marketing investments. Although a marketing professional will, in most cases, be recommending a particular approach, the non-marketing professional must be able to evaluate whether the strategies and expected returns are realistic.

This is where the discipline of marketing discussed in chapter 2 and chapter 3, 'Brand Management Fundamentals,' meets the function of marketing. To ensure that the marketing plan delivers the optimal financial returns, the marketing function must be aligned with the marketing discipline. This is the concept behind the Point C Principle introduced in chapter 2.

To ensure that the marketing plan is in alignment with the discipline of marketing and delivering optimal performance, the non-marketing manager should confirm that

- the marketing team has a thorough knowledge of the organisation's goals, desired brand reputation and expected financial returns, and that it has benefitted from the knowledge gathered throughout the organisation relative to the market and its needs;

- the marketing plan is based on marketing strategies and related objectives that will clearly contribute to the business objectives;

- the tactics or activities identified to support the marketing strategies and related objectives are appropriate for the market and the brand;

- the marketing plan is evaluated in financial terms both prior to approval and after execution.

Whether a non-marketing manager has been asked to help develop a marketing plan or simply provide input or approval once the plan is presented, the Marketing Alignment Map can be a useful tool to assist in evaluating its potential effectiveness. Shown in abbreviated form in figure 4-2 that follows, the Marketing Alignment Map begins with the discipline of marketing as led by the company's executives. Based on the company's target markets, business objectives and brand reputation, the tool facilitates a process of evaluating what the marketing investments are designed to do, how they are expected to work, what activities and investments will be required in order to generate a return and what return is expected. In short, the Marketing Alignment Map ensures that the investments the company makes in marketing activities will help the company achieve both its business objectives and its expected financial return.

Figure 4-2: Abbreviated Marketing Alignment Map

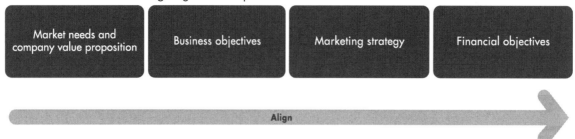

Ensuring alignment using the Marketing Alignment Map or a similar process helps organisations improve the returns they receive on marketing investments by

- improving the chances that marketing plans will not be abandoned before they have the opportunity to become productive;
- minimising inadvertent brand damage;
- providing an efficient tool for evaluating unexpected opportunities; and
- ensuring that the marketing strategies and tactics selected are strong matches for the organisation, its brand and its business and financial objectives.

Endnotes

1 York, Emily Bryson. 'Starbucks Marketing Push for Via Begins with Taste Tests,' *Advertising Age*, September 28, 2009. http://adage.com/article/news/advertising-starbucks-begins-marketing-push/139319/

2 *Ibid.*

3 *Ibid.*

4 Starbucks Press Release: Starbucks VIA Ready Brew Hits Grocery Aisles Around the World, September 7, 2010. http://news.starbucks.com/article_display.cfm?article_id= 436

5 Ferguson, Mike. 'Instant Convenience, Mermaid, Good Enough?' Coffeegeek.com, February 20, 2009. http://coffeegeek.com/opinions/professionals/02-20-2009

.5

UNDERSTANDING WHAT INFLUENCES MARKET BEHAVIOUR

Figure 5-1: Marketing Alignment Map

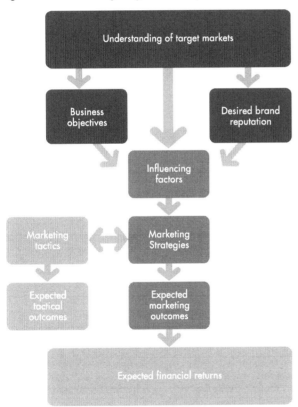

One of the most common reasons plans are misaligned with the market and the company's objectives relative to serving it is that the marketing function does not benefit from the executive team's or management team's broader management of the marketing discipline. The marketing discipline provides the marketing function with critical insight into what is influencing the customer's purchasing decisions, how the company is perceived relative to those criteria and where the company should focus its marketing efforts in order to generate the biggest impact. This information is a crucial part of forming a marketing plan that is based on facts.

DO YOU KNOW WHY YOUR CUSTOMER CHOOSES YOUR COMPANY—AND WHY NON-CUSTOMERS DON'T?

Think back to your most recent new customer acquisition. Do you know what prompted him or her to start buying products or services from your company? Are you sure? Have you asked?

Many people assume they know, but they don't. For example, in service-based companies, people often cite service quality as the difference. However, that's unlikely to be the reason people made the switch from your competitor to you. They didn't know whether your service was good or bad before they became your customer. They had never used your services before. So, what was the real reason? Was it a referral? Was it your reputation? Unless you ask people why they chose your product or service when they first do so, you are unlikely to have an accurate picture.

You might have a better idea of why people remain customers. After all, this is the 'good stuff' you hear back from customers. This is what prompts many companies to think their customer service makes the difference. That's what they hear when things are going well.

What about your former customers? Do you know why they left you? The real reasons, rather than the polite ones they gave you as excuses?

The answers to these questions are called *influencers*. Some of them are things you can affect through marketing such as reputation, product benefits or features or your choice of distribution channels. Others can be affected by addressing issues that aren't traditionally considered to be part of marketing, like quality control issues or manufacturing capacity. Finally, some will be completely outside of your scope of influence, like the economy or their underlying need for the solution your company provides.

Understanding influencers is more difficult than it sounds. Influencers are different for people who are making a purchase decision and people who are currently customers. People remain customers for different reasons than when they initially choose your product or service. Also, they often don't tell you what those underlying reasons are, especially when they constitute bad news. You are more likely to have an accurate depiction of what you do well, when you do it well, than what you don't.

Yet, having an accurate understanding of what influences a customer's purchasing decision is critical to having a well-aligned marketing plan. After all, if the objective of your marketing team and its marketing plan isn't to positively affect the criteria that influence your customers' and prospective customers' purchasing decisions, what is it?

The Danger of Assumptions

To perform well, the marketing function needs to have the information about what influences purchasing behaviour. In companies that are market leaders, that information often comes from the discipline of marketing, either through market research or through informal but systematic gathering of data. Among average performers, the answers to these questions are often based on assumptions, rather than on well-researched information or fact. If those assumptions are wrong, the plan and function of marketing are misaligned, and the company is wasting its marketing dollars.

> By making assumptions about the segment based on mass-level common knowledge, the company can lose its focus and its competitive edge.

Some time ago, I facilitated a business retreat during which we planned to discuss the company's positioning and marketing plan. It was relatively easy to determine what the company's objectives were. They clearly understood who they wanted to serve and what they believed made them different. However, they were quite reluctant to have me speak with their client base and insisted that they had a solid understanding of how they were perceived by the market.

This isn't unusual. Many companies hesitate to 'bother' their customers with questions about their performance. Some are genuinely concerned that the customers will become irritated with the process. Others are more concerned about negative feedback. A few have declined because they would prefer that their customers not be reminded of their competitors.

Fortunately, in this case, a research company serving the industry had conducted some broad-based market research to assess relative competitor positions. Although the research didn't answer all of our questions, it did help us minimise the impact of the executive team's assumptions. It also revealed a problem.

Several of their assumptions about how they were perceived by the market were not correct. Because these assumptions were related to market perceptions about some of the most important competitive criteria, the difference between market perception and executive assumptions was significant.

Understanding the market accurately is important both for understanding how a customer makes his or her purchasing choice, in general, and for understanding how the company is perceived relative to the purchasing decisions. When I meet with a new client to discuss their marketing plans, I often ask them how their customers make a purchase decision. Many times, the answer is a shrug and a dismissal of the question. 'We just know,' I'm told. 'It's just common knowledge in the industry.' However, the industry data to which they are probably referring often represents the mass market, the combination of all segments, not the segments a particular company wants to serve.

For example, industry-wide data about what patients want from doctors is interesting but not sufficient to help position any particular physician within the market. That's because what a patient looks for in a particular type of doctor might vary. For example, for a general practice doctor, convenient location and office hours, bedside manner and referrals from friends might be priority influencers. However, when a patient needs a delicate procedure to address a serious health issue, experience with the procedure, referrals from physicians and the hospital with which the person is associated might be far more important than bedside manner. If the clinic with which the specialty physician was located tried to position the doctor on the basis of what mattered to most patients in general, they might miss the opportunity to distinguish the clinic in a way that was important to the patient.

By making assumptions about the segment based on mass-level common knowledge, the company can lose its focus and its competitive edge.

In addition, because the market is continually changing, with new entrants, new solutions to customer needs, and new needs arising, watching competitors for guidance is like trying to win the Tour de France by following the seat of the bike in front of you. It is a sure way of remaining in the middle of the competitive pack.

To understand what the market's decision criteria are, identify criteria that might influence a specific niche or signal future opportunities and accurately assess where a company stands against those criteria, the company's managers and marketing team need to spend time talking with the market and soliciting direct feedback. Otherwise, the marketing plan may neglect the factors most likely to change customer purchasing behaviour, and as a result, won't deliver the returns it otherwise could.

WHAT YOUR MARKETING FUNCTION NEEDS TO KNOW

So, what information does the marketing function need in order to create plans that are well-aligned?

In addition to knowing what influences purchasing decision behaviour, the marketing function needs to know how those factors connect to the customer's purchasing decision process and criteria. Although influencers are broad groups of factors, both within and outside the company's control, an analysis of the purchasing decision process looks at criteria actively used in the decision to make a purchase. This effectively ignores external factors that prevent a person from becoming a customer, such as an absence of the need, and assumes that the prospective customer is weighing a company's product or service solution against those of competitors. In the preceding physician example, this process would eliminate any person who does not have the health issue the specialist is trained to address and look strictly at those who are prospective patients.

To ensure alignment, the marketing team must understand:

- what the customer's purchasing decision criteria are;

- the relative importance of each influencing factor to the purchasing decision process;

- whether different segments within the market favour different criteria;

- what the market expects from merchants relative to performance;

- how the company and its competitors are performing relative to those purchasing decision criteria;

- whether there are other influencers, outside of the purchasing decision process, that are serving as barriers; and

- what the potential impact of a change in market perception might mean in terms of the company's performance.

The purchasing criteria that prospective customers use in their purchasing decision process are the most important criteria for the company's current business objectives. They are the conscious and subconscious reasons the customer chooses one competitor over the other.

Within the purchasing criteria, some will be more important than others. For example, customers always value strong customer service, but it may be more important when purchasing a product that is complex and technical than it is when purchasing paper towels. By understanding how customers prioritise purchasing decision criteria, marketers have a better understanding of where the company should focus its attention.

When customers have very different prioritisations for their purchasing decision criteria, this may signal that there are different market segments within the market. If the company serves multiple segments, it should understand how the purchasing decision process and criteria differ between them. More information on how segments can be identified will be addressed later in this chapter.

In addition to knowing what those purchasing decision criteria are, the marketing function must have a strong understanding of the acceptable range for those criteria, given the value proposition the company offers, how it is currently performing and how its competitors are performing relative to that criteria. For example, Sam Walton, Wal-Mart's founder, knew that what attracted customers to his stores was having the lowest prices on products used every day, such as milk. He was well-known for touring not only his own stores but also those of his competitors, checking prices on milk and other 'loss leader' products to ensure Wal-Mart's were the lowest. If his competitors' prices were higher, when the local Wal-Mart opened its doors the next morning, its prices would be even lower than the competitor's prices were the prior day.

The marketing team needs to know what other factors influence the company's ability to serve the customer, even if they are outside the traditional scope of the marketing function. For example, if a manufacturer has capacity constraints relative to meeting aggressive business objectives, the marketing function should understand the timeline for addressing that issue because it will affect expectations relative to potential marketing impact.

Finally, the marketing team should have a solid understanding of the type of impact they can have if they change market perception relative to the influencing factor. For example, assume that a manufacturer is evaluating the primary barriers to increasing purchasing behaviour relative to a particular product. Through conversations with prospective customers, it has become clear that the broader set of benefits offered by the company's product is highly valued, but one particular feature is missing. Because that feature is important, customers have been selecting a competitor instead. However, if the feature was added to the current product offering, the combined impact would cause the customer to prefer the manufacturer's offering.

Although this information is helpful, more information is required to effectively assess the impact. The size of the market, the frequency with which orders are placed, whether there are strong barriers to changing providers, other anticipated moves by competitors and the cost of the potential change are all important considerations. The marketing team must have access to, and a command of, this type of information in order to effectively assess the impact they could have if they made the associated change. In many cases, the most effective marketing strategies are based on a combination of influencers that have a smaller but more immediate financial impact and those that have a more substantial impact but that are more time consuming, expensive or complex.

The information that the marketing function gathers through its understanding of the market forms the basis of the company's marketing strategies. Because the company's marketing (and non-marketing) investments are based on this understanding, if the decisions about purchasing decision criteria, priorities and impact are based on mistaken assumptions, everything the company does in support of these strategies will be less effective than it otherwise would have been. Developing strategies is inexpensive. The substantial expense associated with marketing is in taking action on those strategies. If the strategies are flawed and the resulting tactical activity selection is based on those strategies, the company is certain to be wasting marketing dollars.

PURCHASING DECISION CRITERIA

The most important factors influencing a company's success in meeting market needs are the customers' purchasing decision criteria. *Purchasing decision criteria* are the factors a prospective customer considers, consciously or subconsciously, when choosing between available alternatives.

Clip-Level and Competitive Criteria

There are two levels of purchasing criteria: clip-level criteria and competitive criteria.

Clip-Level Criteria

Clip-level criteria are those purchasing decision criteria that are required by the market in order to be eligible for consideration. Once an organisation meets the minimum, there is typically little to no value in placing additional emphasis on them in your marketing plans. They serve primarily as barriers to entry to competitors within a specific market.

Clip-level criteria qualify a company's product or service for consideration as a viable alternative.

Competitive criteria are the basis upon which a company's product or service is selected from among the viable alternatives. Although any of the products might be satisfactory, meeting more competitive criteria makes a particular product or company preferable.

For example, a CPA firm that wants to serve the needs of small businesses must, in fact, be able to serve the basic needs of small businesses. In addition, it must do so with at least the minimum acceptable level of service. For a construction company that wants to do major projects, the contractors under consideration must be large enough to be able to handle both staffing and cash flow requirements associated with the project. An apparel manufacturer must make clothing for the gender and size of the targeted customer. A company that specialises in children's clothing wouldn't be considered by customers looking for adult sizes. Regardless of industry, a company must be visible to the market in order to be identified among alternatives, and the company must have a reputation for integrity, or at least not have a reputation for dishonesty, in order to be considered.

Although investing in clip-level criteria may not make sense if the market already understands that a company meets the criteria, if a company is failing on a clip-level criterion, attempts to change market perceptions based on other, more differentiating factors will be unsuccessful. In some cases, the solution may be a gradual shift. For example, even if a construction company has the capability to take on large projects, the market may not believe it if they have not previously done so. The best evidence of success against that particular clip level criterion may be case studies featuring successful major projects. To accomplish this, the company may choose to aggressively bid on projects of increasingly larger size and then actively promote those successes after completion, gradually gaining the reputation it needs. In this case, it is important to be aware of the market's clip-level criteria and factor them into long-term planning.

In some cases, weakness relative to clip level criteria is much more serious. If a company does not meet the clip level criteria for its market relative to quality, service and ethics, fixing these basic issues should be at the heart of the company's marketing plan.

Several years ago, I spoke with the managing partner of a company who wanted me to help develop a new marketing plan for his company. We discussed the factors that influenced its success in generating business, and he correctly identified most of the common factors. However, in conversations with both clients and non-clients in the community, it was discovered that his firm had a more serious issue. Many of the work his firm had completed required repairs by subsequent vendors, and the market was beginning to question the basic quality of the company's work product.

My recommendation was that his marketing investment be completely focused on resolving his quality issues, and then, once that was complete, on addressing the damage his brand had sustained. Unfortunately, like many executives who believe they need marketing help, he wanted immediate sales results, and he was unconvinced that spending a year focused inwardly would help the company achieve its goals. Instead, he wanted to focus aggressively on trying to bring in business to replace the customers the company was losing for quality reasons. His decision to ignore the clip level criteria in favour of other activities meant that the brand would continue to cement a permanent reputation for inferior work.

Clip-level purchasing criteria should not be ignored. In fact, every company should strive to deliver at the highest level within the expected range for each clip-level factor. However, regardless of how accurate a tax return is, how friendly the server is who brings the drink to the patron's table or how ethical the management team is perceived to be, these clip-level criteria can only go so far to differentiate a company from its competition. That is the role of competitive criteria.

Competitive Criteria

Competitive criteria is the second category of purchasing decision criteria. Unlike clip-level influencers, this category distinguishes a company from its competitors within its target markets. Like everything else that the company does, distinguishing factors must be consistent with the company's desired brand reputation and value proposition. To effectively differentiate the company relative to competitive criteria, the attributes must be relevant and important to the customer, true about the company and believable within the market.

The most successful competitive criteria are exceptionally important to a purchaser, address an unmet or underserved need in the market and are not being pursued by competitors. For example, the Swedish automobile manufacturer, Volvo, has long been associated with safety, although that wasn't always the case.

In 1971, when the company was trying to differentiate Volvo from its competitors, its advertising agency and marketing team began looking for potential competitive criteria in the market against which Volvo had a particular competitive advantage. As it turned out, they found it in the company's track record for durability.

That year, the company launched a campaign touting the fact that, after ten years, nine out of ten Volvos were still on the road. Although the campaign was designed to promote durability, the market associated longevity with a low crash record and a high automobile survival rate, and Volvo's association with safety was born.

Volvo was a safe car, so this was true. Because Volvo could bring solid statistics to the market to back up its claim, and because Volvo had invented the three-point safety restraint and other safety-related innovations, the market considered the positioning credible. Finally, the position was relevant and important to customers. In the era before automobile safety regulations became prevalent, the market was already concerned about safety. This represented an underserved need in the market, and it had not been pursued by a competitor.[1]

MARKET SEGMENTS

Of course, not every car purchaser prioritises safety in the same way. Some are more concerned about the driver experience and how the car handles. For these drivers, BMW might be a better fit. Other drivers want the ability to haul large loads. For them, a pickup truck made by Ford might be a better fit than a sedan made by Volvo. It's not that safety is irrelevant or unimportant to these individuals, but other criteria are more important.

Groups within a market that prioritise their purchasing criteria differently are called *market segments*. When the market is big enough to sustain a profitable business, and the differences are significant enough to be distinct, market segments present opportunities to competitors who can tailor a solution to a market segment's particular priorities.

Market segments are defined by their differentiating purchasing criteria. However, because asking each prospective customer about his or her preferences is not feasible in large markets, marketers often look for characteristics that make customers easier to identify or group together. For example, a market segment might be defined by geography. Grocery stores tend to have geographic segment distinctions, at least, in part, because shoppers are unlikely to travel great distances for daily purchases.

Market segments can also be defined by demographics, like industry, profession, age, income or gender. Mercedes, for example, targets a higher-income segment of the population. School Employees' Credit Union of Washington targets employees of Washington's public school systems. Facebook's initial market was college students.

Market segments can also be defined by psychographic characteristics, including lifestyle preferences or how a particular product or service is used. For example, Mack Trucks, Inc., now a subsidiary of Volvo, manufactures commercial trucks for hauling large loads of supplies, garbage and other materials. Its market for each product is defined by how the vehicle is used, which may include multiple industries. A quilting supply company targets consumers who are interested in the art and craft of quilting, a shared interest.

In addition to the characteristics that customers within the market segment have in common, a market segment is also defined by its differentiation from other segments. For example, an early adopter of consumer technology may place a premium on being the first among his or her peers to own the latest electronic gadget, paying a premium for the opportunity to explore a new gadget even before the bugs have been exposed and addressed. This segment shares a number of characteristics. They tend to be younger, more educated and more affluent. They also share common influencing factors, including where they learn about new technology. By contrast, later adopters place a premium on reliability, looking for a proven product. They tend to look in different places and may rely on the feedback of early adopters to guide their purchasing decisions.

Market segments are quite specific to the product or service. Although an early adopter of technology might value being first to try the latest gadget, he or she may be slow to adopt new apparel trends. Within any market segment, there will also be exceptions. A person who does not fit the demographic profile of an early adopter may still share his or her purchasing criteria.

When a company is evaluating the competitive criteria used by customers in its purchasing decision process, and significant differences exist between two sub-sets of customers, the company may, in fact, be serving two segments with different needs, interests and even purchasing behaviours. For example, a theatre might have one set of patrons who are interested in purchasing every show within a season, experiencing new plays they might otherwise not have tried. Another segment wants to know, in advance, that they will enjoy the show. They are less likely to subscribe to a theatre and more likely to pick a performance based on that show's reputation or reviews. In this case, using the same language to appeal to both segments may be less effective than tailoring language to each one, particularly if the segments can easily be distinguished based on demographic information, such as how old they are or where they live.

Even though market segments are not perfect, they do help to refine a company's understanding of who is most likely to respond to a particular company's value proposition and focus marketing plans on the factors that most influence their behaviour, as opposed to those of other segments in the market. By focusing on a single market segment or a group of market segments that will respond to a company's value proposition and brand reputation, an organisation can often drive better financial outcomes from its marketing investments.

UNDERSTANDING RELATIVE MARKET POSITIONS

As a company considers which market segments it will serve, and before the marketing team and/or executive team begins developing marketing strategies, there are three additional pieces of information the team needs. First, the company should understand how much variation the customer will tolerate in a particular criteria and still consider it acceptable. To illustrate with a simplified example, consider your expectations relative to responsiveness from your attorney. If you leave a voicemail for your attorney, how quickly do you expect him to return your call? Within two hours? 24 hours? Does it change depending on how critical the matter is to you?

In all likelihood, the acceptable response time is a range. Although you might expect a response on a critical matter within four hours, you might find anything within the same business day to be tolerably acceptable. On the other hand, if it takes more than that to respond to something critical, you might consider changing law firms—or at least attorneys. And, if they responded in less than four hours, it might increase the chances that you will recommend your attorney to someone else. Understanding the range and the impact of deviations will help the marketing team, and other management team members, generate more specific and measurable expected outcomes related to the marketing strategies they develop and assess the company's performance more objectively than a customer feedback tool might.

Second, the company should understand how it is perceived by the market segments it wants to serve relative to the decision criteria that are important to those markets. For example, assume in this rather unlikely scenario that the customer's top competitive criterion, relative to law firm selection, is responsiveness. If the market's expected performance criteria are consistent with what was described previously, and the company's actual response rates are within the business day, the company might make improving its response rates, reducing them to be within the expected four-hour window, a high priority. By mapping out performance relative to purchasing decision criteria, in priority order, the company is in a better position to prioritise its own marketing activities.

Finally, a company must understand how its competitors are perceived relative to those same criteria. Don't forget: Many times, your company's competitors extend beyond what your company might traditionally define as 'competition.' For example, if you are a temporary service firm, your competitors include other temporary service firms, potential direct-hire employees and the option of not hiring anyone at all to fill a given need.

By understanding how the competition stands relative to each of the purchasing decision criteria, the company can become more effective at identifying aspects of its performance that help distinguish the company from its peers, as well as potential barriers to new customer acquisition. In our law firm example, if the company found, in its competitive analysis, that other law firms never answered calls within the same business day, the company might have an asset it could both improve (by moving response times closer to market expectations) and leverage (by demonstrating that it is more responsive than its competitors). Like Volvo, it may end up finding an undiscovered asset within its existing behaviours.

When the company serves multiple market segments or provides several distinct products or services, this analysis of expectations, acceptable parameters and competitive positioning should happen at the market, product or service level.

By clearly articulating each competitor's relative market position, the customer's acceptable range for each criteria and the current and desired position for the company itself, the executive and marketing teams can more effectively identify areas in need of improvement, anticipate potential competitor reactions to planned marketing initiatives, and sometimes identify potential purchasing criteria on which the company can substantially differentiate itself from its competition.

OTHER INFLUENCING FACTORS

The customer's purchasing decision criteria will clearly influence the organisation's success in meeting its business objectives. However, there may be other factors that are linked to those purchasing decision criteria that also affect the results. Although these are not decision criteria from the customer's standpoint, they directly affect the decision criteria and are influencing factors that should be considered.

For example, if a brand audit uncovers inconsistencies in the brand's presentation to the market, the brand may not be as effective at remaining top of mind among purchasers. Although a clear brand reputation directly affects the decision process because it helps customers remember and positively associate a company with the solutions it provides, the market would not necessarily cite brand clarity as one of its purchasing criterion. Still, brand consistency is an important factor influencing the company's success.

Operational capacity also influences market decisions. Often, when I meet with clients to discuss their interest in growth, I find they have not considered the potential impact growth would have on their ability to serve their current or new customers. For example, if a manufacturer wants to grow by a specific percentage within the next three years (its business objective), it has often successfully identified strategies to do so, such as expanding customer access to its products and increasing awareness of the benefits it offers. However, it sometimes fails to consider capacity issues within its manufacturing operations that might constrain deliveries. If it achieves its growth objective and manufacturing processes fail to keep up, the company's reputation can be damaged by its own failure to fulfil its intrinsic promise to deliver.

When this happens, the issue that was formerly unrecognised by the market becomes a more significant issue to resolve. The company must now resolve the underlying issue and then try to change market perception, often a more substantial challenge. By considering internal constraints in the planning process, the marketing plan can help prevent the need for future marketing expenditures.

Once a list of influencing factors, both purchasing decision criteria and other factors, are identified, the company's marketing team and its executive team should have some idea of the impact they could have, both short-term and long-term, by affecting those factors. This allows the marketing and executive teams to prioritise marketing strategies and associated investments.

PRIORITISING INFLUENCING FACTORS

Once a company has identified factors that influence the purchasing decision and understands how the market prioritises it and where it is positioned relative to alternative solutions, the marketing teams should be able to assess what kind of impact a change in perception will have on market behaviours.

For example, consider Sam Simmons, the owner of Sam's Hometown Gas Station. Using market research, conversations with customers or other techniques, Simmons may determine that a customer's decision to purchase gas from a given gas station is influenced by how well lit the forecourt is, the price of the gas, the cleanliness of the station, the quality of the coffee, the appearance of the crew, convenience to their path of travel and whether they have breakfast sandwiches in the morning. Although there is nothing that Simmons can do to affect the convenience factor because the station has already been built, it does give him important information about the competition. Competitors exist within a relatively small geographic area, and there are two, in particular, that he feels are the primary competition for customers.

Simmons travels to the competitors' facilities, talks with their customers and his own customers. In the process, Simmons determines that some influencers are more important than others. He also asks customers about their expectations of each element and plots those on a chart. The chart, depicted as figure 5-2 that follows, prioritises the influencing factors that make the most impact on the decision from left (greatest impact) to right (least impact). Simmons determines that forecourt lighting, the cleanliness of the station and the appearance of the crew are most important. In fact, these are more important than the difference of a penny or two in gas prices.

Simmons also asks customers how he and his competitors are doing against those expectations and adds those satisfaction ratings to his chart. When evaluated against competitors, he excels at having a well-lit forecourt and good breakfast sandwiches. No one does well at cleanliness, employee appearance or coffee.

Figure 5-2: Performance Against Customer Expectations

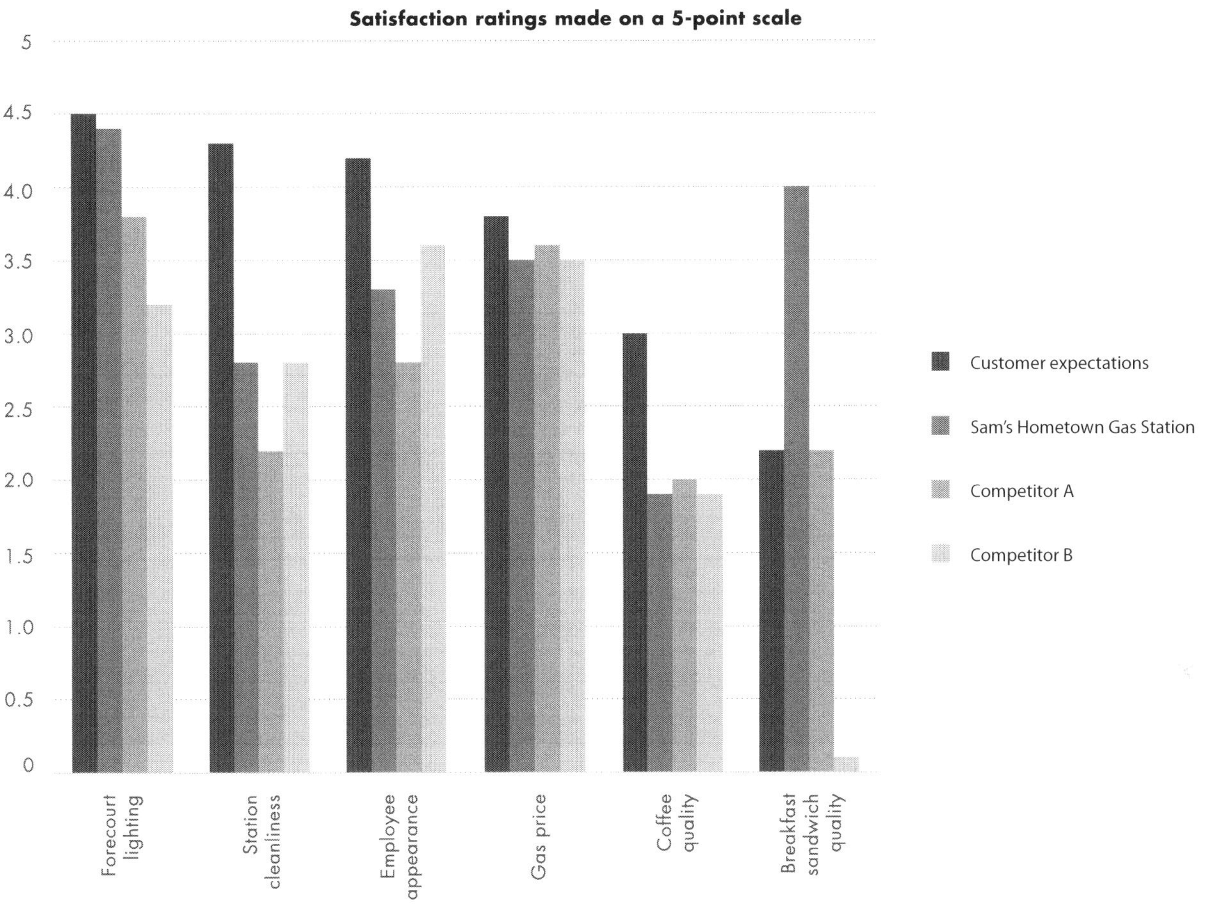

Satisfaction ratings made on a 5-point scale

Based on this information, Simmons determines he will have the most impact on revenues by focusing on customer perception of station cleanliness and crew appearance. He also notes that if the quality of the coffee can be improved, it will further enhance the customer experience. Simmons is now prepared to estimate just how much impact he can have if each factor is improved. Using rough estimates, Simmons determines the impact on revenues and the expense it would take to get there. With estimates of impact associated with each one, he is now prepared to prioritise his potential marketing strategies.

In some cases, as in the Sam's Hometown Gas Station example, the potential impact can be assessed relative to a single factor. In other cases, two or more influencing factors may be combined, either because the impact together is more powerful than the impact of either independently or because they are closely related.

To illustrate this with another example, let's assume that Heart & Home, a non-profit health education organization, is trying to improve major gift donor retention. Its marketing team has identified three influencing factors that have an impact on its donors' decision to repeat their gifts the next year. These factors, or influencers, include the strength of the relationship with the major gift officer, whether they feel their gift was appreciated and whether they feel connected with the organisation in between gifts. When Heart & Home assesses its performance against these factors based on feedback it has received from donors, the management team decides that it is doing well at expressing appreciation at the time of the gift.

However, Heart & Home received mediocre scores in feedback from donors relative to maintaining strong relationships with major gift officers and maintaining the connection with the donor between gifts. Anecdotal feedback supported what they learned directly. Major gift officers frequently reported that by the time they reconnected for the following year's gift, the donor's giving levels and chosen organisations had already been set. Heart & Home decides that these two influencers are its priorities. Focusing on either one is likely to generate a sizeable increase in donations.

The management team also recognises that the two influencers are connected. Improving the relationship with the major donor officer will naturally require more continual contact, and by extension, increase the frequency with which the organisation reaches out. Conversely, the major gift officer is likely to be involved in any other outreach efforts to donors, which will also improve the strength of their relationship. The two influencing factors can, for the purpose of evaluating impact, be combined.

In general, factors that have the most significant positive impact on profitability, are of higher importance to the target market segment and will be more effective in differentiating the company from its competitors should receive the highest priority in the development of marketing strategies and the marketing planning process.

THE CONNECTION BETWEEN INFLUENCING FACTORS, MARKETING STRATEGIES AND RESULTS

The most successful marketing strategies should focus on positively affecting influencing factors. In fact, the strongest marketing strategies should simply restate, in proactive terms, the impact that is expected on the influencing factor. In addition, each marketing strategy should have measurable outcomes associated with it.

> Marketing strategies should always be tied to the influencing factors they will affect. The expected impact should also be established in terms of measurable objectives, ideally in both financial and marketing terms.

When a company has analysed the potential impact of each strategy, the management team can use that information to determine whether the collection of strategies is sufficient to meet the organisation's business and financial objectives. In the example of Sam's Hometown Gas Station, one of the strategies might be to 'improve station cleanliness,' with two associated measurable objectives. One might be to increase the rating customers give the station on cleanliness from 2.8 to 4.0 within 1 year. The other might be the associated increase in business anticipated as a result of that impact, such as a 5% increase in revenues over the next two-year period.

If Simmons was hoping for a 10% increase in revenues over the same period, he may need to do more than just improve station cleanliness. By assessing the potential impact of other strategies, such as improving employee appearance or the taste of the coffee sold at the station's store, the management team may be able to achieve the owner's objectives. On the other hand, if Simmons cannot create enough strategies to ensure the outcomes he wants, he may choose to adjust his or her expected business and financial results.

Similarly, in the case of Heart & Home, if the business objective is to improve revenue from donors by increasing donor retention, the marketing strategy might be to 'improve donor satisfaction with the relationship between the organisation and the donor,' and the anticipated measurement of success could be a 25% increase in the number of gifts that are repeated the following year. Depending on Heart & Home's overall goals, solid metrics associated with marketing strategies will allow the organisation to assess whether the plans are likely to deliver the expected returns.

As a company identifies the metrics it will use to determine whether or not the strategic marketing objective was met, the management team should also consider whether or not the company has the appropriate systems in place to track data and the skills in place to analyse results.

In the Volvo example, had the safety criteria been a known influencer, Volvo's marketing strategy relative to increasing car sales might have been to 'increase the percentage of the target market that believes Volvo manufactures safer vehicles.' The associated marketing outcome may have been the percentage of people surveyed whose response was 'safety' when asked to name the attribute for which Volvo cars are most well-known. In this case, the company will need to budget for brand awareness research in relation to this marketing strategy. The company will also need to have a sense of what kind of impact this change in perception might have on the customer's purchasing decision process. Market research, previous experience and experienced product managers could all provide guidance relative to estimating the changes in purchasing behaviours that might be associated with a change in perception. This will allow the company to tie the marketing outcomes to financial results.

In the law firm example from a previous section in this chapter, if the business objective was to increase market share, the company marketing strategy might be to become known as the most responsive law firm in town. The metrics to measure success might be responses to a customer survey, new client acquisitions from competitors or average response times. The law firm will also need to budget for the customer survey work, establish a system for tracking new client acquisitions and determine how they can effectively track average response times. (Tracking systems, both at the strategic level and tactical level, will be discussed in more detail in chapter 14, 'Managing Measurement.' Financial measurement approaches will also be reviewed in chapter 11, 'Evaluating Returns on Marketing Investments.')

As you can see from these examples, marketing strategies should always be tied to the influencing factors they will affect. The expected impact should also be established in terms of measurable objectives, ideally in both financial and marketing terms. By asking the marketing planning team, whether it is the marketing department or a broader group of managers, to make these connections, the non-marketing professional is more likely to understand how the investments required to execute on the strategies are going to affect the company's profitability and help it achieve the company's objectives. By examining marketing strategies relative to the factors they are designed to influence, the non-marketing professional can more easily evaluate both the plan's alignment and the marketing function's approach.

THE RELATIVE IMPORTANCE OF PRICE

Before we move from our discussion of influencers and strategies to the selection of tactics to achieve marketing objectives, I want to touch briefly on a common misunderstanding about price.

As the prioritisation of factors is considered, it is often tempting to place price at the top. Price is certainly an influencing factor on almost every customer's list of purchasing decision criteria. However, it is rarely the most important one. *Price* describes the value a product or service delivers relative to its competitors. If the price is too high for the same value, sales will be negatively affected. If the price is too low, you may be leaving money on the table or even losing clients who begin to doubt the value you deliver.

When two products are the same in every other way, price probably is the most important factor. However, unless you trade in commodities, this probably isn't the case. More likely, there are subtle differences between the products you and your competitors deliver.

Although pricing approaches will be discussed in more depth in upcoming chapters, I suggest that you evaluate the influencing factors without including price among them. Instead, assume that your price is roughly equivalent to competitors' prices. Now, what is the customer going to do to select between two options? The answer will depend on what the customer values.

To illustrate, consider the market for denim jeans. As a consumer, you have specific criteria related to your choice in attire. It probably includes fit, quality of the product, design elements, fabric and, perhaps, the brand's name. However, the priorities will vary according to the segment of the market to which you belong. Even for the most price-sensitive consumer, price is not the most important factor. For a utilitarian, the jeans must fit, and they have to meet at least certain quality criteria. They also have to be convenient to purchase. After all, if you are going to spend twice the price of the jeans to have them shipped to you or drive across town to purchase them, the effective price has gone up. There may also be certain product features that are so important that the consumer would pay more to have them, such as pockets. They might also need to be a certain colour.

Conversely, there are people who will pay hundreds of dollars for a pair of jeans that are just as functional as their less expensive competitors, have the same features and are just as convenient, but whose brand makes a statement about who they are. These individuals aren't opting for a product because the price is higher. In fact, they might be thrilled to purchase those same jeans through consignment or on sale, thereby saving money. Price itself isn't the decision criterion. It's simply an indicator of the manufacturer's market and value proposition.

This isn't to say that price isn't important. In fact, it is very important. If Wal-Mart offered generic jeans at designer prices, they wouldn't sell. The market and the value proposition are misaligned. Similarly, if a designer label slashed the price of its product, the market would wonder what was wrong with those jeans, and the value of the product itself might begin to drop.

Although price is important, it is rarely the most important factor. If your company believes it is competing exclusively on price, you should look around at the other competitors in your market. If anyone else is competing on price, you should ask why your cost-conscious customer chooses your product over someone else's. Those are your true influencing factors.

QUESTIONS FOR NON-MARKETING MANAGERS TO ASK ABOUT FACTORS INFLUENCING PURCHASING BEHAVIOUR

As a non-marketing manager, your responsibility when evaluating the marketing strategies developed by your marketing function is to ensure they are consistent with what you understand about the market and how the market makes purchasing decisions. You should also ensure that they strengthen or are consistent with your brand and will produce the highest possible return on financial investments. As you discuss the marketing plan with your marketing team and the other executives within the company, you should feel confident you have acceptable answers to the following questions:

- What influences our customers' purchasing decision process? How do these criteria differ between existing and prospective customers?

- Which criteria are clip-level criteria, and which ones are competitive criteria, with the potential to differentiate our solution from the competition?

- How do we know these purchasing decision criteria are accurate?

- Are there differences between segments within our market? How has this affected our choice of strategies?

- Where do we stand, and where are our competitors, relative to each of these criteria?
- How do we know that these aren't simply our own opinions?
- What other factors, in addition to decision criteria, will affect our success relative to our business goals?
- How much impact will the marketing strategies identified in the plan make on the influencing factors we identified? How will that impact translate into business or financial results? How confident are we that the estimated impact is accurate?
- Are we appropriately prioritising the potential strategies, based on impact, importance to the customer and business constraints?
- Are the associated strategies measurable? How will we know they have been successful?
- Do we have the systems in place to measure outcomes? If not, have we budgeted appropriately for them?
- What financial impact will those changes have on both revenues and profitability?
- Are the marketing strategies the marketing team has proposed well-aligned with our business and financial objectives as a company?
- What impact could the strategies have on our brand reputation?

CHAPTER 5 SUMMARY

In order for a non-marketing manager to ensure that marketing strategies at the functional level are well-aligned with the business and financial objectives that the company's executive team wants to achieve, the manager must first understand the factors that influence the market's behaviour and the company's success. These influencing factors can then be used to evaluate the marketing strategies proposed by the marketing team and the outcomes they are expected to generate.

To develop effective marketing strategies, marketing professionals and other managers responsible for the function of marketing need to understand

- what the customer's purchasing decision criteria are and how they differ between existing customers and new customers;
- the relative importance of each influencing factor to the purchasing decision process;
- whether different segments within the market prioritise criteria in different ways;
- what the market expects from merchants relative to performance;
- how the company and its competitors are performing relative to those purchasing decision criteria;
- whether there are other influencers, outside of the purchasing decision process, that are serving as barriers; and
- what the potential impact of a change in market perception might mean in terms of the company's performance.

This information will allow the company to develop marketing strategies that are well-aligned with market needs and that will optimise potential marketing returns.

Marketing strategies should be crafted to affect influencing factors and tied to the company's overall business and financial goals. In fact, the most effective strategies often restate the impact the marketing function wishes to have on the influencing factor, with a high priority on targeting the influencing factors that will have the most significant positive impact on profitability. The company should also consider factors that are more heavily weighted by the target market segment in terms of their importance to the purchasing decision, as well as factors that will be more effective when differentiating the company from its competitors.

Finally, successful marketing strategies contain intermediate marketing metrics and financial metrics that indicate whether the marketing strategy has met its objectives. The sum of the expected impact of the marketing strategies should produce the company's desired business and financial outcomes. If it does not, either the strategies or the company's expectations must be adjusted to more accurately reflect market realities.

Endnotes

1 Schwartzapfel, Stuart. 'Real "Mad Men" Pitched Safety to Sell Volvos,' *The New York Times*, March 23, 2012. www.nytimes.com/2012/03/25/automobiles/ real-mad-men-pitched-safety-to-sell-volvos. html?pagewanted= all&_r= 0

Brauer, Karl. 'The 50-Year-Old Innovation,' Edmunds.com blog, May 5, 2009. www.edmunds. com/car-safety/the-50-year-old-innovation. html?articleid= 43023

ALIGNING MARKETING TACTICS WITH INFLUENCING FACTORS

Figure 6-1: Marketing Alignment Map

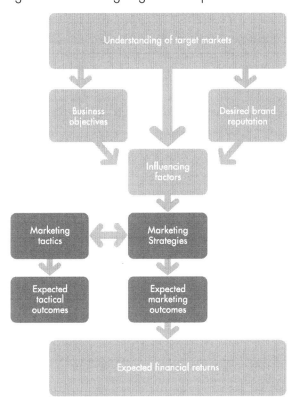

Have you heard the joke about the executive who doesn't understand the value of his marketing investments?

'I know that 50% of my marketing expenditures are productive, and the other 50% are a complete waste,' he quips. 'I just don't know which half is which.'

What he's talking about are the marketing tactics. *Tactics* are the actions a company will take to achieve its marketing objectives, and they represent the bulk of the marketing budget.

Unfortunately, the executive may have good reason to be sceptical. Many marketing dollars are wasted in these efforts.

We discussed the first reason marketing dollars are poorly spent in chapter 5, 'Understanding What Influences Market Behaviour,' which was because marketing plans are based on inaccurate assumptions about the factors that influence purchasing decisions. This chapter covers three additional sources of marketing waste: missing strategies, poorly designed strategies and poorly selected tactics.

TACTICS ARE NOT STRATEGIES

Many companies confuse marketing tactics with marketing strategies. Strategies talk about *what* the company plans to do to influence behaviour. Marketing tactics are *how* the company will make that happen. Tactics are the activities a company can select to reach its marketing goals.

Often, the same tactic can be used to support vastly different strategic objectives, depending on how it is implemented. For example, an advertising campaign could position an automobile as durable and safe (as Volvo does) or as an exceptional drive for the discerning driver (as BMW does). A website can communicate almost any message to the market, affecting a variety of influencing factors, from improving access (through Internet sales) to improving understanding of capabilities (through clarifying information and case studies, for example).

Some companies have a tendency to skip ahead to tactics during the planning process. However, a company should always define marketing strategies first in order to guide those critical tactical decisions. As mentioned in chapter 5, marketing strategies should be crafted to affect influencing factors. The strategies themselves should generally restate the impact the marketing function wishes to have on the influencing factor. They should also include intermediate marketing metrics, financial metrics or both, that indicate what impact the marketing strategy will have on the influencer and overall business and financial goals.

Because tactics are tools that can be used to support or do many different types of things on behalf of a company, an organisation that does not begin with well-defined marketing strategies may apply those tools in ways that don't help the company achieve its business objectives, resulting in wasted funds.

To illustrate, consider this example. After looking at the websites of several of its competitors, the management team at a transportation services company decides its site is dated. The pictures are old, and the site needs an update. The CEO asks the marketing director to tackle the project, and she happily does. After all, she agrees, it does look dated. It hasn't been revised in almost 10 years. She proceeds to execute the request. After four months and a considerable sum of money, the website is launched. She and the CEO are delighted. It looks exactly how they wanted it to look, and it is much faster than the previous site. Unfortunately, once the shine has worn off, this CEO is likely to start scratching his head and wondering about the effectiveness of the money that was just spent.

That's because a website can be used in many ways. By simply executing the activity, the company didn't stop to think about what the company wanted that website to achieve. Did it want the site to help attract new customers? Provide resources to existing customers? Become a recruiting tool for employees? Without this information, the functionality, messaging and design might miss important audiences and objectives.

The company also failed to consider how the website fit among other potential priorities. For example, if the company's goal was to grow its customer base, what would influence purchasing behaviour, and would the website be the most influential tool to make that change happen? If the website wasn't the most appropriate tool, the company may still have decided a website overhaul was required. However, it might also have decided to spend far less on the project than it would if it were the most appropriate way to help the company meet its objectives.

'The use of marketing tactics outside of the framework of focused marketing strategies is one of the most significant sources of financial waste within the marketing function.

Because marketing tactics are simply tools and can be used in many ways, substituting marketing tactics for strategies in a plan is like driving around aimlessly to find a grocery store. You might find the grocery store, or you might not. Regardless, your chances of finding it quickly without wasting gas are small.

The use of marketing tactics outside the framework of focused marketing strategies is one of the most significant sources of financial waste within the marketing function. It also contributes to a company's lacklustre business results because the message the market receives through these tactics is muddled or missed.

WELL-CRAFTED MARKETING STRATEGIES PROVIDE SPECIFIC GUIDANCE

Sometimes, the company believes it has a marketing strategy, but it is not well crafted. My favourite example of this is brand awareness. When executives first approach me to talk about their marketing investments and how to improve returns, I generally ask them what their objectives are. The most common answer is 'to get our name out there.' They want to increase 'brand awareness,' or, more accurately, name recognition.

The problem with this answer is that brand awareness is often a proxy for the real issue. Many companies assume that if everyone knows their solution is available, they will be clamouring for their product or service. However, even an extremely well-known, well-respected manufacturer of exceptionally effective mousetraps is unlikely to generate sales in a land with no mice. The issue, in this case, is really not brand awareness. It's a poor assumption based on inattention to the discipline of marketing.

However, sometimes, even when the company has the right idea, it hasn't driven it to a sufficient degree of precision. For example, in areas where mice run rampant, the mousetrap manufacturer might need visibility to make sure that the community knows that it has a solution to a need. But, unless it has the only solution, visibility alone is probably not sufficient.

Marketing strategies should be very specific in both what they hope to achieve and how that change will impact purchasing behaviours. For example, instead of a vague statement that the company wants to promote visibility, a more precise marketing strategy might state that the company will increase awareness of its mousetrap's effectiveness at attracting and permanently eradicating rodents among restaurant owners in a specific geographic area. In addition, the strategy should include a metric or set of metrics that provides an indication of whether the execution was effective. In this case, it may be a measure of brand awareness in a survey of restaurant owners. It may also be a financial metric, such as a percentage change in sales to restaurants or restaurant supply stores.

> The difference between a strong marketing strategy and one that is less effective is often the degree of specificity around the impact the organisation wishes to have. For example:
>
> **Less specific strategy:** During 2014, we will increase our company's visibility.
>
> **More specific strategy:** During 2014, we will increase awareness among restaurant owners within Los Angeles about the effectiveness of our product in permanently eradicating rodents. By the end of 2014, awareness will have increased from 6% to 75% among decision-makers in this market. As a result, we expect the number of restaurants who become clients to grow from 320 to 1,500 by the end of 2015.

This greater level of precision helps in two ways. First, it clearly specifies what the goal of the efforts is, giving a greater degree of guidance to the person or people responsible for implementing it. In effect, it gives the driver in the previous scenario a map, making it much more clear what route to take to get to the store.

The second advantage is that it makes the outcomes measurable. This allows the marketing function to more accurately estimate how much effort or expense should be invested and makes it less likely that the marketing team will fall short by failing to do enough or waste money by overshooting. When expectations are measurable, the marketing team is better equipped to assess whether the mix of tactics selected will actually work together to achieve the company's strategic objectives.

To illustrate, let's return to the Sam's Hometown Gas Station example we used in chapter 5. One of the marketing strategies the owner selected was to improve customer perception of station cleanliness, moving customer satisfaction rankings from 2.8 to 4.0 within one year and driving a 5% increase in revenues over a two-year period. Assume that the company selected the following tactics:

- Add planters with brightly coloured flowers around the perimeter of the station

- Repaint the bathrooms in brighter colours and add artwork

- Add a sanitation patrol to the staff task list, asking them to pick up garbage and sweep up the doorway every two hours instead of once per day

- Host a campaign asking for customer input into what changes need to be made and offer a free tank of gas to winning suggestions

The owner, Sam Simmons, can now assess whether he believes that these tactical activities will make the required impact, whether the impact will occur in the desired timeframe, whether he needs more customer information in order to know the answer, and, if the activities aren't sufficient, what needs to be added in order to meet the strategic objective. After evaluating the tactics, Simmons might also decide that the number of tactics required would be impractical or financially infeasible. If this is the case, he might revisit the expected impact the strategy might make and adjust expected outcomes accordingly.

The owner should also add into the plan the systems he must develop in order to track progress on both strategies (as mentioned in chapter 5), and tactics. For example, the first two tactics might be measured simply by their completion in a timely manner. However, the third tactic might require a more complicated system to ensure that the sanitation patrol was being conducted and the facility is cleaner as a result. The systems required to support measurement are discussed in more detail in chapter 14, 'Managing Measurement.'

A well-crafted marketing strategy includes the specific impact the company wants to have on the factors influencing the desired behaviour, a measure of how big that change should be and over what timeframe the associated return is expected. With these pieces of information, the marketing team, the management team and anyone else developing marketing plans and spending marketing dollars is well-equipped to pick the right mix of marketing tactics and assess whether they will have the desired impact.

ALIGN ATTRIBUTES TO PICK THE RIGHT TACTIC

Both the absence of strategic objectives and poorly structured strategic objectives cause managers to make poor decisions regarding how they select and implement marketing tactics. In some cases, it may prompt the company to execute the right tactic but miss out on the full potential return. In other cases, it may help the company reach the objective, but with less efficiency than it might otherwise have done.

However, sometimes, the marketing strategies are well-crafted and well-informed by the marketing discipline, but the marketing tactics are poorly selected. In large companies, marketing tactics are generally selected by the marketing team or teams. In small and mid-sized companies, some marketing tactics may be under the control of the executive or management teams, whereas others are the responsibility of a marketing team and external marketing professionals.

In general, marketing tactics managed by the marketing function, whether they are marketing professionals or non-marketing managers, fall into four categories: product or service-related tactics, pricing, placement or distribution, and promotion. These are the four 'P's of marketing mentioned in chapter 1, 'A Market Leader's Definition of Marketing.' Most companies implement multiple tactics simultaneously, and many tactics will affect multiple strategies. Taken together, the group of tactics a company selects to help it execute its marketing strategies is referred to as the company's *marketing mix*.

The selection of tactics is influenced by a variety of considerations related to the marketing strategy itself, including

- the size of the target market;
- market demographics, including where the customer turns for solutions to the specific needs a company addresses;
- whether the customers are businesses or consumers;
- the influencing factor(s) the company is trying to affect;
- the potential impact on a company's brand;
- the competitive environment;
- the cost of the tactic relative to the potential benefit it could deliver and budget constraints;
- the time before such benefits are likely to be realised; and
- how the mix of tactics are likely to work together.

Market Size

This is one of the most important considerations when selecting tactics, especially relative to promotions. Some tactics are best suited to very large, or mass, markets. Others are more appropriate for very small, or targeted, markets or market segments.

For example, billboard advertising is visible to everyone driving past it. Because billboards can't differentiate based on any characteristic other than geography, they are most appropriate for consumer-oriented products or services addressing needs that almost every resident in that geographic area might have.

Billboards are best suited for mass markets, where almost anyone who sees the message on it could be a customer. For example, billboards might be a good fit for paper towels, a consumer-oriented bank, a restaurant or a community event. On the

Sidebar 6-1: Caution: Tactics May Be Complex

In many small and middle market entities, the executive team or management team plays a strong role in crafting the marketing plan. To be successful, he or she will need a solid understanding of the range of marketing tactics available, when and for what purpose they are best used, what costs and potential response rates are associated with the tactic and how they work with the company's brand. To assist non-marketing managers who are serving in this capacity, an introduction to the most common marketing tactics, organised according to the traditional 'P's of marketing, is provided in the next four chapters.

The information in these chapters should be helpful when assessing and even developing marketing plans for a company. However, this information is not meant to serve as a substitute for an experienced marketing professional. The function of marketing is highly specialised and has become very technical, just as the practice of accounting has for CPAs. Although a CPA may have a license to practice in all areas of accounting and tax work, few newly minted CPAs would consider themselves competent providing advice in complex situations. Similarly, with the brief introduction to the tactical aspects of marketing provided in this chapter, you should feel better equipped to ask the right questions but underprepared to serve as chief counsel.

other hand, if the advertised product or service addresses a need held by only a segment of the population, such as accounting services to high net worth individuals, the billboard is likely to be wasted exposure. Most of the people who see the billboard's message will see the message as irrelevant, and the few who make up the market may or may not see the message at all.

Market Demographics

When looking for solutions to a particular need, some demographic segments respond particularly well to a particular type of tactic, whereas others may be less likely to notice. Consider online price discounts. An arts organisation that is strategically targeting a younger, computer-savvy audience would be more successful offering discounts through Goldstar.com or the underground weekly paper in their city, rather than announcing the discount via postcards. On the other hand, if the business objective is to serve seniors, and the strategy is to encourage price-sensitive seniors to attend a performance, print coupons or direct mail would be more effective than an online discount offer.

Some tactics can be good for both small and large markets, but the tactical approach will be different depending on market demographics. For example, media relations can be used for either mass or segmented markets, but the choice of targeted publications will differ. While a mass market outreach might include a broad cross-section of broadcast and print media, if the objective is to educate a specific segment, such as pregnant women, media outreach should be focused on publications targeting that population.

Business-to-Business Versus Business-to-Consumer

Some tactics are more widely used in business-to-business settings, such as trade shows and sales representatives, than in business-to-consumer settings. Others are more common in business-to-consumer environments, like Facebook advertising and other forms of social media, than in business-to-business environments. In many respects, this is simply a variation on the demographics consideration. However, business-to-business marketing plans so often include inefficient consumer-directed tactics that the importance of selecting based on this consideration bears highlighting.

Potential Impact on Influencing Factors

Different tactics affect purchasers in different ways. For example, when Starbucks was preparing to launch its line of instant coffee, Via, it tested some advertising that was designed to influence customer perception about flavour. However, it found that the impact was extremely small. Telling the consumer the flavour was the same didn't work, the customers needed to try it, and they weren't going to spend their own money to do a taste test. To influence their behaviour, Starbucks used very limited advertising, and, instead, opted for in-store taste tests (a promotional tactic) and coupons for free beverages and discounts on the new product (pricing tactics).

Brand Impact

Many tactics carry an implicit message about the brand itself. For example, when a company offers a pricing discount on a product, it sends the market a signal that the true value might be lower. When a premium brand does this, it can damage the firm's brand by suggesting that the price may previously have been inflated. This is why Cartier and Costco products, for example, don't go on sale. Cartier uses its pricing strategies to suggest that the company's products are always worth the high price paid by the customer, and Costco's consistent low pricing suggests that the customer is always getting the lowest possible price within its stores.

The Competitive Environment

Sometimes, a marketing team will select a tactic purely in response to their competitors' marketing initiatives. For example, if a competitor has a strong and lucrative social media presence, a company serving a related market segment might choose to pursue social media as a defensive measure or proactive measure if it believes it might expand to serve a new segment. At an even simpler level, it is not uncommon for a company to register all the URL variations on its name in order to prevent a competitor or squatter from registering it instead.

By contrast, a company might also choose a tactic because competitors have *not* done so. For example, the founders of the board game Cranium knew that they would be one of many, many options in the toy stores. They also had a solid understanding of their customer base and what other retail outlets those consumers patronised. Instead of pursuing the traditional channels, they opted to take their game to their customers. They partnered with Starbucks to sell the game in 1,500 of its stores and also with the bookstore chain Barnes & Noble to become one of the first board games sold in bookstores. By choosing a distribution (placement) channel in which their competitors were not present and their target market was, they were more successful at driving awareness.[1]

Cost-Benefit Analysis

Another reason Cranium's marketing tactics were so well-selected is because the benefits were exceptionally high relative to the costs incurred.

Toy manufacturers typically spend incredible sums of money promoting their products through advertising. Because Cranium was a small player up against giant competitors like Mattel and Hasbro, the company would have needed an incredibly large advertising budget to compete with these players. Instead of advertising, it selected a marketing mix of unique channels, aggressive media relations, celebrity endorsements and events.

The cost of these programmes was an amazingly low $15,000, compared to the hundreds of thousands they might otherwise have spent on advertising. In addition to the cost advantage, the benefits of the unique marketing mix allowed them to drive better results than an advertising spend probably would have.[2] From a cost-benefit perspective, this approach drove superior results.

Return Timeline

The amount of time required for a particular tactic to begin delivering a return, and the timeline over which that return is realised, range from relatively short to very long, depending on the tactic itself and the length of the customer's purchase cycle. In some cases, such as with new product development, a significant investment is made prior to the product launch when no revenues are realised. Once the product is launched, it will still take months or years to recoup those costs. Other times, such as with advertising, the investments may begin to generate revenues fairly quickly, but the revenues will still be far lower than the costs for some time. Of course, advertising often continues to generate revenues after the *advertising flights* have ended. Finally, some tactics, such as coupons, might deliver an immediate uptick in sales. On the other hand, the effect of coupon promotions, particularly on products with which the customer is already familiar, is likely to be short-lived.

Complimentary Marketing Mixes

The strongest marketing plans actively look for tactics that complement other tactics, producing superior returns as a result.

Consider professional service firms, such as CPA or law firms. Their clients typically purchase services from someone with whom they have a relationship, or who was referred to them, and whose services they believe to be high quality. If these are the influencers toward which the company's marketing strategies are directed, the company would be wise to increase the amount of time individual professionals spend building personal relationships with clients and prospective clients.

However, this tactic becomes even more effective when coupled with other tactics that focus on positioning the person as an expert in his or her area of expertise or providing added opportunities to connect with new prospective clients. Seminars, for example, might be an appropriate tactical choice. Taken separately, each of these will provide some help to a firm. However, when combined together, their impact is greater than the sum of the individual parts.

Tactics that focus on promoting visibility and the perception of expertise make it easier for the professional to make connections. They give him or her more immediate credibility and keep him or her top of mind. They effectively reduce the cost of the 'sales' efforts by decreasing the time required meeting and maintaining relationships with prospective clients. Conversely, because relationships are critical to the sales process, the personal relationship management reinforces the less personal outreach tactics, making them more memorable to the client.

As a company selects its marketing mix, it should consider the balance between short-term and longer-term tactics. It should also consider how different tactics might complement one another.

'HOW' IS AS IMPORTANT AS 'WHAT'

How a tactic is executed is as important as what tactic is selected. Without careful forethought, much more than 50% of the cost may go to waste. In many cases, the marketing or executive team has simply failed to consider the potential outcomes. For proof of consequences, one has only to look at the outcomes of larger companies whose public failures have become case studies of the potential impact of poor implementation. Consider the following examples of negative financial impact caused by poorly planned and executed tactical approaches.

Sony Corporation: In order to grow its own online retail operations, Sony Corporation, the Japanese entertainment company, included hyperlinks and promotional information in compact discs they produced and sold through traditional music retailers. However, it failed to let its retail channels know that it planned to include the promotions. Incensed at the idea that Sony was trying to redirect its customers to Sony-owned retail channels without their prior knowledge, retailers banded together through the National Association of Recording Merchandisers to file a lawsuit alleging illegal price discrimination, unfair competition, false advertising and other violation of fair trade laws.[3]

Although the suit was withdrawn two years later, the negative press and ill will the decision generated among distributors posed a cost to Sony. The National Association of Recording Merchandisers indicated that its objective was not to prohibit Sony from becoming a competitor. Instead, it wanted more direct communication about the products Sony was selling so that it could make an informed decision about distribution. More careful consideration in advance of the decision may have prevented this channel conflict issue.

KFC: Fast food restaurateur KFC offered customers the opportunity to download a coupon for a free grilled chicken breast at one of its thousands of restaurants across the United States. When the pricing promotion was announced on The Oprah Winfrey Show, a popular American television programme averaging 10 million viewers, the company's systems were overwhelmed. Restaurant franchisees were unprepared for the long lines of impatient customers demanding a free meal, and KFC's distributors ran out of chicken, forcing franchisees to close their doors for the remainder of the day. In an attempt to fix the issue, KFC told diners they would need to complete a form to receive the certificate by mail. This further frustrated customers. In the end, KFC pulled the promotion, sheepishly apologising to its market.[4]

Cadbury Schweppes: In 2002, Cadbury India, the Indian subsidiary of Cadbury Schweppes London, the world's fourth largest manufacturer of sweets and soft drinks, developed an advertising campaign positioning Cadbury as a premium candy brand with exceptional value to the consumer. To do so, it compared the value of its sweets to the entire value of the Kashmir region, the politically charged, disputed lands jointly governed by China, Pakistan and India. The advertisement proclaimed Cadbury and Kashmir both 'too good to share.' Although this was designed to play well to the Indian market to which it was targeted, it instead provoked anger both inside and outside India, including China and Pakistan, where Cadbury Schweppes also has operations. In the end, the political blunder produced sputtering apologies, embarrassment and a rapid withdrawal of the politically insensitive advertisement.[5]

Qantas Airlines: In 2007, Australia's Qantas Airlines developed a Twitter contest asking participants to describe their idea of a 'dream luxury in-flight experience,' offering a pair of Qantas in-flight pyjamas and a toiletry kit to the most compelling description. Although the concept itself may have been sound, its timing was not. It launched, undoubtedly according to a prearranged schedule, the day after they broke off discussions with union labour and grounded their fleet, leaving thousands of angry customers stranded and unable to reach their destinations. The tweets reflected this anger, exacerbating an already challenging public image situation. To manage the situation, the company hired four, full-time social media professionals to monitor the onslaught of angry tweets.[6]

Although the product, pricing, channel and promotional approaches may be managed by marketing or product marketing teams, the non-marketing executive has a responsibility to be vigilant for potential issues related to execution, particularly if a programme goes awry, and the stakes are high.

SPECIAL CONSIDERATIONS FOR INTERNATIONAL AND MULTI-CULTURAL MARKETS

Organisations that operate internationally and large companies whose products and services appeal to populations that have varied cultural values or norms even within their native country are particularly prone to execution errors. In some cases, the mistakes are brushed off as the naïve efforts of a culturally insensitive company. However, in other cases, the mistakes can be extremely offensive. Either way, they are likely to affect sales and profitability.

For example, according to *CFO Magazine*, the Japanese consumer products company, Panasonic, licensed the cartoon character Woody Woodpecker to use as a promotional icon for its company. It planned to use the character in conjunction with the rollout of a new computer with touch capabilities, which it named the 'Touch Woody,' emphasising its unique features. It also used the character as a search icon, planning to advertise the woodpecker as 'The Internet Pecker.' Fortunately for Panasonic, just before the launch of the marketing campaign, an American employed at Panasonic alerted the company to the connotations of those phrases to English-speaking markets. The company delayed the campaign and renamed its new computer the Woody Touch Screen.[7]

In another example, when United Airlines took over Pan American Airline's Hong Kong routes and launched a new first class service, all its flight attendants wore white carnations in their lapels. However, in Hong Kong, and many other Asian countries, white carnations are funeral flowers, symbols of death and bad luck. When the airline discovered its error, it switched to red carnations.[8]

Not all cultural misunderstandings happen when a company is entering a foreign market. Sometimes, they happen within an organisation's own country. The Cadbury India example, with its politically charged ad created by an Indian ad agency comparing its chocolate bars with the contested Kashmir region, is one example.

The Holiday Inn, a hotel chain based in the United States, provides another cautionary tale. After completing a comprehensive renovation of its hotel facilities, the Holiday Inn wanted to let its market know how transformative the process had been to its appearance. To do so, it launched an advertising campaign set at a high school reunion featuring a transsexual whose name was Bob Johnson. When a former classmate recognises her as his high school male friend, the narrator quips that 'it's amazing the changes you can make for a few thousand dollars. Imagine what Holiday Inns will look like when we spend a billion.'[9]

The advertising campaign angered gay, lesbian and transsexual groups, who were already frustrated with media stereotyping of people with those sexual orientations. However, it also offended socially conservative groups. Both boycotted the chain in the wake of the campaign.[10]

To avoid falling into these types of situations, the non-marketing management team member should ensure that the company has spent the requisite time trying to understand the market in which it plans to operate. It would be a mistake to believe that consumers of a particular product or service base their decision on the same criteria, use the product in the same way or even use it to address the same need they do in the company's native country. When developing everything from the name of the product and its packaging to the promotions used to introduce it to the market, the non-marketing executive should ensure that marketing professionals exercise particular sensitivity to the cultures in which the company is doing business. The use of a particular phrase, colour or image may carry significantly different meanings to different cultures, even within the same country.

In general, it is wise to use local management and creative talent, including copywriters, to develop and execute promotional campaigns and other marketing activities when going into foreign markets. Natives of the region are more likely to be sensitive to the cultural issues and language nuances than non-native professionals or individuals for whom the country's language is not their native tongue.[11]

Regardless of where a company's marketing efforts are aimed, careful consideration should be given to the potential impact when incorporating political, religious or controversial social references into a promotional approach.

SPECIAL CONSIDERATIONS FOR NOT-FOR-PROFITS

Because many of my clients are not-for-profit organisations, I have heard people claim that marketing for not-for-profits is significantly different than marketing for for-profit organisations. However, that simply isn't true. Marketing is the same in almost every respect.

Both for-profits and not-for-profits must ensure their bottom lines are positive. Both must understand who their markets are and what motivates the behaviours they seek to achieve. Both must make challenging decisions about the tactics they employ, whether they involve pricing choices around services, the promotions designed to appeal to donors or clients or where to locate service facilities. They are both equally interested in getting the best possible returns on their investments in market-facing activities.

However, there is one difference that should be understood. Unlike most for-profits, the individual who benefits from the products or services delivered by the not-for-profit is not always the person who pays for those services. A not-for-profit food distribution service for families in need might provide food (its products) to poor families without payment from those individuals. Instead, it turns to donors, where it 'sells' the human service it offers in exchange for a donation.

This bifurcated payment and service model can make marketing more complex because the organisation must now understand and service two often different markets. Although we advise many small businesses struggling with multiple market segments to narrow their focus to a single market, that advice is not practical for many non-profits who must appeal to both donors and beneficiaries (see figure 6-2).

Figure 6-2: Traditional For-Profit and Not-for-Profit Models

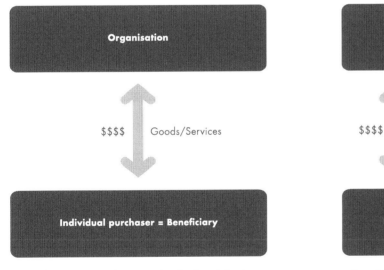

Occasionally, I'll meet with a not-for-profit organisation whose executives clearly understand one of their market segments but have forgotten about or failed to understand the other. As a not-for-profit organisation identifies its strategies—and selects the appropriate tactics—it must remember both markets and develop appropriate strategies for each one.

QUESTIONS FOR NON-MARKETING MANAGERS TO ASK ABOUT ALIGNING MARKETING TACTICS WITH INFLUENCING FACTORS

The greatest expense in marketing is associated with the tactics undertaken to achieve strategic objectives. To ensure that the marketing strategies are aligned with influencers that will make a positive impact on the market's purchasing decision process and the tactics selected will be effective in helping achieve the organisation's strategic objectives, the non-marketing manager should consider asking the following questions about his or her company's marketing plans:

- How do the marketing strategies our company is pursuing tie to the influencers we hope to affect?

- Given the importance of the influencer, how much impact will each strategy have on our business and financial objectives?

- Are the objectives within the marketing strategies clearly measurable, so that we know when they have been achieved?

- Will the tactics we have chosen allow us to meet our strategic marketing objective? Do we need to add additional tactics? Or, is our marketing objective unrealistic given what we can feasibly achieve?

- Do the tactics selected make sense given our market's size and demographic characteristics?

- How will the tactics reinforce or detract from our corporate brand reputation?

- What are our competitors doing? What will they do in response to these tactics?

- How long will it be before the tactic or group of tactics associated with a strategy begin to deliver a return? At what point do the expected returns surpass expected expenditures?

- Do the total returns, net of costs of sales, exceed the anticipated expenses associated with the tactics selected? What alternatives were considered?

- How do the tactics in our plan work together? Is there anything else that could be done to increase the results or reduce the risk that the company won't achieve its objectives?

- Is there anything about what we are doing that could be construed as culturally insensitive within the target population? If there is something questionable, what impact will that have on our organisation's performance if we decide to pursue it?

CHAPTER 6 SUMMARY

In most companies, much of the expense related to marketing is invested in marketing tactics or activities, including pricing promotions, new channel ventures and partnerships, product development or packaging design, or promotions such as advertising, media relations and other activities. Together, these are called the marketing mix. It is the substantial cost of these activities, and particularly those related to promotions, that prompt executives to joke that they know 50% of their marketing is ineffective; they just don't know which half of their activities to eliminate.

The non-marketing manager can help a company prevent waste relative to the selection of its marketing mix by understanding the three most common reasons marketing tactics fail to deliver a return:

- In some cases, marketing plans are comprised entirely of marketing tactics, without any strategic guidance to specify desired returns.
- In other cases, the marketing strategies that are included lack the specificity relative to outcomes required to effectively select tactics.
- Sometimes, the marketing tactics themselves are a mismatch to the strategic objective the company wants to accomplish.

At the end of the selection process, the team planning the marketing activities, whether this includes the marketing team, the executive team, or both, should be confident that the impact of the tactics, when taken together, meets the objective of the marketing strategy. In other words, the team should be confident that the tactics will have the financial or marketing impact on the influencing factor that is required to meet the company's business and financial objectives.

The selection of marketing tactics is particularly complex, in part, because the function of marketing, like many other aspects of business, has become highly specialised. Although the non-marketing manager will probably rely heavily on marketing experts to identify the specific tactics the company will pursue relative to the strategies it has identified, it is helpful to understand the attributes on which marketing tactics should be assessed.

Specifically, the selection of tactics should be influenced by

- the size of the target market;
- market demographics, including where the customer turns for solutions to the specific needs a company addresses;
- whether the customers are businesses or consumers;
- the influencing factor(s) the company is trying to affect;
- the potential impact on a company's brand;
- the competitive environment;
- the cost of the tactic relative to the potential benefit it could deliver and budget constraints;
- the time before such benefits are likely to be realised; and
- how the mix of tactics are likely to work together.

Even well-selected tactics can fail to deliver returns, and occasionally do more harm than good if they are not effectively executed or are insensitive to cultural issues. Although the execution may be done by marketing professionals, the non-marketing manager should remain vigilant for potential operational or other problems with implementation.

Endnotes

1 Sources:

Presentation by Richard Tate, co-founder of Cranium, to the Seattle # 4 Rotary Club on Wednesday, September 26, 2012.

Bloom, Jonah. 'Smart PR and Distribution Via Starbucks Power Cranium,' *Advertising Age*, March 29, 2004. http://adage.com/article/jonah-bloom/smart-pr-distribution-starbucks-power-cranium/39748/

2 Bloom, Jonah. 'Smart PR and Distribution Via Starbucks Power Cranium,' *Advertising Age*, March 29, 2004. http://adage.com/article/jonah-bloom/smart-pr-distribution-starbucks-power-cranium/39748/

3 Sources:

Complaint filed by the National Association of Recording Merchandisers, Inc., on February 1, 2000. http://legal.web.aol.com/decisions/dldecen/sonycomplaint.pdf

Macavinta, Courtney. 'Music retailers charge Sony with unfair competition,' CNET news, January 31, 2000. http://news.cnet.com/2100-1023-236277.html

'NARM Withdraws Anti-Trust Suit Vs. Sony Music,' *Billboard*, date unknown. www.billboard.com/articles/news/77551/narm-withdraws-anti-trust-suit-vs-sony-music

4 Sources:

'KFC cancels free chicken deal after Oprah promo,' Reuters, May 8, 2009. www.reuters.com/article/2009/05/08/television-oprah-idUSN0848545420090508

Brody, Meredith. 'KFC Grilled Chicken Freebie Turned into an Oprah-Size Debacle,' SF Weekly Blogs, SFoodie, May 15, 2009. http://blogs.sfweekly.com/foodie/2009/05/kfcoprah_free_grilled_chicken.php

5 Sources:

'Cadbury Regrets controversial Kashmir ad,' *The Times of India*, August 21, 2002. http://timesofindia.indiatimes.com/world/Cadburys-regrets-controversial-Kashmir-ad/articleshow/19779847.cms;

Cozens, Claire. 'Cadbury's ad upsets India,' *The Guardian*, August 20, 2002. www.guardian.co.uk/media/2002/aug/20/advertising.india

6 Sources:

Taylor, Rob. 'Qantas Twitter Competition is Huge PR Mistake for Beleaguered Airline,' Reuters Canberra, November 22, 2011. www.huffingtonpost.com/2011/11/22/qantas-twitter-competition_n_1107537.html#s496134&title=The_Straits_Times

Miller, Daniel. 'Qantas Twitter campaign takes nosedive,' ABC News, November 23, 2011. www.abc.net.au/news/2011-11-22/qantas-twitter-hashtag-backfires/3686940

Schneider, Kate. 'Fail! Qantas red-faced after Twitter campaign backfires,' news.com.au, November 22, 2011. www.news.com.au/travel/news/fail-qantas-red-faced-after-twitter-campaign-backfires/story-e6frfq80-1226202445747

7 Sources:

Lincoln, Adam. 'Lost in Translation,' *eCFO* magazine, April 15, 2001. www.cfo.com/article.cfm/3000717/1/c_3046576

Boyd, John. 'Naming Names,' *Japan Inc.*, December 1996. www.japaninc.com/cpj/magazine/issues/1996/dec96/indstey.html

James, Geoffrey. 'World's Dumbest Branding Move,' CBS News, March 28, 2007. www.cbsnews.com/8301-505183_162-28540029-10391735/worlds-dumbest-branding-move/

8 Sources:

Wooten, Adam. 'International Business: Wrong flowers can mean death for global business,' Deseret News, February 4, 2011. www.deseretnews.com/article/705365824/Wrong-flowers-can-mean-death-for-global-business.html?pg=all

Feldman, Joan. 'The Dilemma of "Open Skies",' *The New York Times*, April 2, 1989. www.nytimes.com/1989/04/02/magazine/the-dilemma-of-open-skies.html?pagewanted=all&src=pm

9 To see a clip of the original ad, which aired in 1997, go to www.youtube.com/watch?v=0FhjgxjAJxU.

Endnotes, continued

10 Sources:

Salomon, Alan. 'Holiday Inn Boots "Bob Johnson": Lead ad in "makeover" campaign pulled after Bowl: Had been lead spot: "$10 million in publicity",' *Advertising Age*, February 3, 1997. http://adage.com/article/news/holiday-inn-boots-bob-johnson-lead-ad-makeover-campaign-pulled-bowl-lead-spot-10-mil-publicity/69284/

Hartlaub, Peter. 'The 10 worst Super Bowl ads of all time,' NBC News, January 26, 2007. www.nbcnews.com/id/16790823/

11 While researching examples for this section, I ran across a blog posting with additional counsel and more examples of cross-cultural blunders. If you are interested, it is worth looking up for the advice it provides. However, additional research revealed that some of the examples provided there, and in many marketing textbooks as well, are urban legends rather than facts, including the stories of General Motors' Chevy Nova in Mexico and Gerber baby food in Africa.

Doman, Damian. 'Disastrous International Marketing Failures and How to Avoid Them,' New Frontier Digital blog, June 3, 2010. www.nfrontier.co.uk/blog/disastrous-international-marketing-failures-and-how-to-avoid-them/

PRODUCTS AND SERVICES: THE FIRST 'P' OF TACTICAL MARKETING

Figure 7-1: Marketing Alignment Map

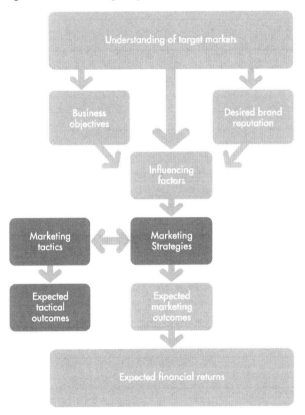

The first, and arguably most important, decision made relative to the marketing mix is how the company will address the market's needs with the product and/or service it will offer. Most companies are launched with a specific solution in mind. Often, it's a product or service that will better address the market's needs. In other cases, it's the same product or service, modified to suit a particular niche in the market or delivered in a different way. The founder of a company wanted to build a better mousetrap, bank or law firm. Or, he or she believed he or she could do a better job preparing Italian food, staging performing arts that appealed to an underserved market or addressing world hunger. He or she started with specific products or service offerings in mind.

For many companies, decisions about core products and services remain the responsibility of the executive team, as an outgrowth of the discipline of marketing. This is especially common in small and mid-sized companies and in business-to-business, service-based organisations. In larger organisations, a professional product management expert might step in to help the company manage its product or service mix. (See box 7-1 for a refresher on the four 'P's of marketing.) Regardless, the executive and management teams need to have a solid understanding of the principles of product management to ensure that the decisions being made are well-aligned with the market and the company's marketing strategy.

A company's *marketing mix* is a group of tactics a company selects to help it execute its marketing strategies. The most common categories of tactics within the marketing mix are the four 'P's of marketing:

- Products and services
- Place or distribution approach
- Pricing approach
- Promotions initiatives

If your company isn't a product-based company, don't assume that this chapter doesn't apply to you. Many of the same concepts that apply to product-based companies also apply to service-based ones. In fact, many service companies very successfully use traditional product concepts to differentiate their services from competitors. Of course, companies are rarely in one camp. They aren't just product companies or just service companies. Most companies include both. The value and perception of a product offered by a particular company can be enhanced or damaged by the services surrounding the purchasing experience. As a result, product-based companies should have a solid understanding of how the services they offer as a part of their product experience reinforce or detract from the market's perception of the product, and service-based companies should have a solid understanding of how products can be used, in some cases, to complement and expand their service offerings.

Product management includes more than just the initial selection of a product or service. Although some companies choose their product and stick to delivering the same product for the company's entire life, market leaders are constantly improving this aspect of the marketing mix. This doesn't mean they continually change the core of what they do. Instead, they leverage what they know, both about the market and the company's core competencies, to constantly improve and expand their ability to serve their market's needs. There's a strong business reason behind this. By continually expanding and improving what they do, they are more likely to stand out from their competitor, gain greater market share and avoid becoming a form of *commodity*, a product or service that can be acquired at virtually the same price from any of a number of competitors.

PRODUCT MANAGEMENT AND INNOVATION

How do you reinvent milk? If you are a dairy farmer and your primary product is already a commodity, one that is combined with the outputs of other farms and sold through a cooperative to companies who package it under their own label, how do you move your company to the front of the competitive pack? Creative product management provides many options, whether your product is available to the few or as ubiquitous as milk. For example, as the dairy farmer, you can do the following:

- **Sell the same product under your own private label.** Private labels are typically used to sell products manufactured by another company under a brand name that is owned by the retailer. For example, UK-based McBride PLC is Europe's leading manufacturer of private label products. They manufacture and package household and personal care products that are sold by retailers such as Tesco and Carrefour.[1]

   However, private labels can also be used to sell something under your own name as a retailer. For example, a dairy farm might sell milk under the farm name. In the Seattle area, Smith Brothers Farms, a family business, produces and delivers milk directly to the consumer, touting it as a fresher alternative to the dairy products found in the grocery store.[2] This requires an investment in a delivery system and additional promotional costs, but they have also been able to command a significant premium over similar in-store products.

- **Differentiate the commodity.** For example, if the milk appeals to a particular need or preference within a market segment, like local sourcing or certified organic pastures and processes, you may be able to sell the product at a premium over what you earn selling milk to the masses.

- **Find new markets for your milk.** You may be able to identify companies that use milk in their manufacturing processes or produce milk derivatives. For example, you could sell directly to cheese or butter manufacturers or to companies that sell products like milk-based bath soaks.

- **Expand the types of milk products you offer.** In other cases, it may make sense for you to expand into new milk products. You could, for example, offer a low sugar, flavoured milk product that is healthier

Sidebar 7-1: Products Are Tactics?

Sometimes, when I talk about products as marketing tactics, people are surprised. But they are, indeed, tactics.

Your organisation doesn't exist to sell a product. It exists to meet a customer's need. That is *why* you are in business. Marketing strategies are reflections of that overall goal, broken into smaller pieces.

Tactics, on the other hand, are *what* you will do to meet your customers' needs. Like other tactics, or tools, they can be used in any number of ways.

For example, let's say that up until this point, watches have been strictly utilitarian. You know there is a group of people that would love to have a watch that is as lovely as it is useful. So, you launch a new company to address their needs.

The exact product you develop, the tool you build, could have a variety of different features. After all, not everyone has the same perspective on beauty.

In fact, you might produce several different watches to reflect different tastes. These products are the tactics you are using to satisfy the underlying market need. They are simply one way to meet your overall strategic objective: to produce watches that are both beautiful and useful.

for children or lactose-free products for customers who are lactose intolerant. You could also expand your own product line to include other dairy products like cheese or butter. By leveraging your core competencies to produce related products and serve related consumer needs, you effectively expand the market you serve. Again, there will be some investment in infrastructure, but selling other dairy products in addition to milk can help generate more return on your existing farm investments.

- **Expand into new products in the same category.** Finally, you could look at the broader need for beverages, the product category to which milk belongs, leveraging knowledge and assets (physical and intellectual) related to milk production. Companies that do this carefully consider trends that affect whether someone chooses milk or another product and develop a new beverage that leverages their competencies and addresses the needs of a new market segment.

For example, consider the approach taken by Indiana dairy farmer and veterinarian Mike McCloskey, owner of Fair Oaks Farms. Leveraging proprietary milk separation and recombination technologies, Fair Oak Farms, under the Fair Oaks Farms Brands label, created a new energy drink that combined the benefits of milk with the portability and appeal of a sports hydration beverage. In 2009, under the leadership of veteran beverage CEO Steve Jones, McCloskey launched Core Power, the first of several planned beverages created and manufactured by Fair Oaks Farms Brands. Core Power is now distributed by Coca-Cola in several regions within the United States.[3]

Product or *service innovation* includes both the creation of new products or services and the improvement upon or variations on existing products and services. Innovation is important for a number of reasons. Not only does it provide opportunity to gain market share within existing markets, leverage assets to expand into new markets, and provide the potential to propel an organisation into a market leadership position, but it can also be a more fundamental requirement of survival. As Bill Gates, founder of the technology company Microsoft, is famously quoted as saying, companies must 'innovate or die.'

THE ALTERNATIVE TO INNOVATION IS DEATH

Companies that do not proactively improve the products or services they offer or look for new and more effective ways to serve their customer will eventually fold or be acquired by companies that do.

The Polaroid Corporation provides a perfect example. Polaroid was founded by Edwin Land, who invented the instant camera as a way for people to capture and share memories more quickly than they could using conventional film processing in the 1940s. The initial product, the Polaroid camera, improved over the years, and Land knew that the future for film would be quite different.

In fact, in 1970, his understanding of what the market wanted in a camera was captured in a documentary film. 'We are still a long way from the...camera that would be, oh, like the telephone: something that you would use not on the occasion of parties only, or of trips only, or when your grandchildren came to see you, but a camera that you would use as often as your pencil or your eyeglasses.'[4] He then described something that would be as easy as taking his wallet out of the breast pocket of his shirt, holding it up in front of his eye and pressing a button to take a picture.

Unfortunately, the corporation Land built did not share his ability to understand the market and envision the product or service that would better meet its needs. After he retired in 1982, the company was less adept at listening to the market and innovating its product line based on what it heard. It slipped from market leadership to an average performer as it copied competitors' entries into the digital film market and held on to its original product too long. By 2001, the company filed for bankruptcy, and its assets were acquired by an investment firm. The Polaroid company that exists today is virtually unrelated to the market leader that Land formed in 1937.[5]

Polaroid illustrates this issue clearly because it is such a large company, but the rise and fall of innovators is more evident when small and mid-sized companies are studied, primarily because there are more of them. Companies that fail to meet customer expectations relative to the products or services they offer fail or are acquired by competitors every day. Their products become obsolete, their services fail to meet the ever rising standards that the public expects or their management simply gets tired of the everyday struggle of an average performer and sells to a more successful competitor. This isn't the only reason companies fail, of course, but it is a significant one.

IF INNOVATION IS CRITICAL TO SURVIVAL, WHY DON'T COMPANIES DO IT?

There are two primary reasons that companies don't innovate when it is so critical to survival. The first is that the management team defines their business by the product it delivers rather than the needs it addresses. As a result, when the needs change, the management team fails to keep pace.

This was, I suspect, part of Polaroid's problem. The management team saw themselves as the company that created instant processing solutions for cameras. They defined what the organisation did by the solution it originally created for the market. As a result, it failed to continue to look for ways to make the experience even better, and creating the solution Land predicted would replace the one he had originally created. Polaroid may have survived had it defined itself according to the need it was trying to solve: allowing customers to capture and share images immediately and easily, wherever they were.

Many newspaper companies are experiencing similar problems. Although newspaper companies faced change over time, the core product remained fairly consistent: a printed document that addressed consumer needs for news and businesses' needs for advertising media. The needs that the company's product addresses still exist, but customer expectations about the format of the media have changed dramatically, with the broad access to, and acceptance of, the Internet as an information access tool. Unfortunately, many newspaper companies missed that shift, remaining committed to the paper document they had traditionally produced. As advertising revenue followed customer preferences, businesses have also become less interested in newspapers as an advertising media. Across the United States, and in other countries around the world, newspapers are merging together for survival, struggling to redefine their companies in ways that leverage digital media or permanently closing their doors.

The second reason that companies fail to innovate is that their management team doesn't understand that the market will continue to do so, even if they don't. Customer expectations change over time, and market leaders identify those trends and adapt to those expectations. From a product management perspective, this steady evolution of products to meet needs, and the death of products that no longer do so, is described as the *product life cycle* depicted in figure 7-2.

Products that do not change in response to changing customer needs have a natural life cycle without innovation. They are introduced, become widely adopted within that market and then plateau as the market's needs and expectations shift. Some products and services become commodities: goods that are virtually indistinguishable from one another with little to differentiate them from competitors, such as oil, coffee beans or milk. Commoditised products and services are very price sensitive, and many companies, particularly smaller companies, make below-market returns, which encourage them to sell or fold. Other products simply become irrelevant and fade from use. Companies that only offer that product fade with them.

Figure 7-2: Classic Product or Service Life Cycle

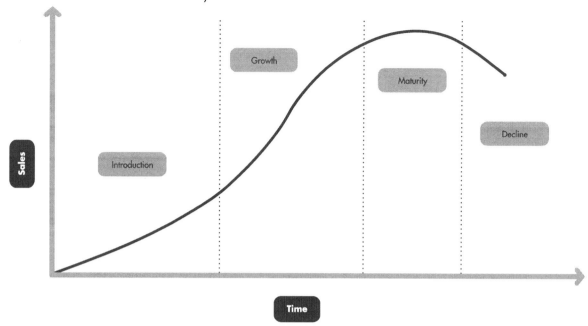

The product or service life cycle is typically described in terms of four phases, each of which carries specific implications for companies competing to serve the market's needs with the same product. In the first phase, market introduction, the new, innovative approach is introduced to the marketplace. If the new product is based on proprietary technologies, takes significant time to emulate or is protected by patents or other legal barriers, and the product is the first in its category, the company may enjoy a brief monopoly within the market. During this period, sales are slow but growing, and the consumers are typically early adopters who are willing to try a new solution. Because the solution is new, the company can typically charge a premium, and per-unit revenues are relatively high.

In the growth phase, the market accepts the product, competitors enter the picture and begin producing the same or substitute products and prices begin to fall. Segment profits are at their highest, as volume grows substantially, while prices are still higher than they will be when the market is mature.

The final two stages of a product or service's life cycle are maturity and decline. When the market segment hits maturity, competition is fierce, profits are dampened and profitability drops. Finally, in the decline stage, new products replace the old, effectively reinventing the industry. Of course, reinvention can happen at any time in the process.

The length of the product or service life cycle varies according to how broadly the product or market segment is defined. The more narrowly the market and product range are defined, the shorter the life cycle will typically be. Many would argue that the rate of innovation among companies is compressing product life cycles in general, creating an increasingly fierce competitive environment. This suggests that a company that defines itself by its products, rather than the underlying need, and neglects innovation is likely to fail more quickly than it might have historically. It also argues even more persuasively that a company should define its market broadly, by the need, rather than the solution.

Exhibit 7-1: The Life Cycles of Mobile Phone Products

To illustrate the life cycle of a series of related products and how they build upon one another, consider mobile phones. Early inventors of wireless phones were responding to a specific market need: the desire to be able to place a call from anyplace the customer happened to be.

The earliest, Mobile Telephone Service (MTS) products were available only to small populations on ships and in private automobiles. Protected by patents and with limited access to traditional switches, early providers, like AT&T, could charge a premium for the product and associated services. However, the devices were hefty, weighing 80 pounds for the equipment alone, and slow, requiring up to 30 minutes to access a free line. In addition, the number of mobile phones that the system could accommodate was limited. Because the need was broader than the current solution, companies continued to innovate.

After almost 30 years of testing and Federal Communication Commission petitions, the first analogue cellular services became commercially available in 1978, facilitating the development of lighter, faster and better products and services.

Subsequent innovations, including digital services, have continued to build upon prior successes. In recent years, the innovation has focused more intently on the services and features of the phone itself, but there is little doubt innovations have continued. Only by continuing to innovate ahead of competitors can companies seeking to address customers' desires to communicate anywhere, anytime, with anyone, continue to survive and thrive in the face of competition.

Simplified Illustration of Impact of Innovation on Mobile Communication Product Life Cycles

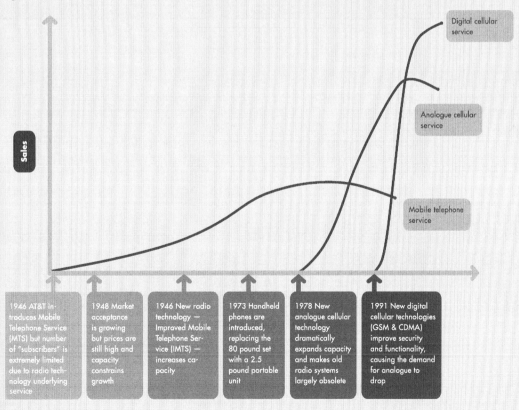

Sources: AT&T Website: www.corp.att.com/attlabs/reputation/timeline/46mobile.html; Wikipedia on AT&T Wireless Services: http://en.wikipedia.org/wiki/AT%26T_Wireless_Services

A broader definition of the market served extends the product life cycle by allowing subsequent innovations to lengthen the amount of time the solution is relevant. For example, if you consider the life cycle of a particular form of mobile communications technology, such as Mobile Telephone Service (MTS) radio-based telephones, the product life is relatively short. However, if you define the market in terms of the market's desire to communicate wherever they are, a series of innovations continues to build on and extend predecessor product life cycles. Each innovation, as it refines the previous version of the product, will gain market acceptance more quickly, compressing the product or service life cycle. (See exhibit 7-1 for more details.)

To benefit from this extended product category growth, companies must look at the need and the solutions more broadly than a single product. AT&T, for example, defined itself as a communications company and continued to innovate to find better solutions. Had the company defined itself a land-line operator, it would have missed the entire move toward mobile communications. Instead, it defined itself more broadly and continued to innovate to meet market needs.

Whereas the rapid life cycles and impact of a company's definition of the needs it serves are most apparent in the product environment or among services that are based on technology or other patentable processes, they are also true of service environments. Many services have very long life cycles. For example, the demand for mechanical engineering services in the construction of a building has remained consistent for many years. However, even in this very mature, fairly price-sensitive market, innovation is a key to success. Proactive anticipation of market needs, like greater energy efficiency and environmentally friendly solutions, has spurred some competitors into leadership roles over peers. These small innovations effectively extend the service life cycle, giving the innovator an opportunity to benefit from the less competitive and more lucrative growth phase, thereby improving corporate profitability.

The United States Postal Service (USPS) provides another example of a service-based business whose failure to define its market broadly and innovate to meet those needs has resulted in the erosion of its business. Once the primary U.S. mail delivery service, USPS has seen its market share of the delivery business steadily eroded by several innovators.

The first significant innovation came in logistics, as local, national and international companies emerged to meet the needs of shippers who wanted faster, more reliable delivery. Federal Express, DHL and other companies grabbed a significant share of the shipping market for both packages and letters, often charging a premium in exchange for guaranteed rapid delivery. Although express services caused some challenges for USPS, the bigger damage came from the invention of alternative means of delivering paper-based information, first with the invention of the fax machine and then with the introduction of e-mail. Although some deliveries must still be made through traditional postal services, far fewer packages, letters and promotional mail is being distributed, and USPS is haemorrhaging funds.

It is hard to speculate what the outcome might have been had USPS defined itself as a delivery service, a communications service or in some other broad-based way. However, it is clear that understanding the market, defining the solutions a company provides broadly enough to innovate on new frontiers and understanding where a company's existing products or services fit within the product or service life cycle are key to the non-marketing executive charged with reviewing product or service investments within a company.

As critical as innovation is to a company's success, it is important to note that a company need not create entirely new products in order to be exceptionally successful. In fact, there are many examples of companies who were second-to-market, or even late entries, and have become market leaders. Starbucks was not the first coffeehouse. Apple did not invent the PC, MP3 player, smart phone or tablet computer.[6] Many generic drugs enjoy greater market share after the patent expires than the drug's inventor and manufacturer enjoyed. However, in every case, they brought something new to the table. They improved the coffeehouse experience. They improved the user interface. They made the same product at a lower cost. Improving the value delivered to customers by looking for better ways to deliver a product or service, even in mature markets, is still a key to success.

Customer expectations change over time. In general, people want access to information, services and products more quickly, more conveniently, and with better customer service than they ever have in the past. Innovation does not have to be dramatic to meet changing customer needs. In fact, most innovation is quite subtle. It's the sum of all the small decisions managers, especially non-marketing managers, make every day. But even the most subtle innovation is necessary innovation. At the very least, the company has to keep up with those clip level criteria on which purchasing decisions are made. However, to be or remain a market leader, the innovation must be more significant and deliberate. This requires active attention to product management as a part of the marketing function.

KEY PRINCIPLES IN PRODUCT MANAGEMENT

Product management, like other aspects of the marketing function, has become a very complex discipline. However, there are several key project management principles a non-marketing manager should understand to more effectively and efficiently manage marketing within their organisation.

How the Product Life Cycle Affects Other Aspects of Marketing

Where a company's products or services are relative to the product life cycle will, in many respects, dictate how the company should invest money relative to the marketing mix, both in the product or service development areas and in promotions, pricing and distribution investments.

Before a product is launched, it is in the development phase, and the company will be investing heavily in research and development, product testing and related research. The costs may be lower if the product is mature because the company will be copying or making minor changes to its own or its competitors' existing offerings. However, if the product is new, companies will spend considerably more money ensuring that the product or service meets the purchaser's needs and requirements. Companies, such as technology companies, which are known for new product introductions, tend to spend more money in this phase of the individual product's life cycle than those who play in mature industry markets.

When the product is launched, the company will spend more money on distribution and promotions as the company demonstrates the value of the product to its market. If the product provides a new, innovative solution, the company will probably charge a price premium. However, it will also spend more on promotions than a company whose product is an addition to a mature, competitive environment. After all, if a company introduces a new yoghurt label to consumers, it does not have to explain what yoghurt is. The public already knows. But if the product is completely different than something that consumers already have, the company will need to work harder to encourage consumers to try it.

When an innovative, new product enters its growth phase, and the market is beginning to be very lucrative, competitors will position themselves to compete. As new products, imitators of the innovators, enter the market, prices will drop. The marketing function will continue to focus on building distribution channels to sell the product, and promotional expenditures will continue.

When the market, or the product, is mature, promotional expenditures are likely to peak, and the company will increase its spending on new product development in an effort to reinvent or extend the product life cycle. Finally, during the product's decline phase, a non-marketing executive should expect extensive expenditures on new product development and decreasing expenditures in other areas.

Box 7-2: Life Cycle Implications for Four 'P's of Marketing

STAGE	COMPETITION	PRODUCT	PRICE	PLACEMENT	PROMOTION	PROFIT POTENTIAL
MARKET INTRODUCTION	Limited: Company may be only player	Single, innovative product	High	Building channels	Focusing on informing and building awareness	Losses
GROWTH	Growing: Competitors offering similar or competing products	Create variations to compete	Medium	Expanding channels	Focused on positioning the product against competitors and building brand recognition	High
MATURITY	Fierce: More competition on price	New product development should be underway	Low	Expanded distribution	Intense promotions to influence consumer preferences	Moderate to low
DECLINE	Fierce	Launch new products and phase out old products	Low	Sustain or contract channels	Sustain promotions to influence consumer preferences	Low to loss

From an executive perspective, an understanding of the product or service life cycle, including a sense of the likely length, can help guide other decisions. For example, some companies enter a market with a single product or service. If the product or service is unique enough and the company does not have the resources or interest in innovating, the executive team may choose to exit the market during the growth phase by selling the company, the product or service or the product or service line, when it is most profitable.

Cranium, the game company formed by Whit Alexander and Richard Tait with a single product, is a great example of this strategy. The market for games is mature. Cranium was entering with a new type of product: a multi-dimensional game. Sustaining a market and innovating to compete long term would have been difficult. They solved this problem by creating their innovative product, introducing it to the market and growing it substantially before selling their product—and the company—to Hasbro.

The Impact of New Product or Service Introductions on Existing Products or Services

Non-marketing executives should also consider the potential impact the introduction of new products or services, or new variations of existing products or services, will have on existing sales. In particular, the executive team should understand whether the new product or service is intended to steal market share from other solutions offered within the marketplace or cannibalise sales of one of the company's existing products or services.

Many times, *cannibalisation*, or moving share from one product to another within the same company, can be a positive attribute. For example, persuading the market to move from an existing product to one with a higher margin might result in higher profitability, without greater market share. In other cases, if a company is faced with a dying product line, as Polaroid and Kodak both were with the advent of digital photography, cannibalisation can be a way of remaining financially viable.

The British discount retailer, Tesco, offered its first private label products under the name 'Value.' The Value label offered products at a discount to the brand name products it carried in its stores. After some analysis, the company discovered that there were opportunities to gain market share among customers who would purchase a private label but preferred a premium product. In response, Tesco launched its Standard and Finest brands. Although there may have been some market cannibalisation from those individuals who were previously purchasing some Value label products, the impact was low because these purchasers still preferred, and were purchasing, more of the products not labelled by Tesco.

However, not all of Tesco's decisions to cannibalise its own markets have been as positive. During the economic recession following 2008, Tesco found it was losing market share among its most price-sensitive customers. In response, Tesco created a fourth private label brand: 'Discount.' Although this move may have retained some of the market share they were losing to bargain hunters, it caused many Value label shoppers to purchase Discount label instead, substantially cannibalising sales of the Value label and negatively affecting profitability.[7]

Many companies intentionally cannibalise existing market share by selling existing customers a product with new features and benefits before their previous purchase has lasted through its useful life. Sometimes, this is done through planned obsolescence, when companies plan to phase out existing, successful products after a certain period of time to encourage consumers to purchase an updated product. The objective is generally to encourage consumers to make a repeat purchase prematurely. Although this can be a strong product management approach, it also has its risks.

If planned obsolescence is an industry standard, as it is in packaged software, consumers faced with reduced functionality may choose to repurchase the same product. Software producers like Sage, owner of Peachtree accounting software, are well known for their use of planned obsolescence. Sage phases out its support of accounting packages after just three years, discontinuing access to critical payroll tax updates and forcing the replacement of otherwise useful software. However, if this is not an industry standard, there may be consumer backlash, and they will choose competitors with similar product functionality even in the face of some conversion barriers.

Discontinuing or Changing a Product or Service

Non-marketing executives often play a critical role in helping a company to decide whether to discontinue or innovate on a particular product or service. Often, the first indication of a need for change is the product's profitability stream. When a product or industry is in decline, some companies hold onto the product until it puts the company at risk or until the company is losing significant money.

Other times, the company simply has too many products available, each drawing customers from the other in ways that are expensive to maintain and less profitable to the company. However, the non-marketing executive should be sensitive to the unintended consequences a change might have on brand loyalty. Although having too broad a selection of products can fuel unwanted cannibalisation, discontinuing or changing a product with strong consumer loyalty can also have negative financial impacts.

One of my clients is a not-for-profit organisation that hosts a fundraiser running event every year. The run is organised by volunteers, with some oversight from the not-for-profit organisation's marketing staff. The profit from this particular 'product' is relatively small considering the time invested by volunteers and staff. However, the event has tremendous loyalty from runners and volunteers alike, many of whom donate considerable sums of money through other fund-raising vehicles offered throughout the year. It also attracts a crowd of donors who do not participate in other fundraisers. Without this event, they would not make charitable contributions to the organisation.

As we considered this event from the life cycle perspective, it was clearly in maturity and approaching decline. The question was whether the value of the revenue from donors who would not participate in another fundraising 'product' was greater than the cost of adding another offering and providing donors with more options. Although phasing out the existing product might have seemed a better choice because of staffing constraints, the organisation ultimately decided to retain the event for several more years, thereby retaining loyal donors. As the loyal volunteer base aged and lost interest, the organisation planned to phase out the event and replace it with lower-cost fundraising products designed to appeal to the same donor audience.

The decision to phase out a product can be a complicated one and involves more than just financial analysis. The market's reaction to the elimination of a product it likes can be significant. Perhaps the most famous example of this was the introduction by Coca-Cola of its New Coke formula in 1985 that was mentioned in a previous chapter.

Coca-Cola had been losing market share for many years to its rival Pepsi, and consumer feedback (as well as Pepsi's own promotions) indicated that Coca-Cola was losing its customers because they preferred Pepsi's smoother, sweeter flavour. In the meantime, the market for sugar-based colas was shrinking, and diet colas were gaining market share. In an effort to reposition Coke relative to Pepsi on flavour, Coca-Cola decided to update the formula, creating a flavour that was closer to its rival cola product.

Because of the shrinking market for sugar-based colas, and based on market research that suggested most consumers preferred the updated formula to their classic approach, the Coca-Cola company decided to replace its existing product with the new, updated product.

However, because the market research was conducted as a blind study, it did not take into consideration the commitment consumers had to the original Coke product. When it launched the product and eliminated the original formula, the consumer backlash was substantial and dramatic. Ultimately, the launch was deemed a failure, and the product reverted to its original formula. The new formula was renamed 'New Coke,' and then 'Coke II,' and was discontinued altogether in 2002.

By reverting to their original formula, Coca-Cola was able to regain its lost market share. It also experienced an unexpected benefit. Because of the visibility the product change created, the company began regaining market share, reversing its 15-year history of decline. The positive outcome caused some to speculate that the debacle was an elaborate marketing strategy to rebuild interest in Coca-Cola. That seems unlikely. It would have been a very risky approach.[8] Tampering with a successful brand for promotional purposes could easily result in extensive market cannibalisation or market share losses.

Brand Considerations

When considering whether to approve proposals to introduce or change services or products within the marketing mix, executives should also consider the impact on the company's brand reputation. In particular, the non-marketing executive should consider whether the new product or service is consistent with the company's basic brand attributes.

For example, for more than 100 years, Harley-Davidson has manufactured motorcycles and related equipment and built a strong and loyal customer base. Ask consumers about its reputation, and they respond with words like *adventure, power, Hell's Angels, cool* and *manly*. Few logos are as requested of tattoo artists as the Harley-Davidson logo. So, when Harley-Davidson tried to extend its brand by offering women's perfume, it didn't fit the brand's reputation and soon failed.[9]

As a non-marketing executive with responsibility, at least in part, for brand oversight, it is critical to consider the potential impact product decisions will have on the company's brand and whether the company's brand reputation will support the products or product extensions under consideration. Brand conflicts, either in new product introductions or in brand extensions, can be extremely costly.

Sometimes, the product itself is a good match to the brand's reputation, but the packaging isn't. In a consumer environment, the packaging must convey what is inside, especially when the product can't be seen. The colours and images on the outside should be consistent with the company's visual identity, and the messaging should communicate clearly the benefits of the product inside.

Just as importantly, the choice in packaging should reflect the company's values and those of its customers. Natural and organic products are, for example, frequently packaged in recycled or unbleached paper packaging, with limited use of plastic. This ecologically friendly packaging is consistent with the psychographics of the market that purchases these products.

In a business-to-business context, product packaging is often little more than a means of labelling and storing the contents. However, packaging approaches that cause delays in manufacturing processes or require costly disposal processes communicate a lack of understanding about customer needs. Again, packaging should be designed with the customers' perspectives in mind.

When your product is a person, as it is in professional services, healthcare and many other service businesses, the company should be concerned about how those skills are 'packaged' as well. Many professional service providers tolerate behaviours from otherwise talented professionals because of their expertise. For example, they might turn a blind eye to an accountant's unprofessional appearance or an attorney's gruff demeanour, but when a client is comparing comparable services, that 'packaging' can make the difference between a win and a loss.

Beyond the Product or Service

Even if your product is not a person, appearances count. My family was in the recycled auto parts business. Their company, Fitz Auto Parts, Inc., was a retail business started in the 1930s by my great-grandfather. Every day, my great-grandfather, my grandfather, my dad and eventually my brother left for work in coveralls with a suit underneath.

Coveralls, my dad explained, were critical to whether or not a customer did business with their company. Customers had a choice, after all. They could go to a new parts store and pay more or pay considerably less through a used parts dealer, like my family's business. However, many used parts companies looked shady. Their stores were staffed by men, and the occasional woman, with grease-smudged faces, dirty hands and dirt-caked jeans and t-shirts. At my family's stores, customers were greeted by people in uniforms that were cleaned daily. Their hands may have been just as dirty, but they were neatly groomed and wore clean uniforms.

In either store, the person could get the same part for about the same price. The employees were just as knowledgeable, and the parts were just as good. The difference was the employees. The neat, clean uniforms conveyed trust. Even though the parts were the same, people felt more comfortable purchasing from the neat, clean, uniformed team. Their appearance conveyed safety and reliability. It inspired trust. It was a part of the product the customer was purchasing. And this attention to the factors that influenced trust and surrounded the product were part of the reason my family's company was recognised for decades as a market leader.

> People, processes and physical facilities, often called the additional three 'P's of marketing, can significantly change customer perception of the product or service a company offers.

There were other aspects, too, that contributed to the customer's trust of the purchasing experience. The stores were neat and tidy. Invoicing was clear, and the return policy was straightforward. The company guaranteed satisfaction. Customers returned to the store because the purchasing experience met their needs and was predictable. Long after my family stopped working directly in the retail stores, when the company was a recognised leader in the industry and their jobs were managerial in nature, they still wore the uniform every day to convey the importance of cleanliness, consistency and teamwork to their entire company. Its market leader position attracted the attention of Ford Motor Company as it was expanding into the used auto parts market, and Ford eventually purchased the company.

The visible aspects of the purchasing experience can be even more important when an organisation sells something intangible, like financial expertise, health care services or a trust that charitable contributions will be used wisely. If a financial services company portrays itself as a cost-effective solution for individuals on a budget, but its office floors are marble and fine art hangs on the walls, the purchasing experience will communicate a far different message about how cost-effective it will be. Similarly, a health care facility that seems cluttered and dirty won't inspire trust in the physician's medical abilities. Not-for-profit organisations whose executives solicit donations over expensive bottles of wine at exclusive restaurants may raise doubts in the minds of donors about how subsequent funding will be used.

As a non-marketing executive considering the product or service aspect of the marketing mix, it is important to consider the purchasing experience and how it reinforces or detracts from both the individual product or service and the brand overall. People, processes and physical facilities, often called the additional three 'P's of marketing, can significantly change customer perception of the product or service a company offers.

OUTSOURCING PRODUCTS OR EXPERTISE

When a company outsources part of its operations, uses external manufacturers to produce products or engages subcontractors to perform services, the company's executive team should carefully consider how those individuals' and organisations' actions might affect the market's perception of their products.

For example, consider the impact of one member of a prominent company's supply chain on its reputation. In 2007, the high-end British department store Marks & Spencer launched a massive sustainability initiative designed to reduce the company's environmental impact and, undoubtedly, to appeal to a market that is increasingly concerned about such issues. To make customers aware of the programme, called Plan A, they launched a national promotional campaign under the slogan 'Doing the Right Thing.' By all accounts, Plan A was (and still is) a great success, both at improving the company's image and attracting new customers and improving the company's economic impact.

Part of the company's sustainability focus is on 'ensuring good working conditions for everyone involved in our supply chains.'[10] However, just a few months into a major media campaign, the British newspaper *The Observer* profiled poor working conditions in one of Marks & Spencer's factories in India. Workers were forced into

16-hour work days with pay under India's required minimum wage rate, and as a result, the employees' children were left unattended for extensive periods of time. The headline read 'Gap, Next and M&S [Marks & Spencer] in new Sweatshop Scandal.'

Of course, it wasn't actually Marks & Spencer's factory. The factory belonged to a supplier, Viva Global, whose name is not mentioned until about one-third of the way through the article. However, Marks & Spencer certainly felt the impact on its brand reputation. The products they produced were negatively affected by the association.[11]

In a professional services environment, your supply chain (and your product) is your employee. If your employee suffers a lapse in judgement, on or off the job, it can cause significant damage to a company's brand—and bottom line. Social media has made this ever more apparent, serving as an easy leak for loose-lipped professionals.

For example, a social media consultant employed by New Media Strategies, a social media consulting firm, sent out a tweet on a client's Twitter account that they managed. The tweet used offensive language to criticise the driving skills of residents in the city in which the client, automobile manufacturer Chrysler, was located. Although the tweet was promptly deleted, followers had already spotted and re-tweeted it. The employee lost his job over the indiscretion, but New Media Strategies suffered even greater financial damages. It lost the Chrysler account.

When asked about his decision to post a tweet that would likely to be viewed as offensive, the employee said that the post was an error. He thought he was logged into a personal Twitter account. As a personal tweet, it would not have been identified with Chrysler, except that a hashtag linked the comment to keywords associated with a major advertising campaign. Had the employee posted the comment in a personal context, it might not have cost him his job or New Media Strategies the client. However, it might still have damaged the relationship with Chrysler.

To many people, terminating an agency relationship because of the use of foul language in a tweet, particularly inadvertently, might seem excessive. However, some Chrysler employees interviewed after the incident indicated that this was not New Media Strategies' first issue with inappropriate employee behaviour. The incident was just a month after New Media Strategies' own CEO was reprimanded by the client for talking about an upcoming Super Bowl ad featuring Eminem before the game, when the client had expressly embargoed public communications about the ad prior to the kick-off.[12]

As a non-marketing executive reviewing the product or service aspects of your marketing mix, it is particularly important to consider how the actions of your supply chain, including your employees, can affect your company. Even when it is 'not your problem,' it could easily become your problem.

QUESTIONS FOR NON-MARKETING MANAGERS TO ASK ABOUT PRODUCTS AND SERVICES

In most companies, non-marketing managers help evaluate proposed additions or changes to the product or service mix. As part of the evaluation or decision-making team, non-marketing managers should be aware of why the company is choosing to make investments in a particular product or service line, packaging approaches or other attributes of the customer experience and alert to whether the company is missing opportunities to innovate and improve its product offering.

As a part of this process, posing the following questions during product or service offering discussions may be helpful:

- Why do our customers choose our products or services over other competitors'?

- What have we heard from customers about how our current products and services address their needs? What are we missing or not doing well?

- What changes do we anticipate making to continue to improve the services or products we offer to customers?

- How well do our operations support the customer experience? For example, does our IT help or hinder a customer's ability to purchase our products?

- How consistent are our products with our company's brand reputation? What about the packaging and facilities our customers see?

- What changes are happening in the market? Are new technologies, products or needs changing customers' purchasing decision criteria? What do we need to do to remain competitive as a result?

- Where are our products or services relative to the product life cycle? Should we anticipate changes in expenditure allocation due to new product innovation, intended cannibalisation, new competitive threats or anticipated divestitures?

- What sales volume, and over what time frame, do we expect from each product or service? How confident are we about these figures? What additional investments must be made in order to ensure we achieve them?

- When introducing a new product, is it consistent with the company's brand reputation? Will customers believe that we can successfully produce a product or service of this type? Will it cannibalise any of our other product or service lines?

- What does our packaging communicate about our values as a company and about the product or service we deliver? In the case of a professional service organisation, do our professionals mirror the image we would like to create, both visually and in terms of their performance? What do our facilities say about the quality and value our products or services deliver?

- How do we ensure that our suppliers' and subcontractors' behaviour is consistent with our company's desired brand reputation? Are we contractually protected against misbehaviour? Do we have a plan in place regarding how misconduct will be handled?

CHAPTER 7 SUMMARY

The products or services a company offers are undoubtedly the most fundamental choices it makes relative to the marketing mix. This first 'P' of marketing includes not only the product or service itself but also the packaging and the surrounding elements of the buying experience. Most product companies have an important service component to their operations. The service aspect, including the way employees interact with the customer, is an increasingly important differentiator among product companies.

Both product and service companies can leverage some of the basic principles of product management:

- **Innovation is critical to survival.** Companies that are first to market with a new solution often enjoy a tremendous competitive advantage. However, even second-to-market or late arrivals can become market leaders by improving the products or services they offer, the way they are produced or the way they are delivered. Without innovation, a product sinks into mediocrity, competition becomes fierce and prices and profitability drop. Consolidation almost invariably follows as companies seek a cost advantage. Innovation differentiates a product from its competitors, providing increased profitability to the innovator and often a longer growth phase of the life cycle to the industry.

- **Products follow a life cycle that significantly affects the company's choice of other marketing tactics.** Almost all products have a predictable life cycle. After the initial, pre-launch development phase, early innovators introduce the product to market, enjoying a premium price as the market learns and adopts its products. In the fiercely competitive growth phase, other competitors enter the market and prices fall. New product variations often grow out of this phase of a product's life cycle, allowing competitors to carve off subsets of broader markets by offering more tailored solutions. In the mature stage, competition remains fierce, prices fall and weaker competitors begin to fail. Finally, in decline, the need the product originally served is being met by a new solution, sales and profitability decline, and remaining players divest or fold.

- **Careful consideration must be given to new product introductions, innovations and divestitures.** Organisations considering changes in the product aspects of its marketing mix must carefully consider not only the operational impact of the changes but also the impact such a change might have on its market or brand reputation. In particular, the non-marketing executive should be aware of the potential for unintended cannibalisation of existing product lines, or the challenges of expanding a brand beyond its existing reputation.

- **The customer is purchasing more than the product or service itself.** A product's packaging significantly influences a customer's perception of the value of the solution it contains. When the packaging does not accurately reflect the contents and the brand reputation of the organisation selling it, the product inside may not appeal to the target market. In a service environment, the product is the employee, and his or her packaging is the level of professionalism, from appearance to communication skills, with which he or she treats a client.

  Similarly, the environment in which products or services are sold can change a customer's perception of the value delivered. From customer service to the appearance of a store, the people, process and physical evidence around the product, often referred to as the *additional three 'P's of marketing*, can complement or detract from the product or services a company offers.

- **The non-marketing executive should remain vigilant about the impact sub-contractors and suppliers can have on public perception about the company and its products or services.** The public often fails to differentiate between a company and the organisations that serve it. Misconduct on the part of an organisation's supply chain can have the same impact as if the company itself had conducted itself poorly. Companies should work proactively to ensure their suppliers conduct themselves consistently with the values the company holds and be prepared to swiftly address misconduct if it occurs.

Endnotes

1 Sources:

Wikinvest information about McBride PLC customers: www.wikinvest.com/stock/McBride_PLC_(MCB-LN)

Berg, Natalie. 'Tesco's private label venture,' PlanetRetail (weblog), June 21, 2011. http://blog.emap.com/Natalie_Berg/2011/06/21/tescos-private-label-venture/

2 Smith Brothers Farms' website can be found at www.smithbrothersfarms.com.

3 For more information about Core Power, Fair Oaks Farms, Fair Oaks Farms Brands, and Select Milk Producers, the milk cooperative co-founded by Mike McCloskey, see

Washington Post Live Speaker biography for Mike McCloskey: http://washingtonpostlive.com/conferences/speakers/mike-mccloskey

Fair Oaks Farms website: www.fofarms.com

PR Newswire press release: 'Innovative New Protein Drink To Be Distributed By Coca-Cola Refreshments in Select Markets,' Chicago, June 21, 2012. www.prnewswire.com/news-releases/core-power-high-protein-milk-shake-breaks-on-to-the-scene-to-provide-the-ultimate-in-workout-recovery-159853965.html

Esterl, Mike. 'Coca-Cola to Distribute High-Protein Milk Shake in U.S.,' *The Wall Street Journal*, June 20, 2012. http://online.wsj.com/article/SB10001424052702304765304577479070452891852.html

4 Bonanos, Christopher. 'It's Polaroid's World—We Just Live in It,' *The Wall Street Journal*, November 9, 2012. http://online.wsj.com/article/SB1000142412788732443980457810884057315 5684.html?KEYWORDS= polaroidKEYWORDS%3Dpolaroid

5 Sources for information about Polaroid Corporation:
Bonanos, Christopher. 'It's Polaroid's World—We Just Live in It,' *The Wall Street Journal*, November 9, 2012. http://online.wsj.com/article/SB100014241278873244398045781088405731 55684.html?KEYWORDS= polaroidKEYWORDS%3Dpolaroid

Lyons, Patrick. 'Polaroid Abandons Instant Photography,' *The New York Times*, February 8, 2008. http://thelede.blogs.nytimes.com/2008/02/08/polaroid-abandons-instant-photography/?hp

'Polaroid Corporation' in the *Encyclopedia Britannica*. www.britannica.com/EBchecked/topic/467177/Polaroid-Corporation

6 Pullen, John Patrick. 'Inside the Success of Second-to-Market Companies,' *Entrepreneur*, October 25, 2012. www.entrepreneur.com/article/224554

7 Berg, Natalie. 'Tesco's private label venture,' PlanetRetail blog, June 21, 2011. http://blog.emap.com/Natalie_Berg/2011/06/21/tescos-private-label-venture/

8 The Coca-Cola Company website: www.thecoca-colacompany.com/heritage/cokelore_newcoke.html; Wikipedia site: http://en.wikipedia.org/wiki/New_Coke

9 'Extension brand failure: Harley Davidson perfume,' on the Brand Failures weblog, November 5, 2006. http://brandfailures.blogspot.com/2006/11/extension-brand-failures-harley.html

10 'Your M&S How We Do Business Report 2012,' by Marks & Spencer, page 10. http://plana.marksandspencer.com/media/pdf/ms_hdwb_2012.pdf

11 Baker, Rosie. 'M&S runs risk of brand damage due to unethical suppliers,' *Marketing Week*, August 11, 2010. www.marketingweek.co.uk/news/ms-runs-risk-of-brand-damage-due-to-unethical-suppliers/3016880.article; Chamberlain, Gethin. 'Gap, Next and M&S in new sweatshop scandal,' *The Observer*, August 7, 2010. www.guardian.co.uk/world/2010/aug/08/gap-next-marks-spencer-sweatshops; Marks & Spencer website regarding Plan A: http://plana.marksandspencer.com/about

12 Kiley, David. 'Chrysler Splits with New Media Strategies Over F-Bomb Tweet,' *AdAge*, March 10, 2011. http://adage.com/article/digital/chrysler-splits-media-strategies-f-bomb-tweet/149335/

PLACEMENT OR DISTRIBUTION: THE SECOND 'P' OF TACTICAL MARKETING

Figure 8-1: Marketing Alignment Map

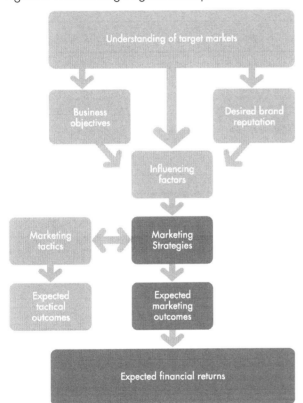

Placement, or distribution, is the way a company ensures its target market or markets have access to its products or services. The goal is to ensure that the customer has access to the products or services a company sells in the location he or she would be most likely to look for that product or service.

The method the company uses to reach the market is called a *channel*, which forms the basis of the second 'P' of marketing. The channel or channels a company selects will depend on the type of product or service, the size and configuration of the market, where the customer will look for the solutions offered by a company, costs and control considerations.

GO WHERE THE MARKET LOOKS FOR SOLUTIONS

Companies should be very familiar with the various places their markets shop for the particular product or service that they offer. For example, service organisations often sell direct to the consumer or business purchaser. In a law firm, the distribution channel is the team of legal professionals who both sell and provide services to customers. If a company tried to set up a professional sales team to sell the services of lawyers the purchaser had not met, it would be less likely to be successful. The market does not expect to shop for legal services through intermediaries.

However, that is how they expect to shop for office supplies. Consumers and business purchasers rarely go directly to a paper clip manufacturer to purchase a box of paperclips. Instead, they look for that product, and others like it, in retail facilities or through commercial office supply distributors. As a result, the paper clip manufacturer will probably sell through wholesalers and retailers rather than attempting to go direct to the purchaser. Wholesalers and retailers are both distribution channels.

Although a company could decide to move away from the classic distribution channels for its industry, it must very carefully consider other places its customers might be receptive to hearing about and purchasing their product. It can be quite expensive to shift customer thinking. On the other hand, it can be—and has been—done at extreme cost savings as well. As mentioned in a previous chapter, the founders of the game Cranium knew they would have difficulty selling through traditional distribution networks because of the significant presence of extremely large competitors. Instead, they sold through other retail environments that didn't typically sell games but were places their target market spent leisure time. Their efforts, reinforced by promotions and an innovative product, were well rewarded and saved the company large sums of money.

BALANCE COST WITH BENEFITS

For many product manufacturers, the cost of getting the product from the manufacturing facility to the consumer represents a significant portion, or even a majority, of the costs relative to the price. Companies must weigh the costs of promoting, distributing and selling their own products, which can be substantial, against the costs of using third-party intermediaries, like distributors or brokers, to help them reach their markets.

Of course, using an intermediary does not mean that the company is excused of all promotional costs. Even when an intermediary's role includes promotion, the manufacturer or service provider must be proactive when promoting their products or services. In fact, most manufacturers factor in the need to promote both to their channel, to encourage them to carry their products and place them in premium locations, and to the end user. By promoting to the end user, they help create demand, which increases the channel's interest in carrying the product.

In some cases, the benefit is related to the company's core competencies. For example, many manufacturers that are extremely innovative are strong at concepting, and manufacturing may not also be as strong at retailing. Developing another strength within the organisation can be costly. In these cases, using a retailer, or combination of intermediaries, makes sense because they lack the experience required to be successful.

CONSIDER THE IMPACT ON BRAND

Control issues are also significant. Although a company has tighter control over its brand, and often, better opportunities to listen to its market, in direct distribution environments, these arrangements are not always practical. When intermediaries are involved, the company needs to invest more heavily in brand management and oversight to ensure the individuals representing the company at the customer-facing end of the distribution chain do not adversely affect the product or the brand.

AN INTRODUCTION TO CHANNEL MANAGEMENT

The management of this second 'P' in the marketing mix, placement (or distribution), is called *channel management*. Like product management, it is a specialty field within the marketing function. However, most organisations do not have a channel manager on staff. Instead, this function is frequently managed by the person who runs the sales team, by someone on the marketing team or by the executive team itself. As a result, the executive team needs a solid understanding of the common distribution arrangements in order to ensure it is generating the best returns on the company's distribution investments.

There are two basic categories of distribution approaches: direct distribution and indirect distribution, which is often called *channel marketing*. When a company uses multiple distribution approaches, it is called *multi-channel distribution*.

Direct Distribution

Many companies use the *direct distribution* approach: The company producing the goods or services sells directly to the customer. For example, a CPA firm typically meets with and sells services directly to its clients. A farmer may sell goods at a local farmers' market or in a retail facility at his or her farm. A restaurant sells a meal and the experience to its diners. An industrial manufacturer might sell its parts to the manufacturers who incorporate them into their products. An insurance company might have its own agents selling to a specific population. In all of these cases, the company is selling directly to the end user.

Direct distribution approaches present several advantages. Common direct distribution approaches are outlined in box 8-1 and the sections that follow. They provide natural opportunities to listen to the market, learn about their needs and improve the company's ability to serve them. They can also be less expensive because the company does not need to pay *intermediaries* to sell products on its behalf.

On the other hand, direct distribution means the company's executive team will need to carefully consider how it ensures its products or services are accessible to the market. There are many common approaches to doing this. Each has its benefits and its drawbacks and will be best suited for one type of product or service over another.

Box 8-1: Common Direct Distribution Approaches

There are many different approaches to selling direct to the customer, including the following:

- Brick-and-mortar facilities
- Sales teams
- Online stores
- Catalogues
- Event-based distribution
- Promotions-based distribution

Brick-and-Mortar Facilities

One of the most common approaches to selling goods or services directly is to have a store, office or other customer-facing facility. These are best used in cases when the customer makes his or her purchase decision based on the physical ability to see the product or connect with someone from the company in person; when the market, within an easily accessible geographic radius, is big enough to support sales; or when the goods or services must be delivered in person.

For example, many retailers, such as grocery stores, have physical facilities because many consumers either prefer, or are accustomed to, making grocery purchases in person. Similarly, it is common for many service organisations to have physical facilities. Health clubs, restaurants and hotels need specially designed facilities in order to deliver their services to their markets. Hair salons, hospitals and not-for-profit human services organisations may need the physical facilities in order to provide their product. In some cases, the facility is also a key part of the product they deliver. A zoo, for example, sells the experience of learning about the animals it houses. Without animals, the value of the product would be significantly lower.

Brick-and-mortar facilities offer many advantages: providing ease of access to local customers, serving in a promotional capacity as customers see signage when passing their facilities, housing company operations and providing many opportunities to converse with customers. Owned properties can also be good corporate assets, providing some income to the company in terms of appreciation upon sale.

However, there are also significant disadvantages. Brick-and-mortar facilities are expensive to construct and maintain, which may not be among the core competencies of the company itself. Leased facilities may include restrictions, are typically more expensive than ownership and leave the company vulnerable in renegotiation processes.

Sales Teams

Most organisations have some type of sales team, regardless of whether they are viewed this way. A sales team, or a sales person, is responsible for helping customers understand the benefits of the solution provided by the company they represent and giving them an opportunity to place an order with the company. The most successful sales personnel understand the careful balance between the promotions end of their job, when they are educating and persuading, and the order-taking aspects of their job, when they are closing the sale.

In a retail environment, the entire customer-facing team is the sales team. If you walk into Tesco, for example, the person who answers your questions and helps you find the solution is also helping the company make the sale. In a restaurant, the server is the sales person, taking your order and offering you an opportunity to add soup, salad, a beverage or dessert to your order. This is called *upselling* or *cross-selling*.

Some product manufacturers have their own sales teams, which may include employees who work in brick-and-mortar facilities like show rooms, sales people who call on customers by phone or in person and team members who respond to inquiries and take orders over the phone. For example, computer component manufacturer Hewlett Packard has a sales team that is dedicated to selling directly to its larger business customers. The Boeing Company's sales team sells its airplanes directly to airlines, the military, corporations and other end users.

In a professional service environment, and in many consumer service environments, the person providing the service or the person who interacts with the customer on behalf of that person or team also acts as the sales professional. In the same respect, doctors, hair dressers, architects and others whose customers buy services delivered by an expert are also serving as sales people.

In the not-for-profit environment, sales people who sell trust in the organisation's ability to accomplish its mission in return for the funding required to accomplish it are called *development officers*. In bigger not-for-profits, as with bigger for-profit organisations, these sales professionals may specialise, focusing on major gifts (large donations), corporate contributions or grants. In all cases, they are the sales team.

There are different types of sales professionals and different skill sets that suit each one. Some sales professionals are proactive, aggressively looking for new customers in a market. These individuals tend to be better at persuading customers to try a new product or solution.

Other sales professionals are better at retaining and nurturing existing customers. This is an extremely important function because it is typically less expensive to sell another unit of product or service to an existing customer than to attract and sell to a new customer.

Some sales professionals are primarily responsive in nature. For example, when I call the apparel manufacturer LL Bean to order clothing, the customer service representative, a sales person, answers my call and takes my order. However, a good order-taker should still understand the value of a cross-sell and try to persuade the customer to purchase a complementary service or product.

There are many advantages to a strong sales force. If they are well-trained and understand your customers' needs, they can customise information and requests to the customer's situations and needs, respond to questions, explain benefits and build loyalty more effectively than automated solutions, all of which can lead to greater sales. In many cases, there is no substitute for sales professionals in the sales process.

However, there are also some drawbacks. First, many companies spend large amounts of money hiring sales people or putting people into sales roles when the people selected are not good at sales. This happens most frequently in professional services, when managers are promoted to senior managers or partners and suddenly discover they must sell business, a skill they have never developed. However, it also happens in other environments.

The second drawback is that unlike the physical facility, or an automated purchasing process like a website, humans are not completely predictable. Even with extensive training, brand indoctrination and great selection processes, sales people can make mistakes. They can misunderstand customers, fail to make an order or fail to represent the brand in the way the executive team would like. They can also simply fail to effectively connect with a customer, client or donor, leading to a lost sale.

To mitigate the risks associated with the human nature of a sales force, companies with strong sales teams often invest both in strong selection systems, to help them identify the right candidates for sales roles, and in extensive training. For example, Starbucks provides baristas with extensive training, educating them about the products they offer, how to make the perfect cup of coffee and how to interface with their customers. See box 8-2 for other ways to fully capitalise on your sales team.

Box 8-2: Ways to Maximise Returns on Investments in a Sales Team

To maximise returns on investments in a sales team:

1. Invest in strong selection procedures to ensure that the person's skills and job duties are a good match.
2. Provide training, both initially and on an ongoing basis, to help improve the sales person's knowledge, skills, understanding of the company and ability to listen and gather customer input.
3. Invest in strong promotions to provide support and leverage to the sales team.

The third drawback to using sales professionals is cost. Sales professionals rely more heavily than other direct distribution mechanisms on strong promotional efforts. Consider a single sales person selling a new or unknown product or service. He or she would need to establish contact with the customer, explain the benefits, persuade the customer to give the solution a try and make the sale. Depending on the amount of time and cost required, this process could require hours or days, translating to expensive compensation, benefits, tax and operational expenses. If the margin on the sale is small, the return on the investment might be negative. The return on a customer service person or order-taker might be higher, but only if the phone is ringing. If it isn't, and the sales person sits idle, the investment is lost.

In order to drive a strong return on sales professionals as a distribution tactic, it is important to invest in strong promotional efforts. Promotions drive down the cost per sale by informing the customer about the benefits of the solution a company offers, predisposing them to try or purchase the product or service, and sometimes even prompting a call to the otherwise idle order-taker. Because promotions are generally designed to reach large portions of a market simultaneously, they can be extremely effective at driving up the return on the company's investment in its sales force.

Many of the other direct distribution approaches require at least some investment in sales professionals. However, if the margins on products are small and the markets are broad, some form of automated sales approach, such as a website or a combination of automated and human distribution approaches, might deliver better returns.

Online Stores

One of the most rapidly growing distribution channels is online stores. For a relatively small investment, almost any organisation whose products or services have a fixed price, and even some that do not, can establish an e-commerce site that allows customers to make purchases on a website. The growth in this area has transformed many industries that once relied on intermediaries to make sales and provided national, and sometimes global, market exposure to small companies offering even just one product. In some cases, direct access to customers has nearly eliminated entire intermediary industries. When airline tickets, hotel reservations and other travel arrangements could be easily made online, travel agencies, an important set of intermediaries for the travel industry, were virtually eliminated.

Many retailers have an online presence to complement their brick-and-mortar facilities. Customers of the clothing retailer Nordstrom can, for example, purchase clothing online or in the store and return or exchange purchases through either channel. Others exist exclusively online, like Amazon.com, which has become the world's largest online department store, selling everything from books to household goods to business supplies.

With overnight shipping, even perishables like flowers and food can be ordered online, opening new possibilities for agribusiness and other companies that previously relied on a complex distribution network. Even online grocery shopping is expanding in many areas, with customers supplementing as needed from their local market. In these cases, companies combine online ordering with delivery from local facilities. Although personal services are offered less frequently, many companies offer gift certificates or gift cards for purchase online, extending their market to gift givers whose friends or family enjoy a particular company's goods or services.

Online stores are relatively inexpensive to set up and manage and dramatically reduce the cost of a sales force. However, they are not an option for every business. Online stores are best suited for companies whose products and services can easily be shipped without being damaged, have little to no customisation, have relatively standardised pricing and can be shipped cost-effectively. Online stores are less effective for professional services and personal services, including health care, hair salons, repair services and other sales that require personal interaction.

Catalogues

Like online stores, catalogues offer customers the opportunity to browse a selection and then place an order either online or by telephone. Catalogues are commonly used by retailers and wholesalers representing a broad selection of items and whose customers might be in the market for one or more of those items. Like online stores, this approach is best for products with fixed prices that are purchased relatively frequently within a market. If a product is not purchased frequently, catalogues can become outdated before the product is needed.

The key advantage to catalogues is that they arrive on the customer's desk or in his or her mailbox without invitation, giving the company an opportunity to introduce itself to a customer it might not otherwise have been successful in reaching.

There are, however, a number of disadvantages. The costs involved in laying out a catalogue, printing and mailing it can be extremely high. In addition, the company must have another channel (Internet and/or customer service personnel, such as a sales team) in order to complete the sale. As with online stores, the company must also have a logistical infrastructure to efficiently ship and return goods.

Event-Based Distribution

Some organisations distribute products to customers through events of various types. For example, smaller farms, artists and other small businesses may use farmers' markets to reach customers. In these cases, the company or individual rents a space, erects a temporary retail facility (typically a booth) and sells products directly to consumers. Not-for-profits frequently use events to generate contributions, either by selling a ticket that includes a contributed amount or asking for a contribution from individuals attending the event.

Auctions are also used as distribution events. Some auctions offer the products of numerous vendors, such as commodity, fish or livestock auctions. In other cases, a business may be auctioning off its own products alone, like collectibles.

Promotions-Based Distribution

Most promotional efforts are designed to drive buyers to a purchase but not to serve as the distribution channel. However, some organisations promote and solicit sales at the same time. Many not-for-profits use direct mail solicitation as a means of collecting donations. More recently, social media campaigns, e-mail campaigns and text message campaigns have all been used to generate donations for not-for-profits, political campaigns and other similar organisations. Other companies, including music, food, wine and book clubs, and more recently, clothing clubs such as Trunk Club, send a box of goods to the consumer who must return them within a finite period of time or be charged for the purchase. Magazine publishers often include an envelope or postcard that the would-be subscriber could complete and mail in, sometimes in a direct mail promotional piece and almost always within the publication itself, as a tear-out card. In each of these cases, the promotional piece is designed to both persuade and collect orders and/or payment.

Advantages and Disadvantages to Direct Distribution

As mentioned earlier in this chapter, direct distribution only works if the company is able to appear in the places where customers are most likely to look for and purchase the company's product. Sometimes, a direct distribution system is simply not an option because building the infrastructure to deliver goods or services to the entire market would be prohibitively expensive. In other cases, the structure of the industry discourages or prohibits direct sales.

For example, prescription drug companies do not typically sell their products directly to patients. Government regulations discourage that behaviour. Instead, they sell indirectly through pharmacies and physicians. A candy manufacturer might prefer to sell its sweets directly to the consumer, but most customers purchase candy in grocery stores or other retail environments. If the candy seller were to limit its sales exclusively to direct channels, like a company website, it would not be as likely to achieve widespread sales. If it constructed physical stores to sell its products, the infrastructure costs would be extremely high. Instead, companies in this situation use a variety of indirect distribution channels to ensure their products reach the market.

When a company could use either a direct or an indirect channel approach, the management team should carefully consider which approach will be best for the company. Although direct distribution allows a company to take its product directly to the customer, the executive team should weigh the benefits of the increased margin with the costs and expertise required to do so.

Successfully owning a distribution system requires several of the following conditions:

- The company promotes its own product.

- The company ensures its distribution will reach potential customers in locations where they look for solutions to the need the product or service is designed to address.

- The company invests in customer relationship development if customers generally make repeat purchases from the same vendor.

- The company is in a position to manage financing or the risk of bad debt.

- The company handles customer service, returns and related issues.

In some cases, it can make more sense for a company to outsource their distribution functions. This is especially true when retail or other direct distribution approaches are the organisation's core competency. Running a retail operation requires specialised expertise that is quite different than, for example, software development or furniture manufacturing. In many cases, it is more economical and practical to use external resources than to develop new internal capacity.

Although working with intermediaries does mean that the company sacrifices some of its profit margin, it can dramatically reduce the company's investments in distribution and promotions, and, in many cases, improve the returns a company generates.

Indirect, or Channel, Distribution

Companies that help deliver and sell the product to the market are called *channel intermediaries* or *distribution intermediaries*. They provide a range of services that may include distribution, sales, promotion and/or financing.

Distribution Channel Configurations

Channels can be relatively short, moving products and services directly to the customer as is true of direct distribution, or relatively long. The longest distribution channel configurations involve multiple steps in which the producer of the product or service sells through several intermediaries before the product or service reaches the actual market. Each has common characteristics, benefits and challenges. In all cases, as noted previously, a company using intermediaries should carefully consider both how it can improve its products appeal to the channel and how it can create and sustain demand in the market to which the channel distributes.

Retailers

Product Manufacturer → Retailer → Business Purchaser/Consumer

Who Uses This: Many companies sell products directly to retailers, who then sell them directly to the consumer or business purchaser. Hewlett Packard, for example, sells its printers and printer products to Sam's Club, Staples and other retailers, who then sell them to the customer. In this process, title for the products typically changes hands, and retailers simply resell what they have purchased.

Cost Considerations: Because the retailer is also taking a cut of the price the consumer will pay, the revenues to the product manufacturer will be less than they would have been had the manufacturer decided to go direct to the consumer. However, the manufacturer will typically have much lower promotional expenses and no retail infrastructure to sustain and continue to focus on what they do best: innovate and manufacture.

<u>Brand and Other Control Considerations</u>: Larger companies who sell through retailers typically collaborate on promotional initiatives and have more leverage relative to the product placement within the store and the shelf space they are given. They may also provide point-of-purchase and other promotional materials that can help ensure consistent brand messaging and positioning. However, smaller companies who sell direct to retailers generally have considerably less leverage. Because the size and placement of products in a retail environment is closely linked to sales, this loss of control can negatively affect sales. The smaller manufacturer often has more limited opportunity to define the brand outside of the product's packaging, as well.

Wholesalers

Product Manufacturer → Wholesaler → Retailer → Business Purchaser/Consumer

Product Manufacturer → Wholesaler → Business Purchaser

<u>Who Uses This</u>: Most product manufacturers, particularly smaller ones, sell through wholesalers or distributors, who then sell the goods to retailers or business purchasers. For example, Fair Oaks Farms sells its milk in bulk to the Select Milk Producers cooperative, which packages it and sells it to grocery stores, institutions and restaurants. The Japanese seafood wholesaler Daito Gyorui provides a similar service to fishing companies, finding purchasers around the world for fish caught in any particular market.

Full-service merchant wholesalers provide a range of services, including packaging products for specific markets. Other wholesalers, such as *drop-shippers*, never actually handle the product. Instead, they play a sales function, identifying markets, selling the products and arranging for delivery direct from the manufacturer. *Jobbers*, or *rack jobbers*, are wholesalers who manage the inventory in the retail environment, freeing the retailer from that responsibility and collecting payment only when something sells. In some respect, jobbers work with retailers in the same way that an individual works with a consignment shop. Some distribution companies are primarily transportation companies, providing shipping, storing and sales services on behalf of manufacturers. In all cases, the wholesaler takes the title of the goods. In other words, they purchase the goods from the manufacturer, and, thereby, assume some level of financial risk if the products do not sell in a timely manner.

<u>Cost Considerations</u>: Like all indirect channel configurations, the wholesaler marks up the product it sells. So, if the company wants the product to be sold to the customer at a specific price point, it will need to sell to the wholesaler at a lesser point. If the wholesaler is, in turn, selling the product to a retailer, the price must reflect the retailer's need to make a profit. These discounts reflect the services the wholesaler and retailer are providing, plus their own profit margin. Because the profit margin is now shared between the manufacturer, the wholesaler and, if applicable, the retailer, the manufacturer has less profit than it would if it owned the distribution process and could manage it with the same financial and operational efficiency. Of course, that isn't generally the case. That is why this approach appeals to many companies.

Because the wholesaler or distributor typically represents many products and cultivates relationships with customers or retailers, a distributor provides the manufacturer with far greater access to customers than the company might otherwise have accessed and often assumes much of the promotional expense the company might otherwise have. The wholesaler might also provide shipping, warehousing or other storage services, assume financing and collections costs relative to product sales and improve cash flows or revenue timing for manufacturers.

<u>Brand and Other Control Considerations</u>: Depending on the wholesale arrangement, a company may lose considerable control using wholesalers to facilitate the distribution process. If the wholesaler handles a broad

array of products, the company may or may not aggressively promote the manufacturer's products, may combine them with other inferior sources or may change the pricing structure or packaging in ways that diminish the value of the brand. Strong contractual agreements with wholesalers can help mitigate these risks, but because the wholesaler is purchasing the products, the manufacturer may have little real clout in negotiations.

Manufacturer Agents/Brokers

Product Manufacturer → Agent/Broker → Wholesaler → Retailer → Business Purchaser/Consumer

Product Manufacturer → Agent/Broker → Wholesaler → Business Purchaser

Product Manufacturer → Agent/Broker → Business Purchaser

Who Uses This: Some manufacturers use *agents* or *brokers* to facilitate the distribution process. Unlike wholesalers, brokers and agents, also called reps or *manufacturers' reps*, do not assume title to the products. They focus on selling and take a commission or a fee when they are successful, acting as an outsourced sales team. The Indian company, Tata Global Beverages, owner of the Tetley Tea label, for example, uses JL International, a food broker based in Ontario, Canada to help extend its reach into North American markets.

Companies use brokers who are experienced in a market to ensure they are well represented. They typically have strong relationships with the companies through which the manufacturer is trying to sell, giving them an advantage in the negotiating process. Also, they know what to expect when an offer is a good one and what additional terms should be negotiated. Unlike the wholesaler or retailer with whom they are negotiating, they represent the manufacturer and help to ensure the company is getting the best possible terms on its channel arrangements.

Cost Considerations: Agents sometimes work on a fixed fee basis. More often, manufacturers pay a percentage of the total value of goods sold. For example, a manufacturer may pay a broker who sells private label orange juice 3% of the total sales and 5% of anything sold under the manufacturer's brand label.[1] In some cases, the agent will sell direct to the end user. However, if the agent sells through other wholesalers or into retail environments, the product price will be reduced accordingly. On the other hand, because the agent's compensation is based on their success rates, this approach can be significantly less risky, and less costly, than hiring a sales force.

Brand and Other Control Considerations: Some agents provide a full range of promotional services on behalf of their client, whereas others simply handle the sales process. Because the agent works directly for the manufacturer, the company may be able to retain more control over brand reputation. On the other hand, using an agent adds one more layer of complexity to a multi-level supply chain, increasing the number of opportunities for brand to be distorted.

Many agents also represent multiple manufacturers, sometimes specialising in a specific type of product offering, like tools. When this happens, an agent might favour one product line over another either because of personal preference or because the commission for that product line is more favourable. Most companies carefully negotiate commissions to be competitive with competing products being sold by the same agent, perhaps offering incentive compensation for sales growth. Other companies negotiate exclusive representation for their product class, limiting the number of competitors who can be represented by a given agent. This is particularly common with products from luxury manufacturers, such as Gucci.

Service Provider Agents/Brokers

Service Provider → Agent/Broker → Business Purchaser/Consumer

<u>Who Uses This</u>: Many service-based companies, such as insurance, employ agents. For example, the Blue Cross and Blue Shield companies generally sell health insurance policies through independent brokers who present their clients with a variety of options.

<u>Cost Considerations</u>: The cost considerations are similar to those listed previously for product manufacturers.

<u>Brand and Other Control Considerations</u>: Although some independent agents serve exclusively one service provider, many serve multiple organisations. In many cases, these individuals act as agents for the customer not the service provider. As a result, any particular service provider's product may not generate the visibility it might otherwise have if a dedicated agent or sales force were representing it. Many companies offer agents incentive commission structures that provide greater rewards for higher levels of sales to help motivate agents to show their products.

Incentivising Sales Through Indirect Channels

In order to encourage agents, wholesalers and retailers to more aggressively promote their products, manufacturers commonly offer a variety of incentives. The most common incentives for agents are temporary incentives, including badges, free products or even vacation travel. Temporary margin increases are sometimes used for wholesalers and retailers.

Many manufacturers also provide some level of promotional assistance, developing *point-of-purchase displays* or other promotional tools for retailer use. Others negotiate a specific dollar amount in *market development funds* or demand generation funds that are used by the wholesaler or retailer to promote the product.

Manufacturers can also use the stick, rather than the carrot, to drive the behaviour they want. Some manufacturers will threaten to change agents or wholesalers, withdraw their products or delay or limit product availability. Of course, these approaches are only effective if the manufacturer has a product that is lucrative for the channel and has strong customer demand.

CUTTING OUT THE MIDDLEMAN

In order to avoid the cost associated with indirect distribution channels, many companies look for ways to reduce the costs of middlemen, increase the control they exercise over their brand, or both. There are many ways these objectives can be accomplished, including *vertical integration, exclusive licensing, franchising* and *disintermediation.*

Vertical Integration

Many companies look for ways to vertically integrate their distribution channels in order to reduce costs and increase control. This means that they create their own, wholly-owned intermediaries to represent their products, either under their existing company name or as separate companies. In some cases, they may also represent the products of other manufacturers or service providers. This allows them to sell their products directly to the consumer, rather than engaging with agents, wholesalers and/or retailers.

Some companies construct their own retail environments. For example, Apple, Inc. sells its products both through its own retail stores and traditional big box retailers, like Best Buy. The retail stores are owned by Apple, so the company eliminates the loss in revenues it has when it sells to a third-party retailer. On the other hand, it has the added cost of building, maintaining, staffing and managing a retail chain. Oil companies, like BP, often own their own distribution channels as well, selling fuel to consumers in company-owned gas stations.

Other companies own one component of the distribution channel, like the wholesaler. Fair Oaks Farms' CEO Mike McClosky was a co-founder of a wholesaler for milk products, the Select Milk Producers cooperative, which purchases the milk from the dairy farmers who own the cooperative and delivers it to their business customers, such as cheese manufacturers.

Anheuser-Busch, the U.S.-based beer manufacturer, works with a range of independent wholesalers, and it also owns its own distributors in major U.S. markets. Although retailers still take a cut of Anheuser-Busch's profits, it is able to retain some portion of what it would otherwise have paid the wholesaler. Because the company has selected only certain markets for this form of integration, there are clearly cost benefits to using other distributors in other markets.

Some companies construct or acquire a distribution network primarily for their own benefit but also provide services to other manufacturers or service providers. For example, Hood Industries, based in Mississippi, was founded in 1983 as a plywood manufacturing facility. The company grew, acquiring additional plywood and lumber manufacturing companies to expand its product offerings. In the mid-1990s, the company saw the opportunity to improve distribution efficiencies and profitability by acquiring distributors that represented both their products and those of other companies targeting the same market. In 1995, the company acquired its first distribution company, McEwen Company. In 1998, it acquired a second distributor. Both distributors, now operating under the Hood Distribution name, serve a variety of wood and related product manufacturers in addition to Hood Industries' own plywood and lumber companies.[2]

The advantage of vertical integration is that the manufacturer, rather than the intermediary, can keep the profit the intermediary would otherwise have made. However, vertical integration can be costly and distracting for smaller organisations.

Franchising and Licensing

Although owning the intermediaries is one approach to improving control while reducing costs, some companies use exclusive licensing agreements or franchising arrangements to more effectively manage their brand. In these cases, the owners of the franchises and licences are independent individuals or corporations. Their contractual arrangement with the franchisor or licensor limits their ability to represent competitors and provides significant marketing, training and other operational support.

For example, the insurance company State Farm sells its products exclusively through licensed agents who train through its programmes and sell exclusively State Farm products. Although they are independent companies, their contract restricts them from selling products other than State Farm insurance. Their offices and operations all bear the State Farm logo, and they have some geographic exclusivity in their representation of State Farm products.

McDonald's owns most of its own restaurants and much of the land on which those restaurants sit. However, in most cases, it doesn't operate the restaurants themselves. It franchises that aspect of the business to individual operator-owners, who have an exclusive contract to operate a McDonald's restaurant in a specific geographic area. This provides the company with substantial control over the location and design of their physical facilities, an important aspect of their brand, while minimising risk surrounding the operations of a food service business.[3]

The Coca-Cola Company licenses many of the beverages it sells from other companies, including Core Power, the power drink owned by Fair Oak Farms brands. Coca-Cola's distribution system, the largest such system in the world, includes wholly-owned wholesalers, distributors in which the company has a substantial or controlling financial interest and independent bottlers to whom it grants a licence. With licensed bottlers, Coca-Cola requires exclusive licensing agreements, allowing it to more effectively manage its own brand image and ensure priority service for its products.[1]

Disintermediation

The most rapidly changing aspect of distribution channel management is the *disintermediation*, which is the ability to remove intermediaries facilitated by the Internet. Companies whose products would not have reached the markets without wholesalers or agents can now be sold directly through online retailers, such as Amazon. com. An author, for example, can take the traditional path, selling his or her work through an agent to a publisher, who manufactures the book and sells it to, or through, national distributors or jobbers, who then sell to bookstores, who then sell to the reader. This process is time consuming, and the author receives only a small portion of the price paid by the consumer. Now, emerging authors can self-publish, taking their books directly to the biggest bookseller in the world and pocketing significantly more revenue as a result. Similarly, small manufacturers of specialty products can reach mass markets without the assistance of an agent or wholesaler.

However, for many businesses, cutting out the intermediary can mean the business assumes unexpected costs. Many small businesses believe that customer access and a good product are sufficient to promote sales and fail to understand the value of the promotional investments made by conventional intermediaries and the credibility they provide. The Internet's capacity to provide direct access to retailers has significantly reduced the costs associated with intermediaries but has not eliminated costs altogether. Companies who bypass intermediaries should anticipate spending most of their cost savings on the promoting, financing and other services the intermediary previously fulfilled.

CREATIVE PARTNERSHIPS

Non-marketing managers considering their distribution channel options can also look at business partnerships, alliances and other relationships formed between non-traditional intermediaries for mutual benefit. Although these types of relationships are common for promotional benefit, they can be developed to address distribution needs as well.

There are some general categories of relationships, but there are no limits to the possibilities. Some of the more common creative partnerships are described in the text that follows.

Strategic Partnerships

Often, two companies can partner to collaborate on distribution in ways that benefit both organisations.

For example, the American Red Cross sells products on its website that help individuals become better prepared for emergencies, which is a part of their mission, and help generate revenues for the organisation, a fund development requirement. Eton Corporation produces a radio that can be operated on batteries, using solar power or using electricity, and includes a flashlight and other capabilities. Eton produces a red and white version, in the colours of the American Red Cross, for sale on the American Red Cross website, giving the not-for-profit a good way to generate revenue. It also sells the same item on its own website in a specially marked 'American Red Cross' section.

Through this strategic partnership, Eton gains access to another channel (the American Red Cross website) and generates goodwill among consumers who appreciate the support of a well-recognised not-for-profit. The American Red Cross also benefits, generating revenues from both its own site and another channel (Eton's website) and helping the public become more prepared for emergencies.

Unlikely partners, the competitors Kraft Foods, Inc. and Starbucks, Inc., both of which sell coffee through retail channels, created a strategic partnership for the distribution of Starbucks' coffee products through Kraft's extensive retail distribution network. Starbucks gained access to retail shelf space it would otherwise have had difficulty securing, and Kraft generated revenue from sales of the popular coffee brand. Unfortunately, 12 years into their distribution agreement, escalating competition caused bitterness between the two coffee vendors, leading to a much-publicised breakup of the partnership.[5]

Value Added Resellers

This type of arrangement is common in many industries when a manufacturer of a product sells it to another company who then takes the product, adds customer value and sells it to the consumer. For example, the software developer Microsoft Corporation sells its Windows software directly to consumers. However, it accesses another channel through its partnership with computer manufacturer Dell Corporation. The Dell Corporation preloads the software onto its computers, which saves the customer time and effort, thus, providing added value. As a result, Dell hopes its computers will be more appealing to consumers, and Microsoft gains another sale.

Joint Ventures

Joint ventures are more formalised agreements to collaborate for mutual benefit. One organisation might benefit from access to distribution channels, whereas the other derives other benefits, such as access to manufacturing facilities. Both organisations typically have an equity stake in the joint venture itself.

For example, U.S.-based Kaman Aerospace Group, Inc., an aerospace manufacturer, wanted to extend manufacturing and distribution into India. Rather than build independent facilities, they formed a joint venture with Indian composite manufacturer Kineco Private Ltd. The jointly owned company, Kineco Kaman Composites–India Pvt. Ltd., manufactures advanced composite structures for aerospace and other industries. The joint venture gave Kaman rapid access to a growing market while leveraging excess capacity in Kineco's existing facilities.[6]

MULTI-CHANNEL DISTRIBUTION

Many companies use a combination of several types of indirect distribution channels, or a combination of both direct and indirect channels to reach their market. For example, Starbucks sells hot beverages, food and products directly to customers in their retail stores. They also sell products through grocery stores and other retailers. Fair Oaks Farms sells milk, butter and cheese directly to customers through its retail facility at the farm and through its website. It also sells its products through a cooperative distributor and through grocery stores and other retailers.

Although almost all professional service firms sell services directly to clients, many join alliances of similar firms in other geographic locations. These firms sell their colleagues' services when local representation is needed in an area they don't already serve. This partnership represents another type of multi-channel distribution approach. In another example, not-for-profit organisations conduct much of their fundraising directly and may also work through third-party organisations, like community chests such as United Way or retailers who solicit donations on their behalf.

When a non-marketing manager or executive is reviewing distribution channels proposed by the company's channel manager or executive team, he or she should consider where their target market or markets look for products, the types of channels that could be used, the advantages and disadvantage each proposed channel presents relative to cost, control, brand consistency and other issues, and whether any of the channels conflict with one another.[7]

CHANNEL CONFLICT

Channel conflict happens when two different channels compete with one another. Because Internet technologies have made it easy for many consumer product manufacturers to sell directly to their customers while maintaining more traditional channels, multi-channel approaches have become more common. Because establishing a website is relatively inexpensive, the online retail approach is appealing. It allows the manufacturer to generate better per-unit profits while benefiting from the promotional efforts of its third-party retail channels.

Similarly, many companies that sell common consumer goods through retailers prefer to sell through as many retailers as possible. By using multiple retailers, all of whom promote their stores and products independently, the manufacturer is effectively increasing its promotional spend. Because the customer will be exposed to the product more frequently, his or her chances of remembering the product name and brand attributes will be greater, and the likelihood of sales will increase.

Although some degree of channel conflict is natural when multiple channels are used, channel conflict can become problematic when one channel receives preferential treatment. For example, consider a cheese manufacturer that has traditionally sold through retail environments and chooses to launch its own website. From the cheese manufacturer's perspective, launching this new channel provides several advantages. The cost is relatively low, and it benefits from the promotional efforts made by the retailers while pocketing the difference between the retail price and the wholesale price it gets from their retail channels. From the retailer's perspective, the manufacturer's website may continue to promote sampling and purchasing behaviours, which subsequently lead to a customer choosing the more convenient local retail solution. However, if the cheese manufacturer offered the cheese for sale online at a price that is lower than the retail price offered in traditional brick-and-mortar environments, the retailers representing the manufacturer might become angry enough to discontinue selling the manufacturer's products.

Differentiated pricing between various retailers can also lead to channel conflict. For example, in 1982, Jockey International launched its incredibly successful women's undergarment line, Jockey for Her. When it was first offered to the public, Jockey for Her was available in traditional retail venues like Nordstrom, with a retail price point reflective of the Nordstrom's premium positioning in the market. Imagine what might have happened had Jockey International, after its first successful year, decided to push the product through a higher volume channel like Costco. As a mass retailer, Costco routinely negotiates low prices with manufacturers and passes along some of those savings to their members in the form of substantially lower prices.

Because Nordstrom would be offering a product that is available at a significant discount through a competitive channel, this would likely represent a significant channel conflict. Nordstrom, in response, might decide to discontinue carrying Jockey for Her products because of significantly reduced sales.

For this reason, manufacturers who offer products direct to the consumer through their own websites or who offer products through multiple channels often carefully negotiate pricing and discount programmes in advance. A manufacturer's own website often carries products at the same price a customer would pay if they chose to make the purchase through the most expensive alternative channel.

To avoid this form of channel conflict, many companies create separate product lines or separate brand names in order to differentiate products. For example, Maidenform Brands, Inc. sells undergarments using different brand names and target price points in order to minimise channel conflict and preserve strong relationships with retailers. It produces the Bodymates collection of bras and panties, which are sold through Costco stores at discounted prices, while offering Maidenform through U.S. department store Macy's at more traditional department store price points.[8]

HOW CHANNEL DECISIONS IMPACT PRODUCT AND SERVICE INNOVATION

An established company's distribution system has an important influence over other aspects of the marketing mix and particularly on product and service innovation. For example, when a company is considering new product or service offerings, it should consider whether the target customers will be likely to turn to the existing distribution channels for the new product or service or whether an entirely new distribution infrastructure will be required. The cost of a product or service requiring a new channel approach will be significantly higher than one that can leverage existing channels.

Similarly, the existing channels might suggest potential product strategies. In the Maidenform example, the company was able to appeal to some channels by offering product lines exclusively through their retail environment. For example, Maidenform's Luleh product line is sold exclusively through Macy's, while Sweet Nothings are sold exclusively by Wal-Mart.

QUESTIONS FOR NON-MARKETING MANAGERS TO ASK ABOUT PLACE OR DISTRIBUTION

Many larger companies have channel managers who specialise in managing distribution approaches for their organisations. Other companies use their product marketing team or their sales teams to manage distribution channels. However, in middle market and smaller companies, non-marketing managers and executives may find themselves very involved in the decision-making process.

Whenever a non-marketing manager is asked to provide input on channel selection decisions, it may be helpful to ask some or all of the following questions:

- Where do our customers look for products like ours? Are we missing any channels we should be considering? Likewise, are there channels from which we should consider withdrawing?

- What other places might our customers be receptive to seeing and purchasing our product or service? Are there places our competitors don't sell that might present new opportunities as channels or distribution partners?

- When considering a new channel: What are the advantages and disadvantages to this channel? Will it conflict with any of our existing channels? Does it require product modifications, special pricing structures or promotional investments or other expenses that hasn't been included in our analysis?

- What incentives do we provide for our sales force and/or our channels to excel at selling our products or services?

- What are the common barriers our sales force and/or channels are encountering in selling our product or service? How can we address them?

- What feedback are we receiving from our customers about the channels through which they acquire our products or services? Should we be making any changes as a result of that feedback?

- How can we ensure that our brand reputation is not tarnished or distorted through our indirect distribution channel partners? How do we ensure that our channel personnel's behaviour is consistent with our company's desired brand reputation? Are we contractually protected against misbehaviour? Do we have a plan in place regarding how misconduct will be handled?

- What sales volume, and over what time frame, do we expect from each channel? How confident are we about these figures? What additional investments must be made in order to ensure we achieve them?

CHAPTER 8 SUMMARY

Placement or distribution is the way a company ensures that the market has access to its products or services. The routes the product takes to get to market are called channels, and this area of marketing is often referred to as *channel marketing.*

Placement choice is a factor of

- the type of product or service being offered;

- where the consumer looks when buying that type of product or service;

- the size and configuration of the market; and

- the degree of control the company wants to have over the customer experience.

There are two basic types of channels: direct and indirect.

Direct distribution approaches sell directly to the consumer. These include traditional brick-and-mortar stores, online stores, sales teams, catalogues, event- and promotion-based distribution and other methods in which the manufacturer or service provider has direct contact with the customer. Direct distribution has both pros and cons, as follows:

Pros and Cons of Direct Distribution

PROS	CONS
Easier to listen to needs. Greater control over customer experience. No middleman costs.	Greater costs related to • promotions • facilities and other channel costs • distribution costs • financing costs • customer service expense

Indirect distribution approaches sell through one or more other companies. With the addition of each additional channel component, the product manufacturer pays a portion of the revenues from the consumer's price and also passes along some of the responsibilities and related expenses for getting the product to the purchaser. Although it is not uncommon for many channels to assume the responsibility for promotions, most companies will still need to consider how they make their own products and services appealing relative to others that the channel might carry. This is particularly true of indirect channels that represent competitors in the same product or service category. In addition to appealing to the channel, the company should also consider how it will create and sustain demand within the broader market because this will improve both the appeal of the products or services and the company's negotiating power relative to prices and other terms.

When a company uses multiple distribution channels, their approach is called *multi-channel distribution.* Multi-channel approaches provide manufacturers or service providers with great opportunities, as long as they avoid channel conflict.

Channel conflict can happen when a company uses multiple channels or competitors within a channel to sell its products or services. Channel conflicts happen when a company's channel approaches favour one channel over another or cannibalise too much of one channel's market. This can cause disruption in market access to products as retailers, wholesalers or other middlemen discontinue or limit sales of the company's product.

A company's channel approach plays an important role in the company's consideration about product line expansion. Because of the costs associated with developing a completely new distribution infrastructure, many companies favour product or service extensions that leverage existing channel relationships.

Endnotes

1 This particular example was taken from the FAQ section of the Food Brokers USA website. Food Brokers USA is an online directory of food brokers in the USA. Their website can be found here: www.foodbrokersusa.com/

2 Source: Hood Industries' websites: www.hooddistribution.com/index.html and www.hoodindustries.com/about/.

3 Source: McDonald's Corporation Annual Report 2011. www.aboutmcdonalds.com/content/dam/AboutMcDonalds/Investors/Investors%20 2012/2011%20Annual%20Report%20Final.pdf

4 From the Coca Cola Company's website and its 2011 Form 10K filing: www.thecoca-colacompany.com/investors/pdfs/form_10K_2011.pdf

5 Neuman, William. 'Starbucks and Kraft Escalate Battle Over Marketing Pact,' *The New York Times*, December 6, 2010. www.nytimes.com/2010/12/07/business/07coffee.html?pagewanted=all&_r=0

6 MDM Staff. 'Kaman and Kineco Agree to Form Joint Venture in India,' Modern Distribution Management, October 9, 2012. www.mdm.com/kaman-and-kineco-agree-to-form-joint-venture-in-india/PARAMS/article/29307

7 Distribution channels and channel management are topics that are complex and interesting. This book only touches the surface of this important topic. However, as I researched this topic, I ran across several articles and other resources I found to be helpful. Here are the ones readily available on the Internet:

Dalao, Bernadette. 'The Ten Types of Wholesalers: Understanding Their Functions, Strategies and the Role They Play,' from Ground Report blog: www.groundreport.com/Business/The-Ten-Types-of-Wholesalers-Understanding-Their-F/2868350

Kilter, Philip. 'Distribution and channels: Kilter on marketing,' an article on the MaRS website, published with permission from John Wiley & Sons, Hoboken, New Jersey. www.marsdd.com/articles/distribution-and-channels-kotler-on-marketing/

Lecture notes prepared by David Gerth, from a variety of sources, for his marketing class: http://ww2.nscc.edu/gerth_d/MKT2220000/Lecture_Notes/unit13.htm

8 Source: Maidenform's 10K filing on March 9, 2012: http://ir.maidenform.com/phoenix.zhtml?c=190009&p=IROL-secToc&TOC=aHR0cDovL2lyLmludC53ZXN0bGF3YnVzaW5lc3MuY29tL2RvY3VtZW50ZW50L3YxLzAwMDEwNDc0NjktMTItMDAyMzgwL3RvYy9wYWdl&ListAll=1&sXBRL=1

PRICING: THE THIRD 'P' OF TACTICAL MARKETING

Figure 9-1: Marketing Alignment Map

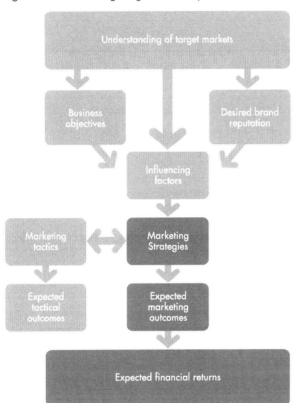

Are you leaving profits on the table because your price is too low or too high? Are you sure?

Pricing is one of the aspects of the marketing function that often receives heavy input from finance, operations or other areas of the company. To state the obvious, prices have a very direct connection with revenue, operating budgets, cash flows and profitability. Yet, many non-marketing managers have only a casual understanding of the complexities of pricing theory.

If you have responsibility or influence over pricing decisions, you should have a solid understanding of this marketing discipline. After all, there is an optimal price point for your product or service, and identifying it may be more complex than it seems at first. If your price is higher or lower than that optimal level, particularly if it is there for a sustained period, you could be leaving significant profits on the table.

THE IMPACT OF A DOLLAR (OR POUND, OR YEN OR RUPEE)

Of the traditional four 'P's of marketing, pricing has the most immediate impact on a company's bottom line. A change of even a modest amount, when multiplied across all of a company's sales, can make a dramatic impact. This is quite evident in the most basic financial equation:

$$(Price \times Units\ Sold = Revenue) - Expenses = Profit$$

If price increases by $1, revenue increases by the number of units sold. If expenses do not change, profits increase by the same amount.

Of course, the true equation isn't that simple. Setting aside cost implications, demand generally changes as the prices change. Consumer and business income constraints, the customer's perception of the value the company delivers and the cost and availability of substitutes will all affect a customer's decision about whether to purchase a particular product or service at a given price or find an alternative. The resulting change in demand associated with changes in price is called *price elasticity of demand.*

Revenues are a function of the resulting price elasticity of demand, and, typically, an optimal price point for any product or service exists, given the company's cost structure and per-unit production or service costs. This relationship is illustrated in figure 9-2. For example, in most cases, a company that raises its prices will reduce demand, driving customers away. If the company was not at the optimal price point, it may lose customers that generate less revenue and gain customers that are willing to pay a higher price for the goods or services. Several years ago, I worked with a professional service firm whose pricing was to the left of its optimal point due to a large group of small, unprofitable clients. Although it is never easy to let existing business go, by doing so, the firm could accommodate other, more lucrative clients and improve its profitability. On the other hand, if the firm was to the right of its optimal revenue level, dropping the price may increase volume in ways that positively affect revenues.

In addition to the impact of price elasticity on demand, a company must consider its cost structure. Sometimes, the optimal pricing point is different than suggested by the price elasticity of demand because of the cost structure under which a company operates. For example, the revenues may peak at a certain price, but if an additional factory must be added to produce sufficient product to meet demand, the company may, in fact, be better off maximising revenues for the quantity it can produce.

Figure 9-2: Price Elasticity of Demand

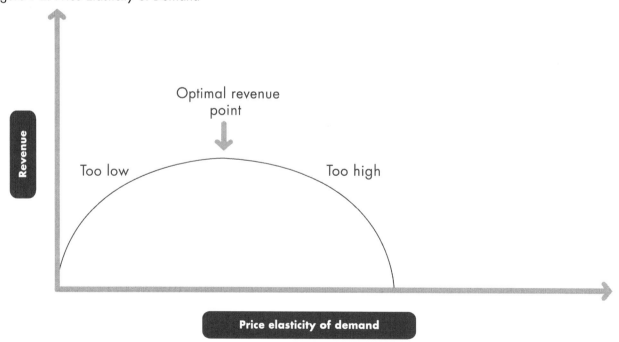

Given this discussion of the optimal pricing, it would appear that any decisions about price should be based purely on market demand, the company's ability to supply products or services and the cost structure under which the company operates. Certainly, this financial analysis is critical, but it's incomplete.

That's because the *demand curve* can shift.

In fact, the entire model has the potential to be very fluid. Demand changes with customer expectations. When new solutions, solutions with better features or attributes or solutions that are more accessible or are delivered with better service enter the market, customers begin to expect those same benefits from competitors, and the demand curve shifts. Changing customer demographics in the company's market, as well as other factors such as the economy, can also affect demand. Of course, a company's own demand curve will also be affected by its brand reputation within the market.

Proactively managing pricing approaches takes a combination of the vision acquired through the discipline of marketing and the financial analysis of the marketing function.

As a result, pricing is not as simple as the mathematical equations behind price elasticity suggest. Proactively managing pricing approaches takes a combination of the vision acquired through the discipline of marketing and the financial analysis of the marketing function.

To pick the optimal pricing approach, a company must have a strong finance team to crunch the numbers. However, research[1] indicates that companies with the strongest ability to set prices at the optimal level share two other characteristics. First, they base their prices on the market and their customers' perception of the value of the products or services they deliver to them. Second, their executive team is actively involved in their pricing strategies, building a culture that reinforces key aspects of their pricing objectives and develops motivational structures to support them.

By contrast, the management teams of average performers base price on competitive or cost issues and are involved in subsequent pricing decisions only to the extent that they need to approve a substantial deviation from list prices or to participate in substantial contract negotiations. Unfortunately, very few companies deliberately consider their pricing approach. Research also shows that fewer than 15% of all companies do systematic research.[2] In my experience, the number is significantly smaller. As a non-marketing executive, it is within your purview to assess your company's pricing strategy and determine whether the value of your products and services is aligned with the expectations of your market.

COMMON APPROACHES TO EVALUATING PRICE

Most companies use one of three approaches to set their list prices and parameters for discounts, sales incentives and other price reductions. *Cost-based* and *competition-based pricing* are the most common approaches. However, market leaders more often use a *market-driven* or *customer value-based* pricing method.

Cost-Based Pricing

In cost-based pricing, the price is established based on the cost of producing the goods or services, plus a specified mark-up. For example, a manufacturer might add a certain percentage of the product's basic manufacturing cost (the mark-up) to each product in order to cover the company's overhead expenses and

Sidebar 9-1: What is Price?

Price is defined as what the customer actually pays. Sometimes, the price is the *list price*, or the price the company set for the product or service. However, more often, the customer pays less or even more than that amount. This is the *realised price*.

For example, customers pay more than the list price when they must pay for delivery associated with receiving the product or service. Although shipping is often a direct cost passed along to the customer, it still represents an incremental increase in price. When customers are evaluating two comparable products, they are more likely to factor in shipping costs and purchase the one that has a lower total price.

Many customers pay less than the list price because companies offer discounts through coupons or promotions, provide incentives to sales people, give advertising or promotional allowances to the channels that purchase their products or allow sales people the latitude to negotiate.

Often, these reductions in price are carefully considered. The most successful pricing approaches have structured parameters for the types and sizes of price reductions that can happen. However, in some businesses, particularly in the service industry, discounts are less carefully monitored. For example, a CPA firm might have established billing rates for each professional within its firm, and, yet, its staff might not bill all the hours they spend on a particular client's work in an effort to reduce fees or manage to an established budget. This problem is compounded when a partner further reduces the fees in an effort to appeal to a client.

Certainly, clients appreciate this practice. However, without careful planning and accurate tracking of all hours, including unbilled hours, a company can inadvertently reduce the value of its work product below what is competitive, much less optimal. When unbilled time is common at all levels of the organisation, with each individual deciding how much he or she should leave unrecorded, the company's realised price can be an extremely small fraction of the actual services rendered. Because this time often slips by unrecorded, it can result in unpredictable or inaccurate financial forecasting.

profit. The mark-up might be consistent across all products or specific to certain products or product categories.

In some industries, businesses follow common rules of thumb, which are relative to mark-ups. For example, in the advertising industry, agencies typically mark up purchases of advertising space, photography, printing and other expenses by 17.65%. This mark-up is designed to cover the cost of capital, the financial administration, bad debt expense and, in some cases, taxes that apply to the purchase. On the labour side of the equation, mid-sized and larger agencies typically charge 3.5–4.5 times the employee's hourly wage, or the equivalent of that figure if the person is on a salary, as the hourly rate. This is intended to cover business development, personal development and administrative time while delivering a profit to the business.

In many industries, cost-based pricing is the accepted standard. For example, many companies in the construction industry outline an acceptable cost-plus approach and reserve the right to audit their contractor's books to confirm compliance. This is particularly common in government contracting relationships and relationships with larger customers.

However, as a general practice, cost-based pricing has some significant drawbacks. Most importantly, it does not account for customer demand and available alternatives. If a company decides to produce a product, then uses a cost-based pricing method to establish its profit threshold, it might hit the peak on the pricing bell curve. On the other hand, it might fall on one side or the other. A company that delivers more value than its price suggests may leave profits on the table, whereas one whose manufacturing or production costs exceed market expectations may find itself struggling financially due to poor sales.

In highly competitive markets, the *margin* that competitors are receiving may be lower than the one targeted by the company. If the targeted margins are higher and the costs are similar, the price may be higher, and the company will get fewer sales. On the other hand, if the solution is new and unique, the market may be willing to pay a premium to access the product or service. An internally-set mark-up that is lower than what the market would accept might forfeit profits that could otherwise have been generated.

For example, Parker Hannifin, the U.S.-based manufacturer of motion and control technologies, developed a pricing approach that was extremely popular internally due to its simplicity: Add up the costs, and tack on a 35% profit margin. Although this pricing tactic was simple to use, it meant that innovative solutions introduced to the market were not offered at their value to the market, a price greater than the price calculated through the company's formulaic approach. Similarly, operational improvements that decreased the cost per unit to produce a product resulted in a price reduction, often to rates below market. In both cases, the company was leaving profits on the table that customers would have been happy to provide. In 2007, their new CEO, Donald Washkewicz, identified the issue and began determining prices according to what customers were willing to pay, adding a senior position for pricing within the company. Although there was significant backlash within the company, the company's operating revenues increased by $200 million in the five-year period following the change in strategy.[3]

Competition-Based Pricing

Companies using this approach look at the market for similar products or services, identify the range of prices and set their prices relative to what they believe the market will accept relative to what their competitors are doing.

This approach is particularly common in mature marketplaces, where competition is perceived to be fierce. For example, if a law firm launches a new practice group, its management team is likely to consider the rates its competitors charge for similar services when setting its billing rates and practices. A fast food restaurant might consider the costs of alternative products available to its customers, such as hamburgers at the US-based chain McDonald's or the French chain Quick, before setting its own prices. Manufacturers who are competing to produce and sell common office supplies will consider their competitors' pricing structure when approaching channels with special pricing.

However, like cost-plus pricing, this approach also neglects the customer's perspective. In fact, it often encourages an assumption that price is the customer's primary decision criteria when that might not, in fact, be the case.

Value-Based Pricing

As the name suggests, companies who use this pricing approach consider the value their customers might place on their solution, the relative elasticity of demand and their understanding of market trends and use that information to identify the optimum pricing model.

Although not as prevalent as the other two approaches, this pricing model is most common when companies develop a new solution to an existing need or have unique knowledge or skills. In these cases, there is no direct competitive information upon which to rely, and, as was the case with Parker Hannifin, the cost-plus approach would not produce optimal results.

To illustrate, consider the pricing approach Josephine Cochrane would have needed when she invented the first functional dishwasher in 1886. This new device had no direct parallel in the market. Servants, dishwashers in hotels and restaurants and housewives were the functional equivalent, so competition-based pricing would have been difficult to assess. At the same time, it was a vast improvement over the drudgery of washing dishes by hand and significantly reduced both the cost of labour and the number of pieces of china that were chipped by servants doing the task. This machine had greater value, in several respects, than current alternatives. By all accounts, the design was relatively simple, and the original unit was built from readily available supplies. A pure cost-based pricing structure would have undervalued the new invention. To price it accurately, Cochrane would have needed to consider customer value.

New products are not the only components on which value-based pricing is more frequently used. Expertise-based organisations, in which the knowledge is highly technical and there are few alternatives, are more likely to base their prices on how valuable the solution is than the cost of delivering it or their competitors' fee structures. For example, two physicians may spend the same amount of time and expense treating a patient. However, if one of the physicians has exceptional expertise with a rare ailment and develops a reputation for addressing it more effectively, the value of his or her services may rise relative to other physicians. Although he or she could keep his or her prices at the same level, he or she might be forfeiting profits. Instead, the physician is likely to charge a premium reflective of his or her expertise.

In some industries, value-based pricing is quite common. For example, major construction, technology implementation and other customised projects are often negotiated bids based on value. Flea markets, art auctions, and other environments in which prices are not posted or predetermined require direct negotiation with a customer.

Ironically, value-based pricing is often ignored as an option in fiercely competitive industries in which this pricing structure, if appropriately supported, could deliver competitive advantage. When I begin working with clients on their marketing efforts, many of them, particularly in the professional services arena, are quick to dismiss value-based pricing. 'Price,' they tell me, 'is what it is.' The market sets it, and the company can't afford to have a price structure that is higher than the industry norms, regardless of the level of value it delivers.

However, when I've conducted research among these clients' customers, many of them have said they selected vendors in the past whose prices were not the lowest of the bids received. In fact, most customers indicate that although pricing is an important decision-making factor, it is not the most important. By neglecting value-based pricing as an approach, these companies often ignore potential opportunities to differentiate, which might allow them to raise their prices and improve their profitability. Instead, they remain engaged in fierce competition, even pricing wars, with their peers, who are pursuing the same pricing approach.

In my experience, when customer value-based pricing is done effectively, it facilitates conversations about how to improve the value delivered to the customer and allows companies to optimise their pricing structures and resulting profitability. Unfortunately, this approach also has its challenges.

The main challenge of the customer value-based pricing approach is that it requires a deep understanding of the customer base, what they value and how sensitive they are to changes in price (price elasticity). Generating and interpreting this data can be time consuming and challenging, especially if an organisation is not already adept at listening to its markets.

When a company uses a value-based pricing approach, the executive team should think carefully about potential competitor response. When pricing based on customer value results in a premium pricing structure, competitors may also recognise the opportunity. Patents, long development cycles and other barriers to new entrants may discourage some competitors, but if the barriers are minimal, any company generating superior profits will attract significant competitor interest.

PRICE AND THE PRODUCT LIFE CYCLE

Pricing is commonly tied to the life cycle of a product or service. In the introduction phase, when the product or service is new, many companies use *skimming* or *penetration* **approaches**. They are designed deliberately to be below or above the optimal revenue point for a short period of time.

Skimming is designed to grab initial sales from customers who are the least price sensitive, maximising short-term profitability while sacrificing revenues. To do so, the product is priced at a significant premium relative to alternative solutions. This approach is only available when there are few comparable alternatives to customers. It is most often used when a company introduces a new product in a particular category that is a significant improvement on alternatives or when the market has a particularly strong group of price-insensitive early adopters. For example, new technology solutions, particularly those offered by popular manufacturers, are often initially priced at a substantial premium. These prices are designed to take advantage of the relatively small group of people who want the product or service offered so desperately that they are willing to pay almost any price to get it. Tickets to the opening night of popular movies, new consumer technologies and new drug treatments protected by patents all commonly use this approach.

However, this is rarely a long-term strategy because the high pricing structure may invite competition. In some cases, as with movie premieres, the pricing structure might exist for a single show. In other cases, the price drops incrementally as the market becomes saturated or as other entrants begin to offer competing products or services. In some markets, such as prescription drugs, the company may enjoy premium pricing structures until the patent expires and the company's effective monopoly on the solution expires.

Penetration pricing (or introductory pricing) takes the opposite approach. Companies using penetration pricing deliberately choose a price point that is relatively low, intentionally forfeiting profit margins in an effort to get more people to purchase the product or service. The objective of this approach is to get purchasers to try a product or service they might not otherwise have tried. It can be used when the solution is completely new and relatively unknown. For example, some software manufacturers ask companies to test-run their products at a deep discount in exchange for endorsements and the ability to build an early customer list. It can also be used when a company is entering a market with established competitors. The low prices, relative to existing solutions, reduce barriers to sampling behaviour, giving the company an opportunity to snatch customers from competitors and build customer loyalty.

Like skimming, penetration pricing is a relatively short-term approach designed to build market share. At some point, the company increases its pricing to reflect the pricing approach it has selected or to be more competitive with the market.

As a product enters the growth phase of its life cycle, and more alternatives are available for a customer to consider, skimming behaviours are less common. In the maturity phase, pricing tends to drift toward competition-based approaches, easing downward over time, and it becomes more difficult to differentiate products or services. At this point, many companies focus their energies on creating a new set of products or services or creating incremental value within their products or services to address customer needs.

INCENTIVE PRICING APPROACHES

Many companies and industries use creative pricing structures to incentivise purchasing behaviours among consumers, and in some cases, to motivate salespeople or channels to sell. Sometimes, these approaches represent an actual reduction in the price paid by a consumer, whereas other times, they drive down the perceived cost of purchasing the goods or services.

Companies use temporary price adjustments to shift purchasing behaviours or increase demand. Among the most common incentive pricing structures are

- loss leaders;
- freemiums;
- coupons and Groupons;
- rebates;
- sales and other short-term price reductions;
- fixed pricing offers;
- retainers;
- package prices;
- contingency pricing;
- bulk pricing;
- multiple-unit pricing; and
- push money/prize money allowances.

Loss Leaders

Many companies use *loss leader* products to drive customer purchases of other, more lucrative products. Grocery stores, for example, may offer eggs or milk at an unusually low price or even for free with a minimum grocery purchase, as a way to attract shoppers. Their objective is to attract shoppers with low prices on everyday items in the hopes that those shoppers will complete the rest of their shopping at the same store. When this happens, they win profits from competitors. Retailers often lure shoppers into their stores by advertising a low cost item, such as a basic toaster, and then place that item next to a more expensive version on the same shelf as a way to entice the shopper to upgrade.

Cell phone service providers commonly provide a cell phone at a reduced cost, or even for free, to customers who sign a contract. They are, in many cases, betting on a consumer's desire to have a specific type of phone, which may be offered by a select number of service providers, to drive business to their store. By providing the phone at no cost, they reduce the immediate costs to the consumer of a new phone contract while locking in a more lucrative revenue stream for the future.

Printer manufacturers offer laser and ink-jet printers at cost, or below cost, for the same reason. When a customer commits to a printer, he or she must purchase ink from the same manufacturer. Ink cartridges are comparatively inexpensive to produce. If a manufacturer can get a customer to purchase a printer it produces, the manufacturer is assured a steady stream of revenue for the life of the printer.

Professional service providers often use a loss leader strategy, as well. When I incorporated my company, MarketFitz, Inc., my attorney offered to do the work at no cost. He knew that as I was starting my company, and my financial situation would be tight. However, he also knew that if he could gain my loyalty by providing a small service for free, our company would have a steady stream of legal needs, ranging from contract development to personnel policies, which his firm could address. The stream of future purchases was worth the forfeited revenues associated with the services related to incorporation.

The use of loss leader products or services can be very effective. However, there are some risks. In the case of non-perishables, for example, some price-conscious shoppers will spot a bargain and simply stock up. To mitigate this risk, stores often cap loss leader products at a small number. However, in a retail setting, this may not stop a shopper from simply returning on a routine basis and purchasing the maximum at each visit.

The shopper may also purchase the loss leader product but not enough additional products or services to recoup the initial cost. For example, had my company failed within its first few months, my attorney might have lost the investment he made in the services related to incorporation. Some companies, particularly consulting companies, use a variation on the loss leader, promising to apply the initial fees to future services. For example, my attorney might have told me that I would need to pay for the incorporation work, but that by choosing his law firm, he would grant me a credit for future legal services in the same amount. However, if the consumer is price sensitive, this might cause the consumer to price shop before making a choice.

In other cases, the company can create significant ill will among customers by using loss leaders. For example, a consulting firm might win work in a competitive environment by proposing a particularly low bid, only to return to the customer time and again with change orders requesting more fees. One of my clients competes in an industry in which one of the larger competitors is well known for this practice, a form of bait-and-switch. However, the person making the purchasing decision is often heavily influenced by people outside the industry who are often swayed by the low price and don't always see the subsequent change orders that follow. Although this approach has been quite successful, other purchasers who are better informed about these practices report that they add 20% to this vendor's price during the bidding evaluation and block the selection of that service provider when they can. Of course, word will get around about the company's approach, and the ill will that this behaviour creates will result in permanent brand damage as the company develops a reputation for deceiving the market.

Freemiums

A variation on the loss leader is the concept of offering the core product or service for free, and then charging for upgrades or add-ons. This is very common among online service providers, including open source software developers, gaming companies, social media providers and other digital service offerings. The objective of *freemiums* is to build a base of consumers quickly, gaining permission to offer other services or products at an additional cost.

In many cases, freemiums are offered for products or services whose true market is advertisers. For example, Google offers free e-mail services. However, account holders are exposed to advertisements that are tailored to what Google knows about the user and her shopping behaviours as well as the content of the e-mail. The advertiser pays Google for the ability to reach individuals with profiles that most closely align with their needs.

Although freemiums have many benefits, companies must consider the potential impact on their brand of this particular pricing structure. In particular, products and services offered for free are often associated with having a lower value in general. Using freemiums would, for this reason, be inappropriate for any organisation seeking a high-end product reputation.

Coupons, Groupons, Rebates, Sales and Other Short-Term Price Reductions

Whereas loss leaders provide an incentive for the market to purchase other goods or services, coupons and other short-term discounts are offered to try to get the market to purchase the good or service itself. Although they can reduce the price below cost, coupons more frequently reduce the price to something between the list and the cost of producing and selling the product or service.

Coupons and other discounts can be used for many purposes. They can be used to induce initial purchasing behaviour, such as when a product is being introduced to the market. Starbucks, for example, provided coupons offering a discount on subsequent purchases of Via to consumers who participated in its in-store sampling efforts.

They can also be used to accelerate purchasing behaviour. For example, an apple grower that had an outstanding crop might use discounted pricing to ensure it sells as many apples as possible when they are at their peak, thus, avoiding storage costs. Car dealers frequently use price discounts to clear out inventory before new models are released by manufacturers. In these cases, sellers are hoping to accelerate the timing of a planned purchase or to increase the volume of purchases. In professional services, a company might offer incentive pricing to a client that is predicated on signing a multi-year contract. For example, a CPA firm might offer extremely low pricing the first year to accommodate a company's short-term financial constraints and increase the price to market, or above market, in subsequent years.

Some vendors use coupons to attract specific, under-tapped markets. For example, a theatre might offer open seats at plays to young patrons at discounted pricing using Groupon, Goldstar or other discounting mechanisms that disproportionately reach this demographic. Because the average age of theatregoers has been climbing and theatres understand the importance of attracting and retaining younger patrons in order to remain financially viable, the use of discounts to incentivise sampling behaviour and increase patronage is appealing. In addition, these theatres hope younger patrons will spread the word about their 'product' to other young prospective patrons.

Although discounts can be used successfully to drive volume, they do have some disadvantages. For example, in the preceding theatre example, research conducted on behalf of one of our clients suggested that a significant number of younger theatre patrons only purchase tickets when they can do so at a deep discount, and theatres may be inadvertently cultivating a perception that the value of the theatre experience is, in fact, lower than the cost of producing a show. If this demographic, which the arts community sees as its future patron base, persists in this belief and refuses to purchase tickets at full price in the future, theatres may need to adjust their cost structures to survive.

Similarly, although coupons and Groupons are used to attract customers, they might not attract the right kind of customer. In other words, the coupon may attract a customer who would purchase from the company when it offers the product at an extremely low price but would not return to purchase at the regular price either because the *value proposition* offered by the company does not appeal to their needs, or they are simply serial bargain hunters. If the company attracts too many of these types of clients, it will lose money without gaining benefit. At its worst, discounting can also distort the company's perspective about who their customers are, as markets that might not otherwise value the services offered at regular prices move in to take advantage of price discounts. Because these customers are not likely to return when prices go up, they can become a drain on the attentions of the management team and a distraction as the company seeks to tailor products or services to existing markets.

Another disadvantage is that industries or companies with a reputation for incentive pricing at specific times of year or in certain situations may simply be changing customer purchasing habits. For example, many food products go on sale at predictable times.[1] Savvy consumers actively managing their budgets stock up during those periods but do not increase or change their buying habits otherwise. In these cases, the food product manufacturer is not increasing sales from these customers. They are simply reducing the price.

Many companies have benefited from the exposure to new customers generated by *daily deal sites* like Amazon Local, Groupon and Living Social. However, companies should carefully weigh the pros and cons of using these services, particularly when it comes to customer retention. Another consideration is that many of these sites require the vendor to provide a deep discount, sometimes 50% or more, and often expect a significant portion of the proceeds in return.

In some cases, the company offers incentive pricing and then finds itself surprised by the demand. Recall the example of fast food restaurant KFC from a previous chapter that offered customers a coupon for a free chicken meal and then ran out of product because of the overwhelming demand. Even if a company is offering a slight discount, a miscalculation of the price elasticity could have a significant impact on capacity.

Finally, in some cases, the market may interpret a temporary price reduction as an indication that your regular pricing structure is higher than it could or should be. This is a common issue in the consulting services arena, when pricing offered to some clients is lower than at other times, such as when working with non-profits or during periods of slow sales.

This same type of market confusion can also happen when sales incentives clash with pricing approaches. For example, a manufacturer might set a quarterly quota for the sales team. The same manufacturer may also give the sales team considerable latitude to adjust prices as a way to incentivise purchases. However, this can result in unofficial end-of-quarter sales if certain members of the sales team find they are running short on their quota and decide to offer deeper discounts and channel incentive programmes to catch up. If this happens on a sustained basis, it can create a permanent dampening effect on prices when the price adjustments become broadly known.

Fixed Fees or Fixed Prices

In some industries, companies offer *a fixed price* to perform a specific set of services or deliver a specific product at a pre-determined cost, regardless of the actual time involved. By guaranteeing that the cost won't exceed a certain price point, the company reduces the customer's risk and improves the perceived value. In some cases, a customer will prefer a fixed fee even when the competitive fee under an hourly schedule might be less expensive, simply because there is no risk that the fee will exceed the original estimate.

Retainers

Retainers are a variation on the fixed price concept. *Retainers* are sums paid by the customer to the company on a routine basis in exchange for services within a specific scope. The customer's demand for services may vary, and the retainer provides incentive to use the company as often as needed without worrying about incremental costs, while making the costs more predictable. Retainers are common in professional and business services that occur routinely and might otherwise be billed on an hourly basis and make the most sense when the company is confident the retainer will cover most, if not all, the actual time used. For example, public relations counsel and building maintenance are available on a retainer basis.

Package Prices

Restaurants, beauty salons and other companies sometimes offer fixed price packages as an incentive for the customer to purchase more than they otherwise might have. Using a restaurant as an example, a customer may then look at the three course meal, add the salad and entrée that he or she might have purchased and realise that the dessert is only a few dollars more under the fixed price menu and decide to splurge. The restaurant gains an additional sale, often from an item that was relatively inexpensive to add to the package as a whole.

Contingency Pricing

Some companies provide goods or services to a company, and payment is contingent on the satisfactory completion of specific requirements. For example, a lawyer might charge fees contingent on winning a legal case. Some construction contracts include provisions that reduce the amount due if the contractor does not complete the project on time. Some investment advisers charge the client a percentage of their portfolio on an annual basis (a form of payment based on success) because the adviser's earnings will be significantly higher if his or her work is financially productive for the client.

Bulk Pricing

This pricing structure provides a lower price to companies who purchase large numbers of a given product. This type of pricing structure is more common when the manufacturer generates a cost savings if the number of products or services sold is higher. For example, if the cost of distribution or the cost of packaging decreases when larger quantities are sold, the manufacturer may pass along some of those savings as a pricing incentive to the customer. In general, this approach works best when the cost differential is not great enough to encourage the bulk purchaser to turn around and resell the product to the broader market at a reduced price or when the benefits of this sort of arrangement exceed the loss in sales to the manufacturer.

Multiple Unit Pricing

A variation of the bulk purchasing discount is *multiple unit pricing*, which is when a company offers a single product for one price and multiple products for slightly less. For example, candy might be offered at 30 cents each or four for a dollar, or a customer might be given a free car wash if he or she purchases ten washes in advance.

This approach is common with low-priced consumer product offerings that have many substitutes and is designed to encourage purchasers to buy more than they might need immediately. This ensures that the subsequent purchases go to the same company and may produce more revenue if the purchases spoil or are lost before they are used.

It is also common in many business-to-business industrial settings. For example, a commercial printer may charge $0.5945 per tri-fold brochure if the customer orders 200 but drops the price to $0.3445 if the customer purchases 2,000 at one time.

Push Money/Prize Money Allowances

Incentive pricing can also be used to provide incentive to channels. *Push money* or *prize money allowances* give purchasers cash they can use to provide incentives to sales people. A sales person representing multiple tool lines, for example, may be offered a free trip to a sunny destination for reaching a particular sales goal relative to one particular tool manufacturer. These prizes are often funded by allowances from the manufacturers whose tools are being promoted. Although the end consumer does not receive a price break, the manufacturer is providing an incentive to the sales representative in exchange for his or her help 'pushing' the manufacturer's products.

OTHER PRICING APPROACHES

Although incentive pricing approaches are designed to give either the customer or the sales person a reason to make an additional purchase, often in the form of a temporary or conditional price reduction, these are not the only approaches used to maximise revenues to a company. This section covers some of the common approaches that many companies routinely use to help improves sales. Many of these long-term pricing approaches are also designed to change the perceived cost of a product or service. The approaches discussed in this section are as follows:

- Price discrimination
- Dynamic pricing
- Terms
- Guarantees and warrantees
- Return policies
- Advertising and promotional allowances
- Psychological pricing

Price Discrimination

Companies using *price discrimination* offer different prices on the same product to different customers or at different times. For example, florists may offer roses for sale at a higher price during the weeks preceding Valentine's Day. A manufacturer might offer a lower price to companies that purchase products in bulk. Other companies might offer lower prices in areas with lower demand and higher prices in areas with higher demand. For example, the price of a fan during the summer in Arizona might be higher than the price of the same fan in Washington State.

Price discrimination works best in certain types of environments. In cases in which the pricing approach is a seasonal response to demand, as in the case of roses at Valentine's Day, airline tickets during the holiday season or gasoline during summer months, price discrimination must be a common practice within the industry. These sorts of pricing structures are generally demand-driven, designed to ensure the seller does not run out of product during a peak season. Otherwise, customers will simply make their purchases elsewhere. Of course, colluding with competitors to raise prices is illegal in most parts of the world.

In general, when different pricing structures are used for specific market segments, the company must be able to differentiate between purchasers in order to ensure pricing consistency. For this reason, publishers offering student discounts often allow those discounts only in university bookstores and only when a student shows a valid student identification card.

Of course, any organisation offering discounts in these types of circumstances runs the risk of having a member of a particular segment making purchases for members of the non-discounted segments. This is common, for example, with employee discounts in which the employee purchases items for friends and relatives. To manage this, many companies limit the number of items a person can purchase or the total value of discounted purchases an individual can make during a particular time period.

Dynamic Pricing

Flea markets and online auction sites like eBay are ideally suited for *dynamic pricing*. This approach allows the seller to price an item based on the individual consumer's behaviour. For example, a flea market might negotiate a price depending on how eager the purchaser seems to be when purchasing the offered item. As a result, the person who appears less anxious to make a purchase might receive a lower price from the vendor than one who is clearly enthralled with his or her find.

The use of cookies and other tracking tools on the Internet has allowed many companies, from airlines to retailers, to track the number of visits a particular customer makes to a site as an indication of how eager he or she may be to make a purchase. A purchaser who returns multiple times to check on the availability of a particular category of hotel room or airline ticket price might find that the lower-priced categories gradually become less available, even if the vendor still has available inventory. This steadily increasing pricing structure is designed to encourage customers to make a decision by suggesting that the lower priced products might soon be unavailable and to shift purchases from the least expensive alternative to something somewhat more lucrative.

Terms

The terms under which a purchase is made have a strong impact on the perceived price. For example, a company might offer to delay the payment date for a purchase. This is particularly common with large consumer purchases. A company might offer a customer the opportunity to take home a refrigerator with no down payment or no payments for a defined period of time, to purchase a car over time rather than coming up with the cash up front or to purchase a hot tub over time at below-market or zero interest rates. These all drive down the overall price of the product, or at least the perception of how manageable the price is, without negatively affecting its list price.

In business-to-business sales, companies commonly negotiate terms as a part of the price. Payment due dates, discounts for prompt payment and penalties for late payments are all a part of the negotiated terms and the resulting price.

Financial terms are not the only terms that can affect price. Shipping and handling costs can also affect price structures. Internet retailers were initially viewed as more costly because of the shipping and handling fees paid by the consumer. However, with free shipping on purchases and returns, both the total cost of the purchase and the risk are decreased. If a consumer considers the time saved by shopping online instead of travelling to a mall, the price may actually be much lower, even if the list price is the same or slightly higher.

Companies can change the terms under which its products or services are offered as a matter of policy, always offering free shipping, for example. However, changes in terms can also be used as an incentive approach to pricing. For example, a company might offer a delayed payment plan to consumers if they make a purchase within a specified time frame. Or, it may offer free shipping for purchases over a certain amount. This is a common approach with major purchases ranging from furniture to appliances.

Finally, companies can change the terms on a customer-by-customer basis. This allows a company the flexibility to change its pricing subtly to attract sales it might not otherwise have had. For example, a company in a highly regulated industry in which pricing cannot be changed to appeal to a customer might offer delayed payment terms or free shipping as an added incentive to gain a large order. In other cases, the customer demands the concession in terms. For example, many small businesses work with larger businesses whose payment terms are slower than average. If the small business depends heavily on that customer for revenues, it may choose to accept the terms, an effective price reduction, in order to retain the customer.

Guarantees, Warrantees and Return Policies

Guarantees, warrantees and *return policies* can change the effective price of a service or product by reducing or increasing the risk associated with the purchase. A product guarantee or warrantee assures the purchaser that the product will either meet his or her needs, or he or she can recoup some of the cost associated with purchasing it. Return policies have a similar effect, changing customer perception of price. When a product cannot be returned under any circumstances, as is common with clearance items, the cost is perceived to be higher. When returns are easy and the cost is minimal or non-existent, the price is perceived to be lower. For example, if a product can be ordered online but returned either online or at a local brick-and-mortar store, the hassle of a return, and, therefore, the price, will be perceived to be lower than if online returns are limited to online channels.

Even if the absolute dollar cost of the item does not change, the existence of a guarantee, warrantee or easy return policy can have a dramatic effect on sales. This is particularly true when the product or service is purchased unseen or with no prior purchasing experience, as is often the case with online sales. In a 2012 study conducted by Washington and Lee University professor Amanda Bower, customers who were able to return an item using a free shipping return policy increased spending with that retailer by 158% to 457%. By contrast, customers who paid to return an item decreased subsequent spending by 74% to 100%. The perceived cost, particularly given their previous experience, had changed. When there was no cost associated with a return, the price of subsequent purchases was more attractive. However, when a restocking or return shipping fee is associated with purchases, the price of subsequent purchases was perceived to be higher.[5]

Advertising and Promotional Allowances

Manufacturers who sell products to intermediaries, such as retailers, often provide price concessions in the form of advertising or promotional allowances. *Advertising allowances* are pre-negotiated dollar amounts that the manufacturer will deduct from the total purchase price if the retailer agrees to spend those dollars on advertising that promotes the manufacturer's products. *Promotional allowances* are similar; however, the form of promotion may be broader than advertising alone, ranging from *end-cap displays* to coupons or rebates, to direct mail campaigns. In all cases, the exact dollar amount is negotiated in advance, and the recipient of the allowance is contractually bound to execute as agreed.

Psychological Pricing

Have you ever noticed that U.S. gasoline prices end in 9/10 of a cent, even though the smallest currency in use is a full penny? This is a classic example of *psychological pricing*, in which the seller makes a strategic decision to price just under or over a certain price point in order to appeal to customers who want to stay within a certain budget range.

It works, doesn't it? If someone's value threshold is $10, then $9.99 may feel like a bargain, even though the difference is just .1%. In the real estate industry, homes are often priced either above or below a certain threshold in the hopes of attracting buyers within a particular budget. For example, a home targeting a new homeowner might be priced at $399,995 in order to appeal to people who believe they can't go into the $400,000 range. A luxury home might be priced at $1,225,000, with the hope of wooing the customer whose budget range extended $1,225,000 into slightly higher territory.

Psychological pricing can more easily attract shoppers who have a particular value threshold in mind. Because people focus on the first digits, rather than the last ones, a small concession in price, from a round figure to one ending in 9, can cause some purchasers to believe the price is actually much lower.

Some researchers have found that consumers also associate a price ending in 9 with a sale or discounted price. Even when the price is higher than it was previously, the presence of a 9 in the price tag can prompt an increase in sales.[6] This is reinforced by the increasingly common practice of using a price ending in .99 or a similarly uneven number as an inventory tracking tool relative to sales or clearance items.

THE CONNECTION BETWEEN PRICE, PRODUCT OR SERVICE, DISTRIBUTION SYSTEMS AND OPERATIONS

The money paid, and the terms under which it is paid, are only part of the overall price of a product or service. The customer experience, which includes facilities, their experience with the sales person (whether they are employed by the product manufacturer or service provider), policies and processes involved in returns, technologies used to access accounts and other information and other aspects of the buying experience all have a significant impact on the customer's perception of the overall cost of a product or service.

For example, consider the purchase of a cup of coffee. If you want a cup of coffee, and it simply needs to be acceptable, not necessarily gourmet, you might visit your local convenience store to help yourself to a self-serve cup of coffee and expect to pay a price that reflects the lack of service and inexpensive nature of the product.

If you are interested in a premium product, you might visit a gourmet coffee stand. The coffee would probably be served to you, and you would expect to pay more for the combination of service and quality. If you wanted to be seated in a warm environment with a space to have a conversation, read a book or set up your laptop, you would expect to pay a little more for the location and, hopefully, the quality of the coffee than you would at a convenience store. In this instance, not only are you paying for the premium coffee itself, but you are also paying for the premium experience that is expected to accompany it.

A company's pricing approach delivers a clear message about the product or service being delivered. That message needs to be consistent with what customers experience when interacting with your company. A premium price may connote a service or product that is superior to others in its category, and customers will have an expectation that the purchasing experience, service environment and other features will also be better than average. Similarly, a low price may communicate that the product or service itself might be inferior to the average or might come with some hidden inconveniences, like a short useful life, expensive add-ons or repairs or poor service. Each of these is a distinct position within the market and will appeal to a certain segment of the market.

THE IMPACT OF BRAND ON PRICE

Often, a strong value proposition and brand reputation will dictate what pricing approaches will be successful. A brand reputation that is strongly associated with inexpensive products will not sustain a premium price point, regardless of the quality of the product. Remember the Gallo expansion into premium wines described in chapter 3, 'Brand Management Fundamentals'? Consumers did not believe that Gallo could produce a product that would be worth the higher price tag.

Similarly, a premium brand trying to sell a less expensive product under the same name will also suffer from the pricing inconsistency. Consider how you would react if you saw a watch sold by a street vendor at a modest price and bearing the logo of Cartier, the high-end French watch maker and jeweller. You would undoubtedly question whether the product is genuine.

However, a strong brand can allow a company to edge into competing products and persuade the customer that it has created a more valuable solution, with a corresponding premium price. Consider Starbucks' entry into the instant coffee market. It positioned its product, Via, as superior in quality to other instant coffee providers, like Folgers, and set its price point almost twice as high as this competitor's similarly packaged product. Similarly, Starbucks offers ground coffee at a significant premium to pre-existing competitors. Is the coffee really that much better? Customers are certainly not enjoying the environment or service for which they were paying in Starbucks' coffee shops. After all, they will need to take the coffee home and make it themselves. When they purchase coffee in instant, ground or whole bean form at the store, the consumer is paying for the strength of a premium brand.

MARKET REALITIES

In addition to considerations about whether a particular long-term or short-term pricing approach delivers a viable return on the company's investment in a product or service and whether the price is consistent with the company's brand promise, management team members should also consider how competitors will react. Many companies fail to understand market realities, and a temporary price cut originally designed to steal market share ends up igniting a price war that permanently undercuts the revenue and profits both the instigating company and its competitors generate. Price wars may benefit the customer as prices across an industry fall, but they rarely benefit the companies who begin them, and they often have no clear winner.

When a company lowers its prices, its most direct competitors have two choices: lower prices or ignore the price cut and hope that its customers are loyal. When a company enjoys strong name recognition, has a strong reputation so that customers know what they will receive or has the ability to differentiate its products or services from its competitors, it may choose the latter option. Similarly, if the company that lowers its prices is a relatively small player in a crowded and competitive market, a larger, more established company may decide the potential shift in market share will not significantly affect them. In these cases, the company that cuts its prices may benefit from growth as some customers switch from more expensive alternatives to the less expensive solution.

This approach is most likely to be effective at increasing market share when the price-slashing company is small relative to its competition. For example, an attorney starting up a new law firm might accept work at lower rates in order to generate the revenues required to cover initial expenses, gradually raising rates as his or her workload increases. Of course, the attorney must also consider whether the volume of work might prohibit him or her from accepting more lucrative clients with large projects and whether he or she might become associated with low cost and potentially inferior quality work product.

A company's management team should also consider how subsequent price increases might affect the market. If the company plans to increase its prices in the future, but is successful in developing strong customer loyalty prior to that change, those same customers may leave as soon as another player uses the same price-cutting approach. To prevent these issues, the management team must rely on careful analysis to understand how many customers will make the switch, and whether the growth in volume will make up for the decrease in per-unit profitability.

However, if competitors in the market opt to lower prices in order to prevent market share loss, a price war may ensue as each competitor attempts to reduce the price below its nearest adversaries. The results of this situation can be devastating not only to an individual company but also to the industry as a whole.

One of the most famous examples of the impact of this form of competition is the U.S. airline price war of 1992. Fierce competition for a shrinking pool of revenue prompted the major U.S. airlines to try to undercut their competitors' prices in an attempt to gain greater market share. Although the number of passengers travelling by air increased significantly in response to the price drops, airlines suffered enormous losses and permanently diminished fare structures. Every competitor ended up worse off than it would have had none of the participants tried to undercut the others.

Non-marketing management team members reviewing or proposing pricing approaches should carefully consider how competitors are likely to respond and whether a price decrease could trigger a price war. If a price war is likely, management team members should anticipate the outcome such activity might have on their own profitability, as well as that of the industry overall. If the company has a unique advantage relative to cost structure, a price war might benefit them. However, in most cases, a company facing a price war would be better served avoiding it and using alternative approaches to generate additional market share.[7]

LEGAL ISSUES

Although the idea of talking with competitors about pricing approaches may be appealing, especially in the interest of avoiding a price war, doing so may be illegal. Comparing notes on pricing approaches is often considered collusion, which is prohibited under anti-trust laws in the United States, Canada, the European Union and many other countries. Even the most innocent of conversations about pricing approaches may result in serious legal concerns.

Agreements, even verbal 'gentlemen's agreements,' to keep prices within a certain range, trading off opportunities to win bids between competitors in an industry, dividing up sales territories between companies and even discussing pricing approaches at a trade association meeting are considered restraint of trade and are illegal in most places. Although anti-trust violations are most common in industries with a limited number of large players, including monopolies and oligopolies, small businesses and industries with fierce competition are not immune.

QUESTIONS FOR NON-MARKETING MANAGERS TO ASK ABOUT PRICE

In many companies, especially middle market and smaller companies, the management team sets or heavily influences pricing decisions. Even in very large companies, pricing approaches may be reviewed by the executive team. In some companies, the pricing approach is set largely by non-marketing managers based on competitive intelligence or cost data. For this reason, it is particularly important for non-marketing managers to be versed in pricing strategy and the implications of different pricing approaches on the company, as well as its likely revenue stream.

When a non-marketing manager is asked to provide input on pricing approach decisions, it may be helpful to ask some or all of the following questions:

- How does our organisation establish pricing? How do we know we are not leaving profitability behind by using this approach?

- How would a change in price affect demand? How do we know this is the case?

- How would our competitors react if we were to change our prices?

- If an incentive pricing approach is under consideration: How will this approach influence customer perceptions of the value we deliver? What response do we expect in return? What will the financial outcome be? How can we ensure long-term customer retention?

- Are there incentive pricing approaches that we do not currently use that we should be considering? Are there other ways we can affect price, such as changes in products or the surrounding experience?

- What incentives do we provide for our sales force and/or channels to excel at selling our products or services?

- How do our operations support or detract from the value we deliver? What operational improvements can we make that will improve customer value?

- Is the customer experience, including price, facilities, policies and supporting operations, consistent with our price point(s)?

- Is our pricing consistent with our desired brand reputation?

- Are all our managers aware of laws governing discussions about pricing approaches and other behaviours that could be considered collusion?

CHAPTER 9 SUMMARY

Of the four 'P's of marketing, a change in price has the most immediate impact on the bottom line. Price includes the amount charged to the customer, less incentive pricing and other adjustments to price, plus other costs incurred by the customer, including shipping and handling, return policies and other terms, the value of time (proximity and speed of access) and other aspects of the customer experience.

The optimal price is a function of demand, defined by consumer and business income constraints, the customer's perception of the value the company delivers, the cost and availability of substitutes and a company's cost structures and desired brand positioning. Typically bell-curved in shape, the optimal price is sometimes difficult to pinpoint and shifts over the life cycle of a product or service. Changes in price must be evaluated carefully against expected changes in demand. Although a change in price might deliver an immediate increase in revenue per unit, if the demand drops proportionately, there may be no change, or even a negative change, in profitability.

There are three common methods of evaluating a company's pricing approach. Each is appropriate in some cases, and managers should weigh the pros and cons of each approach when selecting among them:

- **Cost-based pricing.** The advantage of this cost-plus-mark-up approach is its simplicity. The drawback is that it ignores the market and competitor behaviour and can result in sub-optimal pricing approaches.

- **Competition-based pricing.** Pricing products and services to match the prices of competitors is common, especially in fiercely competitive, mature markets. Like cost-based pricing, it is simple and ensures competitively viable outcomes. The disadvantage is that it does little to distinguish a company from competitors and may not reflect the company's desired brand reputation.

- **Value-based pricing.** The value-based pricing approach is most likely to maximise profitability if it is done correctly. However, it is also the most complex approach, requiring some significant investment of time and/or funds in research.

The product life cycle affects prices. During the introduction phase of a product or service's life cycle, when new adopters will pay higher prices for a better solution, prices are usually higher. Conversely, they are lower during maturity, when the market competes aggressively for established market share. When a company uses higher prices upon introduction of a new product or service, the practice is called *skimming*. Conversely, when a company introduces a product at low prices, typically to a mature market, in order to gain market share, it is called *penetration pricing*.

Companies use a variety of approaches, such as coupons, rebates, sales and multiple-unit pricing to create temporary and on-going incentives for customers to purchase their products or that encourage customers to change the timing of their purchases. There are also other pricing approaches designed to improve sales outcomes by changing customer perceptions of value, including psychological pricing, guarantees and favourable terms.

Non-marketing managers should be particularly aware of how their operations affect the value they deliver, the price they can charge and how brand and pricing strategies reinforce one another. They should also be cognisant of how their competitors are likely to react to any given change in price. In particular, managers should be particularly cautious to avoid price wars, which rarely benefit the company that starts them and often have no clear winner.

Finally, managers should be aware of federal laws governing pricing in each country in which they do business. In many countries, even a casual conversation among competitors about pricing structures could result in allegations of collusion. Managers should be cautious to keep pricing approaches confidential and within their own company.

Endnotes

1 Hinterhuber, Andreas and Liozu, Stephan. 'Is It Time to Rethink Your Pricing Strategy?,' *MIT Sloan Management Review*, Summer 2012, p. 69–77. Reprint #53413.

2 *Ibid.*

3 Aeppel, Timothy. 'Seeking Perfect Prices, CEO Tears Up the Rules,' *Wall Street Journal*, March 27, 2007. http://online.wsj.com/article/SB117496231213149938.html

4 For example, check out Fanny's posting on the Living Richly on a Budget blog entitled 'Grocery Sale Cycles—When do things go on sale?', February 22, 2011. www.livingrichlyonabudget.com/grocery-sale-cycles-when-do-things-go-on-sale

5 Amanda B. Bower, James G. Maxham, III (2012). 'Return Shipping Policies of Online Retailers: Normative Assumptions and the Long-Term Consequences of Fee and Free Returns,' *Journal of Marketing*: Vol. 76, No. 5, pp. 110–124.

Hausman, Sandy. 'Is Charging Customers for Returns Bad Business?' NPR, November 26, 2012. www.npr.org/2012/11/26/165896139/is-charging-customers-for-mail-order-returns-bad-business

6 For an interesting look at this topic, along with psychological aspects of pricing, review the following article and its source documents: Lindstrom, Martin. 'The Psychology behind the Sweet Spots of Pricing,' *Fast Company*, March 26, 2012. www.fastcompany.com/1826172/psychology-behind-sweet-spots-pricing

7 For an excellent overview of some approaches a company might consider in order to avoid a price war, consider this article from the *Harvard Business Review*.
Rao, Akshay; Bergen, Mark & Davis, Scott. 'How to Fight a Price War,' *Harvard Business Review*, March, 2000. http://hbr.org/2000/03/how-to-fight-a-price-war/ar/1

10

PROMOTIONS: THE FOURTH 'P' OF TACTICAL MARKETING

Figure 10-1: Marketing Alignment Map

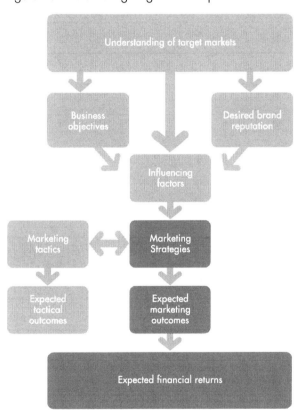

When managers say they are unsure about the returns they are receiving on marketing investments, they are often thinking specifically about their investments in promotions. *Promotions* include the wide range of activities associated with the more commonplace definition of marketing, such as websites, advertising, public relations and a host of other tactical efforts that I will discuss in more detail throughout this chapter.

There are four reasons non-marketing managers remain doubtful, and they are all related to how promotions are typically managed.

The first is that many managers are confused about the two functional roles of promotions. As a result, their expectations aren't consistent with the outcomes that promotions produce. By gaining a better understanding of how promotions work, non-marketing managers will be better able to anticipate potential results.

The second is that promotions are often managed by a team within the company, and sometimes, outside the company, and managers often have limited insight into how decisions about promotions are made. It is not unusual for promotions to be delegated away from senior management. When marketing activities are selected without strategic input, this can result in a significant misalignment between promotional investments and the discipline of marketing. In the worst cases, the company can fall into ineffective 'follow the leader' behaviours.

The third is that many managers don't understand the importance of the message and how it is delivered. Promotions are the most visible aspect of the company's marketing efforts, often reaching the customer before the product or service does. Without careful attention to the message and how it is delivered, even the most effective potential promotional tactic can be rendered ineffective. Non-marketing managers should have a strong understanding of the visual and verbal impact their promotions are having and ensure that they are consistent with the image and brand reputation discussed in chapter 3, 'Brand Management Fundamentals.'

Finally, many managers are relatively unfamiliar with the most common forms of marketing promotions. Although they might be more effective at spotting a poor fit with market needs in a discussion of pricing, product or distribution channels, many non-marketing managers are unsure how to evaluate a marketing tactic effectively. As a result, they approve a plan they do not thoroughly understand and remain unconfident of the potential outcomes. In the worst cases, a non-marketing manager adds to his or her marketing losses by actively advocating adoption of a particular promotional tactic that is a poor fit for the market and related strategies. To address this issue, the non-marketing manager must have a solid understanding of when a particular promotional tactic is likely to be effective and when it is not.

This chapter covers each of these promotional management issues in turn.

UNDERSTANDING THE TWO FUNCTIONAL PURPOSES OF PROMOTIONS

Promotions work most effectively in the context of a well-constructed, broad-based marketing strategy, with a strong product or service, appropriately priced and available in the places in which the customer would look to find it. Assuming those elements are in place, promotions serve two important functional, or operational, purposes.

The first purpose of promotions is to reduce the cost of the sales process. To do so, promotions are used to raise visibility, inform the market about the product or service's benefits and persuade the market that the product or service is a better match to its needs. This reduces the time required to make the sale, improves the odds the sale will close successfully or increases the volume through increased demand.

To better understand why promotions provide leverage and reduce the cost of sales, consider the evolution of promotions. A few hundred years ago, if you wanted to purchase a bar of soap, rather than make it yourself, you purchased it from someone who you knew had a good reputation for quality products, perhaps even a personal friend. Regardless, you could talk to that person individually about the products he or she manufactured.

When soap began to be manufactured by companies, rather than individuals, and sold by multiple sales people, the connection with the value of that particular soap became more tenuous. After all, if you didn't know the person selling it—or even making it—how would you know that it was the same quality or even the same product? The sales person trying to make the sale would spend time trying to reassure the purchaser that his or her product was genuine, costing the manufacturer money in the form of sales personnel, time and lost sales.

In response, manufacturers began to package their products using consistent labelling and brand *logotypes*, so that customers would feel reassured. By making the products look the same, the customer was more likely to feel confident that the product was the same, even if the sales person wasn't the same one who sold it to him or her previously. This helped the sales person make the sale more quickly. Packaging, one of the first forms of promotions, effectively reduced the cost of the manufacturer's investment in their sales, or distribution, approach.

When it became more common for soap to be distributed through retailers, the soap company was even farther away from the customer, with less opportunity to reassure or persuade. To help improve sales to the retailer, the manufacturer needed to further stimulate demand for its product. Advertising, sponsorships and other promotional activities emerged to address the need. The promotions provided leverage, doing some of the selling for the sales person—and even creating demand before the sales person arrived.

The second purpose of promotions is to help shape and manage a company's reputation in order to achieve other business objectives. For example, a company might use promotions to reinforce or develop an organisation's reputation as a great place to work. Several years ago, I worked with the CEO of a regional hospital system to address its greatest barrier to increased revenue: a shortage of qualified nurses. It had applicants, of course. It just didn't have enough of the right applicants: nurses who cared about patients, shared hospital's values and would thrive within its culture.

In order to bring in more nurses and address the labour shortage, the market needed to understand the value a job at that particular hospital could deliver. Because the hospital did not have a list of the candidates it wanted to attract and to whom its staff could speak on a one-on-one basis, it needed a broad-based, one-to-many promotional campaign that would shape perceptions of the hospital as one of the region's premium employers.

Although this might seem to be more of a human resources initiative than a marketing initiative, the CEO of this hospital system, a leader among the region's health care providers, saw this as a marketing concern. From his perspective, the nursing shortage affected the hospital's 'product:' the services it delivered to patients. Without qualified nurses, the hospital's product was compromised, and its revenue was diminished.

Another way companies leverage promotional concepts is by proactively developing reputations as strong corporate citizens in order to facilitate permitting processes and other expansion plans or reinforce relationships with key clients who share strong corporate citizenship as a value. Companies may also use promotions to create a positive image in the community that adds value to their product and enables them to charge a premium price. If a company's market values corporate contributions to community health and welfare, the consumer will often pay a slightly higher price in order to support that organisation. Alternatively, or even additionally, such shared values can increase customer loyalty.

For example, many consumers pay a few cents more per bottle of water to purchase Athena, a product line now owned by DS Waters of America. Athena Waters was created in 2003 to sell bottled water and raise money for breast cancer awareness and research. Formed as a for-profit corporation, the company charged a premium on its product, promising to send the corporate proceeds to not-for-profits whose work focused on breast cancer prevention and research. In 2010, the company was acquired by DS Waters, a manufacturer of a number of bottled waters. DS Waters then further reinforced its community-based image through its other product lines. The company provides bottled water to communities during emergencies, such as floods, hurricanes and other natural disasters, generating appreciation and selection preference. Despite the change in ownership, consumers who are concerned about breast cancer remain loyal to the Athena label because they believe it shares their same core values.

Promotions can also be used to mitigate or repair potential damage to a brand reputation. In 2011, a social media specialist employed by the American Red Cross confused her own account with that of her employer and posted a tweet announcing plans to drink brewer Dogfish Head's beer for the purpose of 'gettngslizzerd' (becoming intoxicated).

The tweet was on the Red Cross site for about an hour before it was deleted. However, rather than ignoring the tweet and hoping it would not be noticed, the Red Cross proactively tweeted 'We've deleted the rogue tweet but rest assured the Red Cross is sober, and we've confiscated the keys.'

Dogfish Head Brewery, which was among the many followers who saw the tweet, successfully encouraged followers of its Twitter account to make donations of blood to the Red Cross and then to 'refill' with Dogfish

Head beer. Both responses were a success. The Red Cross avoided any potential ill will or offense that might have been associated with the initial tweet, Dogfish Head experienced a surge in sales of its beers and individuals in the 30 states in which its beers are sold stepped up to make blood donations. The proactive promotional response allowed them to turn the mistake into money for both the non-profit and the brewery. It also resulted in significant media coverage, providing added visibility to both organisations.[1]

Although promotions can be very effective at providing leverage to a sales or other distribution channel, they cannot compensate for a weak product, inappropriate pricing or poor sales efforts. Yet, that is often the role they are asked to play. When sales sag, companies turn to promotions when other aspects of the marketing mix are more likely to be the culprits. Companies whose management teams expect promotional efforts to compensate for problems in other areas of the marketing mix end up frustrated and disappointed in the outcomes.

Similarly, many companies believe that promotional efforts alone can build a brand's reputation. Although promotions certainly can reinforce or help manage the brand reputation, the brand itself cannot be created by promotions. It must be lived within the company, a reflection of the management team's understanding of the discipline of marketing. Otherwise, like a wolf in sheep's clothing, it will soon be discovered to be something other than what it pretended to be.

DELEGATE, BUT DON'T ABDICATE

The second reason that non-marketing managers are sceptical about the value that promotions deliver is that this aspect of marketing is often delegated away from executive or senior management oversight. The marketing department, or even an external marketing team, is asked to prepare the plan, and the managers are asked to approve it after a relatively cursory review of major budget line items. In some cases, management team members who manage other aspects of the marketing mix, such as sales, product decision, pricing approaches or distribution channel selection, have a limited understanding of how promotions connect with the other elements of the marketing mix.

Because they are unfamiliar with promotions themselves, executives often delegate planning to a marketing team that is not included in the company's strategic or business planning processes. As a result, the marketing team has only limited knowledge of the executives' objectives, or in worst case scenarios, is left to guess what the desired outcomes might be. Similarly, the marketing team may have only a limited understanding of the company's target audience, particularly if they are non-employees or if the company does a poor job of cultivating a market-focused culture.

In these cases, the marketing team is often left to emulate the activities of the market leaders or to create programmes based on assumptions they make about desired outcomes. Neither of these is optimal. Assumptions, as discussed in chapter 5, 'Understanding What Influences Market Behaviour,' can cause a company to invest in areas that will not deliver satisfactory returns. Unfortunately, one of the most common assumptions related to promotions, particularly within companies that do not effectively align promotions along with other aspects of the marketing mix, is that if a promotional approach is being used by a successful competitor, it must be effective.

WHY FOLLOWING THE LEADER IS RISKY

Copycat behaviour is risky for three reasons. First, it assumes the market leader has made a good choice in its promotional efforts. This isn't necessarily the case. Because market leaders enjoy a financial advantage, they may invest in some marketing efforts for speculative reasons. Also, because most promotional initiatives take months, and even years, to deliver results, a promotions blunder may take several years to become apparent. Companies following the market leader's behaviours may be following them off the edge of a cliff.

Even worse, some companies follow average performers, rather than market leaders. They look for companies of similar size and with similar revenues and structure and emulate their behaviour. Pacing your own behaviour with that of other average performers is a sure way to remain in the same position in the competitive race.

Second, the market leader and the copycat company may or may not have the same market. It would, for example, be rather foolish for the French watchmaker and jeweller Cartier to approach promotions in the same way that the discount retailer Wal-Mart has. Of course, that's an obvious example. They clearly target different audiences with different value propositions. However, sometimes, the differences are more subtle. Sometimes, both organisations deliver the same product to similar populations, such as milk, haircuts or patent law, but the audiences to whom they appeal are significantly, or even subtly, different.

In 2011, Starbucks surpassed Burger King and Wendy's to become the United States' third largest restaurant chain. However, it didn't do it by outspending, or even spending equally, on consumer-focused advertising. In fact, it was outspent two to eight times more, relative to its closest rivals. Had it paralleled its competitors' spending, it might not have experienced the success it has. Why? Because Starbucks understands that its market is less likely to be influenced by advertising. Instead, it focused on other promotional, product and pricing approaches.

Starbucks steadily expanded its menu, focusing on healthy food choices that differentiated its offerings from other restaurant chain competitors and appealed to a different demographic. It sustained high prices by offering an experience, rather than just food. They also used other forms of promotions, including social media, sponsorships and other forms of public relations to build brand loyalty.[2]

Starbucks chose its promotional approach based on what would influence its market, which caused the company to stand out from the competition as a result. Non-marketing managers should carefully consider what market they serve and ask marketers how they know the promotional medium will be effective in reaching them before approving promotions-related budgets.

Finally, companies who copy the market leader stand little chance of differentiating themselves from the competitive fray. Market leaders typically have larger marketing budgets, and their size and market share will often make their voice the one customers recall. In fact, a competitor who too closely mimics a market leader's look and message in the same promotional medium may unintentionally reinforce the market leader's message. Although some of the promotional media may still be the same, particularly when the same market is targeted, marketing promotions should be carefully crafted to stand out from the crowd of alternatives.

> The executive team, including non-marketing executives, should retain oversight of promotions just as it oversees other aspects of the marketing mix, evaluating whether the promotional tactics selected are well aligned with the strategies and influencing factors they are designed to influence and whether the expected financial outcomes are likely to be achieved.

The executive team, including non-marketing executives, should retain oversight of promotions just as it oversees other aspects of the marketing mix, evaluating whether the promotional tactics selected are well aligned with the strategies and influencing factors they are designed to influence and whether the expected financial outcomes are likely to be achieved. Companies whose executive teams are uninvolved in this evaluation process are, in my experience, much more likely to question the efficacy of their marketing promotions' investments.

COMMUNICATE SO THE MARKET HEARS WHAT YOU SAY

To deliver a solid return, promotions must be based on a solid understanding of the market and synchronised with other aspects of the marketing mix. They must also communicate a message that is true, credible, relevant to the customer's decision-making process and important enough to make an impact. This topic was discussed in great length in chapter 3, but it bears repeating because so many companies make this mistake in their promotional efforts.

Many companies, particularly smaller companies, have a tendency to describe their product or service, the attributes or features of what it is they offer, rather than the benefits it delivers. Imagine you are at a cocktail party, and you ask two people you have just met what they do for a living. The first says 'I'm a marketing consultant.' Your eyes glaze over. Your brain tunes this person out. You begin looking for the next person you can meet. This person has described what he or she does, and it may be true and credible, but it doesn't seem relevant to you.

But what if the second person said 'I help companies make more money'? Would that get your attention? Probably more than the job description the first person provided. Even if the line seemed so overused that it made you roll your eyes, you would probably still ask the person how. Now, he or she has an opportunity to explain how he or she does his or her job. You are now engaged. That's because what the second person said was relevant. The person was describing the benefits he or she offers to you not just a description of what he or she sells.

If the message isn't relevant to them, or doesn't make a difference in their purchasing process, individuals who see the message are unlikely to connect the product or service with the differentiating benefits it is designed to deliver. Without that mental link, promotional efforts may reach potential clients or consumers, but the efforts are unlikely to make an impact.

However, carrying the right message alone isn't enough. A company could print several true, credible, important and relevant messages, but if they sit hidden in a book's worth of copy, they may never be noticed. After all, the average U.S. consumer is now exposed to as many as 5,000 advertising messages each day.[3] To break through and be noticed, the messages a company tries to communicate in its promotions should be limited in number, concise and repeated frequently.

Finally, when a promotional tactic appears in visual form, as it does in advertising or direct mail, the words can be missed if the reader does not understand the relevance at first glance. Because of the number of visual messages we see every day, we are adept at filtering them out. An advertisement or other printed piece often has only a second or two to communicate relevance to the viewer. In order to do so, the advertising must be designed visually to capture attention. In many cases, the message communicated by the images within the piece is more powerful than the words that support it.

PICK THE RIGHT TOOL FOR THE PURPOSE

In chapter 6, 'Aligning Marketing Tactics With Influencing Factors,' I talked about how the selection of tactics is influenced by a variety of considerations related to the marketing strategy itself, including

- the size of the target market;
- market demographics, including where the customer turns for solutions to the specific needs a company addresses;
- whether the customers are businesses or consumers;
- the influencing factor(s) the company is trying to affect;
- the potential impact on a company's brand;
- the competitive environment;
- the cost of the tactic relative to the potential benefit it could deliver and budget constraints;
- the time before such benefits are likely to be realised; and
- how the mix of tactics are likely to work together.

Although these considerations factored into the discussions of other 'P's, they are especially important in the selection of promotional tactics. However, like many other aspects of marketing, promotions has become increasingly specialised and technical. As a non-marketing executive, your role may not include the development of promotional campaigns. However, you will probably be asked to approve promotional investments, many of which can be quite costly. The next sections of this chapter are designed to give the non-marketing manager a basic introduction to the most common promotional tactics, including planning considerations, relative costs, common *metrics* and, when possible, potential returns.

A GUIDE TO COMMON PROMOTIONAL TACTICS

Literally hundreds of thousands of tactics can be used to promote an organisation. It would be virtually impossible to review all of them, and, most likely, it would be a waste of the non-marketing manager's time even if I could. Instead, this section covers some of the most common categories of tactics, along with information that might be helpful to the non-marketing manager tasked with reviewing marketing plans.

Advertising

Advertising is a broad category of related tactics. In general, *advertising* is when a company pays to communicate a message in verbal and/or visual formats to an audience through a particular media. Advertising can be communicated through traditional mass media, such as newspapers, radio stations, television stations or billboard advertising or through digital media, including paid announcements on blogs or websites associated with mass media, organisations or individuals, banner advertising and display ads. Advertising can also be found in less traditional locations, such as the backs of toilet stall doors, video screens within department stores or shopping malls or towed from behind an airplane. Although advertising is generally paid, some media donate advertising to not-for-profit organisations. These are often called *public service announcements*, or PSAs.

Sidebar 10-1: Advertising Costs

Advertising rates vary depending on the circulation, number of viewers, site popularity and other factors affecting exposure. This column is intended both to satisfy curiosity about advertising rates and provide some guidance when thinking about costs and returns.

In 2012, a 30-second advertisement during the American Super Bowl football game, with 111 million viewers, would cost a company about $3.5 million dollars.

The average cost of a single, 30-second prime time television advertisement in the United States with less than 10 million viewers is about $110,000.

Internationally, television advertising rates vary dramatically. In the Arab world, advertising rates average about $3,300 for a 30-second prime time spot. In the UK, the average cost in 2011 was reported to be £227,500 ($369,000 US) for a 30-second spot.

Placement inside the front cover of a magazine or on the front page of a newspaper will be more expensive than other places in the publication. Similarly, publication in a regional edition of a publication, like *The Wall Street Journal*, will be less expensive than publication in all of its editions.

Running a full-page advertisement in the Japanese newspaper, *Asahi Shimbun*, one of the three most widely circulated newspapers in the world cost JPY 39,855,00 (about $398,750 US). A full-page, colour advertisement in the business section of *The Times*, in the UK, will cost about £27,000 ($40,850 in US dollars). A similar ad in USA Today, published across the US, costs about $200,000.

An advertisement delivered through a mobile device (cell phone) on Black Friday, which is the popular shopping day after the American holiday of Thanksgiving and one of the heaviest American shopping days of the year, cost $.76 per thousand impressions. One week earlier, the same ad would have been $.68 per thousand impressions.

Advertisements appearing on Android devices are less expensive than those on Apple products, as demographic research indicates Android users are more frugal.

Continued on p.175

Who It Reaches: Almost every person sees and notices some advertising over the course of a day. However, to be successful, the advertisement must actually be seen by the target market, which means that it must be in a location that the target market uses as a source of information on a regular basis.

Factors Affecting Success: The most common reasons advertising fails are because the media isn't a good fit for the market and message, the message isn't well developed or the advertisement is poorly designed. These failures were all addressed earlier in this chapter. However, companies using advertising should also consider the following:

- **Repetition.** A single advertisement is rarely successful on its own. There are two reasons this is true. First, even if the advertisement is in a well-chosen location, purchasers in the target market may or may not notice it. They may not read that publication on that particular day, they may be on their phone when an advertisement airs on television or they might not spot the banner behind the airplane. Repeating the advertisement increases the chances people will see or hear it.

  Second, even if a person sees or hears an advertisement once, he or she may not remember it. Have you ever played the game when you are presented with ten items on a tray covered with a cloth? The cloth is removed, and you have two minutes to memorise what you see before the cover is returned to the tray. Depending on the type of items, how they are associated with you and whether you know what they are, you may remember some, or even most, items. However, remembering all of them is challenging.

  Advertising is very similar. Prospective purchasers see or hear an advertisement for a limited period of time, whether it is broadcast on television or printed somewhere. If it is relevant to their needs or they recognise the organisation, they may recall what it said more easily. However, if it is unfamiliar or doesn't quickly strike them as relevant, they are much less likely to recall the contents. By giving the market multiple exposures, you increase its ability to recall both the company and its message.

There is, of course, an optimum level of repetition. Although recall and recognition improve with an increased level of advertising, at some point, the investment no longer produces substantial benefit. To balance this, many experts recommend running advertising consistently for a period of time, then stopping and then repeating the behaviour. These are called *flights*.

In order to broaden exposure, many companies blend different advertising media in order to expand visibility. For example, they may use banner advertising, print advertising and broadcast advertising together to improve the chances that any particular purchaser will see or hear the message. This type of advertising campaign, which should use consistent visual imaging and messaging across all media, may also include non-advertising promotions, such as media relations or product demonstrations that reinforce the advertising messages.

Continued from p.174

Internet-based display advertising, such as banner ads or ads on consumer-focused web pages, have an average click-through rate of 0.024% and an ultimate conversion to purchase rate of just 0.010%, indicating that 10,000 people would need to see a particular ad before one person would make a purchase.

The most expensive place to advertise on Facebook is in Bangladesh, where the cost-per-click is $1.12 (in US Dollars). The US is 7th in worldwide Facebook rates, at $0.77 (in US Dollars). In Vietnam, the rate is $0.06 per click.

Sources: Associated Press. 'Super Bowl ads cost average of $3.5M,' as reported on the ESPN website (www.espn.com), February 6, 2012. http://espn.go.com/nfl/playoffs/2011/story/_/id/7544243/super-bowl-2012-commercials-cost-average-35m

Crupi, Anthony. 'In their Prime: Broadcast Spot Costs Soar,' *AdWeek*, June 22, 2011. www.adweek.com/news/television/their-prime-broadcast-spot-costs-soar-132805

Sambidge, Andy. 'Peak Arab TV ad costs average $3,299 – report,' ArabianBusiness.com, June 8, 2012. http://www.arabianbusiness.com/peak-arab-tv-ad-costs-average-3-299-report-461400.html

Kokemuller, Neil. 'The Average Cost of Advertising,' eHow UK, www.ehow.co.uk/facts_5625807_average-cost-advertising-magazine_.html

Asahi Shimbun website, Display Advertising Rates: http://adv.asahi.com/english/index_image/ratebook2012.pdf

USA Today website, Advertising Rate Sheet: http://adv.asahi.com/english/index_image/ratebook2012.pdf

Peterson, Tim. 'Mobile Ad Rates Inch Up, Slowly,' *AdWeek*, December 11, 2012. www.adweek.com/news/technology/mobile-ad-rates-inch-slowly-145848

Macale, Sherilynn. 'Bangladesh now has the most expensive Facebook CPC in the world,' TheNextWeb.com, October 26, 2011. http://thenextweb.com/facebook/2011/10/26/bangladesh-now-has-the-most-expensive-facebook-cpc-in-the-world/

- **Simplicity.** The saying 'keep it simple' applies well to advertising. To be effective, the number of messages and images included should be limited. Remember the memorisation game? Even after intense scrutiny for a period of several minutes, the participant wants to remember everything on the tray, but he or she is unlikely to be successful. Imagine how that translates to advertising recall.

When a company tries to communicate many messages, the market may miss most, or all, of them. This is especially true when the company itself is unfamiliar. After all, the company's name is one more item the person must recall. To be successful, advertising should be very simple with a limited number of messages to the target market, and the advertisements should be visually consistent and easy to read.

<u>What It Costs</u>: Advertising is generally costly. There are several components in which a company must invest. First, of course, the company must purchase the advertising space or time.

Advertising rates vary substantially. Television advertising can range from a few hundred dollars to a few million.[4,5] The costs vary according to the number of people who will see the ad, the medium and the length or size of the advertisement the company wishes to place.

In print and broadcast media, the rates are generally flat or vary with the size of the ad commitment. The cost of advertising in print media is measured on *costs-per-thousand* also called *costs-per-mille* (CPM) readers. Readers and circulation may not be the same because publications sometimes estimate the number of publications that will be read by multiple people.

In digital advertising, the price may be billed based on the number of people who actually receive the advertisement on their computer or phone. Digital media, including mobile media, is often quoted in *costs-per-thousand-impressions* (CPI) or CPM. In both print and digital advertising, advertisers pay based on the number of times the ad appears, regardless of whether it is actually noticed by the consumer.

The cost of the advertising is only one portion of the expense. An organisation using advertising should also budget for the professional team it will need to develop the advertising itself. In general, this includes both a creative design and production team with experience developing successful advertising campaigns, experienced advertising copywriters and a media buyer who can negotiate the best rates and placements on advertising purchases. Finally, the organisation should reserve budget for the purchase of images or music and other related costs.

Common Tactical Metrics: Several common tactical metrics are used when evaluating advertising campaigns to assess the effectiveness of advertising relative to other comparable programmes but fail to take into consideration whether the medium is appropriate, the message is on point or the creative design is effective.

Among the most common tactical metrics related to advertising are as follows:

- **Impressions.** This term refers to the number of times the advertisement is published or broadcast (frequency) times the number of viewers or readers who will see it (reach).
- **Gross rating points.** This is the number of impressions divided by the size of the target market for the product or service.
- **CPM or CPI.** This is the cost of the advertising buy (the media space only, not the cost of the creation of the advertisement), divided by the impressions, in thousands.
- **Page views.** The number of times a web page is served to a user.
- **Click-through rate.** The number of times a customer clicks on an advertisement to be taken to the company or channel's website, divided by the number of impressions.
- **Cost-per-click.** The cost of the advertising buy divided by the number of times a customer clicks on the advertisement to be taken to the company or channel's website.
- **Cost-per-order.** The cost of the advertising buy divided by the number of orders received as a result.

Potential Returns: There is considerable interest in measuring the returns companies generate on investments in advertising, particularly given the sizeable investment a company must often make. The most accurate numbers will be based on a company's own understanding of its customers' decision-making process, conversion rates, the size of the audience, the specific behaviours that are expected to change, how those changes will affect decision-making behaviour and past experience. In most cases, organisations will need to invest in market research or the incorporation of response codes or other tools to measure impact.[6]

Best Used When: Advertising is almost always a broad-based approach, designed to reach both existing customers and prospects. However, because of the nature of the tool, many of the messages will miss their targets. They will be seen by individuals who are not interested or won't be seen by the people who are. For this reason, advertising is best used when the targeted market or markets are very large, and the company's product or service could be used by most, or all, the individuals within that market.

Advertising is often used to build awareness, inform or interest prospective customers and differentiate a product or service relative to competitors. It can also be used to support other operational objectives, such as advocating on behalf of a particular policy or legislative issue. Advertising can be very effective in helping a company meet any of these objectives. However, advertising is also frequently used for the amorphous goal of generating brand awareness. If this is the primary barrier to increased sales, or at least the most lucrative obstacle to overcome, advertising might be an excellent choice. However, without focus, advertising burns dollars more quickly than any other promotional category.

Sidebar 10-2: Direct Mail Costs and Returns

According to the Direct Mail Association (DMA), the average cost per lead or order varied according to the type of direct mail piece and whether the appeal was sent to prospects or existing customers. In 2012, the average cost of the direct mail campaign per lead or order was as follows:

TYPE OF CAMPAIGN	TYPE OF LIST	AVERAGE COST	RESPONSE RATE
Letter size mailer	Prospect	$51.40	1.28%
Letter size mailer	Existing Customer	$19.35	3.40%
Postcard mailer	Prospect	$54.10	1.12%
Postcard mailer	Existing Customer	$24.53	4.26%
E-mail	Prospect	$55.25	0.03%
E-mail	Existing Customer	N/A	0.12%
Catalogue	Prospect	$111.91	0.94%
Catalogue	Existing Customer	$24.69	4.26%
Telephone	Prospect	$190.49	8.21%
Telephone	Existing Customer	$77.91	12.95%

Although print and telephone campaigns trigger a wider response, when it comes to returns, the DMA says e-mail and digital campaigns are the winners. According to its research, e-mail campaigns generated $28.50 in sales for every $1 of e-mail spending. Telephone campaigns broke even, generating $1 in sales for every $1 spent. This suggests that although e-mail is more expensive than other approaches in generating an order, the size of the order tends to be bigger.

Sources: Bruell, Alexandra. 'DMA Survey Shows Snail Mail, Phone Beat Digital in Response Rates,' Ad Age, June 13, 2012. http://adage.com/print/235364

Haskel, Debora. '2012 DMA Response Rate Report: Direct Mail Shows Well-Rounded Performance,' IWCO Direct blog. Retrieved December 26, 2012. www.iwco.com/blog/2012/07/11/dma-response-rate-report/

'Direct Mail Gets Most Responses; Email Highest ROI,' Rochester Institute of Technology, Print in the Mix blog, June 14, 2012. http://printinthemix.com/fastfacts/show/575

'Direct Mail Tops Email for Response Rates; Costs per Lead Similar,' Marketing Charts blog, June 15, 2012. www.marketingcharts.com/print/direct-mail-tops-email-for-response-rates-costs-per-lead-similar-22395/

For more information, look at the latest edition of the Direct Marketing Association's Response Rate Trend Report. For example, see www.the-dma.org/cgi/dispannouncements?article=1451.

Direct Marketing

Also considered a form of advertising, *direct marketing* uses consumer data to reach out directly to past and potential customers. In the United States, direct marketing expenditures are roughly equal to expenditures on other forms of advertising.

The most common forms of direct marketing include direct mail (via the postal service), direct e-mail and telemarketing. Because the communication goes to an individual, rather than a mass market, it can be more tailored, leveraging information about past purchases, demographics or affinities with similar products or vendors to refine messages and narrow the focus.

Who It Reaches: Direct marketing is used for both business and consumer audiences. In general, it is more effective with purchasers who are already familiar with a company's product or service, but it can be used to inform as well.

Factors Affecting Success: Successful direct marketing is affected by the following:

- **Data quality and use.** Direct mail can be used to reach both existing customers and prospective customers. When targeting non-customers from a purchased list, it is critical to ensure the list is high quality and matches the demographic profile of the target market. If the list is not high quality, mailed pieces may be returned or simply discarded by the postal service, which can significantly decrease the return on investment. Poor quality data in an e-mail list can result in large numbers of bounced e-mails and can sometimes result in a company's domain becoming 'black listed' by major e-mail hosts.

    A poor demographic match can be even more challenging. For example, imagine a list purchased by a baby products retailer. If that list contains large percentages of childless individuals, the mailing sent to those individuals won't be returned, but it probably will not be used. Instead, it is simply discarded as irrelevant. Unfortunately, unlike returned mail or bounced e-mail, when the retailer experiences poor conversion rates, their marketing team will have no way of knowing whether the appeal itself was unsuccessful or the list was inaccurate. All they will know is that the approach did not work.

    Companies using in-house lists of customers, prospects who have shown an interest in their store or website or past customers must also invest in managing their data. Because people change physical and e-mail addresses routinely, an internal list is only valuable to the extent it is routinely maintained. Any company that intends to use direct marketing to reach customers should be prepared to invest in data management to support those efforts.

    Also, any organisation approaching a customer or past customer should be prepared to leverage the data it has about purchasing behaviours to tailor the appeal. Customers expect direct marketing to reflect their history with the organisation. Failure to meet that expectation could damage the organisation's relationship with its customers. For example, a well-crafted appeal letter from a not-for-profit organisation for an end-of-year contribution can be well received by donors. However, if the not-for-profit sends such a letter to a major donor without acknowledging a previous gift, the organisation risks damaging the relationship with the donor and potentially putting future gifts in jeopardy.

    Finally, companies that use direct mail to either customers or prospects should be cautious to follow their own country's laws regarding unsolicited e-mail and e-mailed advertisements. Many laws, including those in the United States, apply to both e-mails to existing customers and to prospects. Links to spam laws for the United States, the UK, the European Union and Japan can be found in appendix A.

- **Design and message.** Like advertising, most direct marketing pieces have only a few seconds to capture the customer's attention. But unlike advertising, direct marketing often offers the opportunity to provide additional information. Perhaps the most common mistake in direct mail is that companies launch directly into the detail before capturing the reader's attention. Direct mail and e-mail communications with cluttered, text-heavy designs often fail to engage the reader and end up discarded. Professional expertise will significantly improve the returns generated on direct marketing investments.

- **Frequency.** Finally, successful direct marketing programmes carefully study and optimise the number of e-mails or other solicitations they send to a customer or prospective customer, along with the timing. Too many communications can cause customers to ignore communications or block them in spam filters, whereas infrequent programmes may leave sales on the table.

Timing is also important. Retailers often send out direct marketing, especially catalogues, more frequently during the holiday season when people are purchasing gifts, and, to the extent their product lines change with the season, as people are considering their needs for each upcoming season. For office supply companies whose customers have a routine purchasing pattern, a reminder e-mail or a new catalogue timed to arrive just prior to their next order may remind them of their previous purchase and the vendor from whom they purchased their supplies.

<u>What It Costs</u>: Depending on the selected campaign method, the primary direct marketing costs may include programme design (concepting, copywriting and graphic design), mail house or postage costs, telemarketing vendor fees, the cost of purchased lists and the cost of database maintenance. In general, the costs are generally higher for business-to-business than they are for business-to-consumer campaigns. None of these costs include the labour or equipment costs related to data management in-house.

<u>Common Tactical Metrics</u>: Several common metrics that marketers use to measure success in direct mail campaigns are as follows:

- **Response rate.** The response rate measures the number of people who made a purchase (or contribution, in the case of non-profits) as a percentage of the total number of individuals to whom the campaign was directed.

- **Open rate.** This measures the number of recipients of a direct e-mail piece that opened the e-mail as a percentage of the number of targets to whom the e-mail was sent.

- **Click-through rate.** The number of times a customer clicks on an advertisement to be taken to the company or channel's website, divided by the number of impressions.

- **Bounce-back rate.** The number of e-mails that bounced because of an incorrect e-mail address as a percentage of the total number to whom the e-mail was sent.

Sidebar 10-3: Worldwide Internet Usage

The United States still has the greatest level of Internet usage. As of September 2012, research by the Pew Foundation found that 81% of American adults use the Internet. 95% of adults aged 18–29 use the Internet, 89% of adults aged 30–49, 77% of adults aged 50–64 and 52% of adults 65 and older.

The Internet has slightly higher usage among whites (83%) than blacks (74%) or Hispanics (73%), and higher usage among those with household incomes over $75,000 per year (97%) and those with a college education (96%), than among those with lower income (less than $30,000, at 68%) or no high school diploma (47%).

In Europe, Internet penetration is slightly lower, at 63.2%. In Oceania/Australia, usage is about 67.6%. In Asia, Internet penetration is significantly lower, at 27.5%.

Sources: Research by Pew Internet & American Life Project, Pew Research Center, conducted in August and September, 2012: 'Demographics of Internet Users' http://pewinternet.org/Trend-Data-(Adults)/Whos-Online.aspx
Research by Pew Internet & American Life Project, Pew Research Center, conducted in June, 2012: 'World Internet Usage and Population Statistics' www.internetworldstats.com/stats.htm

- **Unsubscribe rate.** The percentage of the population to whom an e-mail was sent who requested to be taken off the distribution list.

- **Conversion rate.** The percentage of customers targeted by the campaign who opened the e-mail, clicked-through and made a purchase.

- **Cost-per-lead/order.** The cost of the campaign divided by the number of leads or orders made.

- **Cost-per-click.** Total cost of the campaign divided by the number of click-throughs.

<u>Potential Returns</u>: Because direct mail often includes a call to action, there have been numerous studies relative to return rates associated with direct mail. Although these statistics are helpful, it is important to remember that they vary by industry. In other words, there must still be the appropriate medium to carry the message.[7,8]

<u>Best Used When</u>: Direct marketing works particularly well with existing customer bases and with business-to-business sales.[9] It can also be effective at generating trial behaviour among new customers, if the list used to promote the product or service is strong. Direct mail, of course, can also be used to build goodwill, advocate on behalf of an organisation or solicit new employment candidates. It is a particularly strong choice for companies whose customers are relatively easy to define by demographic or other readily accessible information and who represent a smaller segment of the market.

In terms of its ability to leverage sales, direct marketing can be used at any stage in the sales cycle, from generating new sampling behaviour to prompting repeat sales. Unlike advertising, it provides a more immediate opportunity to encourage a purchase and is commonly used to convert browsers to buyers. For example, not-for-profits send letters soliciting donations to past and current donors via mail and often include an envelope for the return contribution. Retailers and wholesalers send catalogues to likely purchasers of their products to encourage comparative shopping and make a purchase easier. E-mail campaigns advertise specials to repeat shoppers, often including specific products with pricing in targeted advertisements, along with links to their website for purchase. Telemarketers may inform someone about a service but may also double as a sales channel, making appointments or even taking payments over the phone.

Websites

Websites have joined business cards and stationary as a marketing communications staple. Almost every business has a website. However, how it uses the site can and should differ significantly depending on the type of business and the customers it targets.

<u>Who It Reaches</u>: Websites reach everyone with Internet access. In the United States, 81% of adults use the Internet.[10] In Europe, Internet penetration is slightly lower, at 63.2%. In Oceania/Australia, usage is about 67.6%. In Asia, Internet penetration is significantly lower, at 27.5%.[11]

<u>Factors Affecting Success</u>: As with any promotional materials, a company's website should clearly communicate its value proposition to its markets, differentiating itself visually and verbally from competitors. However, there are a number of other factors that influence success:

- **Strong user interface.** The website should be easy to navigate and use. Technology in this area changes continuously, as do customer expectations. This has become a specialty field within the web development arena, and experts are called UI (*user interface*) designers.

  As smartphone and tablet users do more web surfing and purchasing on their mobile devices, it is increasingly important to make sure a website works across multiple platforms. Any website designed for a consumer audience, in particular, should be designed to work on any of the major web browsers and on most common mobile platforms. This is called *responsive design*.

- **Staying current.** Many companies launch their websites and forget about them. However, most websites need at least periodic reviews. Retail websites need to be updated continually to capture shoppers whose purchases are more frequent. On the other hand, a professional service firm might not need to update its website as frequently because its services are unlikely to undergo major changes. Still, both the look of the website and its content should be current, particularly if the content includes professional biographies of team members.

- **Traffic.** A website that has no traffic is delivering little benefit. Companies should track both the volume of traffic to their website and the behaviour of their visitors. This provides helpful information about who is visiting your site and why and may give you an opportunity to follow up with them directly.

Research indicates that 91% of online adults use a search engine to find information on the Internet.[12] Regardless of how a company uses its website, management teams should also give careful thought to whether and how the market will find it when it needs the solution the company offers. There are many ways to do this, some of which are highlighted in sidebar 10-4.

<u>What It Costs</u>: Initial website development costs vary significantly depending on size, complexity, whether the site has a shopping cart, security requirements, platform and design. There are typically three key groups of individuals involved: web copywriters, web designers and developers. Once the site is launched, a company will continue to incur expense in order to keep the site updated.

Sidebar 10-4: Driving Website Traffic

Some of the many ways to drive traffic to a website include the following:

Search engine optimisation (SEO): With pages of results for every search, companies whose websites are at the top of the list are more likely to generate traffic. The algorithms that are responsible for page rankings are proprietary to each search engine, but, in general, it is assumed that effective SEO combines keyword searches with website content and the websites linking to and from a particular site. That is why many SEO professionals encourage companies to refresh web content frequently and to aggressively link to other sites as a way of triggering a response from search engine spiders that crawl the web.

Paid searches: Many companies will pay search engines to list their site above others in response to a search. These results generally appear at the top of the list in a shaded box and are marked 'advertisement' in order to differentiate them from the 'natural' or unpaid responses.

Display ads: These advertisements are placed on search engine sites, social media sites and other locations when the user meets the specific demographic or interest criteria specified by the advertiser. For example, if I visit the website of clothing designer Exclusively Misook, the company might pay Google to place a display ad featuring an item of clothing I looked at when I next conduct a search. Exclusively Misook might also pay for display advertising for new customers whose shopping patterns match those of its existing customers. If I were interested, one click would take me to the company's website.

QRs and URLs: Finally, many companies include their website URL on business cards, advertisements or other materials, or add a quick response (QR) code, a two dimensional bar code, to their advertisements or other materials. QR codes can also be captured on smartphone cameras and will link the user to a website with text, video or other information about the product or service.

Companies that use their websites for e-commerce, provide information or access to accounts or other confidential information or use their website as a portal to a company intranet should also factor in the costs of website security. Companies of all sizes are increasingly at risk for data theft, and security breaches can make a significant negative impact on a company's brand reputation.

Common Tactical Metrics: The most common metrics used to evaluate success relative to websites are as follows:

- *Visitors.* The number of people who view a website during a given period.

- *Visits.* The number of times a website is viewed by all viewers.

- *Hits.* The number of times the website is requested from the server.

- *Page views.* The number of pages a particular viewer visited within the website before leaving. Some companies also track 'unique' page views, which provide data about new traffic, as opposed to repeat visitors.

- *Page time viewed (also known as session duration or visit duration).* These metrics all measure the time a visitor spent on a page or site before leaving.

- *Abandonment rate.* The number of people who begin a purchase but do not complete it as a percentage of the number of people who begin a purchase transaction.

Sidebar 10-5: The Cost of Web Traffic

Paid searches: According to the Direct Marketing Association, the cost per lead or order for paid search listings is $52.58. The response rate is 0.22%, indicating that 1 in every 455 people respond positively to that form of advertising.

Display ads: According to research by Forrester, the average CPM (cost per thousand impressions) for display ads is $3.17 in 2012 and is anticipated to rise to $6.64 by 2017 as placement portals become more adept at guaranteeing placement, and competition for web traffic increases. Research by the Direct Marketing Association indicates that conversion rates for display ads are 0.04%, which suggests a cost per lead or order of $79.25. However, the same research suggests that this number could be low, as only 6% of purchases are made during the first visit via a display ad. The remaining 94% of visitors who first see a website via a display ad and subsequently return to make a purchase may, in fact, have been prompted to do so by the display ad or perhaps because of a combination of promotional initiatives. This suggests that the actual cost per lead or order is as low as $47.31.

Sources: 'Direct Mail Gets Most Responses; Email Highest ROI,' Rochester Institute of Technology, Print in the Mix blog, June 14, 2012. http://printinthemix.com/fastfacts/show/575
Lunden, Ingrid. 'Forrester: US Online Display Ad Spend $12.7B in 2012, Rich Media + Video Leading the Charge,' Tech Crunch Blog, October, 9, 2012. http://techcrunch.com/2012/10/09/forrester-us-online-display-ad-spend-to-hit-12-7b-in-2012-rich-media-video-leading-the-charge/

Potential Returns: The return on a website must be evaluated in the context of how it is used. If the website is predominately a distribution channel, it should be evaluated as such. If its primary function is to provide information about products or services, serving as a part of the company's marketing communications, rather than as a sales channel, the evaluation of the return received would be calculated differently.

Traffic enhancement promotion, such as *search engine optimisation*, paid searches and display ads should be evaluated based on the amount of leverage they provide to the distribution channel or the amount of traffic they contribute to the site. Although the latter is likely to be based on analytics and tracking tools associated with the site and grouped into the website maintenance costs overall, sites that serve as distribution channels can benefit from returns estimates based on industry averages.

Best Used When: Although it has become increasingly rare, I am still occasionally asked by a small business whether it needs a website. The answer is almost invariably 'yes' because a website is one of the first references a prospective purchaser will check to confirm that the vendor is viable. However, the purpose and functionality of the website will vary significantly according to the type of company and the way that the customer makes a purchase decision. The more important the role of the website in the customer's decision process, the more complex a company's website approach, and the more significant the investments are likely to be.

For companies selling a product, online retail websites function as both marketing communications, providing information about products so that consumers can research a purchase or browse products before making a choice, and as distribution channels, allowing customers to make an immediate purchase online. In 2009, online sales represented 6% of all retail purchases in the United States. That number is expected to reach 8% by 2014, growing at about 10% compounding annually, compared to 2.5% growth in in-store sales. Europe's growth rates are expected to be more aggressive, at about 11% compounding annually.[13] As a distribution channel for retailers, websites have been a very effective way to reach consumers in markets in which they don't have physical presence.

Many companies offer other services to customers through their website. For example, hospitals and health insurers often offer online access to medical help. Banks and other financial institutions allow you to manage your accounts online. CPA societies may offer members the opportunity to track continuing professional education online as a member benefit. Some companies offer customer support chat features that allow customers to interact with their support staff whenever it is most convenient for the customer.

Other types of organisations have fairly simple websites that describe their products or services, provide reference materials, manuals or other resources and supply contact information. This is the case with most professional service firms and companies whose products are customised or simply not purchased in an online environment.

Social Media

Social media has been one of the hottest areas of marketing promotions in recent years, the subject of extensive articles, research and financial investment. *Social media* is a loose term referencing digital media that provides for two-way (or community-wide) conversations, as opposed to websites and other digital media that are designed to inform, but not to invite, discussion. As technologies evolve, so do the types of social platforms and formats available. The most common include the following:

- *Social networking sites* such as Facebook, LinkedIn, Google+ , Nexopia, Badoo or XING give people an opportunity to connect with friends and family, reconnect with others and share interests and information regardless of geographic proximity. Social networking sites are the most popular form of social media. Online adults spend about 20% of their personal computer time and 30% of their mobile time on social media websites.[14]

- *Blogs*, short for *weblogs*, provide opportunities for one or more authors to comment on a particular topic and invite feedback through comments. Although many blogs are stand-alone websites, blogs can also appear on an organisation's website, such as a corporation or university or on a magazine or newspaper website.

- *Microblogs* are shorter versions of blogs, allowing authors to post short pieces of information to which others can respond. The most popular applications include Twitter and Jaiku, both of which severely limit the number of characters that can be used within a posting.

- *Wikis* are informational websites that allow users to contribute, modify or delete content using a web browser and text editor, allowing collaborative creation of content. Although there are several public iterations of wikis, such as Wikipedia, wikis are also frequently used within closed communities, such as corporate intranets, for knowledge sharing and management.

- *Digital magazines and news sites* sometimes allow comments on stories. Most print publications have some form of online social media presence, and many publications are moving to, or were created in, an entirely digital format. Although most continue to publish content using the tradition editorial board and observing the same journalistic standards, many offer a place for readers to comment or respond, both to a particular article and to other readers' responses. It is this communication aspect of their websites that makes the social media.

- *Social bookmarking sites*, such as Delicious, Digg and Reddit, allow users to reference and share other content on the Internet. In some respects, they resemble Twitter and other microblogs because they gather an eclectic cross-section of postings.

- *Content sharing sites* allow individuals to share original digital media content, either within a closed community or with the public. Popular sites include the video-sharing site YouTube, which hosts content from individuals, organisations and media companies and photo-sharing sites, such as Instagram and Pinterest.

- *Virtual worlds* are websites that allow people to take on a real or assumed persona (depicted as an avatar) and interact with others in a computer-animated role-play environment. These interactions can include games in which the player assumes a single character, such as Vanguard, and virtual social worlds, where the player can assume several different characters and participate in an on-going social environment, as in Second Life.

<u>Who It Reaches</u>: Internationally, social media has become an immensely powerful way to connect people across geographies. Sixty-six per cent of all online adults use some form of social media platform. In the United States, social media is used more heavily by younger (under 55) and female segments of the population. Most people access social networks on personal computers, but mobile devices and tablets are gaining in popularity, especial in the Asia-Pacific region.[15]

Research indicates that the primary reason people participate in social media is to maintain close ties to friends (67%) or reconnect with people they once knew (50%). Most users also acknowledge that information shared on social media has influenced their purchasing decisions.[16] In particular, Internet users check social media and are influenced by online commentary when making purchases for travel, entertainment, technology, clothing and other major purchases.

<u>Factors Affecting Success</u>: Despite social media's popularity, most companies struggle to find strong financial returns from investments here. To generate promotional profits from social media, organisations need to do the following

- **Confirm the match.** One of the most frequent reasons social media investments fail to deliver returns is that the targeted market or markets don't consider that form of social media as a place to find information about solutions to the types of problems the organisation solves. The key is to pick social media that might be used to help the purchaser make a decision.

  For consumer products, a Facebook approach might be effective because many individuals consult friends using Facebook for recommendations on entertainment and other purchases. However, for a business-to-business service organisation, Facebook makes less sense. Facebook users indicate that their primary interest in that particular media is to connect with friends. The business-to-business company is very unlikely to connect with, or even be noticed by, their target market. And if they do, it's relatively unlikely that their messages will influence a purchase. The communication mechanism is simply too far removed from the purchaser's decision-making process. Instead, they might consider blogs that will give their experts an opportunity to demonstrate expertise or describe their innovative new product, a key influencer in many business-to-business purchasing decisions.

- **Be active.** Many social media, including blogs and microblogs, rely on fresh material to keep people engaged. As with the advertising approach, postings on content-rich sites should be frequent enough to encourage repeat interactions. This can present problems for many companies, especially professional service providers, who launch aggressively into the blogosphere, only to find that their professional commitments constrain activity. Frustrated, they eventually stop, and their investment is largely wasted.

- **Find your fans.** The postings that are most quickly noticed are those that get shared between friends. Although research indicates that social media users are very protective of the people and businesses that intrude on their media, companies can benefit significantly when a person 'likes,' 'friends' or otherwise endorses their company and its products or services.[17] This is the reason many companies encourage customers to 'like' them (or the equivalent) in social networking media.

- **Understand the costs.** One of the greatest myths about social media is that it is free. Social media is not free. In fact, it is often quite expensive. The cost in social media comes not from the technology itself, which is typically maintained by the social media company. Instead, the cost is in the labour required to execute a campaign or plan. Because social media is interactive by nature, most social media approaches will require at least the part-time attention of a smart and articulate communicator. Often, they require much more time and expertise than this.

- **Make it versatile.** According to a 2012 research study by Nielsen, U.S. social media users nearly doubled both their use of social media using mobile apps and mobile web access. In Asia, the Middle East and Africa, the use of mobile devices for social media is even more significant. In addition, there are any number of platforms on which social media can be used. Any social media approach should carefully consider how users are engaging in social media—and ensure that the impression the investment makes is as strong in a mobile environment, and on any particular operating software, as it would be on the systems used by the company developing it.

- **Remember that social media is social.** Companies accustomed to traditional media often make the mistake of using social media to conduct a one-way conversation. However, that isn't the consumer's expectation. Consumers expect social media to be social, an exchange or conversation between a company and its customers. One-way communications are less likely to become interesting or engaging. Even blogs, which provide an easy way for a person or company to express an opinion, should allow for reader response. In fact, successful blogs are judged not only by the number of followers they attract, but the amount of conversation in which their followers engage both on the original blog and beyond.

The social nature of social media provides two other valuable opportunities for organisations. The first is that companies can use social media to address customer needs, answer questions or provide customer service. In fact, 30% of consumers prefer to address customer service needs in a social environment rather than picking up the phone. Because customer concerns, and the approach the company takes to addressing them, are often very visible to the public, this poses both an opportunity and a risk to companies actively engaged in social media. Although the media provides an opportunity to be responsive, the company must actually respond quickly and diplomatically. In this very public setting, there is even less room for error or poor service.

The second opportunity is to engage with and learn about the customer. Social media provides excellent opportunities to learn about the market by soliciting input and feedback, monitoring conversations and mining data for information about customer purchasing habits and process, other products or services

A Different Kind of Social Service

Peter Shankman, CEO of Geek Factory, was at the end of a long day. After a 3.30am wake-up call, a 7.00am meeting, then another three-hour meeting and a return flight to Newark at 4.30pm, all he wanted was a steak dinner. So he tweeted:

'Hey @Mortons - can you meet me at Newark airport with a porterhouse when I land in two hours? K, thanks. :)'

Much to his surprise, when he arrived in the Newark terminal two hours later, he was met by a tuxedo-wearing server with a full steak dinner, all from Morton's Steakhouse, his favorite restaurant.

His next tweet?

'Oh. My. God. I don't believe it. @Mortons showed up at EWR WITH A PORTERHOUSE! http://t.co/bD8k4r0 # OMFG!'

Now that is social [media] service!

Source: 'Peter Shankman Joke Leads to Morton's Surprise Steak Dinner at Newark Airport (TWEETS),' The Huffington Post, August 18, 2011. http://www.huffingtonpost.com/2011/08/18/peter-shankman-mortons-steak-tweet_n_930744.html

he or she likes and purchases, and his or her interests and preferences. Social media provides savvy managers the opportunity to engage in conversations with customers—and with employees—at unprecedented levels.

- **Manage the risk.** In a 2012 study, 'Aftershock: Adjusting to the New World of Risk Management,' Deloitte and Forbes Insight noted that social media is now considered the fourth largest source of risk for executives, on par with financial risk and following risk associated with the global economic environment, governmental spending and budget issues and regulatory changes.[18]

The reasons that executives consider social media to represent such a great source of risk are the same reasons that it can be such an asset for promotions or customer intelligence: Word travels quickly. When that word is positive, so is the impact. However, social media also presents the opportunity for bad news, misinformation or deliberate lies that spread like wildfire among customers and other stakeholders. Company secrets, insider information and rumours spread more quickly and can cause damage more rapidly than they did with e-mail or the traditional media.

Unfortunately, there is little a company can do to prevent malicious misinformation from entering circulation. Employee education and a strong social media policy can, on the other hand, help prevent unintentional breaches of confidentiality or unintended misinformation.

Despite the widely acknowledged risk to brand reputation acknowledged by survey respondents, only about 20% actively monitor their reputation in social media and only about 31% have a social media policy executives have shared with employees.[19] Perhaps one of the reasons that companies are slow to adopt such policies is that employees indicate some resistance to following them. About half of employees (42%) indicate that they don't believe they should be held liable by their employer for damaging or inappropriate content posted on their own social media pages, and 15% believe social media policies invade their privacy.

Despite this resistance, every company should create a social media policy, monitor for compliance among employees and take appropriate punitive actions if it is violated. Every organisation should also actively monitor social media for information that may affect the organisation's reputation and ensure it has thoughtfully-crafted protocols to respond in a timely and factual manner, just as if the situation arose in a press conference or in the traditional media.

What It Costs: It is usually free to set up a social media profile. However, as stated previously, the true cost of social media approaches and campaigns will vary significantly depending on scope. Generally, the greatest investment is in time, either from in-house staff or from external consultants. A company may also incur costs associated with tracking and data collection, paid links or advertising.

<u>Common Tactical Metrics</u>: In addition to monitoring the conversation itself, the most common metrics used to evaluate success relative to social media are as follows:

- *Followers, likes, supporters or friends.* The number of people who have joined your company's social network. Many companies also track changes in the size of their membership base.

- *Mentions.* The number of times your company and/or product or service was mentioned in a particular social media or across the entire spectrum of social networks.

- *Activity, posts, comments, ideas, threads.* The number of comments, retweets or other activities demonstrating social connectivity.

- *Trackbacks.* The number of times someone cited the company's posting in his or her own feed or website and the number of times someone commented on that posting.

- *Active contributors.* The number of people who actively participated in the social conversation in a given period of time.

<u>Potential Returns</u>: Returns, like costs, vary dramatically, and not necessarily proportionately. There are few solid research studies that look at the impact social media makes at a financial level. Most focus on intermediate metrics, such as the number of followers or fans a site has or the number of people who respond to any particular post. Whether this translates to purchasing behaviour is often neglected.

As with other promotional tactics, non-marketing executives should inquire about the impact their marketing team believes investments in social media will have, why they believe the investment will have that level of impact and how those numbers connect to financial returns. Although the model will undoubtedly be based on some assumptions, as all models are, careful consideration of the potential return before an investment is far better than wondering whether the expense was justified after it has been spent.

<u>Best Used When</u>: The term *social media* encompasses a broad cross-section of tools. Each one is appropriate for some audiences and purposes and not for others.

For example, at the point at which this book was written, based on available research on user demographics and behaviours, most social networking and similar media will be most effective when used to reach broad consumer audiences about technology, entertainment, travel and fashion. They are likely to be significantly less useful to professional or business-to-business service organisations or companies that sell products purchased only occasionally. On the other hand, information-based social media, like blogs and microblogs, can be useful to organisations whose primary value to the customer is as a source of expertise, such as professional services, because they present an exceptional way to inform the public or demonstrate capabilities.

Collateral Materials and Related Marketing Communications

Marketing collateral and *marketing communications* are both catch-all terms. *Collateral* generally refers to printed or digital materials used in sales or communications on behalf of a company. A company's collaterals and marketing communications tools may include printed or digital versions of brochures, technical data or sell sheets, newsletters, fact sheets and even stationary and business cards. They can also include point of purchase displays and trade show exhibits.

<u>Who It Reaches</u>: Collateral pieces can be used for any audience and should be tailored to the way the customer expects to receive information. For example, many individuals still exchange paper business cards, but in more technology-intensive communities, v-cards or digital information may be more commonly expected in conjunction with business interactions. In some industries, customers expect printed specification sheets for products. In others, they expect the information to be delivered in a digital document. The combination of collateral materials a company produces will depend heavily on both industry standards and customer expectations.

<u>Factors Affecting Success</u>: Many of the factors affecting success in the development of collateral materials are no different than they are in other promotional efforts. The collateral must provide the appropriate information, in the format most expected by customers, using appealing design and engaging messaging. However, collaterals should also maintain visual consistency.

This means that when a company's collateral materials are displayed next to one another, the visual similarities should be obvious. The use of logo, colours, typeface and images should all readily identify the pieces as being connected with that particular organisation. This substantially reduces the amount of mental attention a customer must give to identifying the vendor, allowing him or her to focus instead on the products or services for sale.

When a company is considering new design standards, it is important to keep in mind how it will translate to all the company's collateral materials. For example, some colours cannot be replicated on certain types of paper, such as newsprint. Some logos, when placed next to those of competitors at an event, appear small or difficult to read. Others use design standards that do not work as fluidly in black and white as they do in print. For more information about graphics standards, refer to the description of the graphics standards document's use and common elements found in chapter 3.

<u>What It Costs</u>: Clearly, printed materials require printing expense. In general, the per-piece price is quite high for small runs and dramatically smaller for large quantities. The company should also anticipate significant design and copywriting costs associated with print collateral development.

Digital media require no printing costs, but some companies do incur a cost associated with producing CDs or DVDs or providing customers with a USB drive containing relevant information. On the design side, it is often more expensive to produce digital materials, especially if interactive features, animation or video production are involved, and digital media other than static information pieces may also require coding or other technical production skills.

<u>Common Tactical Metrics</u>: The most common metrics for collateral materials are related to the sales they facilitate. Either win rates (the percentage of customer accounts won as a percentage of all customer proposals submitted) or the average amount of time required to win an account might serve as good metrics to evaluate effectiveness.

<u>Potential Returns</u>: Because many collateral pieces provide such critical information during the sales process, these materials can be virtually indispensable to a sales person looking to close a deal. Even materials with a more distant connection, such as newsletters or point-of-purchase materials, can have a strong impact on sales. The return will depend on how critical the information or message delivered is to the decision process and how effective the collateral is in engaging the potential customer and prompting them to take action.

<u>Best Used When</u>: Every company has at least some form of collateral, whether it is extremely basic, such as a business card or sales invoice with a logo, or extremely complex, including elements like tradeshow

exhibits, brochures and product specification sheets, or somewhere in between. Collaterals provide important information about the products or services a company offers, the value the company delivers to customers and basic information about how to do business with the company.

Media Relations

In general, the goal of *media relations* efforts is to manage the relationship between professional journalists and an organisation, proactively providing information to them and answering questions they might have. Although the media makes many non-marketing executives nervous because they feel a lack of control over outcomes, ignoring the media, especially when a company is in a crisis situation, can often be more damaging to a company's reputation than providing appropriate information, even if it is misinterpreted.

The term *media* includes consumer and trade newspapers and magazines, television and radio stations, webzines, professional bloggers, publishers of newsletters and others. Media relations work often includes a strong social media component, both as a tool for communicating with journalists and as a way of attracting public attention.

Most companies have a media kit or press kit available to reporters. Press kits include background information about the company, its leadership and its products or services, as well as examples of previous media coverage. Whether or not a company includes elements of media relations in its promotional plans, every organisation should have a crisis communications plan that specifies who will speak to the media. Every company should also identify a media relations professional whose expertise could be tapped, if needed, in such a situation.

Who It Reaches: Almost every audience reads and is influenced by some form of traditional (or professional) media. The audience for each category of media, and for each individual publication, will differ significantly. Most media outlets provide a media kit that profiles their audience. However, the statistics they identify may more accurately indicate generic distribution or geographic makeup than the psychosocial profiles of readers. Media relations professionals often have a deep understanding of the media related to the industries they serve and can help identify media outlets that might otherwise be missed.

Who's Listening?

The media a company targets should be carefully selected to reflect market demographics. In the United States, news communicated through traditional television news media is more likely to be seen by individuals over the age of 64, 63% of whom regularly watch television news broadcasts.

On the other hand, only 28% of people under age 30 watch the news on television. To reach younger people through the news, companies should focus on media who distribute content through social networking sites because 36% visit them regularly for news. By contrast, only 2% of the U.S. population over age 65 uses social media sites as news sources.

Even within a particular medium, the programme, section or topic will appeal to a different population profile. For example, viewers of the television show *The Colbert Report* tend to be younger, with more education and income than average. On the other hand, viewers of Fox News tend to be older and are less likely to have a college degree.

Source: The Pew Research Center for The People & The Press. 'Trends in News Consumption: 1991–2012: In Changing News Landscape, Even Television is Vulnerable,' published September 27, 2012. www.people-press.org/files/legacy-pdf/2012%20 News%20Consumption%20Report.pdf

Factors Affecting Success: Characteristics of the most successful media relations programmes are as follows:

- **They are built on strong relationships with the media.** Like any relationship, relationships with the media should be built on trust and nurtured over time. Professional reporters are trained to check facts before they are printed, and they are constantly battling tight timelines and competitive pressure. If they are covering an organisation with which they have a strong, trusting relationship, they will have greater confidence that the information is accurate and be willing to expedite coverage. This can be a substantial advantage whether a company is launching a new service or product or responding to something negative that has happened.

  As with any relationship, trust is built on sincerity and experience. Companies should provide only true and verified information and not speculate about situations for which they have no information. Whereas an individual reporter may be arrogant, uninformed, negligent or even malicious, most are not. Most reporters are professionals who care about the people they cover and the public they serve. They are under intense pressure to meet deadlines and deliver news that will get readers/viewers to pay attention. Be professional, cooperative, truthful and respectful of their deadlines, and your communications efforts will go much more smoothly.

- **They are carefully managed.** Whether an organisation is speaking to the media about good news, such as an expansion in products, services or locations, or bad news, such as a product failure, accident or management impropriety, external communications should be carefully coordinated and centralised. A single, designated company spokesperson should handle media relations, and others in the company should defer to that individual. Anyone interfacing with the media should have appropriate training, be prepared with all the relevant facts and information and remain professional regardless of public or media response. Timeliness is also important. In an age when information sharing is practically instantaneous, it is important to focus first on media relations if a particular news item is paired with other promotional approaches.

- **Professional help.** If a company does not have strong existing relationships with the media or the experience to manage significant news, the executive team should consider retaining outside public relations expertise. As with any discipline, the media relations professional(s) should have experience handling the specific type of situation involved. The field of media relations, as a subset of public relations, includes many specialists, including individuals who specialise in crisis communications, technology product launches, not-for-profit events and other corporate activities that might be of interest to a specific group of reporters. Finding the team with the right skills and relationships can make a substantial difference in how productive the investment in external resources will be.

What It Costs: Although press coverage is often referred to as *earned media* rather than paid media, like advertising, there is still a substantial cost to effectively working with the press. In particular, the labour costs associated with nurturing media relationships, whether through in-house personnel or external media relations professionals, can be substantial.

Common Tactical Metrics: There are a number of objectives that are used as intermediate, or tactical, metrics for media relations. Some companies engage third-party research companies to gauge public perception of the organisation, measuring improvements against the media relations efforts invested. Other common metrics include the following:

- *Column inches.* The number of inches of earned media printed in news media as a result of proactive media relations.

- *Broadcast seconds.* The number of seconds of earned media coverage on broadcast stations such as radio or television.

- *Clips/impressions.* The number of articles or broadcasts citing the company's name and/or its product or services.

- *Advertising value equivalency.* This is used when someone, usually a marketer or a public relations firm, compares the amount of column inches or broadcast seconds of unpaid, earned media against *rate cards* (*pricing sheets*) for advertising in an effort to give a dollar value to the media relations outcomes. However, this practice is dangerous because it can mislead individuals who are unfamiliar with this metric to believe the advertising value represents income to the organisation.

<u>Potential Returns</u>: Although the traditional media's influence and credibility have both suffered in recent years, it remains an extremely powerful influence on consumer behaviour. Positive coverage is more likely to be perceived as credible by purchasers than its paid counterparts, such as advertising. Negative coverage is more likely to be believed and affect behaviour than if it were not covered by the press. The traditional press also feeds other communications sources, especially social media. Because of this impact, wise investments in carefully crafted media relations efforts can have significant impact.

<u>Best Used When</u>: Every company should be prepared to handle basic media relations, either in a crisis situation or when a reporter calls. However, larger organisations, companies in industries that receive disproportionate amounts of media interest and companies who are interested in expanding visibility or educating target markets will generally benefit from a sustained relationship development effort between media read by their stakeholders and a spokesperson or public relations professional within their company.

Public Relations (Other Than Media Relations and Social Media)

Public relations is a broad term that includes many different tactics designed to educate and build relationships between a company and its various audiences and markets. Originally, the term included primarily media relations and broader publicity efforts (other than advertising), such as trade shows or other events. Over time, it has evolved to include a myriad of activities, all designed to monitor or influence public perception.

Among the more popular public relations activities outside of media relations and social media activities are

- special events hosted by an organisation, including receptions, product sampling events, seminars and lunch-and-learns;

- special events hosted by others in which the organisation participates, including trade shows, sponsorships and conferences;

- third-party endorsements of products or services, including product placement on television shows and in films, celebrity endorsements and client testimonials; and

- *guerrilla* and *viral marketing* approaches, which draw on their uniqueness to expand visibility.

<u>Who It Reaches</u>: When designed with the target audience in mind, public relations efforts can reach virtually any audience.

<u>Factors Affecting Success</u>: In addition to reaching the right audience with the right message, public relations efforts must interest the audience enough to capture their attention and turn that attention into action. The most effective public relations campaigns are creative enough to stand out and still relevant enough to generate

Sidebar 10-6: A Whale of a Tale (And a Very Successful PR Campaign!)

Ivar's, a seafood company and restaurant headquartered in Seattle, Washington, created a hoax that generated exceptional interest and subsequent revenue for the company. Building on the reputation of its founder Ivar Haglund, who was well-known for his creative publicity and his sense of humour, the company led the public to believe that Ivar had anticipated future submarine tourism in the Puget Sound and planted underwater billboards advertising Ivar's products along likely routes.

To support the hoax, the company hauled one of the billboards out of Puget Sound, covered in algae and barnacles, in a very public 'discovery' of one of the artefacts. An unassuming reporter in the area happened to notice the 'discovery' and published photos in the local paper, which only fuelled suspicions. Riding the wave of public excitement, Ivar's persuaded outside parties to join in the hoax, including a respected historian who advised the company on its production of artificial documents. With ample earned media following the exciting 'discovery' and significant paid media, including television ads, radio ads and highway billboards, the company had a surge in sales. In fact, sales of Ivar's most popular products quadrupled during the two months of the campaign.

The company did intentionally leave clues about the fact it was a hoax. The prices of chowder weren't correct for the dates the billboards were supposed to have been planted, the wrong governor was put on the letterhead granting permission to Ivar Haglund from the Department of Fisheries and the falsified documents were a little too polished to be believed. However, the media—and the public—both fell for the hoax, for a while. A few months later, the company 'confessed' to the hoax. Although the media may be leery of similar stories in the future, the short-term payoff was significant.

Source: Lacitis, Erik. 'Ivar's undersea billboards a hoax devised as marketing ploy,' *The Seattle Times*, November 12, 2009. http://seattletimes.com/html/localnews/2010253767_ivars12m.html

sales as a result. Unfortunately, many companies are not as successful in turning attention into action.

For example, many professional service organisations host seminars to help demonstrate their expertise to prospective and existing clients. In general, these professionals know what will appeal to their clients. The clients and prospects who attend are most likely to make a purchase because they have a relationship with a particular service provider, and, yet, most CPAs, attorneys and other presenters dart out the door at the end of a seminar, relieved to have a project off their list. They fail to do the one activity that is most likely to make their public outreach produce returns: build relationships with individuals in their audience. The most effective seminars are hosted by professionals who arrive early, talk extensively with participants during and after the presentation and follow up after the event, building those relationships that will generate sales.

What It Costs: One of the advantages to public relations initiatives is that they can be extremely inexpensive relative to other forms of promotions. However, they do require creativity and coordination, and often, other forms of promotions should be used to gain maximum leverage, driving up cost. If external public relations teams are used, this can also drive up cost.

Common Tactical Metrics: The intermediate metrics used in public relations include those mentioned in media relations and social media, as well as the public perception tools developed by researchers to assess progress. At the individual tactic level, they also include metrics such as the number of event attendees or participants, number of seminars or workshops hosted and other customised metrics.

Potential Returns: The returns depend entirely on how carefully crafted the approach has been. Some companies lose money on public relations efforts because they attract attention, but not from the right audiences, or because they fail to include a strong enough call to action that will produce sales. However, the low cost of public relations outreach can make the returns exceptionally high. The key, again, is creativity and the ability to convert the attention to revenues.

Best Used When: Because the cost of public relations tends to be lower, it is a great fit for smaller companies. However, every company should include some public relations initiatives, including media relations and social media, in their promotions repertoire.

QUESTIONS FOR NON-MARKETING MANAGERS TO ASK ABOUT PROMOTIONS

To ensure that promotions are contributing to marketing objectives, the following questions should be high on a non-marketing manager's list:

- Why did we select the particular tactics we did?

- How do the selected promotional tactics tie to the marketing strategies identified? What impact are they expected to have on the customer's purchasing decision criteria?

- How do we know where our target customer/client looks for information about the products/services we deliver?

- What are the key messages these promotional efforts will communicate? How important are those issues in the minds of customers? Is there anything that is more important? If so, how are we addressing that issue?

- What messages are our competitors communicating? Do we sound like them? Does our proposed campaign look or sound similar to others in a way that could be confusing to the market?

- What intermediate, or tactical, metrics will we use to ensure the plan is on target?

- What impact, in financial terms, should we anticipate from the marketing promotions in which we are engaging?

- Over what time frame will we measure success?

- Will these promotions require changes relative to the other aspects of the marketing mix?

CHAPTER 10 SUMMARY

The fourth 'P' of marketing is promotions, which includes a broad range of tactics, including advertising, public relations, direct mail, social media, websites, collateral materials and other activities. It is also one of the most expensive aspects of marketing, and the 'P' most likely to cause non-marketing managers concern about the efficacy of marketing investments.

This concern is often the result of four mistakes made in the way promotions are managed:

1. Because of a lack of clarity about the two primary functional objectives of marketing, there is inconsistency between expectations and potential outcomes. Working in careful coordination with other aspects of the marketing plan, promotions provides leverage to the sales team and assists in proactive reputation management in the marketplace.

2. When oversight is delegated away from senior leadership, the result is sometimes poor alignment between promotions and other aspects of marketing within either the discipline or marketing the function. It can also lead to risky copycat marketing behaviours.

3. When leaders aren't familiar with how messaging works and how it should be delivered, they are less likely to catch messaging that is inconsistent with their brand reputation or value proposition, or they miss visual inconsistencies that lead to poor brand recall.

4. If they don't know enough about the tactics employed in marketing, it is difficult to ask informed questions about why they were selected. As a result, it is more difficult to effectively monitor recommendations. In the worst cases, non-marketing managers add to their own marketing losses by encouraging their marketing team to engage in tactics that are not a good fit for their market. To be effective, the non-marketing manager must have a basic understanding about common marketing tactics and be prepared to ask informed questions about fit with the company's target market, business objectives, marketing strategies and targeted influencers.

Endnotes

1 Sources:

Praetorius, Dean. 'The Red Cross' Rogue Tweet: #gettngslizzerd On Dogfish Head's Midas Touch,' The Huffington Post, February 16, 2011. www.huffingtonpost.com/2011/02/16/red-cross-rogue-tweet_n_824114.html

Crenshaw, Dorothy. 'PR disasters averted: 7 cases of strong crisis management,' Ragan's PR Daily, March 20, 2012. www.prdaily.com/Main/Articles/PR_disasters_averted_7_cases_of_strong_crisis_mana_11111.aspx#

Segall, Laurie. 'Boozy Red Cross tweet turns into marketing bonanza for Dogfish Brewery,' CNN Money, February 15, 2011. http://money.cnn.com/2011/02/17/smallbusiness/dogfish_redcross/index.htm

2 Morrison, Maureen. 'Starbucks Hits No. 3 Despite Limited Ad Spending,' *Advertising Age*, May 2, 2011. http://adage.com/article/news/starbucks-hits-3-limited-ad-spending/227316/

3 Johnson, Caitlin. 'Cutting Through Advertising Clutter,' CBS News, February 11, 2009. www.cbsnews.com/8301-3445_162-2015684.html

4 Associated Press. 'Super Bowl ads cost average of $3.5M,' as reported on the ESPN website (www.espn.com), February 6, 2012. http://espn.go.com/nfl/playoffs/2011/story/_/id/7544243/super-bowl-2012-commercials-cost-average-35m

5 Crupi, Anthony. 'In their Prime: Broadcast Spot Costs Soar,' *AdWeek*, June 22, 2011. www.adweek.com/news/television/their-prime-broadcast-spot-costs-soar-132805

6 Bruell, Alexandra. 'DMA Survey Shows Snail Mail, Phone Beat Digital in Response Rates,' *Ad Age*, June 13, 2012. http://adage.com/print/235364

7 *Ibid.*

Haskel, Debora. '2012 DMA Response Rate Report: Direct Mail Shows Well Rounded Performance,' IWCO Direct blog. Retrieved December 26, 2012. www.iwco.com/blog/2012/07/11/dma-response-rate-report/

8 'Direct Mail Gets Most Responses; Email Highest ROI,' Rochester Institute of Technology, Print in the Mix blog, June 14, 2012. http://printinthemix.com/fastfacts/show/575

Direct Mail Tops Email for Response Rates; Costs per Lead Similar,' Marketing Charts blog, June 15, 2012. www.marketingcharts.com/print/direct-mail-tops-email-for-response-rates-costs-per-lead-similar-22395/

9 For more information, look at the latest edition of the Direct Marketing Association's Response Rate Trend Report. For example, see www.the-dma.org/cgi/dispannouncements?article=1451.

10 Research by Pew Internet & American Life Project, Pew Research Center, conducted in August and September, 2012: 'Demographics of Internet Users' http://pewinternet.org/Trend-Data-(Adults)/Whos-Online.aspx

11 Research by Pew Internet & American Life Project, Pew Research Center, conducted in June, 2012: 'World Internet Usage and Population Statistics' www.internetworldstats.com/stats.htm

12 Research by Pew Internet & American Life Project, Pew Research Center: 'Search Engine Use 2012' http://pewinternet.org/~/media/Files/Reports/2012/PIP_Search_Engine_Use_2012.pdf

13 Schonfeld, Erick. 'Forrester Forecast: Online Retail Sales will Grow to $250 Billion by 2014,' TechCrunch blog, Monday, March 8, 2010. http://techcrunch.com/2010/03/08/forrester-forecast-online-retail-sales-will-grow-to-250-billion-by-2014/

14 The Neilson Company. 'State of the Media: The Social Media Report 2012,' Nielsen Holdings NV and NM Incite, July 2012. http://blog.nielsen.com/nielsenwire/social/2012/

15 *Ibid.*

16 Smith, Aaron. 'Why Americans Use Social Media,' Pew Internet, November 15, 2011. www.pewinternet.org/Reports/2011/Why-Americans-Use-Social-Media/Main-report.aspx

Endnotes, continued

17 The Neilson Company. 'State of the Media: The Social Media Report 2012,' Nielsen Holdings NV and NM Incite, July 2012. http://blog.nielsen.com/nielsenwire/social/2012/

18 Deloitte Development LLC & Forbes Insight. 'Aftershock: Adjusting to the new world of risk management,' © 2012 Deloitte Development LLC. www.deloitte.com/assets/Dcom-UnitedStates/Local%20Assets/Documents/IMOs/Governance%20and%20Risk%20Management/us_grm_aftershock_062812.PDF

19 Survey conducted on behalf of Workplace Options by Public Policy Polling in May 2012. See press release dated June 5, 2012 and related polling data, both available online atwww.workplaceoptions.com/news/press-releases/press-release.asp?id= 9AAF1BE 9E12D45409F4D&title= Companies Should Think Twice Before Creating Social Media Policy

EVALUATING RETURNS ON MARKETING INVESTMENTS

Figure 11-1: Marketing Alignment Map

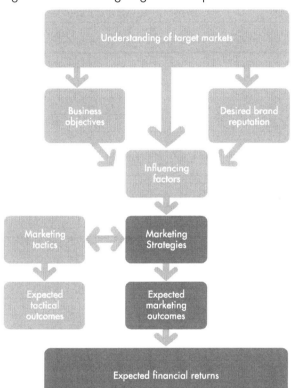

Does your company measure anticipated returns on marketing investments in financial terms? Do you do so before you approve the plan?

If you do, congratulations! You are at the forefront of a trend in marketing management.

If you don't, then why not? There are several reasons companies don't measure returns. The most common one is that they don't believe it is possible. As one CEO once told me, 'marketing is a black art that eludes measurement.'

He was wrong.

DEBUNKING THE MEASUREMENT MYTH

I call this belief that marketing, and particularly promotions, cannot be evaluated in financial terms the *Measurement Myth*. Not only is it untrue, but failing to measure marketing is one of the leading reasons companies fail to maximise returns on their market-facing investments.

Marketing can, and should, be measured in financial terms.

Most executives can figure out how to monetise new product innovation. They simply assume that the units will sell. Pricing, too, is easy. After all, a dollar of change need simply be multiplied out by volume. Of course, the estimator must also assume a change in demand.

Distribution channels are also relatively easy to monetise. The expected volume, multiplied by the price point, less costs gives the company an idea

> Failing to measure marketing is one of the leading reasons companies fail to maximise returns on their market-facing investments.

of how a channel approach might affect the company's bottom line. Executives must, of course, assume their companies' products will sell. They must also make assumptions about how the channel is likely to affect other existing channels and how likely the market is to purchase the product at the price point at which it will be offered.

Although executives are generally comfortable with these types of models, they remain uncomfortable with models projecting financial returns on promotions. Yet, for many, the promotions-related marketing personnel costs and expenses were sizeable portions of their overall marketing budget.

Several common concerns are expressed when I ask executives of both market-leading companies and average performers why they do not measure financial returns on marketing, and particularly, promotional investments.

First, building such a model would require assumptions. After all, just about every financial model does. One of the first lines repeated over and over in business schools when doing financial analysis is to 'assume interest is X%, and inflation is Y%.' These must be assumptions because they are out of our control. We can base them on historical averages, adjusted for our own lending environment and economic conditions. Regardless, they are assumptions.

The models for pricing, products and placement all require assumptions, as well. After all, a company that is investing in the production a new widget assumes that the widget will sell. The company bases this assumption on a series of other assumptions: that the product is correctly based on market needs, a competitor won't arrive on the scene with a better product just before the new widget is launched and the company will succeed in selling the widgets. Because sales are assumed, and promotions are often used to provide leverage to sales, some level of promotional expense is likely assumed in any new product calculation. Similarly, pricing and placement calculations also rely on assumptions about demand, which in turn, assumes a level of promotional investment.

Examining the models from this perspective, and given the role promotions play in providing leverage to the sales force, one might argue that the present value of the stream of promotional investments over the life of the product should be added into expense calculations when estimating potential financial impact. Of course, this is rarely done. Promotions often benefit multiple products or services and can be used for other reasons. The amount of money invested in promotions is also variable and may be difficult to estimate over the life of the product.

Assumptions are both normal and acceptable in financial planning. As the company builds systems and collects data for analysis, the organisation will have more historical performance data and will require fewer assumptions. As long as the assumptions are made consistently, the data should be comparable. When new information validates or disproves historical assumptions, the outcomes of those calculations should be adjusted to reflect the new facts. This is the same approach managers take in any type of financial planning.

The second reason executives say they do not measure outcomes in financial terms is because they already evaluate performance using non-financial metrics. They, or their marketing team, track hits on their website, followers in social media, column inches of news coverage or use one of the industry-wide surveys of brand awareness to track how well the market at large knows their name.

Non-financial metrics may be easier to track, but they can be misleading. First, most of these metrics provide no indication about whether the organisation is reaching the right market. The company may, for example, be receiving excellent news coverage but not in a location that customers would see the articles. No amount of news coverage is likely to move the wrong market to make a purchase decision. Second, the metrics may be appropriate for the tactic, but if someone does not understand how the clicks, inches or awareness translate to revenue for the company, the numbers can lead the company to misinterpret results.

For example, if I told you that a company had 100,000 followers on Facebook, you might think that number was outstanding. After all, that is a large number relative to most small and mid-sized companies' social media. However, if I then told you that only .002% of followers were likely to make a purchase based on what they saw or heard based on the site, meaning that just two of those followers were likely to be customers, the savvy executive might wonder whether his or her social media initiative was paying off. At the very least, it might cause managers and executives to ask why the company generates such a small number of customers and whether the message or approach is effective.

To be useful in assessing potential returns, non-financial metrics must be connected to financial metrics. The company must have some idea of how the followers, hits, column inches or awareness will affect revenues, either alone or in conjunction with other elements of the marketing mix.

This leads to the third common concern driving the Measurement Myth. Many executives and marketing professionals alike will argue that they don't know what the impact of the investments will be. This is generally because they did not think carefully enough through the impacts they expected before they invested in their marketing activities. This is the purpose of the Marketing Alignment Map described in chapter 5, 'Understanding What Influences Market Behaviour.'

A company that focuses on using the Marketing Alignment Map, beginning with a solid understanding of the influencers that affect the purchasing decision process as described in chapter 6, 'Aligning Marketing Tactics With Influencing Factors,' and how changes in influencers will affect sales, can make fact-based assumptions about how its marketing investments will affect customer decisions and company revenues. This is particularly true in larger organisations when more sophisticated analyses can pinpoint with more precision the expected output of an additional investment in a given aspect of the marketing mix. Larger companies should understand the impact of their investments within a few percentage points of actual outcomes. For example, with my company's Fortune 500 clients, our predictive analytics based on historical performance can help optimise marketing expenditures across a range of market-facing investments. We can tell our clients not only how they should allocate funds across activities to achieve the maximum possible return on investment, but also what the financial returns will be.

Small and mid-sized organisations often have a more limited data set, making these sorts of analyses more difficult and/or impractical. However, this does not mean that the outcomes should not be measured. In fact, it makes careful study of marketing returns even more important because historical data will eventually become the strongest guide of future investment decisions.

For example, a small non-profit that does an annual end-of-year appeal can estimate the likely outcome of a similar appeal based on past performance. It can begin by isolating continuing activities from new ones and estimate the expected revenue from sustained activities. Then, it can estimate expected returns based on incremental additions to their marketing plan to estimate the impact those new investments will have. Because this seems like a trial and error approach, and because many marketers are reluctant to be held accountable for financial outcomes, many small and mid-sized organisations fail to estimate or measure the potential outcomes, leaving them no benchmarks for future performance.

The fourth and final common driver of the Measurement Myth is that the executive team and/or its marketing team simply don't believe marketing can be measured. As a result, they don't try. This is, perhaps, the most common reason that the Measurement Myth persists. That old executive joke about being unable to understand which half of their marketing investments are being wasted has established itself, at some level, as truth with a large percentage of non-marketing managers. It is also supported by many marketers who, often for good reasons, are reluctant to be held accountable for financial outcomes.

The reasons for marketers' resistance to debunking the Measurement Myth are described in the next section, which addresses how the marketing function should be managed. The remainder of this chapter describes why and how marketing should be measured as a part of the evaluation of investments in marketing.

THE BENEFITS OF MEASUREMENT

When companies do try to measure marketing, it commonly happens after the marketing investments have been made. They look at the number of column inches of media coverage and try to determine whether that resulted in any new customers, or they look at sales through a new distribution channel, like a catalogue or web partner, and try to determine whether the channel is delivering a solid return.

Although these types of measurements can be helpful, they are often imprecise and not helpful when evaluating a plan before approval. The best approach to understanding the financial impact of marketing is to measure it at least twice: before the plan is funded and after the programmes are complete. In fact, measuring before implementing a marketing plan is often more important than measuring after it has been completed.

MEASURING RESULTS IN ANTICIPATION OF FUNDING

There are several reasons why measuring in anticipation of a marketing activity is arguably more important than specific measurements after execution:

- **Measuring in anticipation facilitates monitoring.** This is because the sum of all marketing activities, if measured in financial terms, should provide two simple metrics that are easy to monitor: revenues and expenses. If the organisation carefully anticipates expected revenues and expenses, it should be easy to monitor outcomes with a quick look at the company's financial statements. If the company is not hitting the revenue goals anticipated in conjunction with marketing expenditures or if the marketing expenses have exceeded their budget, this flags the need for more thorough investigation.

- **Measuring in anticipation facilitates comparison.** When non-marketing management team members are asked to review a marketing plan and budget that include numerous tactics with whose returns they are less familiar, such as social media or public relations activities, it can be difficult to understand the expected impact each component will make. After all, it is difficult to compare eyeballs (or hits on a website) to inches. Asking the team to translate these activities into revenues allows the non-marketing executive to ask more informed questions.

    For example, consider a marketing department for a CPA firm that suggests the firm have a presence at a trade show, engage in social media directed at a particular audience and pursue media relations. Even if the three activities are aggregated, if a dollar outcome is attached, when the non-marketing management team asks about the impact of eliminating one aspect of the plan, the impact can be measured in terms that allow objective evaluation. When financial numbers are not attached, discussions about outcomes can quickly become mired in metrics that are not easily comparable and don't translate to sales.

- **Measuring in anticipation minimises poor investment decisions.** Companies make poor investments in marketing when

    ◦ the marketing activities are not aligned with marketing strategies that are designed to affect the market;

- ∘ the plans are based too heavily on assumptions; and

- ∘ there are other aspects of the company's operations that will affect success but are not identified in the planning process.

Turning anticipated marketing outcomes into financial figures tends to prompt questions that surface these challenges.

When a management team reviews the marketing plan in the context of the Marketing Alignment Map, beginning with the market and the company's business objectives, and ending with anticipated financial outcomes, it can more quickly spot marketing activities that simply aren't aligned. It can also help non-marketing executives identify aspects of the plan that have been based on assumptions, rather than facts. Although assumptions are normal, they represent risk in the planning process, and many can easily be tested or replaced with facts, either from research or from historical performance.

Finally, the discussion of anticipated returns prompts the marketing and executive teams to take a careful look at what other conditions must be satisfied in order to execute effectively. Many times, a marketing plan is created, but some other aspect of company operations becomes a barrier to success. For example, I worked with one manufacturing client whose objective was to grow sales aggressively. We worked together to build a plan, and as we assessed potential returns, I asked whether their manufacturing facilities could accommodate the anticipated expansion. The CEO laughed and told me he would like to have that problem.

However, the issue wasn't a laughing matter. Their capacity constraints were real, and it quickly became evident that if the company's revenue stream grew at the projected rates, demand would exceed the company's ability to supply customers with products, and the company's reputation would suffer as a result. Much to the executive team's disappointment, I recommended scaling back on their market-facing investments and growing at rates that would permit reasonable expansion of manufacturing capacity.

- **Measuring in anticipation improves the accuracy of intermediate and retrospective measurement.**
  Measuring in anticipation makes it easier to develop intermediate metrics and measurement tools. For example, consider a company that anticipates a 20% increase in business due to a combination of more proactive and structured sales activities (a channel tactic) and leverage from specific promotional activities. A discussion of anticipated returns over the longer term allows the executive team to ask about progress points along the way. For example, the executive team might want to track the number of proactive, rather than responsive, sales calls its sales team makes as an intermediate measurement of success.

In the process of this discussion, the company may discover it has a tracking need it has not had in the past. For example, it may not have tracked the number of proactive versus reactive sales calls made by its sales team. The conversations associated with anticipated returns allow the executive and marketing teams to identify these intermediate tracking systems that will help ensure that the programme is delivering on results. In this example, if the number of proactive sales calls was not increasing by a specific date, the marketing and executive teams could reconvene to troubleshoot the problem, helping to ensure that the marketing plan remains on track.

This process also makes it easy to identify tracking systems and reports that are no longer useful. Many companies produce endless numbers of reports to try to track behaviours and activities within a company. By reviewing the anticipated returns in advance, along with the intermediate metrics along the way, it may become clear that some reports provide no meaningful value to managers, allowing the company to reinvest internal resources on more relevant tracking systems.

Measuring Returns During and After Execution

Measuring returns in anticipation of marketing plan approval is the final step in assessing its effectiveness, which is why it is the last chapter in this book's section, 'Evaluating Proposed Investments in the Marketing Function.' It is critical to success. However, measuring returns during and after execution is also important.

Measuring returns during and after execution allows you to improve performance. A professional runner times every run and tracks the food, beverages and training that produced that time result in order to understand how to maximise performance. In the same way, the company that measures the intermediate metrics associated with marketing outcomes, as well as the ultimate financial results on a systematic basis, can improve its ability to compete.

In addition to generating a better understanding of what worked and what didn't, using systematic measurement approaches helps improve accountability by keeping the entire company focused on the metrics that matter and the results the team is trying to achieve.

The planning phase is the perfect time to consider both the metrics you will use to track marketing and financial outcomes and the systems you will use to track actual results. Careful forethought about the information that might be helpful when assessing returns, combined with consistent tracking and analysis, will produce information that will turn assumptions in future planning processes into facts. Because financial models are only as accurate as the underlying assumptions, adhering to this discipline of measurement and analysis will reduce risk and increase the accuracy of future projections.

Best practices related to measurement during the management process are the topic of chapter 14, 'Managing Measurement.' However, many of the approaches used to measure marketing returns after the plan is complete are most effective if anticipated before work begins.

DETERMINING THE APPROPRIATE LEVEL OF ACCURACY

Marketing can, and should, be measured. However, the degree of accuracy with which it is measured will vary from organisation to organisation, and even within an organisation, based on the degree of risk and the cost of estimating or measuring returns of any given tactic. Whereas some situations will merit significant accuracy, in other cases, simple estimates will be sufficient.

To illustrate, consider a few examples. One of our clients is a Fortune 500 manufacturing company that sells its products to businesses and individual consumers through retailers. Because of its size and the ubiquitous nature of its products, its selection of retailers is easy. They sell through virtually every major retailer that sells similar product lines. The company has expected sales based on historical data that is well vetted. If a new retailer emerges, the company can easily, and with relative accuracy, estimate the general level of sales that will result. In this case, the risk of investing resources in the wrong channel is relatively small, so estimates based on historical outcomes are sufficient.

The company also engages in a variety of *point-of-purchase promotions*. Experience has indicated that these programmes are more effective in some environments than in others. Although the cost of the programmes is relatively small compared to the results when invested in a market in which they are successful, investing in the wrong environment would be a significant waste of funds. For this company, the size of the investment and the risk inherent in misapplying promotional dollars make it worthwhile to develop more accurate, fact-based estimates of the potential financial returns the investment might have.

Complex models that accurately forecast outcomes and optimise expenditures dramatically reduce the risk of the company's investment by reducing the money that is invested ineffectively. Of course, these models are not inexpensive. Several hundred thousand dollars can easily be invested in predictive modelling and post-investment assessment. However, for this company, the significant sum that the organisation saves by improving investment decisions through rigorous analysis of anticipated returns is far greater than the incremental cost of the analytics services involved.

However, for a small business, the benefits might not exceed the cost. For example, consider a boutique food distributor that sells specially-blended cheese products through retailers across a region. It, too, uses a retail distribution network and point-of-purchase promotions. However, its sales volume and revenues are small relative to Fortune 500 companies. The complex analytical tool used to deliver information to the larger organisation might provide useful information, but the cost would be disproportionately large when compared to the potential improvement in revenue results. For these organisations, informed estimates based on customer and retailer feedback, along with historical sales data, will probably provide sufficient accuracy in predictive modelling relative to the potential improvements it can make. If the company continues to track investment allocations and outcomes, it will be able to build a simple predictive model for its own point-of-purchase investments over time.

In many cases, companies have operated for years with limited or no tracking of marketing efforts, investments and results. Although they may have historical revenue and profit numbers, marketing expense line items and some recollection of what they have done, reconstructing numbers would be arduous and costly at best and, sometimes, infeasible for all practical purposes. I recently worked with a client whose marketing budget had been divided and merged into a variety of other categories and whose labour costs had been lumped under a general administrative category. Separating these figures to determine what the company had actually spent on marketing and what the impact had been would have been unreasonably costly. The benefits would have been marginal relative to the accuracy the analysis generated. In these cases, it is often best to start anew, assessing what has been done recently and beginning the process of anticipating returns and measuring results in order to improve results.

However, even if a company is completely new to anticipating and measuring marketing returns, it would be foolish to postpone starting this practice. Although establishing metrics, tracking systems and processes might be time consuming, it will become easier with time, and the company's ability to allocate funds effectively—as well as its executives' confidence in the results—will increase.

MEASUREMENT MODELS: SIMPLE TO COMPLEX

Ways of building models to anticipate and measure financial results of marketing activities range from very simple to extremely complex.

The simplest models are designed to ensure plans have been thoroughly vetted before implementation, keep the marketing plan and those who are executing it on track and provide a baseline for future years. These types of models are best for smaller organisations and professional service organisations, companies with simple marketing structures and programmes in which the risk associated with a misstep is minimal.

The most complex models are used to guide resource allocation, provide more accurate financial data for planning purposes, measure outcomes and reward performance. These types of models are best for middle-market and larger organisations, particularly those who serve broad consumer and/or business markets and have extensive marketing data at their disposal. These models are particularly important when the financial investment is substantial, and multiple programmes are running simultaneously.

The best way to illustrate some of the common methods of measurement within the range of options is to use examples. Some are drawn from client experiences, or, as with the other examples in this book, they are fictional, designed to illustrate the case but not intended to be representative of any particular client. They have also been reframed to demonstrate the role a non-marketing manager might play in helping the company effectively assess potential marketing returns.

Case Study #1: Evaluating the Potential Impact of a Website Overhaul

Nick Delacruz, the CEO of Sociedad Española de Fabricación Industrial (SEFI), an industrial equipment manufacturer, meets routinely with his sales team to discuss the status of various customer accounts and how they can improve sales. SEFI is already a leader in its niche field, which serves customers around the world. Most of the customers who have significant need for its products are aware of the equipment it manufactures, and it always makes the short list of manufacturers under consideration.

However, Delacruz wants to tap a broad market of smaller accounts, many of which would purchase only the occasional piece of equipment. Within this category of prospective purchasers, there are a few industries with large groups of potential purchasers, and many purchasers who do not easily fit into a specific product category. At one meeting, the sales team and Delacruz had a lively discussion about barriers to sales, and the sales team was quick to provide input.

'The challenge,' said Juan Perez, the vice president of sales, 'is that customers really doesn't know their options. They know they have a problem, so they do a bit of Internet searching. Sometimes they find our site, sometimes they don't. But even if they do, they may not think we are a good fit.' Perez went on to explain that he, and the other sales people, heard that once a small business prospect landed on the SEFI's site, the company's deep expertise with some of the world's largest manufacturing customers was readily apparent, but it wasn't easy to tell that the manufacturer also served small businesses. As a result, small business customers would leave the site and continue their search.

'It's just not practical to call on them one at a time,' Perez continued. 'Half the time, we get them on the phone and they tell us they saw our site, figured we wouldn't be able to help them and ended up buying something somewhere else. And there are lots of potential customers. They'd be great to have, but calling them one at a time would be very time consuming.'

By the end of the meeting, the sales team and Delacruz had decided that they needed to update their website. The website provided significant leverage to the sales team, both in terms of providing potential examples and identifying prospects before they made a purchase. To be effective, the website had to become more appealing to the small business owner while retaining its appeal to larger customers.

A few weeks later, Delacruz sat at his desk reviewing website design estimates in a state of shock. For the design, development, writing and launch, web design companies were quoting prices that seemed outrageously high. Although it was tempting to revert to easy fixes with their in-house technology team, Carla Rodriguez, the vice president of operations, reminded Delacruz that their current site was the product of that team and the team was busy with other technology priorities. To address Delacruz's concerns, Rodriguez suggested they review the potential returns professional assistance might generate.

In this case, a simple approach was most appropriate. Rodriguez began by reviewing historical performance and forecasting future sales based on the existing marketing mix. Because SEFI had experienced very consistent growth over the past several years, it was easy to predict what the growth was likely to be in the next few years.

Next, Rodriguez reviewed the number of hits received on the current site, looking at where they originated and how they used the site. As it turned out, some of the companies the manufacturer was targeting as customers had looked at the site, but most turned away on the first page. Those who continued looked at just a few pages.

She talked to the sales team and asked them how much time they spent calling on new prospects in these industries in order to estimate the potential time savings. She also asked them to begin asking customers who had already searched for a solution what criteria they had used in their web browser.

Finally, Rodriguez considered the financial impact of an incremental sale on SEFI's profitability. As it turned out, SEFI's margin on the equipment it manufactured was substantial. Most of its expense was in its sales and operational infrastructure not in the incremental cost of another unit. The sale of one additional piece of equipment would easily pay for the website costs.

Sidebar 11-1: Case Study #1: Step by Step

Business Objective and Market: Increase sales to smaller businesses by 15%.

Key Influencer: Small businesses want vendors who serve other small businesses in their industry.

The Barrier: The current website depicts only big companies outside the targeted industries. The website gets hits from small businesses, but most purchase a solution from a competitor. Customer feedback suggests the website is a deterrent. Relying on good timing in cold calls to small businesses is very expensive.

Estimated Returns from Addressing the Barrier: SEFI gets about 800 web hits from qualified small business customers per year. The company's historical win rate on cold calls is 1%. Although the hits are likely to be warm leads, the company estimates on the more conservative 1% rate. Each sale generates profit of $4,000. Executives estimate the website will last 3 years, and cost $45,000 in time, materials and external labor to redevelop.

ROI: Excluding the impact of interest, depreciation and the time value of money, the company estimated the ROI as follows:

> 800 hits × 1% = 8 wins × $4,000 = $32,000 × 3 years = $96,000/$45,000 = 2.13 times the investment or 113% return on the original investment.

Budget to Actual: SEFI will track actual returns by tracking the source of the lead.

To help the CEO understand what she now saw, Rodriguez constructed a financial model demonstrating that if the revised website facilitated the sale of just one additional unit per year, the return on the investment would be in the hundreds of per cents by the end of the three-year measurement period. The sales team, who was even more optimistic about results, believed the returns would be much higher.

Although Rodriguez expected the website to deliver results relatively quickly, she also established intermediate metrics to help monitor the website for potential issues. Rodriguez established tracking and reporting on web hits and the other websites, such as industry organisations, that referred them. She also tracked *conversion rates*, which is the percentage of customers who looked at the website and subsequently requested a call from a sales person. The discussions with her sales and marketing teams led to the identification of several companion promotional efforts that added some cost, but even more dramatically, improved return.

When mapped out in this way, it was clear to Delacruz, the CEO, that investing in a professionally designed website would generate significant financial returns. As you read this case study, it may have been obvious at the very beginning. Why didn't Delacruz immediately make the same leap you did when reading the facts about the market?

There are two reasons he hesitated. First, Delacruz was sceptical about the value of websites and other promotions in general. Other than developing collateral materials, such as specification sheets for the sales team, SEFI had traditionally relied heavily on its sales force to sell its products. This approach was new and, like many CEOs, Delacruz had a nagging fear that the money would be wasted. When Rodriguez demonstrated the potential returns, Delacruz felt more at ease about the solution.

Second, Delacruz was in sticker shock. In his mind, the value of a website redesign was a few thousand dollars. Because web design isn't his business, he didn't understand the complexity of the design, development and writing process and the number of hours that would be required to complete the process. Demonstrating the potential returns helped address this issue.

Delacruz approved the website overhaul, and three months later, the company launched its new site, complete with images of smaller business applications of its equipment, language addressed to the less technical audience and sections dedicated to the industries within which it found the most customers.

Case Study #2: Evaluating the Impact of Changes in Products, Channels and Promotions

In the previous example, the manufacturer was only changing one tactic within one aspect of its marketing mix. However, more often, a company is making a number of changes at once. This is particularly true when the marketing strategy emerges from a time of crisis or change within a company, as it does in this next example.

Several partners from Greeley & Associates, a regional law firm, were talking over lunch at their favourite restaurant. For a while, they reminisced about the firm's glory days. Then, their discussion took a more serious turn. When the firm was founded, 20 years earlier, the first partners were well known in their field, natural rainmakers who brought in all of the firm's business. Now, they were close to retirement, and the company had no clear succession plan in terms of business development. In a professional services environment, this is a placement, or distribution, issue. The partner group, the firm's primary sales channel, wasn't performing as well as required.

'And I don't know what we'll do about the employment law group,' Tony Burns, one of the partners, commented, shaking his head. Greeley & Associates had long been known for its deep expertise in several key areas. Most of their business was generated through referrals from law firms without the required specialty expertise or whose attorneys had conflict issues within their existing client base and were unable to assume responsibility. The service line with poor performance was a generalist practice. Unlike the subject matter experts, this group competed for routine work directly with other firms. This had become quite apparent to attorneys both inside the firm and at the law firms that served as key referral sources to the firm's other practice groups. The result was strained relations, internally and externally, and poor performance due to the lack of available leverage.

'I think we need some marketing help,' Velma Boyle, another partner, finally said. The others agreed. But what kind of marketing? Perhaps a new website? Or an updated logo?

'Whatever we do, it's going to be a hard sell,' Burns warned. The group agreed. The firm's founding *rainmakers* (partners with extensive connections within the legal and business communities), had scoffed at the idea of promoting Greeley & Associates' name and reputation among decision-makers. Because they had a strong reputation and extensive network when they started the firm and were known as subject matter experts among the primary influencers in their business (their peers), they did not see a need for marketing promotions.

Unfortunately, the partners who had been living in the shadows of the rainmakers' success did not have the reputations or relationships their senior partners did. Because Greeley & Associates had always emphasised the success of its founders and made no proactive effort to promote the success of its extremely talented younger partners, the market was less familiar with their capabilities. Younger partners reported uneasily that some clients had been inquiring about the senior partners' retirement dates and asking about their future plans, suggesting that they might be considering their options. This is, of course, a valid concern. Research indicates that when a partner retires, his or her clients are quite likely to consider changing firms, particularly if the more junior attorneys have not been positioned as equally capable of handling their legal needs.

After much discussion, Burns and Boyle asked their marketing department to help them determine what steps to take. The marketing team worked with the partners over the next several months, interviewing partners and clients, reviewing data and facilitating a planning retreat to help them refine the organisation's financial goals. Unlike SEFI, Greeley's marketing efforts had been scattered. They had added and dropped services, launched promotional campaigns and then discontinued them and made efforts to provide business development training and coaching to partners. It took considerable analysis, working hand in hand with the firm's CFO, Anna Hiuuka, to generate forecasts based on previous behaviours.

In the process, the marketing team and partners observed a fourth marketing challenge. Despite the fact that the partners were known for deep subject matter expertise, their billing rates were lower than the market overall. The partners took great pride in their low cost services, but client feedback suggested that this may have contributed to the perception by prospective clients that less senior attorneys were inexperienced. To the market, lower rates didn't mean great value. It meant cheap services, and cheap is rarely associated with exceptional expertise.

Sidebar 11-2: Case Study #2: Step by Step

In this example, components of the plan were evaluated independently.

Practice Group Change

Impact of Practice Group Elimination: The practice's current net revenue contribution is $0. The firm also estimated a negative impact on referred revenue from other firms.

Potential risks: Market perception that the firm is unstable could negatively affect recruitment and retention of talent and clients. Departure of partners could lead to morale issues internally.

Decision: The net impact is close to zero, and the risk is high. The firm will postpone this action until it achieves other objectives.

Pricing Change

Estimated Impact of Billing Rate Change: The firm has 75 attorneys who bill an average of $375,000/year. Market rates are about 20% higher than the firm's existing bill rates. The firm estimated its smallest clients (about 10% of revenues) would leave as a result. The estimated impact is as follows:

$$\$375,000 \times 20\% \times 75 = \$5,625,000 - (10\% \times \$375,000 \times 75) = \$5,625,000 - \$2,812,500 = \$2,812,500 \text{ net impact per year}$$

Potential risks: Raising rates by 20% in one year would cause many existing clients to leave.

Decision: Increase rates to existing clients over 5 years, and immediately to new clients.

Note: Numbers are fictitious to preserve client confidentiality.

The proposed marketing plan developed by the partners and the marketing team contained some very significant changes:

- Spinning off or selling the part of the firm that did not match the company's core value proposition or its existing relationships
- Creating proactive transition plans for clients that would position more junior team members as experts, leaders and primary contacts prior to the retirement of senior partners
- Gradually increasing prices to reflect the value the firm delivered
- Changing the compensation structure to more effectively incentivise and reward new business development
- Supporting partners with a variety of proactive promotional efforts.

Before the plan reached the executive committee, the partners asked the company's CFO, Hiuuka, to take a look at the associated budget and help sell the plan to the leadership team.

Because the recommendations could be taken independently, Hiuuka grouped marketing activities that were related and assessed their potential financial impact as a group.

The service line and pricing changes were the easiest ones to assess. By eliminating the practice group with poor performance, Greeley & Associates would save the costs associated with the salaries of partners and support staff. On the other hand, it would lose the revenue stream associated with the practice. Because the practice had lost more money than it had made, the financial impact of eliminating part of the firm was a net positive.

However, in some cases, such an obvious change can affect other areas of the business. In particular, discontinuing a practice line can affect a firm's perceived stability, making it more difficult to attract and retain top talent, causing clients to question whether the firm is having financial difficulties and prompting referring attorneys to alter their recommendations. After considerable discussion, Hiuuka estimated the negative impact the move might make and developed an anticipated net financial impact.

Because the partners expressed less confidence about the results of these estimates, Hiuuka reduced expectations of the positive impacts of the move to the point that the partners were confident in the likelihood of the outcomes. The net financial impact was still measurable but relatively small. The partners decided to postpone this aspect of the plan until other elements, such as the promotions, could mitigate the risk that the market would react negatively to the change.

The pricing discussion was similar in nature. The proposed increases were gradual and grandfathered in some existing clients. A simple multiplication of the increase in rates over the number of billable hours suggested that the net impact on profitability would be significant. However, Hiuuka knew that many of Greeley & Associates' attorneys had become known for their low cost, rather than their exceptional performance. As a result, clients for whom price was more important than expertise would be likely to leave the firm. Hiuuka reviewed the firm's major clients one by one, assessing the likely impact on their behaviour, and created a model that the partners were confident reflected reality. Although the increase was not as great as it would be if all clients were to remain with the firm, the net impact was still very positive.

Hiuuka assessed the final two aspects of the plan in tandem because they were closely linked. When she asked the partners collectively about the importance of their efforts in developing business, they agreed that most business was generated because of partner efforts. However, independently, many partners seemed to believe that those efforts should or would be made by someone else in the firm.

Culturally, the firm had tolerated poor business development performance among some partners because the senior partners managed to keep the company's pipeline filled with new work. However, those pipelines would undoubtedly dry up when the partners retired, and the culture of tolerance meant little had been done to build business development skills among partners.

In addition, the more junior partners faced a significant image issue. They had spent so long in the shadows of their firm's rainmakers that they were not widely known on their own merits. Fortunately, they had been quite successful independent of the senior partners. This meant that there was much they could say to prospective and existing clients about how their experience would benefit them as clients of the firm. Unfortunately, talking to clients and prospective clients one at a time is costly, especially because the price paid is often in the form of forfeited revenues from other bill opportunities.

To improve their primary sales channel's financial performance, the plan proposed two strategies: improve the way the team was managed relative to business development and provide leverage through increased visibility of individual partners and their success in the marketplace.

Changes in Channel Management and Promotions

Impact of Improved Channel Management and Promotions: Based on partner estimates, each of the firm's 75 partners could add $20,000 in year 1 an incremental $30,000 in year 2 and $45,000 in year 3. Overhead (including salaries) was expected to increase by $3,000 in each of the first two years and $3,500 in the third year, per partner.

Potential risks: The firm had a poor track record of prompting a change in partner behaviour. As a result, it adjusted the expected returns downward by 25%.

Estimated ROI: The estimated change in revenues was $95,000 per partner over the 3-year period. However, the firm anticipated increases in overhead of $9,500 per partner over the same 3-year period. To accommodate risk, the net increase was decreased by 25% as follows: ($95,000 − $9,500) × 75 partners × 75% = $4,809,375

The firm's investments in both channel management and promotions were $525,000 in year 1 and $305,000 in years 2 and 3, totalling $1,135,000 in all.

The estimated ROI was as follows:

$4,809,375 / $1,135,000 = 4.24 times the investment, or 324%

Note: Numbers are fictitious to preserve client confidentiality.

Improving channel management efforts involved structuring incentive-based compensation, adding group training, formalising business development processes and providing individual coaching to partners. The budget for these changes, including the time for partners and staff involved in the process and external consultants, was $340,000 in the first year of the plan and $120,000 for each year thereafter.

To gain leverage, the firm planned to invest in aggressive media relations, small seminars, blogs and a variety of other public relations activities. The estimated cost for this effort, including partner and staff time, costs for materials and costs for external consultants was $185,000 per year for each year of the marketing plan.

Whereas the expenses could be evaluated independently, the outcomes could not. Because the goal of the promotional efforts was to provide leverage to the partners in their business development efforts, the potential returns were dependent on the partners' execution on their business development plans. Similarly, the impact of the partners' business development efforts would be dramatically affected by the promotional efforts involved.

Estimating potential returns took careful consideration. Each partner looked at his or her own record of success, his or her network and the volume of work available and estimated, with the help of the executive team and our firm, what impact an increased focus could have on their revenue streams. On average, the partners estimated that, with focus, each partner could add an additional $20,000 in revenues in the first year, $30,000 in the second and $45,000 in the third year, to their existing performance. Hiuuka compared these estimates with those of similar firms in other geographies and concluded that these estimates were realistic.

Table 11-1 summarizes the financial outcomes expected in conjunction with Greeley & Associates' marketing plan, as calculated by their CFO, Anna Hiukka.

Table 11-1: Anticipated Revenue and Expenses Associated with Greeley & Associates' 3-Year Marketing Plan

	INCREMENTAL REVENUE (FOR 75 PARTNERS)	INCREMENTAL COST OF SERVICES	INCREMENTAL GROSS PROFIT	RISK ADJUSTED GROSS PROFIT (75%)	INCREMENTAL MARKETING EXPENSE
YEAR 1	$1,500,000	$225,000	$1,275,000	$956,250	$525,000
YEAR 2	$2,250,000	$225,000	$2,025,000	$1,518,750	$305,000
YEAR 3	$3,375,000	$262,500	$3,112,500	$2,334,375	$305,000
TOTAL	$7,125,000	$712,500	$6,412,500	$4,809,375	$1,135,000

However, when Hiuuka calculated the net potential impact, she was concerned that the programme might be over-optimistic. Even with focused efforts, altered compensation structures, training and promotional support, she felt that some partners would be likely to fail. For purposes of evaluation, Hiuuka proposed adjusting the calculated outcomes to accommodate the risk of non-compliance. The net anticipated return on investment for these programmes, even after adjustments, was solid at 324%, and she recommended that the partnership approve the plan.

Case Study #3: Increasing Precision Through Analytics

In many respects, small companies and professional service organisations have a significant advantage over larger companies. Because decision-makers are closer to their customers, it is easier to see and understand the impact of specific marketing activities and make decisions as a result.

Middle-market and larger clients tend to be farther from those decision points, with a much larger and more diverse team coordinating a broad range of activities targeted at markets around the world. On the other hand, they typically have the data advantage, particularly if they sell to consumer markets. Middle market and large business-to-consumer companies that sell products either directly or through retail channels often have access to deep stores of sales data that can provide exceptional insight into the outcomes of their marketing activities. The volume of data makes it difficult for a single individual to glance at the numbers and easily spot trends, but more complex analytical models enable companies, or even individual divisions, to make informed marketing allocation decisions and improve the precision with which they measure results. The process is complex, but it yields significant pay off, particularly when investments in channel promotions and selling motion programmes are heavy.

To illustrate, consider the case of the largest global manufacturer of technology components, ABC Technology. This organisation has numerous divisions. One of the largest divisions manufactures products sold to both businesses and independent consumers through brick-and-mortar retailers. To improve sales, the company invests significantly in a variety of point-of-purchase programmes designed to improve the outcomes of specific steps in the purchasing decision process.

The executives at ABC Technology knew that the programmes delivered different returns in different stores, and they suspected there was an optimal investment amount, which probably varied depending on the geography and other factors. Based on experience, they knew that when they invested less than this amount, they would likely forfeit sales to competitors. If they invested more than this amount, the incremental investment would yield less in returns than it would cost to deliver.

Although they had millions of data points about sales and promotional efforts in various retail environments, they had not been successful at determining what the optimal investment level was. In addition, they knew that sales were affected by external factors, such as seasonality in sales, the size and demographics of the geography the store served, as well as other marketing investments, and they were unsure how to isolate those factors from the returns the investments generated so that they were comparing investments on equal terms. Finally, because they were running from one to several programmes in stores, they were also unsure which of the programmes were most effective and how to optimise returns.

Unlike the previous two case studies, the investments ABC Technology was making were very large. How could the company's management team make sure the investments are at the optimal level?

By building complex analytical models.

After reading this case study, you may be wondering how accurate an analytical model can be.

Extremely accurate, as it turns out.

My company constructs models like these on behalf of large organisations that have significant investment risk and big data sources. The models help them determine optimal levels and measure marketing outcomes.

To do so, we use massive regression studies to construct a model that isolates the results of investments made to specific programmes from external factors, such as geography and economy, and from each other. The model was developed using contagion theory, similar to what the Center for Disease Control and Prevention (CDC) uses to anticipate the impact infectious diseases will have on populations. In the CDC's case, its models require the ability to eliminate other factors that might affect public health in order to better understand the true behaviour of a disease. The model we use successfully isolates the impact of a fixed set of point-of-purchase investments in order to understand the impact.

Initially, we used the model to help clients better understand historical performance. Then, we took the process one step further, developing predictive models based on the factors from the optimisation models so that we could accurately forecast sales based on the allocation of dollars to defined selling motions. This allows clients to determine the maximum revenue that would be generated from a specific allocation of funds between programmes and geographies and to optimise that allocation.

In our case, this predictive modelling produces sales forecasts that have been accurate within 3% of actual sales.

Working with marketing, finance and IT professionals, the division's management team developed a model that was able to isolate the outcomes of investments from other external factors and determine how to optimise the returns that could be generated.

Once the tool was developed, they found it had other useful applications. Not only did it help ensure ABC Technology was generating the best possible return on its marketing activities, the management team used it to monitor and compensate vendors on performance. When ABC Technology was ready to introduce new, experimental promotional programmes, the model provided a baseline to analyse impact and helped determine whether the new programmes should be added to the mainline mix of marketing programmes in the future.

Although there is a cost for the development of these types of analytical tools, the benefits are substantial. By optimising investments prior to budget approval, the company avoids poor marketing investments and ensures the optimal results.

This type of approach works best with middle-market and large companies that have significant data regarding sales. Generally, these will be manufacturers whose products have large markets, such as consumer products. However, large consumer service-based organisations, such as restaurant chains or hair salons, might also be able to use sophisticated modelling to improve returns on marketing investments.

RISK ADJUSTMENT

The measurement approach a company selects will depend on the market's decision criteria, the purchasing process, the availability or lack of data, the size of the investment and risk associated with mistakes. In many cases, different models will be used for different aspects of the marketing mix. Whatever the model, there will be some assumptions made, and with those assumptions, varying levels of risk.

There are two ways to mitigate risk associated with assumptions other than building complex analytical models, as in case study # 3. The first is to adjust expected outcomes. To do so, the executive team should ask the team who built the plan and associated financial models about the critical assumptions and their confidence level relative to success. The team can then decide to reduce the expected returns until the team is confident the outcomes are realistic.

Although this, too, entails making assumptions, the process of identifying risk and discussing exposure can both improve planning and cause the financial modelling to become more conservative. With practice, over time, the organisation will become more adept at understanding outcomes, and the financial models will become more accurate.

The second way to mitigate risk is to turn assumptions into facts, or at least stronger assumptions, through formal or informal research or historical performance data. Of course, not all assumptions are risky enough to consider modifying anticipated returns. On the other hand, too many assumptions may indicate that a plan has not been thoroughly evaluated. To determine which assumptions are acceptable and which ones are too risky, use the simple decision tree outlined in figure 11-2.

Figure 11-2: Risk Assessment Decision Tree

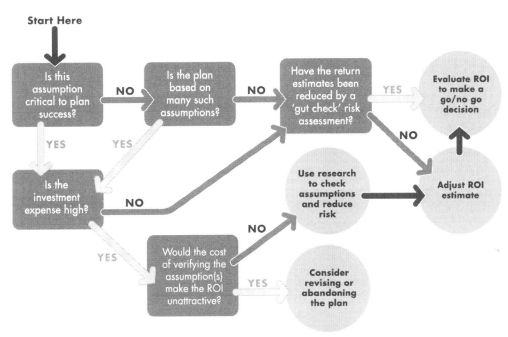

To illustrate, consider a non-profit organisation that is discussing the addition of another development officer for major gifts. A *major gifts officer* is a person who encourages donors to make significant financial gifts to an organisation. These gifts may range from $10,000 to millions of dollars or more, depending on the size and nature of the organisation. In the non-profit world, development officers are part of the placement 'P' of marketing. They are the organisation's sales force.

Let's also assume that the organisation already has two major gift officers. Both were able to develop a certain contribution revenue level within a given time frame. The organisation has a long list of potential donors that they can't nurture because they are too busy. The organisation assumes that an experienced new hire with the right qualifications can bring in at least 80% of that same amount within three years.

Let's say you are evaluating the risk based on the risk assessment decision tree in figure 11-2. Starting at the top left of the decision tree, is that assumption critical? Yes. Is the investment expense high? Let's assume that, relative to other investments in marketing this organisation is making, this investment is small. No, the investment expense isn't high.

Have you 'gut-checked' the returns? Yes—it's reasonable to assume they could do the same, but to account for some doubt, or risk, you've downgraded the estimated returns to 80%. In this case, the executive team can simply evaluate the expected return on investment (ROI) and make its funding decision. However, if the results had not been adjusted based on confidence, this process may have prompted an evaluation of confidence, resulting in an adjusted ROI.

Now, let's assume that this is a material investment for this particular non-profit. In this case, the organisation may want to try to reduce its risk. There are several ways it could do this. It could conduct research about what makes a major gift officer successful in their organisation, and perhaps, increase the pre-employment testing or evaluation process for candidates to make sure it hired a person with the right skills and experience. It could also do some market research to understand how big the market of major donors is, whether the organisation appeals to their interests and what might influence donor decisions. If the cost of mitigating significant risks changes the investment portion of the equation enough that the ROI is no longer attractive, then the organisation might consider abandoning the plan.

If the executive team is so confident in its assumptions that it doesn't consider any single assumption to be critical, it should consider whether the number of assumptions overall is too large. If so, they may want to consider the potential risk of the assumptions overall, rather than individually.

RETURN ON MARKETING INVESTMENT

Many non-marketing managers object to the term ROI as it applies to investments in marketing, largely because marketing expenditures are less frequently associated with fixed or tangible assets. ROI, they argue, can only be associated with a long-term investment, such as the purchase of a building or piece of equipment. However, this argument fails in two ways.

First, in many ways, marketing is a long-term investment. From product development timelines, to the amount of time it takes to generate returns on marketing investments, marketing is often a long-term investment with an even longer-term payoff.

Second, marketing is the hidden assumption in almost every other financial model. When a company estimates the potential revenue associated with a new facility, it assumes that the products produced there will sell, an idea driven by marketing.

Unfortunately, this resistance to measuring marketing outcomes in financial terms is often welcomed by marketers, who often have less experience creating the financial models required to assess impact.

At the same time, marketers have been under greater pressure to demonstrate the impact of their activities on a company's financial performance. As a result, they created a new term, *return on marketing investments* (ROMI), which is an effort to acknowledge the difference between investing in a tangible asset and investing in marketing activities while still providing financial measurement of value.

The calculation is the same as it is for ROI. ROMI is defined as a percentage and is generally considered to be the net revenues attributable to marketing efforts divided by the marketing expenditures required to generate those returns. It is expressed as a number of times the investment is made, or a 1 is subtracted from the results in order to translate it into a percentage format. Written as a formula, ROMI is expressed as follows:

$$\text{ROMI} = \frac{[\text{Incremental Revenue Attributed to Marketing} \times \textit{Contribution Margin Percentage}]}{\text{Marketing Investment}}$$

In this format, the number would be expressed as the number of times the investment is returned. For example, if a company expects to sell $100,000 in widgets, from which it generates incremental revenue of 20%, and will spend $10,000 to do so, the ROI is expressed as follows:

$$\text{ROMI} = \frac{[\$100,000 \times 20\%]}{\$10,000} = \frac{\$20,000}{\$10,000} = 2.0 \text{ times return on investment}$$

More frequently, ROMI is expressed as a percentage. To accomplish this, the marketer either subtracts the dollar amount of the marketing investment from the numerator or subtracts 1 from the outcome. For example:

$$\text{ROMI (\%)} = \frac{[(\$100,000 \times 20\%) - \$10,000]}{\$10,000} = \frac{\$10,000}{\$10,000} = 1.0 = 100\%, \text{ or}$$

$$\text{ROMI (\%)} = \frac{[\$100,000 \times 20\%]}{\$10,000} = \frac{\$20,000}{\$10,000} = 2.0 - 1.0 = 1.0 = 100\%$$

These are the same formulas used to express ROI.

Some marketing professionals argue that ROMI underestimates the long-term impact on the company because it is more difficult to measure the long-term impact of brand awareness or other benefits of marketing. Although brand awareness is an important outcome of many marketing initiatives, it is an intermediate metric. Awareness only has value to the extent that it contributes to financial outcomes. If a company is no longer in business, it does not matter how many people recognise its name. Those marketing dollars have not produced an impact. In addition, brand awareness fades if not sustained over time with additional marketing investments.

Greater levels of brand awareness can increase the anticipated return rates on marketing investments because the products or services they promote will be more readily accepted by the market. However, because the manager calculating incremental revenue is doing so based on his or her understanding of his or her company's market and the potential impact given their existing brand awareness and market penetration, the impact of brand is already accounted for in the calculations.

Whether a company uses ROMI or ROI as its favoured term is irrelevant. In either case, understanding the anticipated return on marketing-related investments can help an organisation make informed investment decisions, both relative to specific marketing activities and to investments in other aspects of its operations.

QUESTIONS FOR NON-MARKETING MANAGERS TO ASK ABOUT MEASUREMENT AND RETURNS

- What return do you expect on this investment? Over what time period?

- How confident are you that we will achieve these returns? What are the greatest risks associated with the plan? What would cause the plan to fail to achieve the anticipated outcome?

- What assumptions are built into the financial modelling of returns? How significant are they relative to the plan's success?

- How will the outcomes be affected if we have a serious economic downturn or other unforeseen event?

- If we have another dollar to allocate to marketing expenditures, where would you invest it in order to generate the maximum return?

- What alternative investments were considered?

- What would happen if we removed a tactic in which we've invested historically? What would we anticipate the impact to be, and over what timeline?

- How will you track progress against the plan to ensure we are on track?

- How does this investment compare with other marketing investments we have made and are making? Does this investment contribute to or enhance other programmes? When adding this investment into the basket of marketing investments we are making, does our overall return go up or down?

CHAPTER 11 SUMMARY

Many executives consider marketing to be more art than science, eluding measurement as a result. I call this the Measurement Myth, and it is both untrue and a sign of poor marketing management. Carefully anticipating financial returns on proposed marketing plans and ensuring that the company has the required systems in place to track outcomes is the final step in the process of evaluating proposed investments in the marketing function.

Financial returns on marketing investments can, and should, be measured at least twice in the marketing process: in anticipation of expenditures (prior to approving the budget) and after the outcomes have been achieved. Many companies measure ROI, or ROMI, more frequently.

Although many companies measure marketing after the investment has been made, or at least try to do so, measuring in anticipation of the investment is even more important. Anticipating returns

- facilitates monitoring;

- facilitates comparison;

- minimises poor investment decisions;

- improves the effectiveness of using intermediate metrics to track progress against plan objectives;

- improves the accuracy of intermediate and retrospective measurements; and

- encourages communication among internal groups about organisational objectives.

A variety of models can be used to anticipate outcomes for all types of marketing efforts. The selection of the model will be made based on the type of business, the size of the market, the availability of historical data, the risk associated with the investment decisions and a variety of other factors. Although all models contain assumptions, assumptions represent risk, and the quantity and significance of those assumptions should be considered when assessing potential financial returns. Because the time frame for experiencing results will vary from one marketing activity to another, the non-marketing manager should work closely with the marketing team to establish a realistic timeline for the returns and the investment.

The most common financial ratio used to assess returns on investments is ROI. Marketers often use a variation on this metric, ROMI, or *return on marketing investment*. However, the math is the same. In either case, ROI and ROMI are calculated as follows:

$$RO[M]I = \frac{[\text{Incremental Revenue Attributed to Marketing} \times \textit{Contribution Margin Percentage}]}{\text{Marketing Investment}}$$

Section 4

MANAGING MARKETING OPERATIONS

12

WHY DO GOOD PLANS FAIL?

Market leaders generate better returns on marketing investments because they manage marketing differently than average performers. They do this in three ways.

First, their management teams are obsessed with understanding and serving the market, and their insatiable curiosity gives them better insight. This insight produces the *Crystal Ball Effect*, an improved ability to accurately anticipate what the market needs and how to communicate effectively with them. Companies that haven't cultivated a culture of curiosity about their market can improve their effectiveness by aggressively identifying assumptions about what influences their success and turning them into facts through research or improved market focus.

Second, market leaders view the purpose of marketing and other operational activities differently. Many average performers 'do' marketing to drive sales. For them, marketing (Point A), results in sales (Point B). By contrast, market leaders align everything they do (Point A), with their desire to provide exceptional solutions to the customer, (Point B). Serving the market better than anyone else is what produces superior returns. For market leaders, financial results are Point C, the outcome of the effective alignment between marketing activities and the market's needs. Companies that don't share market leaders' adherence to the *Point C Principle*, the internal mandate to align everything they do with market needs, can enjoy the benefits of alignment by using the Marketing Alignment Map to evaluate marketing plans.

Basing plans on facts and aligning marketing activities with the market are the first two keys to improving marketing returns in any company. When a company pursues both consistently, it can produce a focused marketing plan with financial returns that exceed industry averages.

Of course, many average performers do both of these things well. In fact, it is not uncommon for companies to produce extremely well-constructed, thorough marketing plans. Yet, many will still fail to produce optimum results. Why is that?

Why do good plans fail?

Because they are missing the third marketing behaviour of market leaders: systematic execution. These plans most often fail simply because they are never completed.

I call this the *Tortoise Law*, and I'll explain why.

The remainder of this chapter will address the various ways in which organisations abandon their marketing efforts, the common causes that drive the behaviour and some of the proactive ways a company can avoid losing the marketing race.

THE TORTOISE LAW

Most people are familiar with Aesop's fable about the tortoise and the hare. The confident hare boasts that he can win any race against his notoriously slow opponent. He shoots out of the gate, quickly leaving the tortoise in the distance behind him. However, at some point, he stops. He stops running the race, pausing instead to take a nap. By the time he resumes the race, the tortoise is within easy reach of the finish line. The hare races to the best of his abilities to beat him, but the tortoise finishes before he can do so. The steady plodding of the tortoise bested the erratic speed of the hare.

Marketing investments are frequently made in erratic spurts, not unlike the hare's approach to the race. Money is poured into the marketing budget when the economy booms or the executive team wants improved sales results. Unfortunately, most marketing investments take some time to succeed. By the time the executive team instructs the marketing team to move quickly, the market leaders are crossing the finish line.

That's because market leaders follow the Tortoise Law. They invest in marketing steadily over time, doggedly pursuing their business and financial objectives. Unlike the hare, market leaders don't take a break to rest when the economy turns downward or shift directions in response to the competitive environment. Market leaders are steadfastly focused on Point C, and they make steady investments in marketing energy and effort until they reach it.

One of the market leader executives interviewed explained his approach to marketing efforts quite succinctly. In economic booms, he said, everyone invests. No single voice is heard well from among the din of competition. Market leaders continue to invest in marketing during economic booms because they understand it is the lifeblood of their organisation, but that is not when they generate the most benefit from their investment.

The greatest benefit, he explained, comes from marketing investments during economic downturns. That's because most companies slash marketing budgets to sustain or improve profitability. Like the hare, they take a break from the competitive fray. But not the market leader.

The market leader knows that this is when the market will be most able to hear what the company has to say. It is during economic downturns that market leaders acquire market share from their sleeping competitors. Then, when the market rebounds, their profitability soars. This longer-term focus on the finish line, rather than the short-term focus on competitive activity or the bottom line, pays off when market leaders finish in first place.

Intuitively, most clients understand the Tortoise Law. When I talk to them about investing in longer-term strategies, it makes sense to them. If this is the case, why are so many average performers still taking naps during the race?

There are a number of reasons, and they typically manifest in one of three ways. First, the company's executive team makes a deliberate decision to discontinue investing in the plan they had previously approved. Second, the company simply fails to carry out the plan, and it simply drifts away from its investment commitment. Finally, the company finds itself unable to execute and is forced to discontinue its marketing activities.

WHY COMPANIES VOLUNTARILY ABANDON THEIR PLANS

Many companies go through the process of developing a marketing plan, executing it and then discontinue funding it. Many companies do this in response to tightening budgets or other financial constraints. When they are considering how they can trim expenses, marketing and human resources typically top the list. However, sometimes companies deliberately change paths for other reasons.

The most common reasons companies voluntarily abandon an otherwise well-constructed and previously approved marketing plan are addressed in the following paragraphs.

Lack of Executive Commitment

The most common reason that marketing plans are intentionally abandoned is because the executives who approved the plan and corresponding budget were not committed to its execution, either because they didn't see the investment as important or because they never fully understood how the company would benefit when they approved it.

Several years ago, I worked with a regional construction firm's marketing and operations team, including their president, to help them construct a marketing plan. We used the Marketing Alignment Map and carefully identified key customer decision process factors we wanted to influence and estimated return. In order to facilitate execution, we identified, recruited and helped them hire an experienced marketing manager to oversee execution.

After about six months, I called the marketing manager to see how she was progressing on the plan. She said she wasn't. The CEO, who had not been involved in the planning process and who had previously approved the plan, had been talking with a friend who told him the future in marketing was all about social media. When he returned to the office, he told the marketing manager to discontinue several of the more substantial portions of the plan and reallocate the funding to a social media manager his friend had recommended. The other components of the plan, which were designed to work together, were virtually useless independently, and the manager was scrambling to deliver some returns on the CEO's newly found marketing passion.

This is a common outcome when an executive is not involved in the planning process. In some cases, this can be averted if the executive team is integrally involved in marketing planning. Because they are engaged in the planning discussions, they understand how the components work together, have the opportunity to voice concerns or make suggestions early in the process and have a better understanding of the expected outcomes.

When it is not practical for the executive team to participate in the development of marketing strategies, they should at least take the time to thoroughly understand how the strategies and tactics will affect outcomes and over what time frame. Before the plan is approved, every executive should be able to connect the dots between the market's needs and the company's goals, the marketing strategies and related tactics and the expected financial returns.

Leadership Changes

A large not-for-profit organisation once retained me to help them develop a marketing and development plan and corresponding budget to help guide the organisation while they were seeking a new development director. Because we knew a new development director would bring his or her own preferred approach to the table, the plan was relatively short, just 18 months long, which emphasised the continuity of successful programmes, gradual discontinuation of programmes with low or negative returns and relatively few additions. It was designed to span the length of time that the position was open, plus the first few months of the development director's tenure.

Happily, the organisation was able to identify, recruit and hire the new development director more quickly than anticipated. Unfortunately, she decided to abandon the plan, working from scratch to create a new one.

Although the ultimate results were very similar, the time she spent reworking her plan had the same effect as the nap in the tale of the tortoise and the hare. Nothing happened during the transition.

Leadership changes in marketing or in the management team are often unavoidable. To avoid a negative outcome, the remaining team should clearly communicate both its expectations about the new leader's commitment to the existing plan and the logic behind its development.

Failure to Plan for Change

Sometimes, a plan is deliberately abandoned because it failed to accommodate for changes in the economic or competitive environment. This is often the reason plans are abandoned during economic downturns. During the planning process, no one thought to ask what would happen if the economy suddenly began to sag.

To prevent the need to slash marketing budgets during economic downturns, the executive team, and particularly the financial team, should ask what might happen if the company's financial resources were more constrained, or, conversely, if the company found that it had more funds available. By preparing both best and worst case scenarios as a part of the planning process, the executive team can be confident that the plan would accommodate economic change.

Marketing plans should also include funding for unexpected opportunities. I once worked with a manufacturing company whose executives wanted to aggressively grow market share. As we developed their marketing plan, we deliberately allocated funds to 'unexpected opportunities,' which we agreed might include acquisition opportunities, previously unidentified channel opportunities or technology-driven product innovation opportunities. The expectation was not that these funds would be spent. Instead, we wanted to make sure they would not have to discontinue part of, or its entire, existing marketing plan in order to pursue potentially lucrative, but previously unidentified, activities.

Planning ahead for potential changes, both good and bad, can help a company avoid abandoning an existing plan before it delivers returns.

No Evidence of Progress

The loose use of the word *marketing* to describe sales has the distinct disadvantage of leading some executives to believe that marketing delivers immediate financial returns in the form of increased revenues. Although this may occasionally be true, it is more common for marketing investments to deliver returns over an extended period, frequently beyond the timeline for the investment itself. For example, investments in product innovations will not pay off until the product is actually purchased by a defined number of customers. Advertising, and many other promotional investments, must be made continually over a period of 12–18 months in order to generate a payoff, and the associated revenues will continue to be recognised after the advertising run is complete.

> Marketing is not a short-term investment. It is a longer-term strategy.

Unfortunately, this delay in revenue impact causes some impatient executives to second guess their strategies, especially when profitability sags due to upfront investments. If they do abandon the marketing plan, they are often abandoning much of the investment they made before generating any return. This is part of what has caused marketing to develop a murky reputation for dubious returns.

Marketing is not a short-term investment. It is a longer-term strategy. To prevent frustrated executives from cutting funding before the investments can generate a return, the marketing plan should include both clear financial projections regarding required investments and the timeline for expected returns and intermediate metrics, often non-financial in nature, that can help provide reassurance that the plan is on track.

Executive Distrust

Finally, many executives abandon marketing plans before they have delivered a return because they do not trust that marketing will deliver a financial return. They see marketing expenditures as highly speculative and, when funds are tight, the most appropriate expenses to cut.

Unfortunately, marketers often do little to reassure them. Often unversed in the financial language used by executives, many marketers, particularly in smaller organisations, are ill-equipped to provide the type of financial analysis that usually accompanies recommended investments in other aspects of operations. In addition, marketers are often resistant to being held accountable for results. This isn't entirely surprising because marketers are typically only one portion of the equation. In order for marketers to be successful, the product or service must be produced and delivered to the customer's satisfaction. Other portions of operations are often out of the control of the marketing team.

In order to address this type of distrust, executives, particularly finance and operations executives, must work with marketers to complete the appropriate analysis and identify other aspects of operations that must be coordinated in order to generate the anticipated results.

WHY COMPANIES DRIFT AWAY FROM THEIR PLANS

Whereas some companies intentionally abandon their plans, others simply drift away. It's not that they weren't interested in executing it. They thought it was a good plan when they approved it, and when they discover the binder on their shelf two years later, they wonder why it was never executed.

In fact, it might even be difficult to determine exactly how the company got off track. Often, the company starts with great enthusiasm, but then, slowly, everything reverts to the way things were before the plan was approved. There are several common reasons this happens.

Lack of Executive Commitment

The same lack of executive commitment that can cause an executive to slash or eliminate budgets can cause other executives to drift off course. However, when companies drift off course, the lack of executive commitment is less about deliberately questioning previously approved plans and more often about a pursuit of the latest shiny marketing object. In these cases, the executive isn't necessarily telling his or her subordinates to discontinue acting on the plan. More often, he or she heard about something exciting or new or have seen something a competitor is doing, and he or she wants the marketing team to add it to the mix.

However, very few organisations operate with significant excess capacity, especially relative to marketing activities. When the executive returns with his or her newest idea, he or she adds it to a very full plate of activities, and something else is pushed off as a result. Sometimes, the most senior marketing person simply makes a prioritisation decision independently. Other times, more junior staff responsible for execution and faced with time constraints simply set aside something already on their plate to make room for the executive's new pet project.

Consider a large health care system that wanted to improve its marketing department's efficiency. My company was engaged to conduct a time and motion study and recommend improvements to its operations. As we dove into the project, we found projects that were not within the organisation's existing marketing plan. For example, one physician, the head of one of the major departments at the hospital, had asked the design team to put together an invitation for his daughter's school's auction. Although this project alone may not have been enough to force reprioritisation of the workload, it wasn't the only one. In fact, the department was handling dozens of special projects, including brochures and other promotional materials deliberately excluded from the organisation's marketing plan during the planning process. Because the physicians were considered by the marketing department to be their superiors within the management structure, the marketing team members who had been asked to comply were reluctant to refuse.

To help the organisation address this issue, a change order process was designed that gave employees a more formal means of establishing priorities and dramatically reduced the number of extraneous requests. The change order process required that requests outside the plan be presented in writing, along with a budget for time and materials. The request then needed to be approved not only by the person asked to perform the work but also by department management. As a result, the number of project requests dropped, and the management team was better able to evaluate true unexpected opportunities.

In general, organisations can reduce the likelihood that the marketing plan will slide off course by

- creating a similar change order procedure;
- creating a process for evaluating and funding new activities that takes into account both labour and material costs; and
- monitoring progress and investigating departures from planned activities.

Poor Accountability

Often, no one is holding the team accountable for performance. To illustrate this point, consider what happened to a professional services firm. The marketing plan developed and approved by the partner group at a strategic planning retreat included a strong business development (sales) component requiring the participation of its partners. In particular, the plan involved developing personal business development plans for each partner, focusing on the expansion of business among existing clients and the development of new prospective client relationships. Once the plans were completed, the marketing team would pull the common elements from all the plans and create cohesive programmes that would provide leverage to the partners in the sales process.

Unfortunately, no one held the partners accountable. The marketing team tried. They stopped by the partners' offices, asking, imploring, begging, demanding and otherwise attempting to influence their behaviour. But the marketing team members aren't partners, and they had little influence on compliance. The managing partner might have had more impact, but he was simply too distracted with his own work. He meant to follow up but never quite made it to his partners' offices to ask. The initial momentum from the planning retreat began to fizzle.

Without the individual marketing plans, the marketing team could not do its share of the work. They couldn't sit around doing nothing, so instead, they, too, reverted to old behaviours. Within six months, it felt as if the firm had never created a plan at all. Nothing had changed.

Accountability issues are serious and a common reason for poor performance in many organisations. To improve accountability, the non-marketing executive should focus on more than just asking subordinates to do their jobs. They should

- **clearly communicate expectations relative to performance, so that each member of the team knows exactly what they must be doing and why it is important.** By communicating clearly and repeatedly about the benefit of the marketing investments a company is making, executives can inspire accountability among those whose compliance is required for successful execution. These communications should be very clear about expectations. Too often, we find that the executive team thought it was clear, and its subordinates all believed someone else would be completing the task. As a result, nothing moved forward.

- **address any internal barriers to satisfactory performance.** If one group's process depends on timely execution by another team and that other team does not perform, it will be difficult to hold the waiting team accountable for its performance. The executive team should proactively identify and address potential barriers to marketing success.

- **ensure evaluation and reward systems reflect the company's priorities.** The old adage that we get what we measure is as true in human resource management as it is in marketing management. If a company's performance evaluation and compensation programmes do not reflect the importance of marketing to the company's success, individuals will continue to prioritise other activities over newly-added marketing activities.

- **refuse to tolerate dissent after agreement.** Sometimes, especially in professional services environments, team members will agree to an approach while in a planning retreat with their peers, allowing their silence to be perceived as agreement. Then, after the meeting has concluded and the plan has been approved, they will quietly dissent, ignoring the agreement that has been made and continuing their previous behaviours. In other cases, they will quietly express their disapproval to like-minded parties, building up steady resistance to activity until they become a solid barrier to progress. In either case, this behaviour is disruptive and disrespectful, and it should not be tolerated by the executive team.

- **establish a schedule for progress reports.** Having a fixed schedule for progress updates, along with defined metrics at each stage, helps keep the team focused and improves accountability.

Incremental Changes

Sometimes, communications about marketing plans resemble the children's game of Telephone. An executive asks the vice president of marketing to tackle a project. Because it's not clearly spelled out, and both the executive and vice president believe they know what the other means, the vice president communicates a different message to the communications director. By the time it reaches the fourth or fifth person, the entire intent or scope of the project may have changed.

Although this example may be more extreme than is often the case, the problem is not uncommon. It is especially common in organisations with multiple reporting layers, when junior level team members are uninformed about the broader strategic objectives of the company's marketing plan and when external agencies or consultants are used, because they may or may not have a complete understanding of the company's market or marketing plan.

To prevent incremental changes from pulling a plan off course, companies should

- make sure the marketing plan is in writing, reducing the risk that the original intent will be changed;

- include enough detail that the plan cannot be misinterpreted by successors or subordinates;

- exercise particular care when communicating about projects, anticipated outcomes and key requirements with agencies and other vendors;

- ensure that the company's staff has the skills and resources available to complete the tasks as outlined in the plan, which will reduce the likelihood an individual will adjust the plan to match his or her own capabilities; and

- establish metrics to monitor progress and identify potential drift before the plan is significantly off course.

WHY COMPANIES INVOLUNTARILY ABANDON THEIR PLANS

Some companies with well-aligned, market-based plans fail to execute because they are forced to abandon them. Unlike companies who deliberately abandon their plans, these companies must change plans because they simply cannot execute the marketing plan as approved. The most common reasons organisations involuntary abandon their plans are included in the following paragraphs.

Inadequate Staffing

The most common reason companies are forced to abandon or rewrite their marketing plan is because they failed to plan accurately for the required human resources. This may be because they do not take the time during the planning process to create estimates for the time required for each tactic and related step. It is also common for both marketing professionals and marketers to underestimate the amount of time required to complete a task.

As a consultant, I see this first hand when we hire new team members. After sitting down with a prospective client to discuss a project, I will often ask the most junior team member in our company to create the budget. In most cases, even a team member with extensive experience as an in-house marketing professional will dramatically underestimate the time required to complete the work. Most people are optimistic about how quickly they can accomplish a task and forget about the time required to set it up and wrap it up, as well as the extra time associated with scheduling or collaboration.

The same problem occurs inside organisations. Marketing plans and budgets often exclude a detailed breakdown by skill set or staff member of the amount of staff time that will be required. When they do, the estimates are generally low. For example, a marketing communicator might estimate that the time required to write a specification sheet will be four hours. However, this excludes the time to conduct the interview with the product manager, the marketing director's time to review the document and the time required to manage printing and upload the final document to shared network drives.

As a result, the marketing communicator commits to the project, assuming it will take just four hours, only to find it is closer to seven. The marketing director also has another hour of unanticipated work on his or her plate. Although these numbers are small, when they are multiplied across hundreds or thousands of projects, the impact is significant.

A related challenge emerges when heavily leveraged resources decide to leave the company. In some companies, turnover among marketing staff is quite high. In one industry within which I work, the average tenure of a marketing professional is about nine months. The volume of work he or she is asked to do by non-marketing executives who have no sense of the time required to accomplish these tasks results in burnout, and the ensuing turnover wreaks even more havoc on the marketing plan.

To avoid this problem, I recommend creating an operating plan for the marketing plan before approval. The operating plan should include a detailed breakdown of who is responsible for which activities and the deadline for completion. It should also include a breakdown of the time required to complete each task, totalled by employee, so that the workload is manageable for all current team members. If new employees are added, this approach also allows more accurate assessments of the type of staffing that might be required: temporary, contract, agency, part-time employee or full-time employee.

Failure to Anticipate Significant Changes

Some companies are forced to abandon their marketing plans for reasons entirely outside of their control: a natural disaster, the death of an owner or some other dramatic change. However, many times, companies are forced to abandon their marketing plans because a more predictable change occurred that left them without the financial resources required to continue execution.

For example, the United States has experienced an economic recession about every ten years for more than a century. Economic downturns are not only a normal economic occurrence, they are relatively predictable. Market leaders not only anticipate economic downturns, they plan for them. After all, they see those periods as times of marketing opportunity.

Unfortunately, most companies fail to plan for economic downturns. Then, when a downturn occurs, they find themselves without the resources to continue normal operations and no reserves upon which to draw. As they scramble for financial dry ground, they abandon every discretionary 'weight' on their operations. Typically, the first among them are human resources and marketing expenditures.

This is short-sighted in more than one way. First, it abandons any outcomes that might have been generated on sunk cost marketing investments. Second, and perhaps more importantly, it eliminates the company's ability to enjoy the growth in market share that can be the result of decreased marketing competition. On the other hand, this isn't a voluntary choice. The company undoubtedly faces significant financial pressure. Unless some expenses are eliminated, the company may suffer even more dramatically as a result.

At the same time, this problem can often be avoided. I recognise that it is exceptionally difficult for many small businesses, including start-ups, and companies with narrow margins. However, businesses that are no longer in those vulnerable first years should be able to begin anticipating, and even building, financial reserves to protect against shifts in economic conditions.

In many cases, proactively anticipating what would happen if the company experienced a dramatic shift can allow the company to build contingencies into the existing plan. This has several benefits. First, it allows the company to sustain critical marketing initiatives, remaining on plan in some sense, while preserving its financial viability. Second, it conveys a sense of assurance to both employees and the market during times of uncertainty. Finally, it reduces the possibility that reductions will be made in haste, without appropriate reflection about which remaining mix investments will deliver the greatest returns.

Failure to Anticipate Opportunities

Similarly, some organisations are forced to abandon marketing plans midway because they fail to proactively plan for opportunities. This is especially common in small organisations in which a given opportunity is likely to consume a greater portion of available dollars. For example, consider a restaurant chain that hosted a popular wine tasting celebration at one of its locations. The company had a strict planning and budgeting process and managed its finances closely. After the budget had been approved, one of my colleagues identified a unique partnership opportunity that could yield significant exposure and dramatically increase event revenues. Although the potential was significant, it would require additional expenses not originally anticipated.

Companies that have limited reserves or whose marketing plans contain limited flexibility might have been forced to abandon the plan, rewriting it to accommodate the new opportunity or to pass on the proposed partnership. Fortunately, the restaurant chain was not in this position. They had reserves allocated for just such opportunities and criteria for evaluating opportunities to determine when and if the reserves should be used.

Other companies with no funding available for reserves use a different approach. They determine, before the plan is approved, which activities could be eliminated in a downturn or during other financial challenges and use the same list when considering unexpected opportunities. They evaluate the new opportunity against pre-established criteria and make the substitution determination based on comparative returns.

By anticipating opportunity as well as challenges, organisations can respond more fluidly to changing situations without completely abandoning their marketing commitments.

QUESTIONS FOR NON-MARKETING MANAGERS TO ASK ABOUT KEEPING A PLAN ON TRACK

In order to win the marketing race, organisations should be consistent and focused in their efforts. The most successful companies follow the Tortoise Law, mimicking the deliberate, consistent, focused approach of the tortoise, rather than the erratic behaviour of the hare from Aesop's famous tale. To successfully apply the Tortoise Law, non-marketing executives should carefully consider the following questions before approving a marketing plan:

- Is the executive team able to articulate why the company is investing in specific marketing activities, and what return is anticipated as a result?

- If we needed to cut budgets, how would this affect the plan? Have we planned for this situation? What would the impact be on outcomes?

- If we had another dollar to allocate to marketing, how would it be used and what incremental return would be realised?

- Do we have a process to evaluate unexpected opportunities? How would we identify and fund such an opportunity?

- How can we tell that the plan is on track?

- What other aspects of our operations need to change or be adjusted in order for the plan to be a success?

- How will we handle proposed changes to the plan?

- How will we monitor work product managed by external vendors?

- How will we communicate with internal audiences about the plan? Is there anyone from whom we expect resistance? If so, how will we prevent actions that will derail the plan?

- Have the individuals to whom responsibilities for activities are assigned accepted those responsibilities? Do they have the skills and time available to complete them?

- Do we anticipate any significant leadership changes? If so, how do we ensure that the plan remains intact?

- Under what circumstances would it be appropriate to abandon the plan?

- How did we estimate the staffing required to execute the plan? Will we need to add any additional team members?

CHAPTER 12 SUMMARY

Market leaders listen to their markets and align their marketing function with their desire to deliver better solutions to those markets. These two behaviours help them develop solid marketing plans. However, they distinguish themselves from other companies that have developed solid plans by exhibiting a steadfast commitment to marketing, in good times and in bad. I call this the Tortoise Law because, like the focused, consistent winner of the race between the tortoise and the hare, the market leaders' consistent investment and execution of marketing plans is a key reason they are the winners of the competitive race.

Average performers don't do this. Like the hare, their performance is erratic. They tend to develop plans but fail to complete them. Because of the nature of marketing, which requires sustained investment to optimise returns, they abandon any potential benefit they may have gained and have less money to invest in subsequent initiatives.

The reasons these companies have problems consistently executing their plans are the same reasons they fail on other strategic planning initiatives. These include poor communication, lack of commitment, poor accountability, incomplete planning, inflexibility in the face of obstacles or opportunities, insufficient or inexistent metrics to measure progress, operational barriers and mixed messages about priorities.

To address these issues, it is helpful to understand the common reasons plans are abandoned and address them proactively.

In some cases, plans are voluntarily abandoned after they are approved. The reasons this happens include the following:

- **Lack of commitment from the executive team.** To address this, managers should involve the CEO in plan development, whenever possible, and ensure all executive team members can connect the dots between plan activities, objectives and anticipated business and financial outcomes.

- **Leadership changes.** Although management changes are inevitable, careful communications about why a plan was developed can help a new team member remain committed to the plan.

- **Failure to plan for changes.** Situations do change. The economy booms or sags, unexpected opportunities arise and competitors' behaviours threaten current plans. The most effective plans incorporate contingency plans and funds to allow companies to sustain forward momentum while addressing these shifts.

- **No evidence of progress.** Sometimes, executives cut funding because they don't see progress. To avoid this situation, managers should ensure the plan includes a clear timeline for success and defined intermediate metrics that help assure the executive team the plan is on track.

- **Executive distrust.** Executives sometimes cut funding because they don't understand the value marketing delivers. Companies can avert this cause of abandonment by ensuring complete and appropriate financial analysis took place and was shared with the executive team prior to plan approval.

In other cases, companies simply drift away from their plans. The reasons this happens include the following:

- **Lack of commitment from the executive team.** In this case, the lack of commitment manifests as internally-mandated changes to marketing plans that are not consistent with its strategies. To avoid these issues, a solid change order management process, along with a process for evaluating newly proposed activities and a means of monitoring progress on existing commitments, can help keep the plan on track.

- **Poor accountability.** This leads to a lack of performance and can be prevented with clear and consistent communications about the plan's value and associated performance expectations, evaluation and reward programmes that reinforce the importance of execution and routine reporting that highlights executive commitment and dissuades dissent.

- **Incremental changes to the plan.** Plans often drift off course because the company inadvertently changes the original intent. To prevent this, plans should be in writing, with adequate staffing an established intermediate metrics.

Finally, some companies are forced to abandon their plans. This is often because of the following:

- **Inadequate staffing.** Many times, an organisation's plan fails for human resource reasons. They do not have enough staff or the right skills on hand. To prevent this, marketing plans should include operations plans for staffing that forecast human resource needs.

- **Failure to anticipate changes.** As noted previously, situations do change. Established companies can often avert a negative impact by building reserves. Companies of any size should build contingency plans into their marketing programmes.

- **Failure to anticipate opportunities.** Sometimes, a plan is abandoned because what appears to be a better opportunity arises. This issue can also be averted with careful planning.

13

STAFFING THE MARKETING DEPARTMENT

Have you ever been asked to do something, either at home or at work, that you just didn't have the time available to do? What happened?

Maybe you decided it wasn't all that important, and it didn't get done. Or, maybe you did it, but you didn't do the job well. You did the very least you could do to check the task off the list. Or, perhaps you did the task, but something else got put on the back burner.

As I mentioned in chapter 12, 'Why Do Good Plans Fail?' when this happens within the marketing function, it can cause a plan to be abandoned involuntarily. This frequently happens because

- the plans are insufficiently staffed;
- the staff or marketing department does not understand or accept the responsibility for executing on the plan; and/or
- the staff or marketing department has the wrong mix of skills available for execution.

As I will discuss in this chapter, staffing is crucial to the success of a marketing plan and, therefore, the marketing function. Without an adequate team to carry out the tasks within a plan, all the work the company does aligning its plan with market needs and mitigating risks to assure success will be lost.

ESTIMATING HUMAN RESOURCES REQUIREMENTS

When I develop marketing plans on behalf of clients, I work with them to break down marketing activities into steps, estimating both the skills and the time required at each level. I also assess the impact of activities that are abandoned or reassigned as a result of the planning process. I referred to this process when I described the operating plan for human resources in chapter 12. In this chapter, I'll provide a more detailed example.

Consider the simplistic example of a fictitious client, Fleurs d'Emilie, a chain of florists whose added marketing activities include a website overhaul, updating collateral materials, constructing a new tradeshow booth and adding a sales person. The executive team is confident that the company's technology team can handle any programming requirements, and their marketing communications person can handle the writing. An initial review of the plan by the executive team suggests that the company has all the resources required internally, except the website designer. An initial list of the plan elements, without the related strategies, is shown in table 13-1.

Table 13-1: Fleurs d'Emilie's Corporate Marketing Plan

MARKETING TACTICS	BUDGET (EXCLUDING EXISTING STAFF)
Website overhaul	$12,000 for website design only
Collateral update	$6,000 for design elements, plus $3,700 for printing
Tradeshow booth	$18,000 for design, plus $4,500 for supplies
Additional sales team member focused on an industry segment	$78,000 plus 38.5% for benefits and taxes

The executive team is on board with the budget, but the IT manager, Louis Tolbert, is worried about whether the staffing is realistic. He suggests that the company also prepare an operating budget for staff time. As they go through the process, the validity of Tolbert's concerns becomes evident.

Writing is often the most time consuming element of a website overhaul, and if the marketing communications professional, Olivier Babineaux, is also responsible for managing the request for proposal process to secure the designer and managing the various elements of the project, 275 hours is a realistic budget. Babineaux will also have responsibilities in some other areas.

Often, executive time is omitted from the time budgeting process, and the executive team's busy schedules become a constraint on progress. In this case, the executive team will spend a considerable amount of personal time interviewing and providing on-boarding services to the potential sales team member.

When revised to account for staff time, a list of the plan elements looks more like table 13-2.

Table 13-2: Fleurs d'Emilie's Corporate Marketing Plan With Staff Time

MARKETING TACTICS	BUDGET (EXCLUDING EXISTING STAFF)	BABINEAUX'S TIME (MARKETING COMMUNICATIONS PROFESSIONAL)	TOLBERT'S TIME (IT PROFESSIONAL)	EXECUTIVE TIME	EXPECTED COMPLETION DATE (FROM APPROVAL OF PLAN)
Website overhaul	$12,000	275 hours	65 hours	15 hours	4 months
Collateral update	$9,700	60 hours	2 hours (uploading to website)	10 hours	2 months
Tradeshow booth	$22,500	35 hours (writing and managing)	0 hours	2 hours	2 months

Continued on p.235

Continued from p.234

MARKETING TACTICS	BUDGET (EXCLUDING EXISTING STAFF)	BABINEAUX'S TIME (MARKETING COMMUNICATIONS PROFESSIONAL)	TOLBERT'S TIME (IT PROFESSIONAL)	EXECUTIVE TIME	EXPECTED COMPLETION DATE (FROM APPROVAL OF PLAN)
Additional sales team member focused on segment of industry	$108,030	0 hours	0 hours	80 hours (for interviewing and training)	3 months
Totals:	$152,230	370 hours	67 hours	107 hours	

Although 370 hours may not seem like a substantial amount of time, if Babineaux, the sole marketing communication professional, has an existing plate of responsibilities, and the web and collateral update projects are expected to be completed quickly, the hours may be unrealistic. Adding 370 hours to a four-month period, for example, would be adding another part-time job to his existing position.

The executive team members who are involved should also review the employee's time commitments in light of other responsibilities. In some cases, duties may be able to be delegated. In other cases, the timeline may require adjustment. Either way, Fleurs d'Emilie has an opportunity to identify weaknesses in the potential workflow based on human resources constraints before the plan is approved. The result is reduced risk of derailment.

In this case, let's assume that a discussion of the additional workload with the development team and executives suggested that the incremental workload was acceptable. However, Babineaux was less enthusiastic. Already fully employed with proposal writing, internal communications and other responsibilities, the 370 hours seemed unrealistic both to Babineaux and, after an examination of his workload, to the executive team.

After some discussion about priorities and budget, the executive team opts to engage an external contractor to complete the work. This revision would change the budget for the organisation and for the marketing communications team member, as shown in table 13-3.

Table 13-3: Fleurs d'Emilie's Corporate Marketing Plan With External Contractor Time

MARKETING TACTICS	BUDGET (EXCLUDING EXISTING STAFF)	BABINEAUX'S TIME (MARKETING COMMUNICATIONS PROFESSIONAL)	TOLBERT'S TIME (IT PROFESSIONAL)	EXECUTIVE TIME
Website overhaul	$12,000 + $13,750 for contracted support for copywriting	25 hours to review copy	65 hours	15 hours

Continued on p.236

Continued from p.235

MARKETING TACTICS	BUDGET (EXCLUDING EXISTING STAFF)	BABINEAUX'S TIME (MARKETING COMMUNICATIONS PROFESSIONAL)	TOLBERT'S TIME (IT PROFESSIONAL)	EXECUTIVE TIME
Collateral update	$9,700	60 hours	2 hours (uploading to website)	10 hours
Tradeshow booth	$22,500	35 hours (writing and managing)	0 hours	2 hours
Additional sales team member focused on segment of industry	$108,030	0 hours	0 hours	80 hours (for interviewing and training)
Totals:	$165,980	120 hours	67 hours	107 hours

With the updated and more accurate budget in front of them, the executive team can update its anticipated return on investment calculations and make an informed decision about how to proceed.

In some corporate cultures, a marketing coordinator or other team member may be able to object to the assignment and press for additional resources, ensuring that important activities were not neglected. However, in many cultures, this type of pushback is discouraged. In these settings, employees are more likely to set aside other projects or neglect new priorities in order to manage their workload. By reviewing the workload in advance of plan approval, a company can identify and prevent a common cause of plan failure.

ACCEPTANCE OF RESPONSIBILITIES

A related weakness of marketing plans relative to human resources surfaces when plans are developed without input from, or acceptance by, the individuals who will execute them. Although collaboratively developed marketing plans are often impractical, plan developers should, at the very least, discuss the added workload with team members and confirm that they are willing to accept it.

The previous example illustrates this point. In many cases, a marketing communications coordinator would not be at the table to develop a marketing plan, even in an environment in which he or she was the only marketing professional on staff. In small and mid-sized businesses, particularly those that do not target broad consumer markets, the marketing promotions team is likely to be small, and marketing plans are often developed by the executive team or by a sales leader. Sometimes the planning person or group does determine a time budget as well as an expense budget, as the preceding team did. However, if they simply assume the individual has time available, rather than asking the question directly, they risk assigning the task to someone who will not accept it or who will flail at execution due to competing demands on their time.

Marketing professionals are not the only team members who will reject acceptance of responsibilities, particularly if not asked directly to do so. In fact, many marketing plans fail because non-marketing managers reject responsibilities assigned to them. For example, in a professional services environment, partners or other professionals whose background is not marketing or sales are asked to take an active role in business development (sales) on behalf of their firms. In most organisations with which I've worked, the marketing plans assign networking activities, presentations and other public relations work to various associates, professional staff or partners. Although this is a necessary part of the job for most professional service providers, it is also one for which many professionals are ill-equipped. After all, they became accountants or engineers or architects not because they enjoyed sales, but because they enjoyed their area of expertise.

When plans such as these are developed, they are often approved by the partner group. The same team members being asked to do the work are being asked to approve it, and they do, because the need seems obvious. But when it comes to execution, nothing happens. When the partners in these firms are asked why they aren't executing the plan, they shrug it off. They believed it was someone else's responsibility. When they approved the plan, they assumed that those roles would be filled by people who 'are good at it,' or 'like it,' and not by them. The result is that the plan fails.

As another example, consider an IT department in a consumer-focused business. In the marketing plan development process, leaders identified the customer interface of the company's primary platform to be a barrier to customer retention. From a marketing perspective, improving the interface is critical.

However, if the technology team already has a heavy workload and the importance of accepting this responsibility and executing the agreed timeline is not accepted by the technology team's leadership, the department may not give it the required attention. As a result, the plan slips or is eventually abandoned.

In these cases, it is particularly important for the company's leadership team to communicate the importance of the plan, review workload and confirm that the technology team is willing and able to shoulder the additional work. Communicating clearly in advance will help prevent the issue, and consistently assessing progress and holding team members accountable for execution will reduce the risk that previous work habits or other priorities will derail marketing efforts.

ASSESSING THE REQUIRED SKILLS

In some cases, the failure to execute is related to the misalignment of skills with needs in the plan. Have you ever volunteered on a non-profit board? If you have, you were probably asked to do some level of fundraising.

How comfortable are you asking friends to give you money? Some people are very comfortable with this role. They are happy to ask others to provide financial backing to a cause to which they feel committed. Others are not. They are more likely to decline a board role with a heavy fund development component.

But what if the expectations change? What if the organisation decides that each board member should be responsible for a more significant level of revenue? Some of the existing board members might feel torn. They recognise the need and

Marketing Failures Related to Staffing

Marketing plans often suffer from poor human resource planning, including

- plans that are insufficiently staffed;

- plans in which marketing or non-marketing employees do not understand or accept the responsibility for executing on the plan; and/or

- plans for which the existing staff has the wrong mix of skills available for execution.

support, but they don't have the skills—or perhaps the contacts—to provide the added revenue. If they quietly assent but fail, a development plan that was counting on increased board development will also fail.

Non-marketing professionals are not the only group affected by this issue. Marketing professionals, particularly marketers whose expertise is related to promotions, are highly susceptible to misaligned skill sets. One underlying reason is because marketing has become highly specialised. For example, a writer is not typically just a writer. They specialise. One writer might excel at advertising copy, which requires a concise, creative style. Another might excel at writing press releases, which follows a standardised format. Still another might excel at writing technical manuals, which requires a detailed, process-oriented writing style. One writer is rarely versatile enough to cover all three.

Similarly, designers specialise in certain media. Some are experts at print; others excel in online formats. Some designers can translate a concept into a visually inspiring advertisement, whereas others are better at laying out websites, which requires a certain level of technical knowledge. Each of these types of activities requires a different style and skill set.

Unfortunately, most companies with smaller marketing departments try to make a single person span a broad set of needs. For example, as the local marketing director for an international accounting firm, my staff was limited in number. Although I needed skills in several different types of copywriting, I only had enough in my budget for a single, in-house writer. As a result, I picked the most versatile writer I could find. This person could adapt to most styles but was excellent at none of them. The outcome was compromised quality and substantial inefficiency.

Both marketing and non-marketing team members whose workloads are affected by a marketing plan must be willing and able to accommodate the additional workload, and they must have the skills to do so. If they do not, the marketing plan will fail. As a non-marketing executive, it is important to either understand the skill sets required for each task within the marketing plan or ensure that they have been comprehensively reviewed.

USING EXTERNAL RESOURCES TO ADDRESS SKILL GAPS

Many companies address skill misalignments or human resources deficiencies, especially in promotions, by supplementing internal staff with external resources ranging from advertising and public relations agencies, to contractors, to temporary employees.

The Benefits of External Resources

Clearly, external resources can help keep a marketing plan on track. However, external resources can also deliver two additional benefits. First, the careful use of external staff can help compensate for the inherently episodic nature of many marketing efforts. By using variable resources, rather than fixed resources, the company can save money on staffing costs. Second, industries with high marketing turnover rates can reduce costs by leveraging external staff on a more consistent basis. Let's look at each of these benefits in turn.

Compensating for Fluctuating Needs

The need for marketing skill sets, especially specialised ones, fluctuates based on plan requirements at various times. By contrast, staff levels are typically static. (See figure 13-1 for a visualisation of fixed staff versus fluctuating needs.) As a result, the company suffers inefficiencies when the staff is underutilised, in terms of excess capacity, and ineffectiveness, when the staff has too much work for the size of the team. Supplementing marketing staff with external resources can fill these gaps.

Figure 13-1: Fixed Staff vs. Fluctuating Needs

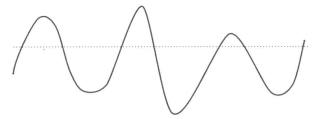

Consider, for example, a company's advertising needs. Many companies use some form of print or broadcast advertising as a part of their promotional mix. However, hiring and retaining a full-time advertising team would be financially unfeasible for most companies. Advertising development requires several specialised talents, including designers, copywriters, creative directors, media buyers and other skills. Using generalist resources already in-house to address these needs would likely sacrifice effectiveness of the end product, whereas few firms would use a full-fledged advertising team consistently enough to justify the expense.

Managing Performance Issues

Companies can also use external resources to reduce costs when the company is experiencing turnover or has performance issues. In some industries, turnover of marketing professionals is quite high. For example, in the mid-1990s, the average tenure rate for marketing directors in some professional services organisations was about ten months. Given the time required to recruit and train new team members, it is doubtful the organisation was recouping its investment in recruiting and training the team member before that person left the firm.

In other cases, when companies are experiencing internal dissatisfaction or significant inefficiency, using external resources or completely outsourcing a marketing department may be the right move. In the case of both inefficiencies and dissatisfaction, performance is less than optimal. As a result, the cost of the department may be higher than what it would cost to use an external agency or on-site outsourced solution.

Finally, companies may consider using external resources, rather than hiring new staff when the organisation has hiring constraints or is experiencing significant organisational change. In these situations, the immediate cost savings may be less, but the company's marketing efforts remain on track.

How to Decide When to Use External Marketing Resources

The choice about whether to use internal or external resources should be based on a number of considerations.

Core Versus Non-Core Business Functions

In general, the more integral a function is to its business, the more appropriate it is for internal resources to be used. For example, some professional services organisations have tried to use external contract sales personnel to sell services. However, the client's decision-making process is influenced significantly by the strength of the relationship between the individual professional and the client. The use of an external sales person, paid based on the business he or she generates, is likely to be marginally or completely unsuccessful. In this case, relationship development, or sales, is core to the business, and internal resources should be used.

Strategic Versus Tactical Services

Similarly, companies should consider how strategic the decisions and processes used are to the company's core ability to meet its customers' needs. For example, product or service decisions are typically reserved for in-house teams. Because products and services are so closely tied to the way the organisation serves its customers, most companies consider them too critical to outsource to external vendors. By contrast, website management is often appropriate to outsource. It is tactical in nature, rather than strategic, and the risk of missteps is generally less significant.

In some cases, certain aspects of the function can be performed by external vendors, whereas other portions should be performed in-house. See box 13-1 for a list to help determine if outside services are beneficial. For example, some aspects of channel management, such as the selection of appropriate channels and the negotiation of terms, may be handled most appropriately by in-house personnel, whereas other aspects, such as the legal documentation of channel arrangements, the development of a web-based retail outlet or the management of brick-and-mortar facilities may be managed by an external company.

Box 13-1: Outside Services Checklist

CONSIDER USING OUTSIDE SERVICES WHEN ONE OR MORE OF THE FOLLOWING ARE TRUE:	COST SAVINGS	IMPROVED EFFECTVENESS
Workloads fluctuate and/or skill needs change	✓	✓
Highly specialised skills are needed.	✓	✓
Function is experiencing performance issues or internal satisfaction issues.	✓	✓
Staff turn-over is significant.	✓	✓
Significant organisational change and/or innovation is needed		✓
Headcount or other organisational limitation creates a need for outside assistance.		✓

Selecting a Resource

As a company considers how it will match skills to needs in order to execute consistently on a marketing plan, there are a variety of options from which to choose. The most common staffing approaches include full-time and part-time employees, *interim (temporary) employees*, independent contractors or consultants, agencies or consulting firms and complete outsourcing solutions. Each approach has benefits and challenges and is best applied to certain types of situations.

Because of the breadth of services required within the marketing function, organisations can tap a wide range of solutions, from employees to independent sales representatives, public relations agencies to fully outsourced solutions. As the company considers its options, it may choose to leverage the following components.

Employees

Most organisations have at least some full- or part-time employees with marketing responsibilities. Employees are the least flexible solution but can also be the most cost-effective when their skill sets are fully utilised. They are also the best choice for core and strategic needs within the company. Because they are culturally engrained in the organisation, they are also in the best position to help the company nurture and sustain its brand reputation. Box 13-2 depicts the attributes of full- and part-time employees.

Interim or Temporary Employees

Some companies supplement existing staff using skilled personnel
employed by an outside service. Although they behave similarly to
employees, they offer the advantage of increased flexibility. They can be
added or removed from the job as needed, without fear of employment-
related issues. They have the disadvantage of being less likely to adopt
a company's market-focused culture or understand the company's value
proposition at a deep level, and for this reason, are most effectively used
for tactical work. They are also more costly than employees and require
a higher level of management oversight. See box 13-3 for attributes of
interim employees.

However, using interim personnel
can be a good way to address
temporary instability in a
department, staff a company
during a period of transition or
test a prospective employee before
making a long-term job offer.
Of course, the company will still

**Attributes of
interim or temporary staff**

Tactical effectiveness	
Strategic effectiveness	
Cost effectiveness	
Short-term solution	
Long-term solution	
Oversight required	High

need to invest some time in the recruiting process and may be at greater
risk of loss if the employee receives a permanent job offer from another
organisation. Companies using temporary employees as a recruiting
approach should also be aware that most temporary firms charge a fee for
converting a temporary employee to a direct hire. Temporary employees
are best used when the need is substantial, lasting more than a week or
two and consuming a full-time employee, but not long term.

Independent Consultants or Contractors

Many companies use independent contractors or consultants to fulfil a
wide range of needs within their organisations. Generally, this approach
is most successful when the project or activity has a specific start and
completion date or has specific desired outcomes and requires specialised
skills.

Independent consultants can be used for strategic work, but it is more likely to be tactical in nature. For example,
a company is unlikely to outsource new product development but may use an independent patent attorney to do
the critical work of protecting its investment.

There are a few disadvantages to using independent consultants. First, they are typically more expensive than
employees on a per-hour basis. Second, in many countries, co-employment, employment tax, employee benefit
and business liability issues may present risk exposure to the companies who retain them. Third, if they become
incapacitated or unwilling to work, there may not be a readily available substitute to take their place. Finally,
although the management of a single contractor is typically not burdensome, managing multiple independent
contractors working on a single project can be time consuming. See box 13-4 for the aspects of independent
contractors.

Box 13-4: Attributes of Independent
Contractors

Attributes of independent contractors

Tactical effectiveness

Strategic effectiveness

Cost effectiveness

Short-term solution

Long-term solution

Oversight required **Medium**

Agencies or Firms

The use of *agencies* and other *consulting firms* is common in marketing, particularly relative to specialised promotional fields, such as advertising and public relations. Although these organisations can take on small projects, the larger agencies typically manage larger-scale projects or on-going needs on behalf of their clients. Because of the complex and long-term nature of the relationship between agencies and their clients, the work can be more strategic in nature.

In general, agencies provide the flexibility offered by temporary employees or independent contractors, often coupled with multiple levels of expertise in a particular field. They reduce the time required selecting team members because the organisation recruits and retains the various skill sets required. They can also be held accountable for outcomes and terminated for non-performance more easily than an employee. However, their pricing structure is likely to be significantly higher. Although independent contractors may be 70% to 100% more expensive per hour than the fully-burdened cost of an employee, agency billing rates can be 120% to 300% more than the employee equivalent.

Agencies and consulting firms are best used for complex projects and services requiring multiple specialised skill sets, such as public relations, advertising or investor relations and for projects that require an independent perspective, such as strategic planning, analytics and market research. See box 13-5 for attributes of agencies.

Outsourcing Services

In some cases, an entire department can be outsourced to an external vendor that is tasked with managing to specific performance expectations. This has become common with some forms of direct sales, customer service and other functions that require less sophisticated skill sets. However, the outsourcing of more complex functions, such as marketing communications, graphic design and public relations functions, including both internal and external teams, is becoming more common.

In traditional outsourcing arrangements, whether handled by domestic or off-shore service providers, the supplier provides the same services without significant process change or improvement. Although this arrangement reduces risk and management requirements and allows the company to focus on its core competencies, it results in limited savings. In *business process outsourcing*, the supplier works with the client to evaluate and re-engineer the solution. This is the process applied when an organisation outsources a function that combines both static (internal) and flexible (external) resources into a single *just-in-time* labour solution. This type of arrangement generates the same operational benefits as traditional outsourcing but can result in significant cost savings as well.

Box 13-5: Attributes of Agencies

Attributes of agencies

Tactical effectiveness

Strategic effectiveness

Cost effectiveness

Short-term solution

Long-term solution

Oversight required **Low**

I recently spoke to a group of non-profit leaders about another variation on the outsourcing concept, *source-sharing*. In this case, a group of non-competing non-profit organisations entered into a formal agreement to share the costs and benefits of employees with specific skills needed on a fluctuating basis by all the organisations. For example, every non-profit in the partnership needed some form of human resources support, but none could justify hiring a part-time team member, much less a full-time team member. The group of non-profits agreed that one of the partners would hire the individual, and he or she would be paid by that organisation. However, the other partners would each reimburse the hiring organisation for a portion of the costs, and the person would serve all the member organisations. Although this example is related to human resources professionals, a similar structure could be used for marketing and other personnel.

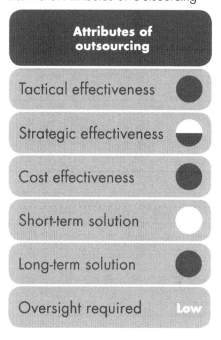

Box 13-6: Attributes of Outsourcing

Attributes of outsourcing	
Tactical effectiveness	◐
Strategic effectiveness	◓
Cost effectiveness	◐
Short-term solution	○
Long-term solution	●
Oversight required	Low

Using outsourced services is best when there is an opportunity for significant savings, significant quality improvement and/or significant service improvements. For example, a company might have needs for skills within the marketing function, such as trade show expertise, which tends to be seasonal, have a single employee it is trying to stretch over many different job responsibilities or have a department with operational problems that needs to be overhauled. All of these situations make strong cases for full or partial for outsourcing.

Traditional outsourcing can be a particularly strong choice for companies with functions that are neither core nor strategic in areas with strong histories of outsourcing performance. Business process outsourcing is a strong fit for organisations with small and mid-sized in-house departments with turnover or performance issues and a variety of external vendors.

Outsourcing, particularly business process outsourcing, is a long-term solution. Most contracts are generated for a period of years, rather than months, and it may be difficult to hastily extract a company from such an arrangement. On the other hand, outsourcing offers the greatest opportunity to manage by results and hold the team accountable for outcomes. For both of these reasons, it is important to select a company that has the relevant outsourcing methods and tools and a track record of successful engagements as a provider of outsourced marketing services. It is also critical to ensure that the organisation's culture and understanding of the target market match your own.

Making cultural awareness management a part of the outsourcing process is critical to protecting a company's brand reputation and integrity. This is even more important if the services are performed by overseas providers. If a company's employees and customers are all in one country, and it is outsourcing to an off-shore service provider, the company could be at significantly higher risk for inadvertent cultural insensitivities, language barriers and misrepresentations of the brand's key attributes. Although this can still happen in domestic outsourcing, it is a less pervasive issue. See box 13-6 for attributes of outsourcing.

OVERSEEING EXTERNAL RESOURCES

Using external resources can effectively resolve the skill alignment issues that can derail marketing plans. However, poor management of those resources can present its own set of problems. Brand consistency, marketing alignment, quality and efficiency can all suffer without careful consideration about needs and monitoring of outcomes. The following are ways to make the most of your investment in external resources:

- **Provide training to external resources.** If a project is significant, and especially if the results will be easily visible to the market, it is wise to provide a comprehensive orientation to external vendors. After all, they often don't enjoy the benefits of the company's marketing discipline: its constant feedback system. The content included in the orientation may include the organisation's history, primary markets, value proposition, desired brand reputation, graphics standards, key messages, marketing plan and, in some cases, elements of the company's business plan. If the external resource is an outsourcing organisation or a temporary team member, this orientation should also include technology policies, security and company standards, such as document naming protocols.

- **Be deliberate in your governance and oversight.** Sometimes, simply defining the roles and responsibilities of both your external resources and your internal team before beginning an engagement can help ensure no details are overlooked and prevent subsequent contract disputes when one side or the other believes the scope has changed.

- **Establish processes for managing change.** When an engagement is large, like an outsourced sales team, product design work conducted by an external agency or an advertising campaign managed by an independent contractor, there are likely to be changes along the way. If these changes affect the scope of the engagement, it is easy for costs to escalate before they catch senior management team members' attention. To prevent scope creep, it is helpful to have a carefully defined process for managing changes, including a process for budget approval.

- **Establish communication methods.** Every company has slightly different communications approaches and habits. So does every agency, outsourcing organisation and independent contractor. Does your company prefer to have communications funnelled through a single oversight manager? Or would a decentralised communication approach be a better fit? Whatever approach best suits your company, you should be sure that your external resources know how best to communicate with you. If you don't establish your preferences early in the process, communications could be less effective, less efficient or both.

  You should also consider the timing and types of communications you wish to receive. For example, there may be certain intermediate metrics associated with the plan that you wish to monitor, such as the number of sales calls per week or the number of coupons redeemed. Clearly establishing what types of metrics and other information you want to receive and how frequently you would like to receive them facilitates both management and quality control.

- **Establish quality control procedures.** It can be very embarrassing, and sometimes extremely damaging, when a company's vendors don't meet its quality standards, and the work product is highly visible to the public. Consider the recent advertising debacle with Ford Motor Company and the unauthorised and offensive ads produced by their Indian advertising agency, JWT India. Employees at the agency created the ads, which depicted disturbing images of women gagged and bound in the back of a Ford automobile, and posted them online. They also submitted the ads to India's top advertising award programme. Even though Ford did not authorise the ads, and the agency has since fired the employees who created and released them, Ford's reputation has suffered because of their actions.[1]

  Companies using external resources to perform highly visible marketing activities on behalf of their company should ensure that the agencies with whom they work have strict policies prohibiting the misuse of a client's name or logo. It is also wise to establish quality standards and practices to ensure that work products meet or exceed the company's expectations. Written work product standards, deliverable review and approval processes and project objectives reviews based on intermediate marketing metrics are all examples of these types of quality control procedures.

QUESTIONS FOR NON-MARKETING MANAGERS TO ASK ABOUT STAFFING THE MARKETING DEPARTMENT

When a non-marketing manager is involved in reviewing the staffing requirements related to a marketing plan, he or she should ask the following questions:

- How were our internal and external team members selected? Do they share our core values? Do they understand the importance of listening to, and aligning marketing with, our market's needs?
- Did we accurately estimate the number of hours required for existing team members to complete this plan?
- Do we have enough team members to execute on this plan? If not, does the budget include the related human resources investments?
- Did the team members who will be asked to execute on this plan review the additional workload and accept responsibility for their assignments?
- What is the cost to engage external resources, if necessary, and do the potential financial returns offset these investments?
- What types of activities will be assigned to them, and who will review their work product?
- How will we hold team members accountable for performance? What impact does performance failure have?
- How will we ensure external resources have a thorough understanding of our market, value proposition, brand and marketing strategies?

CHAPTER 13 SUMMARY

In some cases, the primary obstacle to successful execution on a marketing plan is a human resources problem. The company cannot execute because it has insufficient staff to carry out the plan, the individuals who are responsible for specific activities can't or won't accept responsibility or the company doesn't have the required skill sets.

To prevent issues related to insufficient staff, organisations should implement a process for evaluating the time budget for each marketing activity during the planning process. Once complete, the executive team or other management group will have a better understanding of whether the workload is feasible and whether additional budget should be included to accommodate additional human resources.

Marketing, particularly the promotions aspect of the function, has become highly specialised. Companies who try to stretch a single resource over a diverse set of needs often sacrifice effectiveness, incur additional expense or both. To improve returns, organisations should carefully consider how they allocate workload between potential human resources, tapping both internal and external resources as required.

Fortunately, there are many sources of skills from which to choose, both internal and external to the organisation. Each is best used in specific types of situations, which are summarised in box 13-7.

Box 13-7: Human Resources Approaches

APPROACH	BEST USED WHEN
Employees	• The hours of a specific skill set are equal to or greater than the employee hours, and the hours are evenly spread throughout the year. • The function is core to the business, strategic and/or long-term in nature.
Temporary or Interim Services	• Team members are needed to supplement existing staff on a short-term basis. • The company is considering hiring into a position and would like to see if a particular candidate is a fit before making an offer of employment.
Independent Consultants or Contractors	• Highly skilled resources are needed to complete specific tactical marketing activities.
Agencies or Consulting Firms	• A company has more complex marketing activities that require many specific and highly specialised skill sets, such as strategic planning, market research, analytics, public relations, advertising or creative design. • A company's marketing activity requires an impartial perspective or highly specialised expertise, such as market research or pricing analyses. • A company wants to deal with one set of vendors over multiple geographies.
Outsourcing Solutions	• A company has extremely variable demand for a broad range of marketing skill sets. • A company perceives a need to reorganise or restructure a team.

Once a staffing approach has been developed, the management team must carefully manage external resources to ensure the work they do benefits from the company's understanding of the discipline of marketing, positively reinforces its desired brand reputation and is aligned with the market's needs, the company's value proposition and the company's core values.

Endnotes

1 Hennigan, Andrew. 'Ford's ad debacle offers important lessons for brands,' Ragan's PR Daily, Marcy 28, 2013. www.prdaily.com/Main/Articles/Fords_ad_debacle_offers_important_lessons_for_bran_14158.aspx#

14

MANAGING MEASUREMENT

There is an old business adage: What gets measured gets done. Yet, marketing frequently isn't measured.

In chapter 11, 'Evaluating Returns on Marketing Investments,' I discussed the importance of estimating returns on marketing investments as a part of the plan evaluation process and anticipating the needs for systems or processes that will support information gathering during the execution phase so that outcomes can be evaluated. During the plan evaluation process, the management team outlines what *should* happen.

However, a company's marketing plan can drift off track, or even become abandoned, if those expectations and the actual results aren't continually present in discussions and assessment throughout the process. This is where measurement and management intersect. Effective management of measurement in marketing can vastly improve returns on marketing investments—and improve the company's ability to forecast future performance. It takes some advanced planning and discipline to be effective. This chapter looks at some of the practices required for effective management of measurement on an on-going basis.

More specifically, to effectively manage measurement, managers must

- address language barriers;
- agree on metrics in advance;
- build the processes and systems required to measure performance, if the company does not have them;
- remain focused on metrics throughout plan execution; and
- coordinate the team members whose participation is required for success.

ADDRESSING THE LANGUAGE BARRIER

Marketing professionals speak a different language. It's true.

Of course, so do finance and accounting professionals, operations team members, and others whose area of expertise has become highly technical and specialised.

The problem with the jargon and three-letter acronyms developed by these internal teams is that they pose a language barrier when it comes to measurement. And if no one is really sure what is being measured, it is less likely to be realised.

To illustrate the problem, let me provide a real example from a client we worked with many years ago. This Fortune 500 company engaged our firm to help develop an approach to measuring financial returns on investments (ROI) in marketing and set goals to track performance. As we sat around the table with its marketing and finance teams discussing marketing ROI, it became increasingly apparent that team members were using at least two very different definitions of ROI. For part of the group, including the marketing team and part of the finance team, the definition of ROI was the same as *sales uplift*. The ROI was the increase in sales over previous performance, so a 200% ROI meant sales doubled.

Others around the table, including some of the finance team members, considered ROI to be the increase in sales, net of the required investment, divided by the incremental investment in marketing efforts required to achieve that increase. This is, of course, the traditional financial definition of ROI.

Had our project leader not called attention to the definitional difference and worked with the team to establish a common definition, this language difference may have led team members, particularly in the marketing group, to focus on the wrong thing. They would have focused on increasing sales, regardless of cost, rather than optimising sales based on incremental investments.

ROI is not the only term that can be misunderstood. Marketing and finance are both replete with terms that may mean something else, or nothing at all, to their colleagues in the other department. Many marketers talk about hits, eyeballs or column inches, all common metrics within the marketing field, but finance professionals interpret them quite differently. Similarly, marketing professionals without financial training may be baffled by some accounting terms or simply have difficulty interpreting common financial metrics. For example, they may know the definition of *account receivable days* or *current ratio*, but are uncertain how it should be interpreted or applied to their planning.

Several years ago, a vice president of marketing for a large regional company approached me to ask if I would teach a class on finance to marketing professionals. He felt frustrated by his inability to ask informed questions when sitting in on executive team meetings. It also damaged his ability to justify his own department's expenditures because he found the interpretation of financial data to be so challenging.

Similarly, I am frequently asked to speak about marketing to non-marketing executives. When we arrive at the question and answer period, often, the questions are definitional in nature. They want to know what their marketing team is talking about when they discuss *cause marketing*, collateral, brand architecture or *cost-per-lead* (also known as CPL), for example. It is one of the reasons that this book includes a glossary of terms commonly, and even less commonly, used in the marketing field.

Many individuals, particularly in leadership roles, don't take the time to clarify definitions, either because they make the assumption that everyone knows what the term means or because they are afraid to look uninformed when they ask for a definition. When these misunderstandings are not resolved prior to plan approval, they can result in inaccurate estimates of potential returns, subsequent second-guessing of marketing investments and even turnover among frustrated personnel.

To avoid these problems, executives should encourage their team members to ask questions about definitions they don't understand and ask for clarification when a definition is critical to success or likely to be misunderstood. Cross-training marketing, finance and operational professionals on the basics of the other areas of expertise can also help improve communications, measurement and outcomes.

AGREEING ON METRICS

Marketing managers and non-marketing managers should agree, in advance of plan approval, on the metrics that will be used to evaluate plan success. There are three types of metrics that are commonly used: completion metrics, intermediate marketing metrics and financial metrics.

Completion metrics identify when a particular activity will be complete. For example, if the company's marketing strategy is to expand access to the product, and the company decides to add retail facilities in new geographies, the completion metric might be whether the retail facilities were open for business by a certain date.

When I facilitate retreats with leadership teams that focus on building cohesive marketing strategies, there is a tendency to want to measure marketing success exclusively in terms of the completion of activities. Although completion metrics are useful and should be included, they do not present a complete picture of the success of a particular investment.

For example, the team might decide to launch a public relations campaign. When asked how they will determine whether the campaign has been a success, the response is frequently related to the on-time, on-budget execution of a plan. This is a great response to the question 'How will you know you are done?' but a rather poor answer to the question 'How will you know your efforts were successful?'

Effective management requires more than the knowledge that work was completed. It requires an understanding of whether the investment was a success.

To make sure that a post-plan evaluation can answer both of those questions, the company needs both intermediate marketing metrics and financial metrics.

Intermediate marketing metrics are the traditional approach marketers have taken to assessing marketing outcomes. They range from the number of products sold, to the number of coupons redeemed, to the volume of business from particular channels, to the myriad of intermediate metrics associated with promotions, some of which are listed in chapter 10, 'Promotions: The Fourth 'P' of Tactical Marketing.'

Intermediate metrics are typically not financial in nature, and they are useful indicators about whether a plan is on track. For example, a company might be using a coupon to develop new repeat customer behaviour. The number of customers who redeemed the coupon might be a good intermediate metric to evaluate whether the pricing approach was on track, whereas the real financial outcome, subsequent sales volume, might not be known until several months or years later. The intermediate metric provides useful ways of determining whether the plan is on course to meet its financial metrics, the anticipated financial outcomes of the marketing investments.

Intermediate metrics should be tied to activities known to influence the customer purchasing decision process. For example, if a company is using coupons to encourage sampling behaviour, the management team should have some idea about whether sampling will increase purchases, and, if so, by how much. The management team should also be able to estimate how much impact a change in the influencing factor will have on the financial performance of that product or service line or on the company. As discussed in chapter 11, this is how financial metrics and goals are developed.

Sometimes, a group of intermediate metrics will have a combined impact on a particular influencing factor. In other words, a single activity does not directly drive behaviour. Remember Starbucks and the Via introduction? They needed sampling behaviour, coupon redemption and probably other actions working in collaboration to change market behaviour. There may have been numerous intermediate marketing metrics, but they might connect with just one or two financial metrics, like sales or gross margin.

To illustrate the different forms of metrics, let me return to one of the cases used in chapter 11, the example Sociedad Española de Fabricación Industrial (SEFI), a small manufacturer that wanted to increase sales to small businesses in certain segments. Its analysis of barriers within the purchasing decision process led the manufacturer to decide to overhaul its website.

Sidebar 14-1: Case Study 1: Agreeing on Metrics

This case study is a continuation of the SEFI example in chapter 11.

Completion Metrics: Website launched by specific date; expenses within budget of $45,000.

Intermediate Marketing Metrics: Web hits and conversion rates

Marketing Goals: 800 web hits from the targeted market segments; 1% conversion rate.

Financial Metrics: Sales to smaller businesses; profit margin on those sales.

Financial Goals: 15% increase in sales to small businesses in three industries; profit margins consistent with existing gross margin.

Its completion metric was simple: whether the website was completed on time and on budget. The intermediate marketing metrics were based on the expected intermediate outcomes from the website and structured similarly to a sales funnel: leads generated and per cent converted to sales. The financial goals reflect the expected outcomes of the marketing efforts: improved revenues and consistent gross margins.

Nick Delacruz, the CEO in the example, can use the completion metrics to keep the marketing plan on task and manage budget, the intermediate marketing metrics to determine whether the plan is producing the expected outcomes and the financial metrics to assess whether the objectives were met when the plan is complete.

However, simply having metrics isn't enough. It's equally important to pick the right metrics. Failing to focus on objectives can cause a plan to drift, but focusing on the wrong metrics is certain to lead the plan off course.

The metrics should also be meaningful. Many presentations of data include a list of static numbers when, to be interpretable, the numbers only have meaning when compared to previous performance. Thus, a trend line, percentage change figure or series of numbers would be a more appropriate way for metrics to appear.

For example, imagine a CFO who informs the marketing team that their accounts receivable aging is now at 28 days. Should they be celebrating success or commiserating over their failure? In order to understand the situation, the outside observer needs two additional pieces of information: the previous performance of accounts receivable and the goal set by the team relative to that objective. Only with these pieces of information will it be obvious whether the team should be celebrating an early success or taking steps to improve their collections.

The key to successful coordination is to ensure that conversations about both intermediate marketing metrics and financial outcomes include both marketing and finance leaders within the organisation, and that the metrics selected are relevant and actionable. By establishing all three types of metrics (completion, intermediate marketing and financial), a company's leadership team will have a better understanding of how the latter two connect, when results might be expected relative to completion dates and what type of impact is expected. In addition, the team will be able to more effectively monitor progress and take action to correct issues when they arise.

BUILDING PROCESSES AND SYSTEMS TO MEASURE PERFORMANCE

Another advantage to a joint conversation on metrics is that it can help identify places where the company will need to create measurement tools. Without advance consideration of the types of feedback that will be needed, the company might miss an opportunity to gather important information.

For example, marketers and financial managers alike might be interested in understanding response rates from a direct mail campaign. If the direct mail campaign is the only change to the company's marketing mix, the company might decide that it could measure response rates simply through a change in the volume of inquiries or sales. However, if the company is making multiple changes to its marketing mix, the company may wish to understand the direct mail campaign's impact independent of other activities. In this case, the company might choose to establish a new website, e-mail address, phone number or other way for the company to track individuals responding to the direct mail piece. Leads and sales generated through this new contact approach are likely responding to the direct mail campaign. Without these dedicated response mechanisms, the company will be less able to determine the actual performance of the tactic.

Shell Oil Company, the U.S. subsidiary of Royal Dutch Shell, dominated the United States in retail gasoline sales for many years. It got to the top by focusing on what mattered to its customers: clean restrooms and attractively-decorated, well-lit forecourts. But it did more than just initiate a plan to make improvements. It established specific intermediate marketing metrics and hired a team of individuals to inspect bathrooms, measure the lumens emitted by their retailers' lighting systems and count the number of plants and other features that added colour and beauty to their gas stations' locations. Shell invested in the inspection team and tracked performance over time in order to allow the company to evaluate the effectiveness of these improvements and draw a correlation between investments made and financial outcomes. Without advanced planning and appropriate tracking mechanisms, Shell might have missed this opportunity to better understand not only how it was performing against plan but also how specific differences affected financial outcomes.

Because marketing professionals look at market segment performance whereas financial professionals look at performance within a product or service category or division, in some cases, a discussion about metrics may reveal a need to revise the chart of accounts or create a separate financial reporting system. For example, many accounting firms have a tax department and an attest or audit department. Many also have a consulting group or simply track revenues and expenses related to consulting projects. However, clients don't segment themselves according to need. After all, most audit clients also need tax work, and tax clients may need consulting services.

It's also not how clients choose a service provider. They generally don't choose a CPA firm simply because they have a tax department. They generally choose the firm because they have a relationship with a particular partner or because they have a reputation for expertise that serves their needs. To measure marketing's effectiveness or understand penetration within a particular segment, departmentally-based financial data is relatively worthless.

By identifying the need to track financial progress by market segment, rather than department, before the plan is executed, the company can establish financial analysis tools that will be more effective for the marketing team and increase the likelihood that both the marketing team and the financial team will be focused on achieving the desired financial results. This type of improved financial analysis is also a significant milestone in the transition from average performer to market leader status. In the preceding CPA firm example, the finance team might make the marketing team more effective by providing financial data by industry.

DON'T FORGET THE INVESTMENT SIDE OF THE ROI EQUATION

So far, these examples have focused on metrics that track revenues. But many companies are also lax in tracking marketing investments. In some cases, expense items related to marketing are assigned to other general ledger codes. For example, some companies consider the compensation and benefits associated with its marketing team to be part of administrative overhead. As a result, the company's overhead costs are higher than they should be, and its investments in marketing are systematically understated.

This is particularly common in professional and other business service organisations, when relationship development is an important part of the sales process and is commonly managed by the professionals themselves. In many cases, these expenses, in the form of time, are simply assigned to a general administrative code, rather than being allocated to a business development or marketing expense line item. Again, this systematically understates the cost of the firm's marketing efforts and makes it particularly difficult for marketers to assess the effectiveness of any given programme or collection of programmes.

In many cases, the problem isn't the assignment of marketing budget items away from marketing, it is the inclusion of expenses in the marketing budget that are not directly associated with the company's marketing efforts. For example, many executives choose to sponsor non-profit organisations whose causes they support personally. Although these may be strategic efforts to reinforce the company's brand, occasionally, they are simply an executive's personal interest and are unconnected to the company's marketing efforts. When personal interest sponsorships or contributions are included as marketing expenses, it effectively overstates the cost of marketing, thereby diminishing financial returns. These types of expenses would be more appropriately allocated to charitable contributions, if the company has such a budget.

Another expense commonly assigned to the marketing function but not directly related to marketing is the expense of advertising to attract candidates for open jobs within an organisation. Often, the costs associated with recruitment, including advertising, promotional branded items (also called tchotchkes), trade show materials and collaterals are assigned to marketing ledger codes. If these activities are not directly associated with the marketing plan, a related budget and anticipated returns, this process makes it difficult to determine whether the marketing plan as written is on budget and can skew estimates of financial returns. Expense related to these types of activities should be accounted for within the human resources budget. In cases in which the purchases serve dual purposes, such as the purchase of promotional branded items used for a tradeshow booth, it may be appropriate to allocate expense to more than one cost code.

To ensure the company has the capability to accurately assess the impact of its marketing investments, executives should encourage thoughtful planning discussions between the marketing, operations and finance teams. These discussions should include a conversation about the types of data the organisation will need to accurately assess financial returns and the types of intermediate metrics the organisation will use to track progress against goals. It should also encompass budget management issues, such as expense allocation, so that financial returns are accurately calculated.

REMAINING FOCUSED

Once the company has identified the metrics it will track and developed the tools with which to do so, the key is execution. By keeping everyone focused on the metrics and tracking progress against plan, the company will be more likely to catch a plan when it first begins drifting off course or encountering barriers to success.

Create a dashboard to track metrics against plan. Like the dashboard of an automobile, a marketing dashboard provides users with a quick assessment of the company's performance against plan. Dashboards typically feature the most important indicators of performance and should include both financial and intermediate marketing metrics. In some cases, they may also include completion metrics.

To be useful, the metrics should be presented in a way that is easy for the targeted audiences to read. The particular format will vary depending on the type of data and the users themselves. Some people need very visual depictions of performance data, and graphics, charts and other pictures will be more effective than numbers or narrative. Other audiences prefer words or numbers to images. In many cases, the optimal display is a combination of both styles.

Depending on the scope of the plan, the size of the company and the number of metrics, the dashboard could be as simple as a single, letter-sized piece of paper with several key performance indicators or metrics identified. An example of a simple dashboard appears at the end of this chapter.

Larger companies with complex marketing programmes are likely to have more sophisticated dashboard needs. These organisations may prepare multiple dashboards or use computer software to track performance against metrics. When a company's needs are sophisticated, it should still prepare a single high-level dashboard that can be used by senior executives to monitor performance but may also have more detailed dashboards for use by the next tiers of leadership. In almost every case, a user can drill down to look at more detailed information supporting, or related to, a particular metric. See figure 14-1 for an example of a team's dashboard.

For instance, a company might visually depict the volume of initial inquiries about products or services, conversion rates and customer retention rates, along with sales figures and profit margins, each by market or product line. This type of dashboard might be used by the company's executive leadership to monitor progress overall.

Divisional leadership might dive more deeply into a specific metric, or their own division's performance against a specific metric, looking at how their portion of the organisation performed relative to overall corporate performance. For example, if the organisation identified that customer retention was heavily influenced by how fast customer service calls were returned and the absolute number of calls, which serve as an indication of initial customer satisfaction, the customer service and product development teams might be particularly interested in those metrics and their impact on customer retention rates.

Figure 14-1: Using Dashboards to Maintain Focus

Dashboards should reflect the data most relevant to the viewer. In this example, the team responsible for the online channel might use a dashboard that looks something like this:

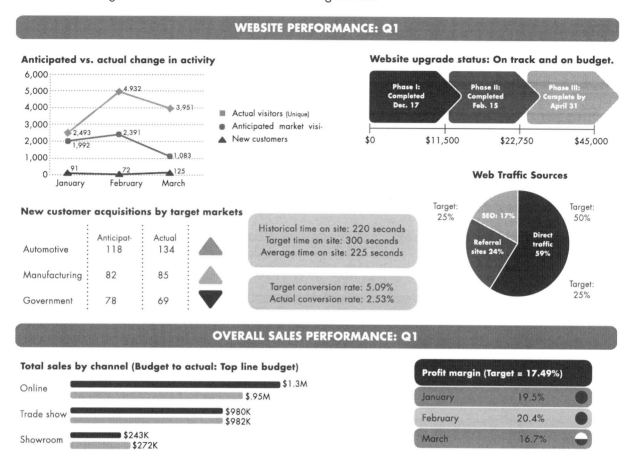

To be effective, a dashboard must be easy for the audience to read and interpret. When the dashboard is complex and will be used by dozens or hundreds of managers, a company may decide to retain a usability expert. Usability professionals focus on how easy and intuitive the interface of a particular software or web tool is to the user.

Regardless of whether a company uses a dashboard or another form of reporting to keep the plan on track, the process will be most effective if the information is easy to access, visually appealing, provides the appropriate amount of detail and is routinely reviewed by the organisation's leadership team.

COORDINATING EFFORTS

Finally, the effective management of performance and related measurement requires careful coordination of roles. It should be clearly understood before the plan is approved not only who will be responsible for each task relative to execution but also who will be responsible for which aspects of measurement.

When performance measurement is left to chance, managers sometimes discover that the data is not reliable or not available or that the effort to gather it is unnecessarily time consuming. Each person or team responsible for a component of marketing plan measurement should understand the metrics for which they have measurement responsibility, the data sources they will use to generate their assessment, how often the data should be presented and how it will be used. By reviewing needs and assigning responsibilities before execution begins, the individual with whom measurement responsibility begins has added incentive to confirm that the task is manageable and propose alternatives if it is not.

For example, a law firm may only be able to track the source of leads if the attorney who wins the work remembers to ask the client. In addition, the client might not remember exactly how he or she was first introduced to the law firm. Because the attribution may not be completely accurate, some attorneys may resist compliance, leading to missing or inaccurate information.

In this case, the management team will need to decide whether the attribution information is helpful as a general indicator of visibility and awareness of expertise within the target market, both contributors to the purchasing decision process. If it is, the marketing and finance teams will need the buy-in of the attorneys in order to accurately track the information. On the other hand, if the organisation decides that it cannot secure partner participation, alternative intermediate metrics may need to be selected.

Many times, historical data is needed in order to provide insight about change. When a company is new to measurement, this data may not be readily available. The executive or management team responsible for the process will need to determine whether the effort of sorting previous period data is required, or if the company will simply begin tracking data on a go-forward basis, understanding its limited usefulness in the current period.

THE CEO'S ROLE IN MEASUREMENT

The CEO and other executives play a critical role in *marketing measurement* by setting the tone and holding team members accountable for measuring activities and results. As the leader of marketing initiatives within their organisations, the executives of market leading companies understand the importance of consistent execution. In order to ensure the marketing plans their teams craft are executed, they monitor performance and take action when marketing plans begin to slip.

Many companies begin tracking marketing performance, but their efforts fizzle when the company encounters its first barrier. Few companies can execute a plan without running into challenges. Employee departures, busy work schedules, staffing constraints and unforeseen challenges all throw wrenches into the marketing machinery. If the executive team ignores these issues, either because they are not monitoring performance or because they are not willing or able to hold people accountable, the plan will be shaped by the barriers in its path instead of taking a temporary detour before resuming the path to success.

QUESTIONS FOR NON-MARKETING MANAGERS TO ASK ABOUT MANAGING THE MEASUREMENT OF MARKETING PERFORMANCE

To be effective in this oversight role, the non-marketing executive should ask the following questions:

- What completion, intermediate marketing and financial metrics should we be tracking to ensure that our plan stays on track?

- How do we plan to use the information?

- Where will the information come from?

- Do we have the appropriate systems and processes we need to ensure the information is collected?

- Have we established baseline metrics against which future performance can be compared?

- Who will be responsible for gathering it?

- How often should we review it?

- Who should review it?

- In what format should the data be presented?

- Do we already have a process for handling departures from the plan? If not, how will we address this possibility?

- Does our executive team hold our marketing function accountable for performance against the plan? If so, does the marketing function have control over all aspects of performance, or should other teams also be held accountable for their contributions to plan performance?

CHAPTER 14 SUMMARY

In marketing, as in so many other aspects of business, what gets measured and evaluated by the executive team becomes a focus for the rest of the company. To make sure a well-designed marketing plan stays on track, the executive team should make sure that

- the entire company uses the same definition to describe the metrics identified in the marketing plan, encouraging cross-training as needed.

- everyone agrees on the metrics the team will use and has identified meaningful metrics for each aspect of the plan. This includes not only completion metrics, which answer the question 'How will you know you are done?' but also intermediate marketing metrics and financial metrics, which answer the question 'How will you know your efforts were successful?'

- the company has the systems and processes required to effectively track marketing efforts. Many companies stumble in their measurement efforts because they did not determine how they would measure results, and build the appropriate processes to do so, in advance. These issues should be resolved before the plan is approved.

- the company has a clear communication tool, such as a marketing dashboard, that will let the executive team and others with responsibility for managing against specific marketing objectives know how well they are performing.

- before the plan is approved, individuals with responsibility for tracking performance against metrics know what they will be tracking, where the data will come from and how it will be reported, and have agreed to track the data required.

- the CEO and other members of the management team are actively engaged in monitoring measurement and hold team members accountable for marketing performance.

CULTIVATING SYSTEMATIC LISTENING

Market leaders are exceptionally good at listening to their markets. It's one of the reasons they are market leaders. In fact, it may be the most important reason. Listening to the market gives market leaders the next best thing to a crystal ball. It gives them what I call the Crystal Ball Effect: a greater level of understanding about the market that allows them to more effectively anticipate market needs, understand how to respond to them and generate better financial performance as a result.

To generate the Crystal Ball Effect, market leaders don't just listen occasionally. They do so systematically. Every team member is taught to gather information and pass it along.

Not only do they listen, but market leaders act on what they hear. The feedback they get from their customers is one of the key drivers of decisions about the products and services they offer, the pricing structures they use, their distribution channel selections, the technology systems they use and how they promote their products.

Unfortunately, the average performers in the market, which is what most companies are considered, don't listen. Worse yet, some companies solicit input and then ignore the feedback. There is little difference between this situation and that of a friend who asks for your advice and then ignores it. It frustrates the customer and may eventually cause them to stop giving advice or remaining your customer.

The reason companies ignore what their customers say isn't because they don't care. They do care. In fact, many think they are listening, and, sometimes, they are. But they aren't listening systematically, they're listening sporadically. Their CEO may listen, and perhaps, the executive team or sales team, but the organisation's culture as a whole doesn't focus on listening as a core value. Thus, the information they hear may not make it to the individuals who are in a position for driving critical business decisions.

Market leaders build a listening culture in three ways. First, the executive team models the behaviours they want to see within the organisation. Second, they build processes and systems internally to listen and incorporate feedback. Third, they use market research, when needed, to improve accuracy and gather additional feedback. This chapter explores each of these aspects of listening organisations in more detail.

MODELLING THE WAY: THE EXECUTIVE'S ROLE IN BUILDING THE CRYSTAL BALL EFFECT

Costco Wholesale Corporation focuses on providing what it calls 'the extreme value proposition' to members. Its customer is a value seeker who wants quality but opts for price over brand as long as the product meets quality standards.

To make this possible for customers, Costco combines no-frills, warehouse-style retail facilities, strong vendor negotiation strategies and the economics of a gym membership. Members pay an annual membership fee that gives them access to its physical and online stores and provides Costco with a direct communication channel to its customer base. Like a gym membership, this fee is paid annually, regardless of whether Costco's services are used.

This steady stream of income helps facilitate the low prices members find inside, which reinforces member usage. The result is a cult-like following from members. According to Jim Galanti, Costco's executive vice president and CFO, 'We don't tweet. We don't buy banner ads. We rely on the fact that we've got 30 million member households that are loyal to us.'

The model has been extremely successful. Since it was founded in 1983, the company has grown from a single warehouse in Seattle to nearly 600 warehouses in nine countries, with 64 million members worldwide and over $100 billion in annual sales. In just 29 years, Costco has become the third largest retailer in the United States and the leader in the warehouse retail sector. Costco is a market leader.

When asked why Costco has enjoyed such exceptional success, Galanti emphasised the importance of understanding their customer and looking for ways to serve their customer's needs. And how have they done so through their rapid growth? In part, it is because of their executive commitment to understanding who they serve.

Costco Wholesale Corporation's co-founder and CEO Jim Sinegal began his warehouse retail career as a stock boy, working directly with customers. Many of his fellow executive team members also got their start in the 1950s or 1960s as box boys or cart pushers at Fed-Mart or Price Club, some of Costco's predecessors in the warehouse retail business.[1] Although experience at this level isn't a requirement to understand the customer, it certainly helps. But what is more important is that the executive team's active interface with customers didn't stop when they joined the corporate office.

In 2012, as Jim Sinegal was preparing to retire, he still visited each of Costco's 600 locations at least once each year, talking with employees from store managers to forklift drivers and gathering information about the customer experience. Sinegal was not the only executive committed to listening personally to input from customers and employees. 'Each and every one of the senior executives of Costco, including me,' Galanti explained, 'have a [customer] phone call or receive an e-mail or a letter on a weekly basis that we're responsible for responding to. No matter how big we are, if you don't know what's going on out there in the stores, or in our case, the warehouses, you're missing something.'

And the conversations don't end with goodbye. Costco's management brings that information to the table as it talks over what else can be done to help meet customer needs. Galanti goes on to say, 'We're constantly going back and looking at what we're doing. We operate in a healthy state of paranoia. It sounds a little perverse, but [we recognise] that we don't invent things that have patents or [are proprietary]. Once it's out there, on the very next day, not only you, the customer, but every competitor can see it. So we have to remain a moving target.'

Jim Sinegal and Jim Galanti both see listening to customers as a key reason that Costco is a market leader. Their own behaviour as executives reflects that belief and they serve as models for others.

Bill Ayer, the recently retired CEO of Alaska Airlines concurs. Listening is critical, and one of the most important lessons the airline has learned is 'to be totally and completely customer focused.' Ayer continues, 'I would tell you that the primary motivation for all of the changes that we've made, all the improvements we have made in our operations, have been driven by customers. Customers are the only reason we're in existence. They drive every decision that we make, directly or indirectly, and at the end of the day, they decide how successful we're going to be.'

Ayer modelled the behaviour he wanted within the company. Before his retirement, he still visited airports routinely, often stopping by on his way to work, a heavy travel time for the airlines. When he got there, he watched and listened. He listened to customer complaints about waiting lines, anxieties about missing flights, concerns about bags and desire for different amenities. Then, he took action. He returned to work with insights and input and encouraged others to do the same.

The result was innovative improvements that helped improve the customer experience. One example is the approach Alaska Airlines took to expediting the ticketing process by using ticketing kiosks rather than a ticket counter. 'That all came from just talking to customers and watching customers,' he said. 'I used to stop at SeaTac [airport], in fact, I still do, at 6:00 in the morning and watch people get in line at our old ticket counter. People that are running for a meeting, maybe running a little late [because] they hit traffic, and they're just scared to death when you look at them and talk to them, and they say "darn, I wasn't counting on a 20-minute wait at your ticket counter line. Can't you do this better? I may miss my flight, and my day is destroyed if that happens."'

He took that feedback to his team with a mandate to remove customer stress from the existing system. The result was a self-service kiosk system used in some foreign airports but completely unused within the U.S. airline system, and it has dramatically improved the speed with which passengers can go through the ticketing process. Is this part of marketing? According to market leaders, it is. It may not be part of the marketing function, but it is definitely part of the discipline of marketing. It is part of aligning everything the company does with customer needs and expectations, and it is critical to success.

The CEOs and other executives of companies that are market leaders spend time in the market talking with customers, listening to the feedback they receive and taking action to improve. As Ayer said, 'it's all about continual improvement' of the customer experience based on feedback from the customer, and the executive team must lead the way for improvements.

BUILDING A LISTENING CULTURE

Listening has to happen at more than the executive level. In fact, many average performers are led by executives who are very good at listening. They talk with customers, and they take action on aspects of their business that they learn need to change. The challenge is that when a company grows, if the executives are the only ones listening, they are likely to hear only a small percentage of the feedback. If the population of customers is very large, and the number of customers with whom the executive team has relationships is very small, especially if the customers have an existing relationship with the executives who speak with them, the information the leadership team receives is not likely to be representative of the population overall. This means that without a company culture that reinforces listening, these leaders may be missing extremely valuable insights that might give them the Crystal Ball Effect, the edge they need to become leaders in their industry.

Most companies need more than executives who listen, they need a culture that systematically listens to customers and passes along feedback internally. The executive team plays a critical role in building that culture, and they do it in two ways: informally, by recognising employees who help the company listen, and formally, through systems and processes designed to help companies gather information.

> Most companies need more than executives who listen, they need a culture that systematically listens to customers and passes along feedback internally.

Employees at every level within an organisation have conversations with customers or prospective customers every day. These provide excellent opportunities to gather feedback, if the employees know that doing so is important and valued and if they have the training to do so well.

At Alaska Airlines, Bill Ayer and his management team focused on helping employees understand the importance of a listening culture informally through subtle changes, feedback and persuasive conversations. Because many of the changes the process prompted were hard on employees or existing operations, the change was challenging, and when we spoke in May 2011, Ayer said it still wasn't complete.

He said the key to change was to frame the conversation in terms of the benefits to employees. If they wanted the company to remain independent, which most employees did, the company needed to be profitable. To be profitable, they needed loyal customers. To have loyal customers, they needed to be completely focused on what customers want and need.

Although many of those conversations happened at employee only meetings or in other venues where leadership could address multiple employees at the same time, it also happened individually. Ayer said that he often had conversations with front line team members, asking them how they were helping to improve the customer experience. If their feedback reflected an operational focus, he corrected them.

If they responded by saying, 'that's not what my supervisor said to do,' Ayer said his next visit was to the supervisor. This process takes time, but the outcomes are literally paying dividends for Alaska Airlines. Since 2008, Alaska Air Group's stock has outperformed every other stock in the Pacific Northwest, including Amazon. com. By explaining the importance of a customer focus to employees one conversation at a time, Ayer and his team changed Alaska Airline's focus, and the airline became a market leader and improved returns for investors.

Other companies have learned the value of customer conversations through experimentation and now provide more formalised training to help improve the impact. For example, the marketing team at Ford Motor Company's European division understood that the next generation of automobile purchasers would be teenagers, but they didn't know as much about this age group's lifestyle or priorities. To gain more insight, a group of Ford engineers and marketers spent time at a hair salon in London that also hosted experimental techno-pop music sessions.

They spent time talking to their target market, discussing their priorities and then went out together to experience their lives first hand. When they started connecting at a more personal level, they were able to get a better understanding of what mattered to the teens, and they incorporated the feedback into designs. The teens continued to provide input to the Ford team until they produced a design for a car that was both simple to drive and inexpensive to purchase.

The programme was so successful that Ford employees in North America are now being trained on how to communicate with consumers wherever they meet them, whether they happen to be in a dance club, a hair salon or a department store.[2]

Many companies, especially consumer-focused companies, are leveraging social media to communicate with customers. By some estimates, 61% of U.S. companies use social media to 'listen' to their markets at least occasionally.[3] Unfortunately, most of what happens using social media is more aptly labelled 'hearing' than 'listening.' In these cases, internal teams are more focused on the number of likes or followers or communicating to the customer than on actively listening to what they say. Yet, social media provides an unprecedented opportunity for employees within a company to gather real-time feedback.

The computer maker Dell, Inc., has been listening—and training its employees to listen—to conversations on social media. In 2010, Dell opened a social media university where employees could learn to participate on behalf of the company in social media initiatives. Within ten months, 9,000 employees had taken a course through the programme, and more than 1,000 had finished the four courses required to become a certified participant in Dell's social media programme. Dell also created a social media centre that scans the online conversations between their market and their employees, looking for patterns and developing additional ways to promote conversation. According to Manish Mehta, vice president of social media and community at Dell, the company uses the conversations as 'a systematic early warning system' for product flaws and other issues.[4]

In each of these cases, the executive team led the way by modelling the behaviour they wanted. They followed up that behaviour with formal and informal programmes that encourage employees to listen to, and take action on, what they are hearing from customers.

VALIDATING INTERNAL INFORMATION WITH THIRD-PARTY RESEARCH

The third tool that market leaders use to listen to their market is third-party research. Market research, conducted by an impartial third party, can bring valuable insights to an organisation. It can also be quite costly. The key to effectively using research is to remember that the primary purpose of market research is to reduce risk. It acts as an insurance policy, reducing risk by turning some assumptions into facts. Market research allows a company to shift from making decisions on assumptions to making decisions based on facts, or at least a reduced level of uncertainty, by testing the assumptions made by inherently biased internal decision-makers before using them to make strategic decisions.

Many companies resist market research just as they resist planning processes because they both cost time and money and don't deliver an immediate return. However, the outcome is like building a home without plans that have been reviewed for compliance with building codes. By neglecting the facts of the environment, in this case,

> The primary purpose of market research is to reduce risk. It acts as an insurance policy, reducing risk by turning some assumptions into facts.

the required building codes in the building process, the builder is highly likely to have to tear down part of what has been built in order to fix it. Although the building process may begin more quickly, the house will cost more money and time to complete.

Market research provides insight into the market's code, so that whatever is built by the company will be readily accepted by the market for which it was designed. It reduces risk by reducing mistakes and shortening the time between execution and realisation of financial returns.

Why Market Research Reduces Risk

Market research works to reduce risk in several ways. First, using a third party to listen to customer input can eliminate a company's natural tendency to filter feedback based on what the company's executive team wants to hear. Even the most adept listeners can fall into the habit of hearing what they want to hear and neglecting other information. Those who perform third-party research listen with a fresh perspective and may catch feedback that internal sources have inadvertently ignored. This reduces risk by improving the chances that the executive team will appropriately prioritise initiatives according to what the market truly wants.

Second, third-party research can improve the quality of the research results. Some audiences will resist providing direct feedback, particularly negative feedback, to a person or company with whom they have a significant relationship. As a result, the answers to questions about service quality may reflect satisfaction when, in fact, they are searching for a new vendor. However, when a third party asks and assures the respondent of anonymity, the respondent may be more forthright with his or her feedback. When a company is using satisfaction metrics to project future revenue or assess whether processes need to be improved, misinformation can result in miscalculations or missed opportunities. Market research reduces the risk of these issues by providing more accurate results to decision-makers.

Third, many companies are simply not good listeners. In these cases, market research can play an important role in helping address that shortcoming and improving the organisation's ability to respond to market needs. This substantially reduces risk by allowing companies to drive decisions from a market perspective, rather than an internal or operational perspective.

Fourth, many companies, especially national and international companies, have many markets across multiple geographies. When the geography is large, companies are often faced with trying to make sense of massive quantities of data or managing the collection and analysis of data in multiple languages or cultural environments. In these cases, using third-party researchers to help handle the workload or provide interpretation of data through a local lens can reduce workloads and improve results.

Effective Research Keeps the End in Mind

One of the reasons many executives are sceptical of the value of market research, and particularly third-party research, is that many research studies are expensive and, yet, fail to deliver actionable information that effectively reduces risk or improves return. Unfortunately, neither of these problems should exist. Market research can be quite inexpensive relative to the risk it is attempting to mitigate, and well-constructed market research always provides value, even if the results simply validate existing beliefs.

In many cases, companies who have experienced problems with expensive or ineffective market research have themselves to blame. As with other forms of outsourcing, external research firms can only perform well if they thoroughly understand the questions they need to answer, the budget available to answer them and the format of the information required at the end of the process. When the commissioning company does not accurately brief the market research firm, selects a market research firm that does not have sufficient general business knowledge in addition to marketing and technical research skills or is not very clear about their own expectations, the market research investment is less likely to provide the insurance coverage the company expected.

To be effective, market research projects should be managed carefully, keeping the desired outcomes firmly in mind. In particular, managers who are responsible for market research, whether internal or external, should do the following:

Identify Assumptions and Define Risks

Chapter 11, 'Evaluating Returns on Marketing Investments,' addressed the importance of assessing risks in the process of estimating potential returns. Risks in the planning process emerge from assumptions about the market on which marketing strategies are based.

In many cases, the risks are small. For example, a health care organisation that wishes to promote its cancer treatment capabilities may be considering a brochure to be distributed in doctors' offices that targets patients considering alternative treatment venues. The message and aspects of the hospital's services that are featured must be appropriate to the audience, or the brochure is unlikely to make an impact. On the other hand, the cost of this particular marketing tactic might be quite low. If it fails, the resulting financial failure is similarly low. Because the risk is low, any research conducted regarding placement, response or stylistic preferences could quite easily be performed by someone within the health care organisation itself.

On the other hand, some risks are quite significant. If an international consumer product manufacturer is considering a major change to a product with strong brand loyalty, as Coca Cola once did relative to its traditional cola beverage, the risk of failure is quite high. If the product change is significant and loyal customers switch products as a result, it may be difficult to regain their trust and encourage them to resume their purchasing behaviour, even if the change is reversed. If the investment in the change is also quite large, the financial loss in the event of a poor decision might be substantial.

In most cases, the risks are somewhere in between, and they may be more difficult to pinpoint. For example, we recently conducted a research study on behalf of a client whose executive team and company culture are not market-focused. This isn't to say that they aren't good at what they do. In fact, the company is one of the largest in its industry, with a track record of successful performance. They are also extremely conscientious about performance, a strong factor in their success. Nonetheless, they recognised that they were not systematically listening to their market, and they were about to embark on a strategic planning process.

The strategic planning process would result in important decisions about operations, investments and marketing over the upcoming years. If the company's understanding of its market was accurate, the results were likely to be good. However, if the company was missing something, the company might slip relative to its competitors in a highly competitive market, resulting in significant financial losses. The company wasn't sure what it didn't know or what the risks might be, but it did understand that if it made incorrect assumptions, it could lose footing against competitors. The executive team worked with us to develop research that helped them better understand the market's perception of the value they, and their competitors, brought to the market.

Assess the Appropriate Investment

In the previous hospital example, the low potential loss justifies a low investment in risk mitigation. Just as it would be expensive and potentially impossible for an individual to insure against every possible risk, it is impractical to eliminate all risk from marketing decision making. In this case, the organisation might determine that the investment of a few hours of time on behalf of medical professionals and marketing team members, for which the hospital would incur little or no incremental expense, is sufficient to mitigate that level of risk.

In the consumer product example, in which the risk is substantially higher, the company might invest more heavily in market research. It might, for example, invite customers to compare the two products and provide feedback, followed by a limited roll-out in a single geography to assess the reaction. Although these two programmes might involve more substantial financial investment than the informal, internal feedback in the hospital example, if the research averts a Coca-Cola-sized calamity, it would be well worth a more substantial financial investment.

Regardless of whether the risk is large, small or in between, the key is to understand the size of the financial risk first and then assess the level of investment that would be appropriate to convert assumptions to facts and reduce those risks. This helps ensure that the investment remains proportionate to the potential benefit associated with eliminating or reducing the risk.

Start With the End

There is an old saying that if you don't know where you are going, any road will get you there. This is particularly true of market research. If you are simply looking for information, there is plenty to be had. I have seen dozens, if not hundreds, of market research studies that are full of interesting, but completely useless, data. Most often, this is because the researchers did not understand the types of information that would be required to make the decisions for which the research was originally requested.

When working with a market research professional inside or outside the organisation, it is important to be extremely clear and specific about the type of information you need, and the format in which you need it, in order to make a decision. For example, if you will be interested in whether there are differences in answers based on gender, usage, geography or any other factor, these should be identified in advance so that the researcher can design the study with these requirements in mind.

Similarly, many researchers will include a variety of demographic or segment-based data as a part of the data-gathering process. If that information is not practical or relevant, it should not be asked. For example, many organisations ask my company's research team to include questions about respondent income in research studies. Sometimes, the data reveals interesting information about the income levels of participants, but often, that is the end of its relevance. Many companies find they cannot use the data because their databases don't track the income levels of customers or prospective customers. In these cases, when the results cannot be used for any practical purpose, it would be best not to ask the question.

It is also important to anticipate how you will respond to information when it is received. Many researchers sit across from clients who, at the end of an expensive study, hear the results and say, 'Yes, but did you ask them what would happen if we did it this way instead?' To prevent this issue, the market research team and the management team should talk through how they would respond to the potential range of responses, particularly relative to questions with a limited range of responses. If additional information or options should be presented, it is more cost effective to identify these before the research begins.

The managers responsible for market research should be specific about the format in which the data should be delivered in order to be useful. In some cases, static numbers are sufficient. In other cases, the information is only useful if it can be compared to industry data, historical information from previous studies or in other formats. When the data will be compared to the results of other studies or the information will be gathered routinely to track progress, the researcher will need to format the question appropriately for this purpose.

When a company does solicit input, it should also be prepared to act on what it hears. For example, if a company retains a research firm to inquire about customer satisfaction and receives a low score, it should be prepared to take action. Although many individuals are happy to provide feedback to the companies who serve their needs, they will be less likely to respond in the future if they see no response to their concerns. When a service business conducts this type of study, especially if the population is small, I often recommend that the company send a thank you note either directly or through the third-party researcher that summarises the action the company will take as a result of the feedback the customers provided.

KEY MARKET RESEARCH TOOLS AND CONCEPTS

Like other areas of marketing, market research has become very sophisticated and specialised over the past 100 years. It also suffers some of the definitional issues that are prevalent in marketing in general.

Marketing research and *market research* are often used interchangeably. However, many marketing experts consider them to be different types of research. Market research is generally considered to be systematic research designed to uncover or validate information about markets overall, including customers and non-customers, market segments, competitors, market perceptions and market trends. Marketing research is much more focused on the specific processes, activities and intermediate metrics of your marketing efforts. Marketing research is used to assess brand familiarity, measure ad views, test concepts or copy or measure customer satisfaction, among other things. It can also be used to test new marketing initiatives that are under development prior to actually launching them.

From my perspective, market research is the more comprehensive term because it includes both listening to the market overall and listening for specific information about marketing activities. For the purposes of this chapter, marketing research will be discussed only as a subset of market research.

Types of Research

Two basic types of market research are primary research and secondary research. *Primary research* relies on data gathered directly from the market itself. *Secondary research* is gathered from libraries, census information or other sources that gathered the information, often for different purposes. Although both types of research are valuable, when the financial risk of an assumption is significant, it may be more appropriate to gather primary research, rather than to rely strictly on secondary data.

Two types of primary research are *qualitative* and *quantitative studies*. *Qualitative studies* focus on generating a deeper understanding of market perceptions and opinions through conversations. It typically involves a small set of market participants, which means that the results can generally not be statistically relied upon to be representative of the overall population. However, *qualitative* approaches typically provide the researcher with an opportunity to explore information in greater detail. Common qualitative approaches include *one-on-one interviews, pilot or beta testing, observational research* and *focus groups*. In general, the results provide directional guidance, rather than definitive answers.

By contrast, quantitative studies focus on generating more statistically representative, numbers-based data. Quantitative research is mathematically based and may be used to test a particular hypothesis or theory. It relies on the selection of a representative subset of the population of sufficient size to be statistically reliable at a level acceptable to the organisation requesting the research. Because of the size of the population and the desire to have comparable data, the researcher asks defined questions, with limited opportunity to probe responses in greater detail. The most common quantitative approaches include mail, e-mail, telephone and *intercept surveys*.

The results of quantitative data are generally expressed with a level of statistical reliability, such as 95% + / - 5%. The *confidence interval*, expressed as a percentage, indicates the *margin of error* in which the answer is likely to lie. The confidence interval is the second percentage: + / - 5% in this case. For example, if 55% of the population responded 'yes,' and the confidence interval is 5%, the actual percentage of the population that would answer 'yes,' if the entire population were asked, is likely to be somewhere between 50% and 60%. Fifty-five per cent less 5% is 50%, the lower end of the confidence range, and the upper end is 55% plus 5%, or 60%.

The *confidence level* indicates how sure you can be that the response is, indeed, within that range. The confidence level is indicated by the first percentage, which is 95% in this case. A confidence level of 95% indicates that there is a 95% chance that the actual answer is within that range and a fairly small chance (5%) that the actual answer is outside of the margin of error range. Most researchers strive for a 95% confidence level for market research.

Three factors affect the size of the confidence interval. The first is the sample size. The larger the sample size, the more likely it is to reflect the population overall, and the smaller the confidence interval will be. However, the relationship is not linear. For example, if the population is 1,000, the sample size is 100, and the percentage responding 'yes' is 55%, the confidence level in our previous example would be 95% + / − 9.26%. However, if the sample size were to double, the confidence level improves, dropping to 95% + / − 6.17%.

The second factor that affects the confidence interval is the percentage of the population that selects a particular answer. If 99% of the sample size responded yes, the margin of error is reduced because of the overwhelming response rate. Using the previous example, with a sample size of 100, if 99% of the sampled population said 'yes,' the margin of error would be 99% + / − 1.85%. If 50% of the population said yes, the confidence interval would be + / − 9.30%.

Finally, the size of the population overall affects confidence intervals. If the population is small, the confidence interval will be smaller. For example, if the population in the previous example was 100, instead of 1,000, and the sample size remained at 10% of the population, the small size of the overall population would cause the confidence interval to rise dramatically. If 50% say 'yes,' the confidence interval at a 95% level rises to + / − 29.55%.

Bias Risk in Research

Both qualitative and quantitative research approaches are subject to bias. In fact, it is almost impossible to completely avoid bias in research design. However, an understanding of the most common forms of bias can help the non-marketing manager more effectively identify potential problems, particularly with internally-conducted research.

The most common types of bias include the following:

- *Selection and sampling biases.* Confidence levels and confidence intervals assume a random sampling of the population. If researchers only conduct research at certain times or in certain places, the sample population may not reflect the actual population. Researchers who sample on a convenience basis, polling only people who are easily accessible during their work day, are more likely to be subject to this bias.

  Another common source of this type of bias is the selection process. When a sample selects itself by opting in or out of a study, the responses may be biased because there may be a difference in opinions between those who choose to participate and those who decline.

- *Interviewer or moderator bias.* In qualitative studies in which the interpretation depends heavily on the facilitator who is asking questions in response to what he or she hears, one of the most common sources of bias is *moderator bias.* This occurs when a moderator interprets participant comments or responds in non-verbal ways to what is said based on his or her own perception of the topic. This can also happen in telephone interviews when an interviewer modifies a response based on his or her interpretation of the respondent's reaction.

  This can also arise in the interpretation of data, when a person allows their personal opinion to influence their interpretation of either qualitative of quantitative data. This type of bias can be a particular concern for internal market research functions in which individuals may interpret results based on what they wanted or expected to see and are not specifically trained in the art of unbiased research interpretation.

- *Design bias.* Bias is introduced in the design process in many ways. Often, the source is the question itself, which may lead the respondent to answer in a particular way or in the array of responses from which the respondent may choose. For example, the question 'How significantly will the following action affect you?' assumes that the respondent will be affected by the action. If he or she might otherwise have answered that it would not affect him or her at all, he or she may feel more likely to interpret an impact with this form of question. Similarly, if a survey asks 'Which of the following do you read?' and does not offer a 'None of the above' or similar response, it may be prompting inaccurate responses.

Confusing language or a lack of parallel construction in survey questions can also result in inaccurate responses. For example, if the question asks about the number of times per month a respondent purchases a product, but the response options are outlined in times per week, the respondent may miss the change.

- *Measurement and response biases.* These issues arise when respondents shape their responses in a way that they suspect will please the researcher or beneficiary. For example, it is common for researchers asking about intent to donate or volunteer for a non-profit to receive overly positive response rates. Although respondents may respond with rosy intents in the survey process, the actual participation rates are often considerably lower. This problem is particularly pervasive in studies asking about socially undesirable behaviours, such as violence or criminal activities, or when participants know their behaviours are being tracked or observed.

Research Design

The effectiveness of a research instrument is typically assessed for both validity and reliability. *Validity* refers to whether the research answers the question or questions for which it was designed. *Reliability* addresses whether the research will deliver data that is representative at the expected level. Qualitative research is less representative of the overall population, but the research team should still take precautions to minimise bias and ensure that the information is at least directionally accurate. Quantitative research should be more accurate, and researchers should take particular care to address potential sources of bias in the design and execution of the research.

To mitigate the risk of certain types of biases, researchers often alternate the use of qualitative and quantitative research. For example, a researcher might interview or host focus groups with clients or prospects to get a better understanding of the range of possible responses to various questions and then use that understanding to design questions for a quantitative survey. This initial qualitative step reduces the risk of overlooking response options that a typical respondent might expect to see in a quantitative survey.

In other cases, companies may conduct *blind research studies* in which the respondent does not know who requested the research. This reduces the incidence of response bias because the respondent cannot tailor responses to an unknown audience. In *double-blind research studies*, both the respondent and the individual conducting the interview or survey are prohibited from knowing the organisation for which the research is being conducted. This design structure is intended to reduce both response bias and interviewer bias.

Although researchers are trained to develop research tools to be as free of bias as feasible given the budget constraints and the importance of accuracy, mistakes do happen. It is important for a non-marketing manager involved in overseeing the research process to monitor for sources of bias that may skew the research results.

The Art of Interpretation in Research

Have you heard the story of the woman who met Picasso on the street and asked him to sketch something for her? Picasso agrees, and five minutes later, hands her a piece of paper with a simple pencil drawing.

'That will be $10,000,' he says.

Shocked, the woman protests. 'That much money for only five minutes of work?'

Picasso nods, and with a smile, explains. 'It did not take me five minutes. It took me 30 years.'

The art of interpreting market research is similar. There are many market researchers who can conduct a study and create a set of attractive infographics to illustrate the results. When the project is simple and the risk is low, it is reasonable to hunt for the best price among the many competitors.

However, if the risks that the research is designed to mitigate are more significant, and getting the wrong answer or misinterpreting the answer could have a significant negative impact, an investment in a more sophisticated level of research and analysis is more appropriate.

Insight and interpretation requires a knowledgeable professional with the business experience to interpret the results in the context of your unique organisational objectives and who understands the importance of statistical nuances. It also requires someone with enough marketing expertise to help you translate the data into an actionable plan, which, in my experience, is the most effective way to ensure success. Without that level of insight, the results will stand little chance of providing the risk mitigation that research is intended to deliver.

Sophisticated market research is often more expensive. However, given that the results will be forming the foundation of your strategic planning process, the reduction in risk may be worth the added investment.

When considering options relative to third-party researchers, managers should listen carefully to the questions the researchers ask when planning, particularly when it comes to their understanding of your organisational objectives, and to their experience outside of the simple realm of data gathering.

QUESTIONS FOR NON-MARKETING MANAGERS TO ASK ABOUT CULTIVATING SYSTEMATIC LISTENING

To ensure that your company has the tools and systems required to listen to the market effectively, the non-marketing manager should consider the answers to the following questions:

- How well does our organisation listen to the market? When we get information from the market, do we act on it? Or does the feedback simply get filed with the report that brought it to our attention?

- Do our executives model the way by actively engaging in conversations with the market themselves?

- What processes or programmes support internal communications about market feedback?

- How do we reward people who pass along market feedback? Is their input ignored or valued?

- Are there assumptions about the market that we are making in our business or marketing planning that we have not validated? How much risk do they pose to our organisation's financial health?

- If we are supplementing learning with internal or external market research, how often do we do so? Are we using external resources appropriately? Did we select a research team that has the requisite knowledge to interpret the data in a business context so that we are maximising the value we get out of our research investment?

CHAPTER 15 SUMMARY

Market leaders benefit from the Crystal Ball Effect, the perception among their competitors that they are better at predicting where the market will go and how to get there first. They don't actually have a crystal ball, of course, but they do have stronger listening skills than their competitors.

Market leaders actively listen to the market, asking clarifying questions and pursuing issues and concerns with the eagerness of a friend wanting to help. They do so in three key ways. First, their executive team takes a personal interest in what customers are saying. They pay calls on customers, talk with customer-facing employees, respond to customer complaints or concerns or maintain an active presence in social media. And they do more than listen. They take action on what they hear.

Second, they actively build company-wide processes to gather information and incorporate feedback. In some cases, these processes are informal, encouraged by positive reinforcement and internal communications. In other cases, the organisation builds more formal structures, sometimes within the marketing function and incorporated into other aspects of operations. In all cases, the information these more formal structures gather is systematically reviewed and shared within the organisation, and the input forms the basis of a continual improvement process.

Finally, the company uses formal market research, using either internal or external research resources, to supplement on-going processes. Whereas some research is used to measure outcomes, the market research related to listening is designed to gather market information that reduces the risk involved in business decision-making. To be effective, market research should be budgeted based on the size of the financial risk and the potential impact failure could have on the company and designed with the information required to mitigate that risk firmly in mind.

Market research, like other aspects of marketing, has become highly technical and specialised. Two main types of research are primary and secondary. Primary research is divided into qualitative research, which is based on discussions and concept exploration, and quantitative research, which is based on statistical sampling and numerical outcomes. Market research must be carefully designed to minimise the impact of bias and generate valid and reliable results. In addition, companies should be careful to select a research team that provides the appropriate level of interpretive expertise. If the insight is critical or the risk associated with poor outcomes is significant, a company should identify a research partner who can interpret the data in a business context. Although many researchers are adept at the mechanics of conducting a study, fewer are skilled in the art of interpretation.

This combination of executives who model the importance of listening, systems and processes that facilitate the gathering and distribution of data and formalised research to mitigate risk and provide added insight are the source of the market leader's insight. Together, they provide the insight required to generate the Crystal Ball Effect.

Endnotes

1 Fuller, David W., Telvich, Tim and Shechter, Brenda. 'The Empire Built on Values,' *The Costco Connection*, January 2012. www.costcoconnection. com/connection/201201/u1= issues# pg27

2 Balu, Rekha. 'Listen Up!' *Fast Company*, April 30, 2000. www.fastcompany.com/39485/listen

3 Ritchie, James. 'Most U.S. companies listen to customers on social networking sites,' *Cincinnati Business Courier*, June 20, 2012. www.bizjournals. com/cincinnati/blog/socialmadness/2012/06/most-us-companies-listen-to.html

4 Fowler, Geoffrey A. 'Are You Talking to Me?' *The Wall Street Journal*, April 25, 2011. http://online.wsj. com/article/SB10001424052748704116404576263083 970961862.html

Section 5

CONCLUSION

16

FOUR TESTS TO RUN BEFORE FUNDING

Many non-marketing executives' first glimpse of marketing plans, particularly promotional plans, is when the budget is being prepared for approval. CFOs and financial managers, in particular, often have limited involvement in the planning process. Yet, they are asked to evaluate whether the marketing department or executive team's proposal is a good financial investment for the company. At the same time, when marketing efforts fail, the CFO and the financial management team is most likely to see and feel the fallout as the company scrambles to address missed revenue targets and unanticipated expenses.

Regardless of your level of involvement in developing plans for the marketing function, there are four tests you can run to help you determine whether the proposed marketing investments are solid investments for your company: the Alignment Test, the Assignment Test, the Risk Assessment Test and the Anticipated Returns Test.

This chapter reviews each of these tests and illustrates their use with very simplified case studies.

THE ALIGNMENT TEST

The *Alignment Test* provides a means of evaluating how well the plan is aligned with business and financial objectives. Plans that satisfactorily pass this test are more likely to succeed for two reasons. First, if the executive and marketing teams can both walk through the plan and explain the connection between the marketing tactics they have selected, the marketing strategies they are pursuing, the impact these investments are likely to have on the influencing factors and how these activities will ultimately affect business and financial outcomes, the plan is more likely to be consistent with, and supportive of, the company's overall strategy. If the plan fails this test, it can be an indicator that the plan was developed without sufficient executive input or support or that the team identifying tactics did not clearly understand the objectives.

Second, when executives clearly understand how and why investments are being made and how they work together to achieve business objectives, they are less likely to second guess the planning process or discontinue funding before the objectives are achieved. This test helps ensure that the marketing and executive teams are in agreement on the plan before the plan is executed, improving the odds that it will be completed successfully.

How the Test Works

This test follows the flow of the Marketing Alignment Map introduced in chapter 4, 'Evaluating Marketing Plan Alignment.' However, it approaches it in a different order. The objective is to ensure each key member of the marketing and executive team can explain why the company is engaging in specific marketing activities, like a coupon campaign or a new distribution channel, and what the outcome will be on the market and the business as a result. This test can be performed at the company level, division level or an individual investment level. At each step, all parties should understand and be in agreement with the actions.

To facilitate this exercise, I recommend using a chart similar to box 16-1 that follows:

- **Step 1.** Participants should be able to specifically describe the marketing tactics or activities in which the organisation will be investing and the way in which the company will know that it has been satisfactorily completed. This helps prevent vague tactical objectives and improves accountability.

  For examples of these, return to chapters 7–10, which cover the most common categories of marketing tactics (products/services, pricing approaches, distribution approaches and promotions) and common tactical measurements.

- **Step 2.** Participants should then be able to link each marketing tactic to the marketing strategy or strategies to which it is connected and describe how the tactics will help the organisation fulfil the strategy's objective. The tactics should make sense given what the executive or manager knows about the target market's purchasing decision process and demographics. Like the marketing tactics, the strategies should have clearly articulated metrics associated with them. This ensures that the tactics are based on broader marketing strategies and weren't created as 'one off' activities.

  Additional guidance on confirming a fit between the marketing tactics, marketing strategies and market demographics are included in chapter 6, 'Aligning Marketing Tactics With Influencing Factors.'

- **Step 3.** Each strategy should, in turn, be clearly tied to one or more influencing factors, the purchasing decision criteria that the marketing initiatives are designed to address. This helps ensure that the marketing strategies have been developed and the tactics selected with the company's own market in mind, rather than as mirrors of other players in the market or in an unfocused effort to increase brand awareness. The management team should be confident that if the company pursues the marketing strategies identified, they will have the desired impact on the influencing factor.

  Additional information about this step is the subject of chapter 5, 'Understanding What Influences Market Behaviour.'

- **Step 4.** Next, participants should also be able to describe the combined impact the tactics supporting a marketing strategy will have on the influencing factor(s), described in terms of expected marketing outcomes. Expected marketing outcomes should be stated in the same terms as both the organisational objectives and the expected financial returns. This provides an opportunity for questions regarding expected financial outcomes, timing of results and related expenses.

  This is part of the return on investment (ROI) estimation process outlined in chapter 11, 'Evaluating Returns on Marketing Investments.'

- **Step 5.** Finally, participants should be able to describe how the business and financial outcomes of the plan dovetail with the company's business and financial goals. This confirms that the company is prioritising correctly based on the factors most likely to affect its success. If the sum of the impact of all marketing strategies is insufficient to meet the organisational and financial objectives of the organisation, either the business and financial objectives or the marketing plan must be adjusted.

Box 16-1: Sample Alignment Test Chart

	DO THESE …	TIE TO THESE …?
Step 1:	**Marketing Tactics:** Specific activities the company will take	**Expected Tactical Outcomes:** metrics and related outcomes used to evaluate success
	Identify the primary marketing tactics the company will pursue …	… and the metrics that will be used to determine whether they were successfully completed, along with the measurement processes and systems required to track success.
Step 2:	**Marketing Tactics and Expected Tactical Outcomes**	**Marketing Strategies and Objectives:** The approaches the company will take to favourably affect the factors that influence the customer's purchasing decision criteria, stated with measurable objectives.
	Verify that the marketing tactics and expected outcomes …	… support the marketing strategies, are appropriate choices for the targeted markets and together will deliver the impact expected of the marketing strategy.
Step 3:	**Marketing Strategies and Objectives**	**Influencing Factor:** Aspects of the customer's purchasing decision process that support or impede the company's ability to sell to the market.
	Assess whether the marketing strategies and objectives related to a given influencing factor …	… will have the expected impact on the influencing factor.
Step 4:	**Influencing Factor and Marketing Strategies**	**Anticipated Business Outcomes and Financial Returns:** The measurable outcomes relative to business goals and the financial returns the company expects from its marketing efforts.
	Review the impact a change in the influencing factors …	… will have on business and financial results of the company.
Step 5:	**Anticipated Business Outcomes and Financial Returns**	**Performance Expectations:** The company's targeted performance levels
	Verify that the anticipated impact the marketing programme will have on the company's business and financial performance …	… meets company expectations and merits the investment.

Case Study: The Alignment Test in Action

The subject of this case study is a proposed marketing investment within a mid-sized services company that provides health management services to large companies as a way to lower their client's overall health insurance costs. They are under the leadership of a new CEO, who has commissioned market research to get a better understanding of the factors impeding corporate growth. The research suggests that the market is interested in improving employees' health through proactive management because it will lower health care costs, but there are a number of barriers.

First, the link between the company's services and health outcomes is not clear to prospective customers. Second, many companies use alternative approaches, such as funding gym memberships. Finally, the company's name and the services it offers are not well known beyond its own clients. The research also identified the likely decision-makers for services and other influencers within the organisations whose opinions could sway the decision. Further, the research suggests that if the health management services company can increase awareness of their organisation and the benefits of their services by 40%, they are likely to increase their gross margins by 120% over three years.

The new CEO, with the enthusiastic support of the marketing team, proposed that the organisation invest in its first advertising campaign in order to increase awareness. The associated budget line item was significant to the company, and the CFO was concerned. Most of the company's previous sales had been made by a sales team that had relationships with the decision-makers within their client organisation. To help allay his concerns—or identify issues he can bring to the leadership team—the CFO decided to walk through the Alignment Test, as depicted in the boxes that follow.

The proposed marketing tactic is a significant advertising campaign, using broadcast and print media. The tactical objectives the marketing team has outlined in the proposed plan are fairly clear. They identified the specific media they want to use and the number of impressions they want to have. They have a timeline for execution and know how many commercials and advertisements they want to run before the end of the fiscal year.

	DO THESE …	TIE TO THESE …?	CONCLUSION
	Marketing Tactics	**Expected Tactical Outcomes**	The tactic is very specific and has clear and measurable completion and intermediate metrics.
Step 1:	Advertising campaign, print and broadcast, positioning the company as a leading provider of business-to-business employee health management solutions.	*Completion Metrics:* Three flights of six ads in business journals within the geographic service area over 18 months; one ad running on local broadcast television over two, three-month periods. *Intermediate Marketing Metrics:* X impressions within decision-maker populations.	

The tactics also seem to align with the marketing strategies the marketing team had identified, based on the market research. Increasing visibility among decision-makers is a key strategy, and the advertising campaign's objective is to increase awareness. The local business journals and the broadcast stations were selected based on the media identified in the market research.

	DO THESE …	TIE TO THESE …?	CONCLUSION
Step 2:	**Marketing Tactics and Expected Tactical Outcomes**	**Marketing Strategies and Objectives**	The broadcast media is too broad and would waste funds. The business journals are probably more appropriate. This tactic alone will not make the desired impact.
	Advertising campaign on local broadcast television and business journals. Media sources were selected based on research.	40% increase in recognition of company name and services among decision-makers.	

The research indicated that the target market uses both of these media for information. However, the market is relatively small, with a target client population of 450 companies and less than 2,000 relevant decision-makers. After further discussion about the feasibility of this audience, the management team decides that the broadcast advertising is too broad an approach to make sense. Although it might reach the decision-makers, it would also 'waste' messaging on thousands of individuals outside their target market. They conclude that the business journal advertising alone would be insufficient to meet their strategic objective.

As a result, they ask the marketing team to revisit the research and the plan. A more careful evaluation of the client's decision-making criteria, mapped out through the research, suggests that a referral from a peer would be more influential than simply increasing name recognition. This leads the team to add a referral programme to the marketing mix, shaped by data from the survey. When the management team reviewed the revised plan, the results looked more favourable.

		TIE TO THESE …?	CONCLUSION
Step 1:	**Marketing Tactics**	**Expected Tactical Outcomes**	The tactics are very specific and have clear and measurable completion and intermediate metrics.
	Print advertising campaign positioning the company as a leading provider of business-to-business employee health management solutions. Referral campaign run among existing customer.	*Completion Metrics:* Three flights of six ads in business journals within the geographic service area over 18 months. *Intermediate Marketing Metrics:* X impressions within decision-maker populations. Y referrals within the first six months.	

Continued on p.282

Continued from p.281

	DO THESE ...	TIE TO THESE ...?	CONCLUSION
Step 2:	**Marketing Tactics and Expected Tactical Outcomes**	**Marketing Strategies and Objectives**	The revised tactics match market demographics and customer decision-making processes, and the management is confident they will have the desired impact.
	Advertising campaign in business journals. Referral campaign.	40% increase in recognition of company name and services among decision-makers.	

Upon reviewing the revised plan, the management team was confident that the combination of tactics would increase name recognition by 40%. The company moved to the next step in the Alignment Test. When the management team considers the alignment of the strategies with the purchasing decision process, they seem to be a strong fit.

	DO THESE ...	TIE TO THESE ...?	CONCLUSION
Step 3:	**Marketing Strategies and Objectives**	**Influencing Factors**	Yes. Based on what the company knows about how the market makes decisions, the strategies make sense and will have an impact.
	40% increase in recognition of company name and services among decision-makers.	Awareness that services are an option. Receiving a referral from a peer.	

Although the company has limited baseline information, the marketing team has made an informed assumption using the research about the impact that a change in the influencing factor could have on revenues. After much discussion, the CFO concurs. A 40% increase in the recognition of the company's name and services could allow the company to increase revenues by 22% over the next two years. The company's CEO was targeting a 20% increase in revenues.

	DO THESE ...	TIE TO THESE ...?	CONCLUSION
Step 4:	**Influencing Factor and Marketing Strategies**	**Anticipated Business Outcomes & Financial Returns**	The risk-adjusted ROI seems solid, and the management team is confident that the anticipated change in customer perception will deliver the growth as indicated.
	40% increase in recognition of company name and services among decision-makers and increased referrals from peers.	Expand existing services by 22%. 462% return on investment (ROI).	
Step 5:	**Anticipated Business Outcomes and Financial Returns**	**Performance Expectations:** The company's targeted performance levels	The anticipated business and financial returns meet the company's performance expectations.
	Expand existing services by 22%. 462% ROI.	Revenue growth of 20%. No investment with an anticipated ROI of less than 100%.	

Based on the Alignment Test, the CFO recommends that the management team approve the plan as revised.

THE ASSIGNMENT TEST

Even when a company's marketing plan satisfies the Alignment Test, it can fail for other reasons. One of the most common is that the budgeting process took into consideration materials costs, including advertising buys and other promotions costs, research and development, hard costs associated with channel expansions and the impact of pricing approaches, but failed to consider the incremental time required to execute the plan. In some cases, aggressive new marketing plans pile additional work onto existing employees' plates, increasing the chances of burnout or making it difficult to meet deadlines. In other cases, the budgeted costs do not accurately reflect the actual cost because the company must add additional staff, either internal or external, to support execution. These are the issues outlined in chapter 13, 'Staffing the Marketing Department,' regarding staffing the marketing function.

The *Assignment Test* helps avert failure in execution by ensuring that every activity has been allocated to a specific resource who has, in turn, accepted that responsibility.

When I am facilitating marketing plan development with middle-market companies, I generally complete the Assignment Test with them before presenting the results to the executive team. With small companies, the non-marketing executives with budget responsibility, including the CEO, chief operating officer (COO), CFO and others are often involved in the process itself. Although many executives suggest they simply skip this section, I recommend that they remain involved to ensure the assignment of responsibilities is realistic. In larger companies, this test can be delegated to the marketing team. The non-marketing executive should simply confirm that all additional workload, including oversight and coordination, have been assigned, and the assignments accepted prior to funding.

How the Test Works

Whether conducted by the executive team or delegated to the marketing team for completion, the non-marketing executive should ensure that the time required for additional activities is budgeted and accepted by the individuals to whom it is assigned. To do so, use the following steps:

- **Step 1.** First, review each marketing tactic identified within the plan, breaking it into the steps required for completion.

- **Step 2.** Next, estimate the amount of time required to complete the activity. In many cases, we find marketing professionals are optimistic about the amount of hours that will be required. As a result, the budgeted time figures are quite low. If possible, time requirements should be estimated based on prior experience or the investment of time in similar projects.

- **Step 3.** Once all the activities are outlined and the time required for each step has been estimated, make sure each activity has been assigned to an employee or group of employees for execution. During this step, look at any existing activities that have been removed from an employee's workload. For example, if the marketing planning process identified existing activities that are not a fit to updated strategic objectives, and those programmes are eliminated, the employee should have available time.

  The net number of hours assigned to the employee must be realistic, or the plan is unlikely to receive the attention required to make it a success. Also, the employee to which the tasks are assigned should have the requisite skill sets to complete the job effectively.

- **Step 4.** Finally, confirm that every employee to whom a task has been assigned has accepted the additional workload and believes he or she can complete the task without negatively affecting other areas of his or her workload.

When I am facilitating marketing planning retreats, particularly with small and mid-sized companies, I use box 16-2 to facilitate the conversation.

Box 16-2: Sample Assignment Test Chart

STEP 1	STEP 2		STEP 3	STEP 4
Marketing Tactic This is the specific tactic, whether it is a new product introduction, a temporary pricing approach or a new promotional initiative.	**Specific Activities** The activities that will be required to execute on the tactic.	**Hours and Skills Required** The number of hours required by skill-set.	**Assignment** The employee, or team of employees, to whom the task of completing the activity is assigned.	**Confirmation** Y/N

Case Study: The Assignment Test in Action

The CEO of a national professional service firm wants to conduct a performance audit of his firm's marketing efforts—and then help the company update its marketing plan. Although the company has experienced steady growth, it hasn't kept pace with market growth in many of its markets, and the managing partner feels that the marketing could be at fault.

After interviewing partners, clients and marketing team members and looking at the company's marketing promotions, pricing structure and competitive environment, it becomes evident that the biggest barrier to growth was a channel problem. Clients select among equally qualified professional service providers, in a mature and very competitive market, based on relationships with the key service provider. In professional services, the professionals, whether they are CPAs, lawyers, architects, engineers or consultants, are the primary sales force for the company. In this case, its sales team is primarily responsive in nature. Because of this, its smaller and 'hungrier' competitors had begun to erode the possibility for additional growth through more aggressive business development efforts.

Based on this analysis, and working with a small team of marketers and partners, the CEO developed a new marketing plan for the company that included an increased focus on relationship development. The plan included training for its 'sales force,' the development of personal business development plans, updated collateral materials designed based on feedback from partners about their needs during business development calls as well as clients, client entertainment events, seminars and other elements. The plan satisfied the Alignment Test, and when the plan was presented to the partners, on whose plates the plan laid most of the responsibility for execution, it was heartily approved.

At first glance, it met the Assignment Test as well. After all, the partners, in a company-wide meeting of the partnership, had been presented with and eagerly supported the plan. However, the CEO wisely took one final step before considering the plan complete. He outlined how each office's managing partner would hold the partners in their office accountable and was very specific about the time that would be required. Next, he asked each managing partner to take the outline of responsibilities to each partner in his or her office and request that he or she review and sign a form acknowledging that he or she could, and would, accept these responsibilities. If they would not sign, the managing partners were requested to ask what changes would be required in order to make the plan operational for each managing partner.

Although this effort was somewhat counter-cultural because the firm's partners had traditionally operated largely independently, it paid off. About 10% of the partners signed off. This was roughly consistent with the company's historical performance. The other 90% all had reasons that they wouldn't or couldn't participate, from workload, to their own perception of client relationships or their performance. Approved as it was designed, this plan would fail.

After several more months of work to address the concerns, the firm adjusted the plan, adding in some staffing changes, additional coaching on delegation and time management and including incentives for performance. When the plan was finally approved, most of the partners had signed off on the workload, and the expected outcomes had been adjusted to reflect the expected impact of those who might not carry through.

Although this problem is particularly common among professional service organisations of all sizes, it is also common in other business-to-business settings and with fund development plans for non-profit organisations. In the latter case, the plan usually includes some component of board engagement. When approved, the board is often enthusiastic about the outcomes, but the response of individual board members, when asked about the status of their personal commitments to raising money, is often 'I didn't think you meant *me*.'

THE RISK ASSESSMENT TEST

Many plans fail because individuals responsible for planning have made overly optimistic assumptions about outcomes. This has two negative impacts. First, it can encourage ineffective spending. Second, when the plan's performance begins falling short of expectations because of poor assumptions, it increases the odds that the executive team will cut or eliminate funding of this plan and be more inclined to do so with future plans as well.

Assumptions are necessary in any planning process. However, they do represent risk. Too many assumptions mean that the expected outcomes are less certain. The *Risk Assessment Test* reviews the plan for assumptions and serves as a basis for adjusting estimated financial returns, making them more reliable for financial planning purposes.

How the Test Works

The marketing or planning team is typically the group that assesses assumptions and performs this test. However, the executive team should review the results and evaluate whether any key assumptions were missed. To complete both processes, use the following steps:

- **Step 1.** First, the marketing or planning team should review each strategy within the plan and evaluate the assumptions made relative to potential risk. To do so, use the *risk assessment decision tree* introduced in chapter 11 and reproduced again here as figure 16-1.

Figure 16-1: Risk Assessment Decision Tree

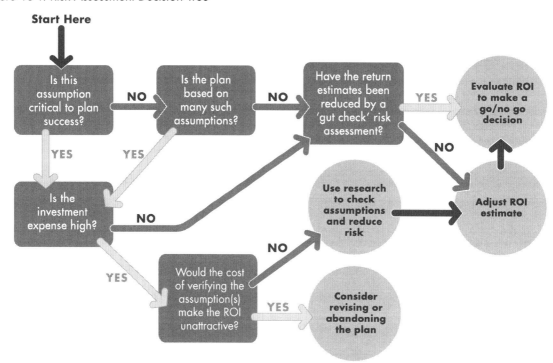

By reviewing each assumption relative to the risk assessment decision tree, the team can evaluate where the plan contains significant risk and work to mitigate those risks through research before reviewing the plan with the executive team. Once the team agrees that there are no further adjustments to the assumptions, the plan or the anticipated ROI, the team is ready to present the plan to the executive team.

- **Step 2.** When the executive team reviews the plan, they should ask team members to review with them the critical assumptions and describe any mitigating actions that have, or could be, taken. Critical assumptions include assumptions which, if incorrect, will cause the marketing strategy or tactic to fail or will result in substantial financial loss. To facilitate the discussion, the planning team might present a list of assumptions in a format similar to the one in box 16-3.

Box 16-3: Sample Critical Assumptions Chart

MARKETING STRATEGIES AND/OR TACTICS	CRITICAL ASSUMPTIONS	MITIGATING ACTIONS
This is the specific marketing strategy or tactic, whether it is a new product introduction, a temporary pricing approach or a new promotional initiative.	These are assumptions that are critical to the plan's success and/or will cause substantial financial loss if incorrect.	These are the actions the team has taken to mitigate the risk. These could include testing through market research, reliance on historical performance or other data which lends credibility to the assumption.

- **Step 3.** Using this information, the executive team can assess whether further adjustment of expected returns or anticipated impact are warranted or whether additional testing is required prior to plan approval.

Case Study: The Risk Assessment Test in Action

Chapter 11, which reviews the Measurement Myth, includes one example of the use of the risk assessment decision tree. To illustrate the process using another, consider a restaurant that is developing a new marketing plan. The owner, also the marketing director for the restaurant, is discussing the plan with the manager.

The owner has been chatting with guests as they come in for meals, asking them how they found out about the restaurant. If someone referred them, she asks for their name, so that she can thank them for the referral. When guests indicate that they have visited the restaurant before, she finds a way to ask what they particularly enjoyed. She has also tracked guests who return repeatedly and knows them by name.

As a result of these conversations, the owner had created an informal tally of results. She found that about 35% of her guests came in based on a recommendation from a friend who had dined there in the past. Another 40% lived in the neighbourhood and noticed the restaurant when they were running errands. The last 25% came in because of some promotional coupons she had distributed at farmers' markets in the region. There were a few guests who referred more guests than anyone else. In addition, a few guests who initially came in because of the promotional coupons returned later without one.

Her restaurant was fairly new, and she had more capacity than she did money for marketing, so she knew that her plan would need to be thoughtfully constructed. Based on what she knew, she felt the key influencers of market behaviour were recommendations, visibility and discounts. However, individuals who came because of recommendations or visibility were more likely to return. Her estimate was that 50% of the individuals in that category eventually returned to the restaurant. By contrast, only about 20% of the promotional coupon recipients would return.

She decided on two primary marketing strategies. First, she decided to work on increasing recommendations by 35%. Second, she decided to maintain her focus on the local farmers' market because it did seem to be producing some sampling behaviour. If that approach was successful, she would have enough returning business that she could eliminate the coupon programme, which was relatively expensive. This programme would, she decided, allow her to meet her growth goals.

To increase recommendations, she decided to begin offering a gift to individuals whose recommendations resulted in a new customer through the door. She planned to offer the programme to anyone who ate at the restaurant. To participate, they would sign up for the programme and when a guest gave their name as the referral source, she would e-mail them a coupon for a free dessert.

In the course of explaining the new recommendation programme, about which she was quite enthusiastic, the manager asked her about the possible drawbacks or risks associated with the plan. After careful considerations, she identified the following assumptions as shown in box 16-4.

Box 16-4: Restaurant Recommendation Programme Critical Assumptions

MARKETING STRATEGIES AND/OR TACTICS	CRITICAL ASSUMPTIONS	ELABORATION
Increase recommendations through a rewards programme	An incentive is required to prompt recommendations. Guests will participate in the programme.	If recommendations happen without incentive, it is possible that adding a recommendation incentive will discourage guests who worry that friends might question their motives. If recommendations happen without a gift, adding a reward programme may simply be adding an expense without substantial benefit. Clearly, in order to be successful, guests must participate in the programme. Success will be measured by the number of new customers that report having tried the restaurant based on a recommendation.

She considered the significance of each of these risks against the risk assessment decision tree, answering each question in turn:

- **Is this assumption critical to plan success?** Yes. The owner decided both assumptions represented risk. The first assumption, that something free was required, was risky because if she was wrong, people who otherwise might have made recommendations would not, and the business would incur added expense with free gifts.

- **Is the investment expense high?** Yes, for her nascent business, the expense of error would also be high.

- **Would the cost of verifying the assumptions make the ROI unattractive?** She considered this for some time. Clearly, third-party research would be inappropriate. She already had some research from her conversations with customers. She wondered if she could do more to reduce the risk using the same approach. She decided to try.

Over the next three weeks, she mentioned her plan to some of the guests that routinely referred guests. The responses were divided. Several told her that they would not participate because taking some remuneration in exchange for a recommendation seemed dishonest. Recommendations needed to come from personal conviction, not payment. Others told her they thought the idea was a good one. Of course, they were already making recommendations and had not needed the extra incentive to do so.

She also talked to guests who, to her knowledge, had not made a recommendation and who were regular diners at her restaurant. Their feedback was also divided. Some liked the programme and assured her they would increase behaviour if they were there, whereas others said they didn't believe it would affect their behaviour either way. A few shared her existing recommender's perspective that payment in exchange for recommendations seemed dishonest somehow.

In response to the feedback, the owner decided to make a few changes to her plans. She decided not to launch the recommendation programme on a formal basis. Instead, she would create an informal reward programme. She would continue to track guests who made recommendations, and slip a note on their table to thank them for the recommendation. She would also give them preferred seating, the occasional bottle of wine or free dessert, in recognition of their assistance.

The programme would not be published, so patrons would not feel they were being bribed to make recommendations. However, based on the feedback, she felt that the gifts would help her cultivate loyalty among her most valuable customers.

The informal nature had an additional benefit. If the owner starts the programme with free items, and none were required, patrons might discontinue their behaviour if the programme was subsequently discontinued. On the other hand, if no incentives were offered or the programme was informal in nature, the financial commitment and associated risk would be lower.

As she walked through the risk assessment decision tree a second time, she decided that because of her 'research,' the assumptions about behaviours were no longer substantial risks to the programme. She was also confident that the results she anticipated, related both to revenues and expenses, were accurate. She was ready to move forward.

THE ANTICIPATED RETURNS TEST

When a company invests in a new manufacturing plant or expands production capabilities, its executive team usually constructs a model to evaluate the potential impact on revenue against the investment required. Of course, they make a number of assumptions in the process. Perhaps most importantly, they assume they can sell more products. Because building a facility does not guarantee that the product will sell, this is a substantial assumption.

Yet, the return on marketing investments, whose components are so directly tied to revenues, are less consistently evaluated on an ROI basis. Of course, there are exceptions. New facilities and products often are exceptions, but without channels through which they reach the market, and promotions so that the market is aware they exist, they are unlikely to sell. Many companies also do financial analyses on pricing strategies or channel decisions. However, promotions are frequently left out of the evaluation process.

When other aspects of marketing are assessed for expected returns before investments, and promotions are not, it exacerbates the nagging doubt executives have about the efficacy of their investments in that aspect of marketing. Worse yet, because there were only vague expectations relative to financial performance at the outset, marketers have little to defend—and executives have few tools to hold marketers accountable.

The fourth test non-marketing executives should run prior to approving funding for a marketing plan is designed to address these issues, and it is called the *Anticipated Returns Test*. This test evaluates the expected returns relative to the anticipated financial investments and provides a simple means of evaluating anticipated ROI. It is introduced in chapter 11, 'Evaluating Returns on Marketing Investments.'

By running the Anticipated Returns Test and discussing the expected returns prior to approving funding, the executive team will be more committed to the investment and less likely to discontinue funding before the returns are received. The exercise can also improve accountability, minimise poor investment decisions, improve the accuracy of intermediate and retrospective measurements and reduce waste.

Before I describe the test in more detail, it should be noted that executives are not the only ones who have neglected measurements of financial returns on marketing investments in the past. Marketers themselves are often reluctant to commit to such a measurement process for many reasons. Some marketers are simply not comfortable with financial analysis, just as some non-marketing managers are confused by terms routinely used by marketers. To facilitate the measurement process, both sides must exercise patience and understand their colleagues' strengths and challenges in the process.

Other marketers are reluctant to commit to measurement because they are concerned that they will be held accountable for outcomes that may not be within their control. For example, in the case study used in the Assignment Test section, the marketing department of the law firm, which frequently manages only the promotional aspects of the marketing mix, might be very reluctant to commit to outcomes given the partners' reluctance to act as an effective sales channel. Without sales, appropriate pricing and quality legal services, the promotional efforts are unlikely to produce at their full potential. As such, these contingencies must be identified.

In other cases, the marketing team hasn't attempted to measure returns because it has simply never been expected. By routinely running the Anticipated Returns Test prior to funding, the marketing team will become more adept at, and more comfortable with, the measurement of returns, and the company's performance will benefit as a result.

How the Test Works

Whether conducted by the executive team or delegated to the marketing team for completion, the non-marketing executive should request that the expected return and any assumptions associated with that return be outlined in conjunction with marketing plan development. To do so, use the following steps:

- **Step 1.** In most cases, companies will need to begin with an estimate of revenue streams that assumes no incremental investment. In other words, the company should estimate what the revenues would be over the same period in which the marketing plan is expected to generate results, if it continued on its existing course, spending the same amount of money on the same marketing initiatives. Similarly, it should understand what the related expenses would be. This provides a baseline against which incremental revenues and expenses can be calculated.

- **Step 2.** Next, the company should calculate a preliminary ROI ratio by dividing the expected returns under the status quo model by the expected expenses under the same model. This provides a good starting point for a comparative ROI.

- **Step 3.** The company should begin its assessment of the proposed marketing plan with the last step of the Alignment Test, noting the projected revenue and related expenses. As discussed in chapter 11, these numbers should be adjusted to account for the perceived performance risk. For example, if the budget includes a line item for overruns, the company should include the budget overrun estimate in the total budget amount. Similarly, if the management team assesses the likelihood that the company will achieve the targeted revenue goals at 80%, the revenues should be reduced by 20% to reflect that risk. By calculating the ROI based on these new figures, the company can more easily compare the new plan to its predecessor.

- **Step 4.** In many cases, it may be helpful to assess the incremental impact the plan will make. In this case, netting out the status quo revenues and expenses from the ROI equation may help the executive team evaluate the effectiveness of the plan.

- **Step 5.** Once the ROI has been calculated, the executive team can evaluate the investment in incremental marketing initiatives against expected return rates on capital and other investments to determine whether the plan meets company expectations.

- **Step 6.** Finally, the executive team should confirm that the marketing team has outlined appropriate completion, intermediate marketing and financial metrics to track progress and measure results.

In the same way that a company can estimate the potential returns on a single piece of equipment, this process can be used to evaluate the investment in an incremental marketing activity. However, the evaluator should be careful to consider whether the returns are tied to other activities or whether the incremental marketing activity will have a positive (or negative) impact on other aspects of company performance and account for these impacts accordingly.

Case Study: The Anticipated Returns Test in Action

The executive team at a mid-sized aerospace component manufacturing company sat around their board room table. The company's new chief marketing officer (CMO) had just finished a presentation of its newly developed marketing promotions plan, which required a sizeable increase in budget over previous years. It was clear from the conversation following the presentation that the CFO was sceptical that the investment was worthwhile, whereas the CMO was equally passionate about the company's need for change. After listening to the conversation for some time, the CEO stepped in and suggested they calculate the anticipated financial returns on the plan.

The CFO began by reviewing historical performance. The company had a small but stable share of its market. The market was mature, but the component was critical, and revenues, when adjusted for the impact of inflation and economic trends, had reached a plateau several years before. Revenues were estimated at about $50 million annually. The gross profits, after costs associated with production were deducted, was $10 million in revenues.

The company's own customers were very loyal but so were their competitors' customers. Because sales had not changed, and the situation seemed unchangeable, the company's previous CMO had focused on efficiency, and marketing expenditure focused primarily on customer retention. The company's marketing budget included some promotional expenditures, three marketing team members and four sales people. With compensation, benefit, payroll taxes and materials costs, the marketing budget had been reduced to $1.5 million annually.

Using these figures, the team calculated the ROI of existing marketing to be about 6.67, or 567% ROI. This level of investment, they agreed, provided a return that was higher than they could get investing the money in other activities or financial markets. Box 16-5 shows the status quo calculations.

Box 16-5: Status Quo Calculations for a 3-Year Period

Gross profits: (3 years × $10 million =) $30 million

Marketing expenses: (3 years × $1.5 million): $4.5 million

Return on Investment: $\dfrac{\text{Gross Profit}}{\text{Marketing Expense}} = \dfrac{\$30 \text{ million}}{\$4.5 \text{ million}} = 6.67$ or 567% ROI

When the new CMO joined the company, he spent the first several weeks visiting existing and prospective customers. These conversations led him to believe there were opportunities to increase the company's market share. In particular, a number of the customers he had visited expressed frustration over the delivery processes. Just-in-time fulfilment practices had not yet been established in this particular industry, due largely to the size and shipping cost associated with the particular components they manufactured. However, the COO and CMO had developed a model that would allow the company to offer just-in-time fulfilment services, with modest additional expense. Unfortunately, the competitive nature of the industry would not allow the marginal costs to be passed along to the customers.

The CMO believed that if the company invested heavily in promotions associated with this innovation, it could snag market share before competitors had an opportunity to imitate the improvement. Because customers tended to be loyal once they had established a vendor relationship, the CMO believed an operational change and a short-term marketing push could deliver long-term financial benefits for the company.

The marketing plan proposed an incremental expense (associated with the revised shipping approach) of .25% of revenues in each year due to storage and higher per-unit shipping costs. In addition, the plan added two new sales professionals, at a cost of $240,000 per year, and $160,000 in incremental promotions.

Based on his conversations with customers, he believed that the new shipping approach would be extremely attractive to their customers and that they could easily increase revenues by 75% by the end of the third year. Specifically, he estimated that revenues would grow from $50 million in the previous year to $60 million in year one, $75 million in year two and $87.5 million in year three. The COO added that the company had the production capacity, so the gross margin percentage was not expected to be affected.

Using these figures, the team calculated the return on the marketing investment to be 6.5 times the investment, or 550% ROI, as shown in box 16-6.

Box 16-6: Anticipated Revenue Under New Plan for a 3-Year Period

	YEAR 1	YEAR 2	YEAR 3
REVENUES	$60 million	$75 million	$87.5 million
GROSS PROFIT (REVENUES LESS COST OF GOODS SOLD, EXCLUDING SALES COSTS)	$60 million × (20% – .25% incremental shipping and storage costs) = $11.85 million	$75 million × (20% – .25%) = $14.8125 million	$87.5 million × (20% – .25%) = $17.28125 million
EXPENSES	$1.5 million (status quo) + $400,000 (incremental costs) = $1.9 million	$1.5 million + $400,000 = $1.9 million	$1.5 million + $400,000 = $1.9 million

Gross profits: ($11.85 + $14.8125 + $17.28125=) $43.94375 million
Marketing expenses: (3 years × $1.9 million): $5.7 million
Return on investment: $\dfrac{\text{Gross Profit}}{\text{Marketing Expense}}$ = $\dfrac{\$43.94375 \text{ million}}{\$5.7 \text{ million}}$ = 7.71 times or 671% ROI

The return was slightly higher than the status quo ROI, and the company had had access to the cash required. The CMO was thrilled, but the CFO was still concerned. The team turned to the incremental ROI, shown below in box 16-7.

Box 16-7: Incremental Return on Investment Under New Plan for a 3-Year Period

	YEAR 1	YEAR 2	YEAR 3
INCREMENTAL REVENUES	$60 million – $50 million = $10 million	$75 million – $50 million = $25 million	$87.5 million – $50 million = $37.5 million

Continued on p.294

Continued from p.293

	YEAR 1	YEAR 2	YEAR 3
INCREMENTAL GROSS PROFIT (REVENUES LESS COST OF GOODS SOLD, EXCLUDING SALES COSTS)	$11.85 million – $10 million = $1.85 million	$14.8125 million – $10 million = $4.8125 million	$17.28125 million – $10 million = $7.28125 million
EXPENSES	$400,000	$400,000	$400,000

Gross profits: ($1.85 + $4.8125 + $7.28125=) $13.94375 million
Marketing expenses: (3 years × $400,000): $1.2 million
Return on Investment: $\frac{\text{Gross Profit}}{\text{Marketing Expense}}$ = $\frac{\$13.94375 \text{ million}}{\$1.2 \text{ million}}$ = 11.62 or 1062% ROI

The results of this test also looked impressive. At over 1000% return on investment, investing in this plan seemed a far better venture than could be obtained elsewhere.

However, the team had not yet addressed risk. After a lengthy discussion, the team reduced projections to 45% growth, a level that even the sceptical CFO felt was likely, given the change. With this level of sales, the CMO said that the marketing budget should also change. The addition of a single sales person would be sufficient to handle both prospective lead generation and order-taking needs in year one. A second sales professional could be added in year two.

The risk-adjusted budget figures provided a return rate of 6.71 times the investment, or 471% ROI, very similar to the original plan. Not surprisingly, the incremental rate was in the same range, producing a 6.16 times the incremental investment, or a 516% ROI. Box 16-8 shows the calculations using the risk-adjusted budget figures.

Box 16-8: Risk-Adjusted Anticipated Revenues Under New Plan for a 3-Year Period

	YEAR 1	YEAR 2	YEAR 3
REVENUES	$55 million	$62 million	$72.5 million
GROSS PROFIT (REVENUES LESS COSTS OF GOODS SOLD, EXCLUDING SALES COSTS)	$55 million × (20% – .25% incremental shipping and storage costs) = $10.8625	$62 million × (20% – .25%) = $12.245 million	$72.5 million × (20% – 1%) = $14.31875 million
INCREMENTAL REVENUE	$10.8625 – $10 = $862,500	$12.245 – $10 = $2.245 million	$14.31875 – $10 = $4.31875 million
EXPENSES	$1.5 million (status quo) + $280,000 (incremental costs) = $1.78 million	$1.5 million + $400,000 = $1.9 million	$1.5 million + $400,000 = $1.9 million
INCREMENTAL EXPENSES	$280,000	$400,000	$400,000

Gross profits: (10.8625 + 12.245 + 14.31875 =) $37.42625 million
Marketing expenses: (1.78 + 1.9 + 1.9): $5.58 million
Return on Investment: $\dfrac{\text{Gross Profit}}{\text{Marketing Expense}}$ = $\dfrac{\$37.42625 \text{ million}}{\$5.58 \text{ million}}$ = 6.71 or 571% ROI

Incremental profits: (0.8625 + 2.245 + 4.31875 =) $6.65 million
Incremental marketing expenses: (280 + 400 + 400): $1.08 million
Return on incremental investment: $\dfrac{\text{Gross Profit}}{\text{Marketing Expense}}$ = $\dfrac{\$6.65 \text{ million}}{\$1.08 \text{ million}}$ = 6.16 or 516% ROI

At the end of the conversation, the executive team, with the CFO's agreement, decided that the plan sounded solid. Before the team was asked to indicate their approval, the CEO asked the CMO to review the metrics the team would use to track progress and indicate what corrective measures would be taken to correct deficiencies if they arose. Satisfied with the responses, the team approved the plan.

CHAPTER 16 SUMMARY

Many non-marketing managers, particularly CFOs, see a marketing plan for the first time when they are asked to approve the budget request. Whether the CFO has a very active role in evaluating marketing investments, or a less integrated one as a part of the executive team, there are four tests the CFO should use to evaluate whether a plan is complete, what kinds of financial returns are expected and whether it is ready to be approved and funded.

The *Alignment Test* provides a means of evaluating how well the plan is aligned with business and financial objectives. My research indicates that this is a key indicator of whether the plan will help a company achieve its objectives and whether the required executive support exists to execute a plan through to completion.

The *Assignment Test* ensures all the activities within a plan are effectively staffed. Even a well-constructed, well-aligned plan can fail if it does not account for staffing needs or secure buy-in from key team members. This test helps avert that issue by ensuring that every activity has been allocated to a specific resource who has, in turn, accepted that responsibility.

The *Risk Assessment Test* reviews the plan for critical assumptions. Although assumptions are normal in any planning process, assumptions constitute risk. This test is designed to ensure that the critical assumptions have been identified and mitigated if possible.

The *Anticipated Returns Test* evaluates the expected returns relative to the anticipated financial investments and provides a simple means of evaluating anticipated ROI. Calculating returns on marketing investments provides two substantial benefits: It makes it easier to compare marketing investments to alternative uses of cash, and it improves accountability and focus in the process of execution.

17

NOW WHAT?

Most managers want their companies to be market leaders. Why wouldn't they? Not only do market leaders outperform the market, but they generally attract the best and brightest talent, have better work environments, provide more opportunities for professional growth and are a source of pride.

The good news is that even if your company isn't a market leader, it can be. You have part of the formula for success in this book: insight about how market leaders define and manage marketing.

My guess is that you looked at some of what you read and thought, 'That's not new. We already do that.' And I'm sure that's true!

Most companies do some, or even most, of these things very well. They listen to the market, cultivating a culture of curiosity and absorbing information about needs and ways the company can serve the market's needs more effectively. They align everything they do with their goal of improving the customer's experience and better serving their needs. Or, they execute unwaveringly on their marketing plans, regardless of the economic environment.

But the difference between market leaders and average performers is that market leaders do all three of the following things consistently. They

- listen to their markets and enjoy the Crystal Ball Effect;
- follow the Point C Principle, aligning everything they do with their goal of meeting market needs (and enjoying superior financial results as a result); *and*
- adhere to the Tortoise Law, executing their go-to-market plans with unflagging commitment and persistence.

If you are doing all of these things, congratulations! But as a market leader, you know there is always room for improvement. I hope this book provided some insights that you can share with your colleagues and will help you drive even better returns from your marketing investments.

If you are not a market leader, you may be looking at the list of topics and trying to decide where to start. As you probably realise after reading this book, everything begins with the customer. If you don't listen to them now, that's the place to start. But if you already do that, or you need some additional assistance determining just how to get started, I have one more test for you.

This one is a self-assessment test. The purpose is to tell you where your company is succeeding and where it needs to focus its efforts. I call it the Marketing Performance Evaluation.

Sharpen your pencil, and give it a try. When you're done, share your answers with me, and I'll tell you how you compare to others in your industry. I'll explain more about that when you're done.

MARKETING PERFORMANCE EVALUATION: HOW DOES YOUR COMPANY COMPARE?

Section I: The Discipline of Marketing

Review each of the following statements and rate how frequently the statement would apply to your company or organisation. At the end, add up the number of statements at each of the indicated point levels to determine how likely your company is to beat your competitors to market opportunities.

	CONSISTENTLY	USUALLY	OCCASIONALLY	NEVER
Our executives solicit customer feedback for the explicit purpose of continually improving the customer experience.				
We use systematic processes for gathering customer feedback, compiling it for distribution and routing it to the appropriate internal team.				
When we identify a trend or theme as we analyse feedback, we take prompt action.				
Our hiring practices reflect a commitment to listening to the market.				
Employees can accurately describe which segments of the market we serve and which segments we do not.				
We can articulate why our customers would buy from us rather than our competitors, and we can support our assertions with measurable evidence.				
What we say, how we look and how we behave in the community is consistent with the reputation of the type of person with whom our customers want to do business.				
In our company, our executive team aligns our operations with an overall vision of how we provide value to the customer.				

Continued on p.299

Continued from p.298

	CONSISTENTLY	USUALLY	OCCASIONALLY	NEVER
Total number of checks in the column:				
Point value per check mark:	**6 points**	**4 points**	**1 point**	**0 points**
Total points by column:				

Total Score for the Discipline of Marketing: _____ out of a possible 48 points.

How did you do?

39–48 points: Congratulations! **You get an A** in the discipline of marketing. You may already be enjoying the benefits of the Crystal Ball Effect. Listening to customers is critical. Keep up the good work!

26–38 points: Great job! **You earned a B** in the discipline of marketing. You do a good job at listening to the market, but there is still room for improvement. With a little hard work, your company could leverage your existing strengths and become even more adept at recognising opportunities in the marketplace.

13–25 points: Nice work. **You earned a C** in the discipline of marketing. Despite the low numbers, your work is in the average range. This isn't an area of strength for you—but it could be! With focus and commitment, you can improve your ability to beat competitors to market opportunities.

0–12 points: You've got some work ahead of you. **You earned a D** in the discipline of marketing, which means you are probably more internally focused than you need to be to become a strong competitor.

If your grade wasn't as high as you would like it to be, review chapters 2 and 3. These two chapters provide insight into how market leaders manage the discipline of marketing and how you can improve your own company's ability to compete.

Section II: Evaluating Marketing Plans

This portion of the evaluation has two parts, part A and part B. Complete both parts and add the totals in the two sections to determine how likely your company is to be maximising the returns it generates on marketing investments.

Part A

Review each of the following statements and evaluate whether or not it is true for your organisation. At the end, add up the number of statements at each of the indicated point levels to determine your score for part A.

PART A	YES	NO OR NOT SURE
We have a clear understanding of our target customers' purchasing decision process.		

Continued on p.300

Continued from p.299

PART A	YES	NO OR NOT SURE
Our marketing plan has contingencies to address unexpected opportunities or challenges.		
Total number of checks in the column:		
Point value per check mark:	**6 points**	**0 points**
Total points by column:		

Total Points from Part A: _____ out of a possible 12 points.

Part B

Review each of the following statements and rate how frequently the statement would apply to your company or organisation. At the end, add up the number of statements at each of the indicated point levels to determine your score for part B.

PART B	CONSISTENTLY	USUALLY	OCCASIONALLY	NEVER
Our marketing strategies are based on our understanding of what influences our target customers' purchasing decisions.				
We calculate anticipated financial returns on marketing investments prior to approval.				
We measure actual returns on marketing investments upon completion of the plan.				
Our executives can explain the connection between our marketing strategies and tactics, the impact on the market and the expected return.				
Our executive team champions the marketing plan.				
Before the marketing plan is approved, we review the plan for risks based on assumptions and take appropriate steps to mitigate them when they are significant.				

Continued on p.301

Continued from p.300

PART B	CONSISTENTLY	USUALLY	OCCASIONALLY	NEVER
Total number of checks in the column:				
Point value per check mark:	**6 points**	**4 points**	**1 point**	**0 points**
Total points by column:				

Total Score for Part B: _____ out of a possible 36 points.

Total Score for Evaluating Marketing Plans (Part A + Part B): _____ out of a possible 48 points.

How did you do?

39–48 points: Congratulations! **You earned an A** relative to how effectively your management team evaluates proposed marketing investments. You are a savvy investor with a thoughtful approach to analysing risk and returns. Your marketing strategies are well aligned with your business objectives and the financial returns you want to achieve. Keep up the good work!

26–38 points: Great job! **You earned a B** for your management team's ability to evaluate marketing investments. You are well positioned to spot investment risks and opportunities, although a few risky decisions probably still slip into your plan.

13–25 points: Nice work. **You earned a C** for your management team's ability to evaluate marketing investments. You do a good job evaluating measurement, but you are probably leaving money on the table. With more careful focus on alignment, you will be able to identify risks and other sources of poor returns and prevent them before you spend any money.

0–12 points: You've got some work ahead of you. **You earned a D** in the discipline of marketing. Your company may be making very poor decisions relative to its marketing investments and sacrificing competitiveness as a result.

If your grade wasn't as high as you would like it to be, review chapters 4–11. These chapters will guide you through the Marketing Alignment Map process and help you evaluate the financial returns your plans will deliver before they are approved. With these best practices around marketing plan development and measurement in place, you will be more likely to maximise the returns your marketing plans deliver.

Section III: Managing the Marketing Function

Review each of the following statements in both part A and part B and rate how frequently the statement would apply to your company or organisation. At the end of each of the two parts, add up the number of statements at each of the indicated point levels. Then, total the two sections to determine how likely your company is to be able to execute effectively on a marketing plan.

Part A

	CONSISTENTLY	USUALLY	OCCASIONALLY	NEVER
The skills and time availability of our internal and external staff match the skills and time required to successfully execute our company's marketing initiatives.				
We ensure that everyone whose participation is required, including non-marketing personnel, has accepted responsibility for executing their assigned tasks in a timely manner before approving marketing investments.				
Our company uses a clear communications tool, such as a dashboard, to track progress against a plan.				
Our executive team and/ or management team ensures accountability and addresses non-performance.				
Our company uses both graphic standards and key messages that are relevant to our customers.				
Total number of checks in the column:				
Point value per check mark:	**6 points**	**4 points**	**1 point**	**0 points**
Sub-total points for Part A:				

Total Points from Part A: _____ out of a possible 30 points.

Part B

	YES	YES	NO OR NOT SURE
Our marketing plan has specific milestones for completion of tactics and/or initiatives, marketing metrics related to activities and financial metrics associated with outcomes, all of which are finite and measurable.			
The company has systems and processes in place to track the marketing and financial metrics associated with our plan, including revenues, expenses and progress against marketing goals.			
We have a crisis communications plan, and our executives and senior management are aware of when and how it should be used.			
Total number of checks in the column:			
Point value per check mark:	**6 points**	**3 points**	**0 points**
Sub-total points for Part B:			

Total Points from Part B: _____ out of a possible 15 points.

Total Score for Managing the Marketing Function (Part A + Part B): _____ out of a possible 45 points.

How did you do?

41–45 points: Congratulations! **You earned an A** in marketing management. Your marketing function is run effectively and efficiently, and your marketing plans are likely to be executed on plan and on budget. Bravo!

28–40 points: Great job! **You earned a B** in marketing management. Your management skills are solid, but there is still room for improvement. To make sure you don't lose your marketing focus, concentrate on those areas with weak scores.

15–27 points: Nice work. **You earned a C** in marketing management. Although you manage some aspects of your marketing function well, you may be inadvertently, or even deliberately, abandoning or drifting away from your marketing plan before it has a chance to deliver the promised returns. You can improve your ability to execute effectively by improving your management skills.

0–14 points: You've got some work ahead of you. **You earned a D** in marketing management. Even with a well-designed plan, you are not likely to be generating appropriate returns. Without improvement, this represents a significant area of risk to your company.

If your grade wasn't as high as you would like it to be, review chapters 11–15. These chapters address some of the management practices that cause companies to forfeit potential returns.

NOW, TAKE IT AGAIN

If you took this before reading the book, as I recommended in the preface, take it again when you're done. See if your answers change when you read more about the discipline of marketing.

If you took this after reading the book, try implementing a few of the concepts, perhaps those found in sections where you received your lowest grades, and take this again in a year. See if you've improved. Better yet, measure the difference.

SHARE YOUR ANSWERS

Now that you've completed the Marketing Performance Evaluation, I have one final suggestion: Share your answers. More specifically, share them with me. In return, I'll share something with you. If you log onto our website and complete this same evaluation online, I'll tell you how you compare to other respondents in your industry and overall.

Here's the website address: www.MarketFitz.com/MPE.

You can also find it by going to my company's website, www.MarketFitz.com, and looking for the icon for this book.

ASK QUESTIONS

Finally, if you have questions about this evaluation or about any of the concepts in this book, please don't hesitate to ask. My contact information follows. I would be happy to help you better understand how your company can become or remain a market leader and improve the returns you generate from investments in marketing.

Heather Fitzpatrick
MarketFitz, Inc.
PO Box 1839
Edmonds, WA 98020
USA
HFitzpatrick@MarketFitz.com
www.MarketFitz.com
+ 1-206-624-7470

GLOSSARY

abandonment rate. A metric used to evaluate websites. It is the number of people who begin a purchase but do not complete it as a percentage of the number of people who begin a purchase transaction.

active contributors. A metric used to evaluate the effectiveness of social media efforts. It is the number of people who actively participated in a social conversation in a given period of time.

activity. A metric used to evaluate the effectiveness of social media efforts. It is the number of comments, re-tweets or other activities demonstrating social connectivity. Also known as *posts, comments, ideas* and *threads*.

advertising. When a company pays to communicate a message in verbal and/or visual formats to an audience through a particular media.

advertising allowances. Offered by manufacturers who sell products to intermediaries, such as retailers, it is a pre-negotiated dollar amount that the manufacturer will deduct from the total purchase price if the retailer agrees to spend those dollars on advertising that promotes the manufacturer's products.

advertising flights. Advertising that is placed consistently over a specified period of time, then discontinued and resumed after a hiatus. Flights are designed to maximise the customer's recall for the price paid, and studies show an appropriately timed hiatus will reduce the cost without significant loss in customer recall.

advertising value equivalency. A metric that measures the effectiveness of media relations. It is an attempt to attach a dollar value to the media coverage generated through media relations. It may, for example, compare the column inches or broadcast seconds in reporters' stories about the company and compare that to what it would have cost to place the same amount of advertising in the same medium. It does not represent income to the company.

agencies. A company that specialises in a particular area of marketing, such as promotions, that can be tapped to handle a range of project needs. Advertising, market research, strategic planning and public relations expertise are commonly tapped through these sorts of organisations. Also known as *consulting firms*.

Alignment Test. A test to conduct before funding a marketing activity, which provides a means of evaluating how well the plan is aligned with business and financial objectives. It is a key indicator of whether the activity will help a company achieve its objectives and whether the required executive support exists to execute a plan through to completion.

Anticipated Returns Test. A test to conduct before funding a marketing activity. It evaluates the expected returns relative to the anticipated financial investments and provides a simple means of evaluating anticipated return on investment.

Assignment Test. A test to conduct before funding a marketing activity that ensures all the activities within a plan are effectively staffed. This test helps avert staffing and execution issues by ensuring that every activity has been allocated to a specific resource who has, in turn, accepted that responsibility.

blind research studies. A type of market research study in which the respondent does not know who requested the research. This reduces the incidence of response bias because the respondent cannot tailor responses to an unknown audience.

blogs. An online resource that provides opportunities for one or more authors to draft content, comment on a particular topic or engage in discussion. Although many blogs are stand-alone websites, blogs can also appear on an organisation's website, such as a corporation or university, or on a magazine or newspaper website. Also known as *weblogs*.

bounce-back rate. A tactical metric used in evaluating digital advertising, direct mail or other digital promotional campaign. It is a ratio and is calculated by dividing the number of e-mails that bounced because of an incorrect e-mail address by the total number to whom the e-mail was sent and stated as a percentage.

brand. The reputation a company has within the market, relative to its corporate values, operating philosophy, value proposition and corporate social responsibility, which facilitates the customer's decision-making process. It is a reflection of how effectively an organisation has managed the discipline of marketing and those aspects of the company's reputation that affect purchasing behaviour.

brand architecture. For organisations managing multiple brands, it is the hierarchical structure that governs the way in which those brand names and personas are differentiated or related within the market.

brand audit. A comprehensive assessment of an organisation's promotional materials, internal or external communications and common visual expressions of the company's brand identity to identify inconsistencies that may damage the brand.

brand identity. The visual, verbal and behavioural cues that an organisation presents to the market as a means of reinforcing brand reputation.

brand management. The tools and best practices used to manage an organisation's brand.

broadcast seconds. A metric that measures the effectiveness of media relations. It is the number of seconds of 'earned media' coverage on broadcast stations, such as radio or television.

brokers/agents. Individuals in a distribution chain who focus on selling on behalf of a manufacturer or service provider and take a commission or a fee when they are successful, acting as an outsourced sales team. They do not assume title to the products. Also known as *reps* or *manufacturer reps*.

bulk pricing. A pricing approach that provides a lower price to companies who purchase large numbers of a given product.

business process outsourcing. An outsourcing arrangement in which the external vendor works with the client to evaluate and reengineer efficiency solution for an entire department or a single process.

cause marketing. A type of marketing, typically promotional in nature, in which a for-profit and non-profit organisation cooperate for mutual benefit.

channel conflict. When two distribution channels compete with one another for sales. Although some channel conflict is normal, it can become problematic when one channel partner, or group of partners, receives preferential pricing or terms.

channel intermediaries. Parties in a distribution chain who sell goods or services on behalf of a company. Their role may include distribution, sales, promotion and/or financing. Also known as *distribution intermediaries*.

channel management. The way a company manages the distribution channels for its products or services.

channel marketing. Promotional efforts that are geared towards indirect distribution channels for a product or service.

click-through rate. A tactical metric used in evaluating digital advertising, direct mail or other digital promotional campaign. It is the number of times a customer clicks on an advertisement to be taken to the company or channel's website, divided by the number of impressions.

clip-level criteria. The minimum purchasing criteria that are required by the market in order to be eligible for consideration

clips. A metric that measures the effectiveness of media relations. It is the number of articles or broadcasts citing the company's name and/or its product or services. See also **impressions**.

column inches. A metric that measures the effectiveness of media relations. It is the number of inches of earned media printed in news media as a result of proactive media relations.

competition-based pricing. A pricing approach in which companies identify similar products or services that already exist, identify the range of prices and set their prices relative to what they believe the market will accept relative to what their competitors are doing.

competitive criteria. Purchasing criteria that distinguish a company from its competitors within its target markets and are consistent with the company's desired brand reputation and value proposition.

completion metrics. A marketing metric that provides an indication of whether an activity was completed on time. It answers the question, 'How will we know we are done?'

confidence interval. Used in market research, it is a percentage that indicates the margin of error in which any given answer is likely to be untrue. It is expressed as a '+/-' percentage relative to the confidence level.

confidence level. Used in market research, it is the degree of certainty about how sure a researcher can be that any given response is within the margin of error range. Most researchers use a 95% confidence level for market research.

content sharing sites. Websites that allow individuals to share original digital media content, either within a closed community or with the public. Popular examples include the video-sharing site YouTube, photo-sharing site Instagram and online pin board Pinterest.

contingency pricing. A pricing approach in which a company provides goods or services to a customer, and payment is contingent on the satisfactory completion of specific requirements.

contribution margin. A financial metric. The contribution margin is the marginal profit per unit of sale.

contribution margin ratio (or percentage). A financial metric. The contribution margin ratio is the contribution margin divided by the total revenues, and the result is stated as a percentage.

conversion rate. The percentage of customers targeted by a digital advertising, direct mail or other promotional campaign who made a purchase.

core competencies. The set of knowledge, skills and experience a company brings to delivering value to the market.

cost-based pricing. A pricing approach. The price is established based on the cost of producing the goods or services plus a specified mark-up.

cost per click. The cost of the advertising buy divided by the number of times a customer clicks on the advertisement to be taken to the company or channel's website.

cost per lead/order. The cost of the advertising buy divided by the number of orders received as a result.

cost-per-thousand or **cost-per-mille.** A unit of measurement to determine the cost of advertising in print or digital media (does not include the cost of creating the advertisement).

costs-per-thousand-impressions. A unit of measurement to determine the cost of advertising in digital and mobile media (does not include the cost of the creating the advertisement).

crisis communications plan. A plan that outlines the response a company will have in the event of an unexpected or potentially detrimental occurrence that generates media interest.

cross-selling. A sales technique that encourages customers to purchase additional items in order to increase the amount of the sale.

Crystal Ball Effect. An improved ability, at the executive level, to accurately anticipate what the market needs and how to communicate effectively with them.

daily deal sites. Websites such as Groupon, Living Social and Amazon Local that allow companies to offer a deep discount on goods or services to entice new customers as long as they are purchased within a defined time period (usually 24 hours). Use of these services typically requires sharing a portion of the proceeds from each sale.

demand curve. A mathematical graph illustrating what the demand would be for a product if it were sold at various price points.

design bias. A market research bias that is introduced during the design process of the research itself, which prompts the respondent to respond in a certain way due to misleading, persuasive or omitted language in a question or in the response options.

digital magazines and news sites. Online versions of news outlets. Most print publications have some form of online social media presence, and many publications are moving to, or were created in, an entirely digital format.

disintermediation. The process of removing distribution intermediaries facilitated by the Internet.

direct distribution. A distribution term used to describe a company that sells its goods or services directly to the consumer or business purchaser.

direct marketing. A form of advertising that uses consumer data to reach out directly to past and potential customers via direct mail, direct e-mail and/or telemarketing.

display ads (online). Advertisements that are placed on search engine sites, social media sites and other locations when a user meets the specific demographic or interest criteria specified by the advertiser.

distribution channels. The various methods a company uses to provide the market with access to its goods and services.

double–blind research studies. A type of market research study in which both the respondent and the individual conducting the interview or survey are prohibited from knowing the organisation for which the research is being conducted. This design structure is intended to reduce both response bias and interviewer bias.

drop-shippers. Companies that play a sales function in a distribution chain by identifying markets, selling the products and arranging for delivery direct from the manufacturer.

dynamic pricing. A pricing approach that allows the seller to negotiate a price based on the individual consumer's behaviour during the sale, such as a flea market or online auction site.

earned media. Media coverage that a company has not paid to receive.

end-cap displays. A merchandise stand placed at the end of a store aisle, commonly found in supermarkets and department stores.

exclusive licensing. A distribution approach in which the company grants a single organisation or individual the right to sell a product or service without competition in a specifically defined scope.

financial metric. A marketing metric that is directly connected to the company's financial performance. It answers the question, 'How will we know this activity was successful?'

fixed price. A pricing approach in which a pre-determined fee is negotiated for a specific product or set of services.

focus groups. A qualitative research approach that assembles a select group of participants in order to engage opinions and feedback via informal discussion about a product or service.

followers. A metric used to evaluate the effectiveness of social media efforts. It is the number of people who have joined a social network. Related to *likes, supporters* or *friends*.

four 'P's of marketing. The four most common groups of marketing tactics: price, product (and services), promotions and placement (distribution).

franchising. An arrangement in which a company (the franchisor) grants permission to another individual or company (franchisee) that allows the franchisee to operate a company, produce a product or sell a product or service under the franchisor's name. Franchises may grant the use of an organisation's trademark or business processes and require compliance with specific standards franchisor standards.

freemiums. A pricing approach that offers the core product or service for free and then charges for upgrades or add-ons.

full-service merchant wholesalers. Companies in a distribution chain that purchase large quantities of goods from manufacturers, process and store that merchandise and resell it to retailers. They may also provide packaging services, manage promotions, provide installation and customer support services and/or offer credit to customers.

gap analysis. The process by which a company assesses its current market realities against its vision and identifies the changes that must occur from an operational perspective in order to achieve that vision.

graphic standards document. A document specifying how the company's logo or logos, taglines, corporate colours, images and other visual elements should be used.

gross rating points. The number of impressions divided by the size of the target market for the product or service.

guarantee. A product guarantee assures the purchaser that the product will meet their needs, or they can recoup some of the cost associated with purchasing it.

guerrilla marketing. An unconventional promotions approach that relies on the element of surprise or word-of-mouth to fuel interest in a product or service. Also known as *viral marketing.*

hits. A metric used to evaluate the effectiveness of websites. It is the number of times a website is requested from the server.

impressions. Refers to the number of times an advertisement is published or broadcast (ie, frequency), multiplied by the number of viewers or readers who will see it (*ie*, reach).

independent consultants. A staffing resource generally used for projects with a specific start and completion date or with specific desired outcomes and that require specialised skills. Also known as *contractors.*

influencers. The various factors that contribute to a customer's purchasing decision. Also known as *influencing factors.*

intercept surveys. A survey that is administered face to face, in a public place, in which a trained interviewer invites feedback from passers-by.

interim employees. Often used to supplement existing employees within a company, these resources provide increased flexibility to manage fluctuating needs. Also known as *temporary employees.*

intermediate marketing metrics. A unit of measurement that is commonly used by marketing professionals to assess marketing outcomes in non-financial terms. They range from the number of products sold, to the number of coupons redeemed, to the volume of business from particular channels, to the myriad of intermediate metrics associated with promotions such as webpage views and impressions.

interviewer or moderator bias. A bias that occurs in qualitative market research studies when a moderator or facilitator interprets participant comments or responds in non-verbal ways to what is said based on his or her own perception of the topic. This can also occur in telephone interviews when an interviewer modifies a response based on his or her interpretation of the respondent's reaction.

jobbers. Wholesalers who manage the inventory in the retail environment, freeing the retailer from that responsibility and collecting payment only when something sells. In some respect, jobbers work with retailers in the same way that an individual works with a consignment shop. Also known as *rack jobbers.*

joint ventures. Formalised agreements between companies to collaborate for mutual benefit, usually relative to distribution channels. Both organisations typically have an equity stake in the joint venture itself.

just-in-time. An operations approach in which the company's suppliers provide products or services upon demand, eliminating or reducing the need for inventory or, in the case of labour, employees.

key messaging. A set of statements that consistently and uniformly define an organisation's value proposition when communicating with the public. The messages must be true, credible and important to the target market(s).

key messaging document. A document defining what the market should hear about the company and what differentiates it from competitors. It typically comprises one or several of the following components: positioning statement, list of key brand attributes, tagline (also known as endline or catch copy), elevator pitch, audience definitions, key messages, proof points, boilerplate and competitive positioning.

list price. The cost of a product or service as set by a company.

logo. A symbol or other graphical representation of a company or the company's name. Also known as *logotype*.

loss leaders. A piece of merchandise that is deliberately sold at loss in order to drive customer purchases of other, more lucrative products.

margin. A financial metric measured by the revenue from sales, less the cost of goods sold.

market development funds. Funds provided by a manufacturer to a used wholesaler or retailer to help promote the product.

market research. Systematic research designed to uncover or validate information about markets overall, including customers and non-customers, market segments, competitors, market perceptions and market trends.

market segments. Distinct groups within a market who prioritise their purchasing criteria differently. Market segments can also be defined by demographics, like industry, profession, age, income or gender. They can also be defined by psychographic characteristics, including lifestyle preferences or how they use a particular product or service.

marketing. According to market leaders, marketing is the profitable management of the interface between the market and its needs and an organisation's ability to meet those needs, for the purpose of producing mutual benefit.

Marketing Alignment Map. A flow chart that describes how each of the components of a marketing plan relates to the other for the purposes of aligning marketing activities with business objectives and assessing financial returns on the marketing function investments.

marketing collateral. Printed or digital materials used in sales or communications on behalf of a company. The most common metrics for evaluating the effectiveness of collateral materials are related to the sales they facilitate.

marketing, the discipline. Cultivated at the executive level, it is the process of collecting and processing customer input in order to more effectively address market needs. It defines all aspects of the direction of the company, the markets it serves, the ways it addresses customer needs and the operations required to support those activities.

marketing, the function. The tactical management of marketing efforts.

marketing measurement models. Ranging from simple to complex, a financial model and associated systems and processes that are used to anticipate and measure financial results of marketing activities.

marketing mix. The combination of tactics that are used to execute a company's marketing strategies.

marketing research. A type of research that is focused on the specific processes, activities and intermediate metrics of marketing. It is used to assess brand familiarity, measure ad views, test concepts or copy or measure customer satisfaction, among other things.

marketing strategy. A concise description of what the company will do to influence purchasing behaviour and achieve business objectives. It should be framed in terms of *what* the company wants to accomplish relative to these influences, rather than how it will do so. Each marketing strategy should have an associated objective, a metric that can be used to evaluate whether the company was successful in its efforts.

marketing tactic. The specific activities a company undertakes to execute its marketing strategies. Tactics should be framed in terms of *how* it will be done and include metrics to measure whether it was completed and whether the market has responded as anticipated. Marketing tactics are most often drawn from the four 'P's of marketing, which includes product and service changes and introductions, pricing approaches and temporary pricing incentives, the selection of distribution channels and the management of the sales team and process and promotional approaches such as newsletters, advertising and social media.

Measurement Myth. The belief that marketing investments, particularly around promotions, cannot be measured in financial terms. Not only is it untrue, but failing to measure marketing is one of the leading reasons companies fail to maximise returns on their market-facing investments.

measurement and response biases. A bias introduced in market research when a respondent shapes his or her responses in a way that he or she suspects will please the researcher or beneficiary.

media. A medium of communication used to reach a specific group of people. Examples include consumer and trade newspapers and magazines, television and radio stations, webzines, professional bloggers, publishers of newsletters and others.

media relations. The management of relationships between journalists and a company.

mentions. A metric used to evaluate the effectiveness of social media efforts. It is the number of times a company and/or product or service has been mentioned in a particular social media.

metrics. A unit of measurement that is used to assess performance of a strategy or tactic. Marketing metrics generally fall into three categories: completion metrics, intermediate marketing metrics and financial metrics.

microblogs. A shorter version of a blog that allows authors to post content within a certain character limit.

multi-channel distribution. The use of several types of indirect distribution channels, or a combination of both direct and indirect channels, to distribute goods or services to a market.

multiple unit pricing. Similar to bulk pricing, multiple unit pricing is when a company offers a single product for one price and multiple products for slightly less.

observational research. A qualitative research technique that gathers market data by having a researcher passively observe customers interacting with a product or service.

one-on-one interviews. A qualitative research approach in which a researcher puts forth questions to participants via telephone, online or in-person conversations.

open rate. A tactical metric used in evaluating digital advertising, direct mail or other digital promotional campaign. It measures the number of recipients of a direct e-mail piece that opened the e-mail as a percentage of the number of targets to whom the e-mail was sent.

outsourcing services. The use of an external vendor to perform specific services, often replacing an entire business process or function.

package prices. A fixed price for a bundle of goods or services offered as an incentive for the customer to purchase more than he or she otherwise might have.

paid searches. Payment to search engines to list a website above others in response to a search. These results generally appear at the top of the list in a shaded box and are marked 'advertisement' in order to differentiate them from the 'natural' or unpaid responses.

page time viewed. A metric used to evaluate the effectiveness of websites. It measures the time a visitor spent on a page or site before leaving. Also known as *session duration* or *visit duration*.

page views. A metric used to evaluate the effectiveness of websites. It is the number of pages a particular viewer visited within a website before leaving. Some companies also track 'unique' page views, which provide data about new traffic, as opposed to repeat visitors.

penetration pricing. A pricing approach that deliberately sets a price point that is relatively low, intentionally forfeiting profit margins in an effort to get more people to purchase the product or service. Also known as *introductory pricing*.

pilot testing. A qualitative research approach that tests the launch of a product or service with a select group of individuals in order to receive feedback. Also known as *beta testing*.

placement. One of the four 'P's of marketing, it is the distribution channel(s) or means by which customers are given access to products or services.

Point C Principle. Led by the executive team, it is the effective alignment between marketing activities and the market's needs in order to achieve superior financial performance.

point of purchase promotions. Promotional displays or demonstrations designed to intercept customers at the location where they pay for goods or services.

price. One of the four 'P's of marketing, it is the amount paid by a company's customers in exchange for a product or service. Although *price* is frequently used to describe the listed or stated price in monetary terms, the true price of a product also includes additional charges, such as shipping, and terms, such as guarantees and return policies.

price discrimination. A pricing approach in which companies offer different prices on the same product to different customers or at different times.

price elasticity of demand. The percentage change in quantity of goods or services associated with unit change in price.

primary research. A type of market research that relies on data gathered directly from the market via qualitative and/or quantitative studies.

product. One of the four 'P's of marketing, it is the product or service delivered to the market by an organisation and the particular features and benefits it offers. This 'P' also encompasses the packaging and/or experience associated with the product or service.

product life cycle. The period of time encompassing the development and introduction of a product, its steady evolution to meet market needs and its plateau or obsolescence. There are four phases to a product life cycle: introduction, growth, maturity and decline.

promotional allowances. Offered by manufacturers who sell products to intermediaries such as retailers, it is a pre-negotiated dollar amount that the manufacturer will deduct from the total purchase price if the retailer agrees to spend those dollars on promoting the manufacturer's products.

promotions. One of the four 'P's of marketing, it is the set of activities that an organisation uses to communicate information to the market about the products or services it offers, such as advertising, media relations, public relations and social media.

psychological pricing. A pricing approach in which the seller makes a strategic decision to price just under or over a certain price point in order to appeal to customers who want to stay within a certain budget range.

public relations. A broad term encompassing many different tactics designed to educate and build customer relationships, such as media relations, social media, special events, seminars, product placement and guerrilla or viral marketing campaigns.

purchasing decision criteria. The factors a prospective customer considers, consciously or subconsciously, when choosing between available alternatives.

push money. Cash or other rewards that are offered to companies as a way to incentivise their sales team to sell a particular product over another. Also known as *prize money allowances*.

quick response code. A two-dimensional bar code that can be captured on smart phone cameras and links the user to a website with text, video or other information about the product or service.

qualitative studies. A type of primary research focused on generating a deeper understanding of market perceptions and opinions through conversations with a small set of research participants. Common qualitative approaches include one-on-one interviews, pilot or beta testing, observational research and focus groups. In general, the results provide directional guidance, rather than definitive answers.

rate cards. A summary of advertising rates charged by a publication or other form of media. Also known as *pricing sheets*.

realised price. A price that is less than list price, often due to discounts, such as coupons or promotions, or other types of incentives.

reliability. A market research term that addresses whether the research will deliver data that is representative at the expected level.

response rate. A tactical metric used in evaluating the effectiveness of digital advertising, direct mail or other promotional campaign. It measures the number of people who made a purchase (or contribution, in the case of non-profits) as a percentage of the total number of individuals to whom the campaign was directed.

responsive design. An online design approach that ensures consistency in the user experience when viewing a website across a range of devices from computer screens to mobile phones.

retainers. A pricing model in which a fixed price is paid in exchange for a claim on the service provider's time, within a specific scope, when needed. This pricing approach helps make the cost more predictable for the customer and the income more predictable for the service provider.

return on investment. Expressed either as a fixed number or as a percentage, it is a financial performance measure of an investment that is calculated by dividing the gross profit (the return) by the investment amount.

return on marketing investment. Defined as a percentage, it is generally considered to be the gross profit attributable to marketing efforts divided by the marketing expenditures required to generate those returns.

return policies. The rules that a company establishes for how, when and where a consumer can return a product after it has been purchased.

Risk Assessment Test. A test to conduct before funding a marketing activity that reviews the plan for critical assumptions. It is designed to ensure that critical assumptions within a plan have been identified and mitigated if possible.

risk assessment decision tree. A decision-making tool used to determine which assumptions are acceptable within a marketing investment and which ones contain a level of risk.

sales uplift. The increase in gross revenues from sales associated with a particular marketing activity.

sampling bias. A statistical bias in market research in which the method used for selecting research participants does not accurately reflect the actual population.

search engine optimisation. The process of affecting the visibility of a website or web page in search engine results.

secondary research. Information about the market that is gathered from libraries, census information or other sources that gathered the information, often for different purposes.

selection bias. A statistical bias in market research in which opinions of a sample group who self-select to participate may differ from those who decline.

skimming. The result of a value-based approach to pricing in which the product or service is priced at a significant premium relative to alternative solutions. This is sometimes used when a company introduces a new product in a particular category that is a significant improvement on alternatives or when the market has a particularly strong group of price-insensitive early adopters.

social bookmarking. Websites such as Delicious, Digg and Reddit that allow users to reference and share other content on the Internet.

social networking sites. Websites such as Facebook, LinkedIn, Google+ , Nexopia, Badoo or XING that give people an opportunity to connect with friends and family, reconnect with others and share interests and information regardless of geographic proximity.

source sharing. Common among non-profit organisations, an arrangement in which a group of non-competing organisations enter into a formal agreement to share the costs and benefits of employees with specific skills needed on a fluctuating basis by all the organisations.

target market. A group of purchasers with a shared need and purchasing decision process to whom the company's value proposition will appeal.

terms. The conditions under which a product or service is sold.

Tortoise Law. The consistent, steady investment in marketing over time, no matter the economic or business climate, which has been shown to improve a company's ability to achieve its business and financial objectives.

trackbacks. A metric used to evaluate the effectiveness of social media efforts. It is the number of times someone cited the company's posting in his or her own feed or website and the number of times someone commented on that posting.

unsubscribe rate. The percentage of the population to whom an e-mail was sent who then requested to be taken off the distribution list.

up-selling. A sales technique that encourages customers to upgrade to a more expensive item in order to increase the amount of the sale.

user interface. The visual and physical means by which a computer and user interact, such as screen menus, icons and mouse and gesture movements. It also includes input devices such as keyboards, mice and game controllers.

user interface designer. A specialty field in the graphic design arena that focuses on optimising the user experience relative to technology.

universal resource locator (URL): A website address.

validity. A market research term that refers to whether the research answers the question or questions for which it was designed.

value added resellers. A business arrangement in which a manufacturer of a product sells it to another company that makes enhancements to the product before selling it to the consumer.

value-based pricing (also known as market-driven pricing). A pricing approach that considers the value customers might place on the company's goods or services, along with the relative elasticity of demand. Also known as *market-driven pricing.*

value proposition. The unique set of skills and abilities that a company brings to the market. It is the company's source of value and differentiation, from the customer's perspective.

vertical integration. The process by which a company creates its own wholly-owned intermediaries to represent their products, either under its existing company name or as separate companies. In some cases, it may also represent the products of other manufacturers or service providers, allowing them to sell their products directly to the consumer, rather than engaging with agents, wholesalers and/or retailers.

vision statement. An aspirational description of what an organisation hopes to achieve or accomplish, with focus, within a defined timeframe. A strong vision statement builds on an understanding of the market and its needs, core competencies and the value that is delivered to market.

visitors. A metric used to evaluate the effectiveness of websites. It is the number of unique people who view a website during a given period.

visit. A metric used to evaluate the effectiveness of websites. It is the number of unique times a website is viewed by all viewers.

virtual worlds. Websites that allow people to take on a real or assumed persona (depicted as an avatar) and interact with others in a computer-animated role play environment.

wikis. Informational websites that allow users to contribute, modify or delete content using a web browser and text editor, allowing collaborative creation of content.

APPENDIX A

REFERENCES AND RESOURCES

For information about spam e-mail laws in various countries, visit the following websites:

COUNTRY OR REGION	RELEVANT LEGISLATION	WEBSITE
UNITED STATES	The CAN-SPAM Act	www.business.ftc.gov/documents/bus61-can-spam-act-compliance-guide-business
UNITED KINGDOM	Privacy & Electronic Communications Regulations	www.ico.gov.uk/for_organisations/privacy_and_electronic_communications/the_guide.aspx
EUROPEAN UNION	Directive on Privacy and Electronic Communications	http://eur-lex.europa.eu/LexUriServ/LexUriServ.do?uri=CELEX:32002L0058:en:NOT
JAPAN	The Law on Regulation of Transmission of Specified Electronic Mail	www.cas.go.jp/jp/seisaku/hourei/data/ACPT.pdf

For an easy reference to other countries' laws, see e-mail spam legislation by country on Wikipedia: http://en.wikipedia.org/wiki/Email_spam_legislation_by_country.

Printed in the United States
By Bookmasters